Apple Pro Training Series

Advanced Editing Techniques in Final Cut Pro 5

Michael Wohl

Apple
Certified

Apple Pro Training Series: Advanced Editing Techniques in Final Cut Pro 5
Michael Wohl
Copyright © 2006 by Michael Wohl

Published by Peachpit Press. For information on Peachpit Press books, contact:

Peachpit Press
1249 Eighth Street
Berkeley, CA 94710
(510) 524-2178
(800) 283-9444
Fax: (510) 524-2221
http://www.peachpit.com
To report errors, please send a note to errata@peachpit.com
Peachpit Press is a division of Pearson Education

Apple Series Editor: Serena Herr
Editor: Bob Lindstrom
Managing Editors: Kristin Kalning and Nancy Peterson
Production Editor: Laurie Stewart, Happenstance Type-O-Rama
Technical Editor: Adam Green
Technical Reviewer: Brendan Boykin
Copy Editor: Liz Welch
Compositor: Craig Woods, Happenstance Type-O-Rama
Indexer: Jack Lewis
Cover Art Direction: Charlene Charles-Will
Cover Illustration: Alicia Buelow
Cover Production: George Mattingly / GMD

ISBN 0-321-33549-X
9 8 7 6 5 4 3 2
Printed and bound in the United States of America

01:07:41:13
07:41:13
1:05:23
PROD. NO.
SCENE
TAKE
ROLL
DATE
PROD. CO.
DIRECTOR
CAMERAMAN
SOUND

Contents at a Glance

Table of Contents

Getting Started

Welcome to the official advanced training course for Final Cut Pro 5, Apple's dynamic and powerful nonlinear editing package. This book is a detailed guide to advanced editing techniques using Final Cut Pro, with a brief section on Compressor. The premise of this book is to build upon your technical knowledge of editing with Final Cut Pro, by introducing you to the aesthetic and structural challenges you will face as you sit down to edit different types of projects.

This book assumes that you're comfortable with the basic operation of Final Cut Pro and aims to takes you to the next level: transforming you from a technician into an artist. Just as knowing how to use a pencil doesn't make you a writer, knowing how to operate Final Cut Pro doesn't necessarily make you an editor.

Like that pencil, Final Cut Pro 5 is an incredibly versatile tool. The pencil can produce a technical manual or a poem, a carrot cake recipe or the notes of Beethoven's Fifth, the Declaration of Independence or *The Iliad*. Similarly, Final Cut Pro can turn out instructional videos or action scenes, dramatic dialogue, or sports documentaries.

This book is organized around editing scenarios just like those and will help you realize them by developing your creative skills alongside your Final Cut Pro skills.

Furthermore, each type of project also requires a different mental approach. The lessons in this book explore *why* editors make the decisions they do and those lessons will get you to think about your own editing decisions in a whole new light.

Section One begins with a simple dialogue scene from the short film "Hope," in which you'll learn the fundamentals of dramatic action and narrative story-telling. Later, you'll explore action scenes, including fight and chase scenes from films such as "Broken Fists" and "Slapdash."

Section Two covers nonfiction material such as interviews, music videos, multi-camera editing, and documenting an event. You'll cut scenes from a behind-the-scenes featurette, a documentary travel show, and a real world music video.

Each of the projects on the DVD contains extra media associated with the lesson; all of it is real-world footage from actual projects. After completing the exercises in each lesson, you are strongly encouraged to continue working with the project, exploring different ways of implementing the concepts. Try different ways of editing each scene, finessing them until you feel they are complete.

Along the way you'll learn many advanced Final Cut Pro tips and tricks such as dynamic trimming, slipping and sliding, and subframe audio editing. But you'll also learn what makes an effective montage, and how to use split edits to tell better stories. This book is unique in its approach, in that it is even more than a guide to improve your level of expertise with the software. It immerses that expertise in the real world scenarios that editors face every day. And learning how to handle those scenarios will not just teach you how to make the most of Final Cut Pro, it will also teach you how to be a great editor regardless of the tools at hand.

The Methodology

The emphasis of this book is hands-on training. Each exercise was designed to help you start editing in Final Cut Pro at a professional level as quickly as possible. The book assumes a basic level of familiarity with the Final Cut Pro interface and with the fundamentals of postproduction. If you are new to video editing, it would be helpful for you to start at the beginning and progress through each lesson in order. Since every section (and every lesson) is self-contained, if you are familiar with basic editing techniques you can start with any section and focus on that topic.

Course Structure

This book was designed to help you master the most critical professional-level editing and postproduction techniques in Final Cut Pro. Each lesson expands on the basic concepts of digital video editing, giving you the tools to customize your project workflows and use the program for your own purposes. Finally, the book delves into features that are not frequently touched on, with a special section on using Compressor to transcode and export files to a variety of formats. The lessons fall into the following categories:

▶ Lessons 1–5: Cutting Dramatic Material

   You will learn the secrets of cutting narrative scenes, including both simple and complex dialogue scenes, basic action scenes, and complex action scenes such as fights and chases. Plus the section includes a special lesson on editing comedy.

▶ Lessons 6–9: Cutting Nonfiction Material

   Covers interviews and associated B-roll footage, documenting an event such as a wedding or tradeshow, cutting a music video, and cutting multi-camera footage.

▶ Lessons 10–11: Working with Audio

   Focuses on the concepts and processes of audio editing, sound design, sound mixing, and other audio finishing techniques.

► Lessons 12–15: Project Management

You will learn essential tools and techniques for managing your Final Cut Pro projects; manipulating, outputting, and transcoding your finished work; and developing a workflow for projects originating on film.

System Requirements

Before beginning to use this book, you should have a working knowledge of your computer and its operating system, as well as a basic level of proficiency with Final Cut Pro.

Basic system requirements for Final Cut Pro 5 include:

► Mac OS X 10.3.9 or later

► G4 or G5 500 MHz or faster

► 512 MB of RAM or more

► AGP Quartz Extreme graphics card

► DVD drive

► Separate hard drive for media is recommended

► To use DVCPRO HD footage, 1 GHz minimum processor speed and 1 GB of RAM are required.

Consult the Final Cut Pro technical specifications page (www.apple.com/finalcutpro/specs.html) for more details on specific system requirements and qualified third-party devices such as cameras, capture cards, and other peripherals.

Copying the Lesson Files

All the necessary files you need to complete the lessons are found on the two DVD-ROM discs that come with this book.

Installing the Lesson Files

1   Insert the *APTS Advanced FCP* DVD 1 into your DVD drive.

2   For best results, drag the entire Adv_FCP_Book_Files folder from DVD 1 to the top level of your computer's hard drive or an attached media drive.

3   Remove *APTS Advanced FCP* DVD 1 from your DVD drive and insert *APTS Advanced FCP* DVD 2.

4   Select the entire contents of DVD 2 and copy them into the Media folder on your hard drive inside the Adv_FCP_Book_Files folder you copied from DVD 1.

There is a total of approximately 17 GB of data on both discs.

NOTE ▶ When you keep all the lesson files and media files from the disc together in one single Adv_FCP_Book_Files folder on your hard drive, just as you find them on the DVD, you will ensure that the tutorial project files for each lesson will open with their media files all correctly linked, and ready for you to begin the lesson.

5   To begin each lesson, launch the application for that lesson and then open the project file or files listed at the beginning of each lesson.

Reconnecting Broken Media Links

For any number of reasons, you may need to separate the lesson files from the media files when you install and use them. For instance, you may choose to keep the project files in a user home directory and the media files on a dedicated media drive. In this case, when you open a project file, a window will appear asking you to reconnect the project files to their source media files.

Reconnecting files is a simple process. Just follow these steps:

1   When you first open a lesson's project file, a Final Cut Pro dialog will appear listing one or more files that are offline. Click the Reconnect button.

A Final Cut Pro Reconnect Files window appears.

2 Click Search.

Final Cut Pro will search any attached hard disks looking for the missing files. When it finds the first file, a Mac OS X Reconnect dialog will appear.

3 Select the highlighted file and click Choose.

In the Final Cut Pro Reconnect Files dialog, all of the offline files will be moved to the lower Files Located pane.

4 Click Connect.

5 Be sure to save the newly reconnected project file, or you will have to perform the reconnect operation every time you open it.

See Lesson 13, "Reconnecting Offline Files," if you have any difficulties when connecting broken links between project files and media files.

About the Apple Pro Training Series

Advanced Editing Techniques in Final Cut Pro 5 is part of the official training series for Apple Pro applications, developed by experts in the field and certified by Apple Computer. The series is the official course curriculum used by Apple Authorized Training Centers worldwide, and offers complete training in all Apple Pro products. The lessons are designed to let you learn at your own pace. Although each lesson provides step-by-step instructions for creating specific projects, there's room for exploration and experimentation. Each lesson concludes with review questions and answers summarizing what you've learned, which can be used to help you prepare for the Apple Pro Certification Exam.

For a complete list of Apple Pro Training Series books, see the course catalog at the end of this book, or visit www.peachpit.com/applebooklet.

Apple Pro Certification Program

The Apple Pro Training and Certification Program is designed to keep you at the forefront of Apple's digital media technology while giving you a competitive edge in today's ever-changing job market. Whether you're an editor, graphic designer, sound designer, special effects artist, or teacher, these training tools are meant to help you expand your skills.

Upon completing the course material in this book, you can become a certified Apple Pro by taking the certification exam at an Apple Authorized Training Center. Successful certification as an Apple Pro gives you official recognition of your knowledge of Apple's professional applications while allowing you to market yourself to employers and clients as a skilled, pro-level user of Apple products.

For those who prefer to learn in an instructor-led setting, Apple offers training courses at Apple Authorized Training Centers worldwide. These courses, which use the Apple Pro Training Series books as their curriculum, are taught by Apple Certified Trainers and balance concepts and lectures with hands-on labs and exercises. Apple Authorized Training Centers have been carefully selected and have met Apple's highest standards in all areas, including facilities, instructors, course delivery, and infrastructure. The goal of the program is to offer Apple customers, from beginners to the most seasoned professionals, the highest quality training experience.

For more information or to find an Authorized Training Center near you, go to www.apple.com/software/pro/training.

Resources

This book is not intended as a comprehensive reference manual, nor does it replace the documentation that comes with the application. For comprehensive information about program features, refer to these resources:

► The Reference Guide. Accessed through the Final Cut Pro Help menu, the Reference Guide contains a complete description of all features.

► Apple's Web site: www.apple.com.

► Stay current: As Final Cut Pro 5 is updated, Peachpit may choose to update lessons or post additional exercises as necessary on this book's companion Web page. Please check www.peachpit.com/apts.advfcp5 for revised lessons.

Dramatic Editing

1

Editing Dialogue

The craft of editing requires a variety of skills and talents, ranging from understanding rhythm and timing to recognizing effective performances. You do need to know how to use Final Cut Pro (or a similar editing program) but a skilled editor also needs to know the medium inside and out. She must distill each bit of visual and audio information down to its elemental core and meaning; intuitively grasp the subtle difference between a close-up and a medium close-up; hear ten distinct sounds in a single ambience; and know how a fifth of a second can be the difference between suspense and comedy.

This volume is an advanced book, and assumes you already have a basic understanding of the tools and commands of Final Cut Pro. While this book will improve your mastery of the software and familiarize you with some of its more advanced and subtle features, the book's true purpose is to get you thinking more about why you make certain editing decisions rather than just how or which buttons to press. In many ways this book will serve as a sort of primer on the language of editing, familiarizing you with common words and turns of phrase as well as identifying the grammatical rules and trends.

Editing is a creative expression, so those rules may often beg to be broken. However, your communication will be most effective if you understand why the rules work, even if you choose to ignore them.

Learning the Language of Film

To be an film editor, you must learn to speak a new language, and to communicate effectively you must be fluent in that language. As a dutiful consumer of media, you almost certainly understand what you watch on TV, but that doesn't make you *literate*. Literacy requires the ability to read and write the language; to disassemble it and then reassemble it; to understand not only what a film means, but *why* it means what it does.

Such literacy takes time and effort. While you can teach yourself through experimentation and trial and error, the best way to learn is by pursuing both formal training and guided exercises. This book and its corresponding Apple Certification Program provide both.

Obviously, training is just a starting point. The exercises provided here are just examples of the types of situations and editorial challenges you might encounter. Every project is unique and every show provides nearly infinite possibilities for telling its particular story. Your skill will grow the more you practice, and eventually your editing will become completely intuitive, just like reading and writing any language in which you are truly fluent.

Using Cinematic Language

The language of cinema combines images and sounds, but otherwise it is just like any other language. This is not a metaphor. A language is any systematic means of communicating information. By choosing different words, or phrasing something differently, subtle differences in meaning are conveyed. The more deftly you choose your words, and the more creatively you arrange your phrases, the more precisely and accurately you control how the story is told.

As with any language, to master this language of film you need to learn the system and syntax. Shots and sequences are just like words and phrases. Cuts and transitions serve as punctuation, controlling the flow and pacing of meaning and message. Grammatical rules such as "starting on a master shot" or "matching similar angles" help your viewer understand what type of story you are telling. The same "words" can construct poetry or prose, novels or training manuals.

Understanding these rules is fundamental to successful editing. Remember, the purpose of editing is to communicate. If your idea or point isn't clear to the viewer, you haven't communicated successfully. Of course, like any language this one is constantly evolving and growing. New ideas and techniques are forever emerging. Idioms and trends arise and fall out of fashion.

Understanding the Editor as Storyteller

Who is a film's storyteller? The writer conceives the world and the structure of the story. The director and the production crew realize that world, capturing its sounds and images. But it is the editor who *tells* the story. It is his "voice" that actually reaches the audience.

Everyone knows someone who's a great storyteller; someone who can captivate you even when describing something mundane. Conversely, everyone knows someone who can hardly tell a joke. Have you ever stopped to think about what makes that first person so fascinating? Or what ruins a joke? If you want to be an editor, you need to think about those questions. You need to understand the mechanics of *story*.

What is a story? A story is way of packaging information so it's easy to understand. In part, a story is a collection of facts constructed in a way that our brains find easy to remember. But stories are more than that. They have a magical quality, and engage us in a special way. Stories resonate in a way that tickles us, terrifies us, makes us laugh, and moves us to tears. But stories are not just fantasy. They are, in fact, how we make sense of the world. Our brains are specifically programmed to understand the world in terms of stories.

Who, what, why, when, where, and how. Are these questions familiar? Of course they are. In fact, they are possibly the six most important words in the language. Those simple questions are the tools for taking apart and understanding a story and, by extension, for understanding the world. They are also the tools for assembling a story.

Good stories are constructed by revealing the answers to those six one-word questions in a thoughtful and deliberate way. The answers must be disclosed just as the listener is ready for them and not before or after. If a storyteller spends too much time explaining *where* something took place, the listener might lose track of *who* the story was about. If the teller spends too much time explaining *why* the three men walked into the bar and doesn't get around to explaining *what* they were doing there, the listener loses interest and the joke is spoiled.

Okay, but how does this relate to video editing? It is absolutely fundamental. Every sequence you construct is a story that answers those six questions. As an editor, you must thoughtfully and deliberately answer each one, and must reveal them just as the viewer is anticipating them. Furthermore, every shot in your film answers one of those questions. One shot might identify the *who*. Another shot might clarify the *where* or even the *why*. In fact, you can nearly count on the fact that different shot types reliably answer different questions.

Close-ups tell us *who* the story is about.

Long shots illustrate *where* a scene is taking place.

Extreme close-ups put the audience inside a character's head, revealing (often with the help of sound) *why* the character is acting a certain way.

And so on. Sometimes a shot will answer more than one question and many shots, such as over the shoulder or two-shots, focus on defining the relationships between characters, answering the question *with whom*. The editor's job is to carefully craft each scene by revealing the answers to each of those basic questions at the precise moment that they will most effectively communicate with the audience.

For example, in the most common scene-opening technique, the first shot is a master wide shot. The *where* and sometimes the *what* questions are answered, but the audience quickly begins to wonder *who* the scene is about. If the editor waits too long to cut to a close-up (CU) to answer the audience's implicit question, the scene will likely lose energy and lose its audience.

Conversely, if you begin a scene on a CU and continue to cut back and forth on CUs without ever backing out to a wider shot, the *who* of the scene remains perfectly clear, but the audience will begin to lose a sense of the *where*, the environment in which the scene is taking place. The reality of the scene will evaporate. At best, viewers will be confused; at worst, they'll change the channel.

Wielding the Secret Weapon

There is one more fundamental component of an effective story that the editor must be fully aware of in order to edit effectively: What is the story about?

The theme or main idea of the story ought to be present in every single shot in the movie. Ideally, the choices of camera angles, the lighting, the production design, and, most of all, the content of the shots will reinforce the theme. Whether they do or not, it is the editor's job to find those shots that illuminate the theme and discard the shots that cloud it.

All the magic of story, all the techniques of teasing the audience with the answers to those six questions—leading them along and engaging their emotions—are just tricks to entice them to listen to the underlying theme. Story is the spoonful of sugar that helps the medicine of theme go down.

Theme doesn't have to be heady or abstract. In advertisements, the theme is usually just the merits of the product being hawked. In many nonfiction films, the theme or purpose is expressly stated. But it's no coincidence that dramatic films are often the most effective and moving expressions of a theme, precisely because the themes are persuasively threaded into the twine of story rather than explicitly stated.

If the editor doesn't know what the theme is, or doesn't understand it clearly, it's unlikely he will be able to edit a scene in the most effective manner.

Pursuing the Invisible Art

Among the most important aspects of the editor's job is the ability to stay out of the way. It's hard for an audience to stare at a two-dimensional movie or television screen and suspend their disbelief long enough to become engaged in the story you're telling. Every time you cut, you potentially make it that much harder. Every edit is a small interruption in the flow of the story; an opportunity for the viewer to disengage and start wondering where her car is parked or if that show she likes on that other channel has started yet. It's a chance to become distracted by a growling stomach or a full bladder. Once that happens, you've lost your viewer, and that precious theme you'd been hoping to communicate is lost with her.

Your editing must strive at all times to hide the artifice of filmmaking. Your goal is to distract the viewer from the edits that keep the story moving forward; to make the action within the scene appear perfectly smooth and realistic; to stitch together the dozen or more individual shots that were recorded over many hours into 2 minutes of seamless storytelling. And you must make it look effortless.

If you have done your job properly, in fact, the film should look like there was no editing at all. Never mind the hours you have to spend finessing one edit in which a door was slammed in one shot and was gently pushed shut in another. Good editing is invisible.

If you crave the limelight, become an actor (or maybe a director). An editor's job is to make those people look good and then to quietly step back into the wings and disappear.

But don't confuse this with thinking that an editor's role is unimportant. Making those invisible edits, controlling the viewer's focus, *telling* the story the writer conceived and the production crew realized is absolutely vital to effective filmmaking.

Of course, there are exceptions to the invisible edit rule. Sometimes edits are deliberately highlighted. Sometimes sound design or other elements of your job are best brought to the fore. Indeed, a whole school of filmmakers believe that the more the artifice of film is exposed, the more effective and moving a film will be. But don't be fooled into thinking that you don't need to master your craft. Even the most glaring jump cut must be made deliberately and with the conscious intention of conveying an underlying meaning and controlling the audience's focus.

Editing the Basic Dialogue Sequence

Enough theory, it's time to start editing!

Not all projects include narrative-style dialogue, but this sequence type is so basic, and incorporates so many of the fundamental tenets of editing technique, that it's an ideal place to start. The techniques described here are the foundation of nearly every other kind of scene you will encounter, in both dramatic and nondramatic projects.

The first step is to get familiar with the footage available to you.

1   Start Final Cut Pro and open the **01_Project_Start** project.

This project contains a dialogue scene set in a diner from the film "Hope."

2   Double-click shot **1-2** and play it in the Viewer.

This shot is a master full shot that shows the entire scene. While it does a great job of answering the where question, once the main dialogue begins, it's too far away and too far *off-axis* to answer much of the who, why, or how.

3   Scroll the Browser columns until the Description and comment fields are visible.

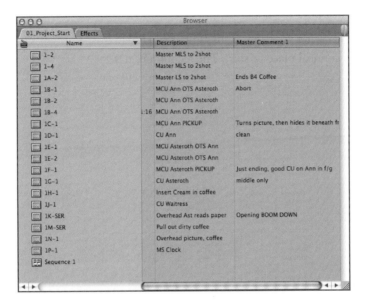

Dialogue scenes almost always contain the same standard coverage: a master shot that shows both parties, usually from a neutral angle; a pair of matching over-the-shoulder (OTS) singles; and a pair of matching clean singles.

> **NOTE** ▶ A *single* is any shot of one person, usually a close-up or medium close-up. A dirty single is an over-the-shoulder shot where just a little of the person in the foreground is visible. A clean single is one where the person in the foreground is completely out of the shot, leaving an unobstructed, or clean, view of the subject.

That's it. Five shots. And it's all you need.

You might think cutting a dialogue scene is boring, or perhaps deceptively easy, but it's not true. Every day, hundreds of scenes just like this are cut and each one is unique—guided by the nuances of the performances, and the actions and reactions within the scene.

At best, the coverage also includes a few *cutaways* and *inserts* to give you some editorial flexibility, and occasionally there'll be a *special*: a shot intended for a transition into or out of the scene. Most of the time, however, you'll work with those five main shots.

But don't worry. There's infinite room for creativity, even with such limited and predictable coverage. Think how many simple dialogue scenes there are in every film or television show. Even though the vast majority of those scenes follow this same pattern, every one feels fresh and unique. Why? Because it works. It keeps the focus on the content, not the camerawork, and it gives the editor everything needed to tell the story.

Organizing Your Clips

It's absolutely critical that you become intimately familiar with all of the available footage before you begin to cut a scene. Get in the habit of watching every take of every shot. Use markers or take notes to identify interesting and important moments.

Usually, this footage analysis begins during logging, when you can also incorporate notes from the director and information from the camera log. But if an assistant logged the footage for you, you must take some time to study the footage before diving into the scene.

One easy way to build this step into your process is to begin every scene by identifying and categorizing all of your shots. You can do this by moving clips into different bins or by making notes in one of the many comment fields. Presumably the shots have already been grouped according to scene, but now you can further categorize them by shot type, angle, or other pertinent information.

In the next example, you will use Final Cut Pro's colored labels to identify which characters appear in which shots.

1   Select all of the **1B** shots, as well as **1C-1** and **1D-1**.

These are all of the shots that favor the character Ann.

2   Control-click the selected clips and from the pop-up menu choose Label > Best Take to turn the clips red.

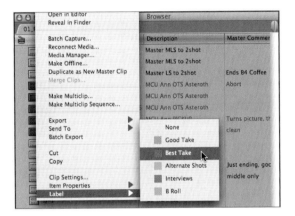

Right now, it's easy to remember that for this sequence, "Best Take" simply means "Shots of Ann". However, this might prove to be confusing if you are sharing this project with another editor, or if you put it down and return to it several months from now. To prevent any such confusion, you can change the text associated with the labels.

3   Choose Final Cut Pro > User Preferences and choose the Labels tab.

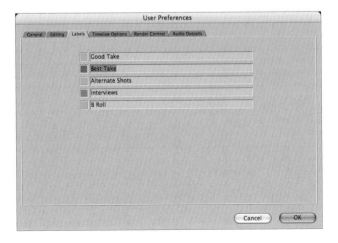

4   Change the text next to the red color to *Ann*, change the blue label to *Asteroth*, and change purple to *Both Ann & Asteroth*.

The color purple is a good visual clue, since purple is a combination of red and blue. If you prefer, you can set the labels however you like. Rather than ignore the two remaining labels, you can put them to good use, too.

5   Change the text for the color orange to *Cutaways* and the text for green to *Inserts*.

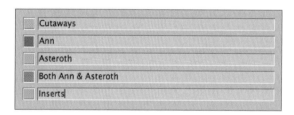

Don't worry if you don't know exactly what cutaways and inserts are. You'll learn that in a moment.

6   Click OK to close the window.

7   In the Browser, select the **1E**, **1F** , **1G**, and **1K** shots. Choose Modify > Label > Asteroth.

1K is a *special* that doesn't fit into the standard coverage categories, but because it's a shot of Asteroth, it is helpful to label it with his color.

8   Scenes **1** and **1A** are both versions of the master scene, so make them purple.

That covers the basic coverage of the two actors, but a few clips are still unaccounted for.

9   Double-click **1H-1** and play it in the Viewer.

This is an insert shot of Ann pouring cream into her coffee. An *insert* is any shot that focuses on an action that occurs within other shots.

10 Double-click **1N-1** and play it in the Viewer.

The subject of this shot is the photograph. This is clearly another insert. These inserts are a bit wider than typical inserts. A more traditional insert of the photo probably would have been an extreme close-up (ECU) from Asteroth's point of view (POV). Still, they serve the classic purpose of an insert: to draw attention to a detail within the scene, and to provide options for the editor.

11 Select **1N-1** and **1H-1** and label them as green inserts.

Alternatively, a shot of something in the environment but not visible in the other shots (such as a shot of the jukebox or the rotating pie display) would not be an insert but a *cutaway*. Cutaways are typically more flexible than inserts. Inserts must be used at the precise moment when the action occurs in the scene or not at all, but a cutaway can be used almost any time in the scene.

12 Double-click **1P-1** and play it in the Viewer.

This is a classic example of a cutaway.

13 Label **1P-1** as orange cutaways.

All that remain unlabeled are shots **1J-1** and **1M-1**.

14 Open and play shot **1J-1**.

Shot **1J-1** is a CU of the waitress pouring coffee. Technically, this is neither an insert nor a cutaway, but it serves similar purposes. The scene could play perfectly well without ever showing the face of the waitress, but it gives the opportunity to provide an outside perspective on the conversation between

Ann and Asteroth. It also provides further editorial flexibility. Leave this shot unlabeled.

15 Open and play shot **1M-SER**.

This shot is not really of Ann, and the pullout makes it not just an insert of the coffee. In fact, it's another special that mirrors the overhead shot of Asteroth, and is designed specifically to end the sequence.

The director carefully chose these overhead bookend shots to lend unique-ness and style to the scene. Since the movie overall is about heaven and hell, this overhead POV offers a subtle reference to an omniscience that will be reflected later in the film. Leave shot **1M-SER** unlabeled.

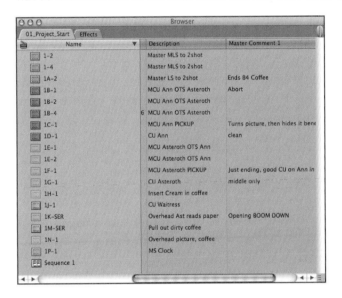

Although this bin only contains 18 clips, doing this sort of organization before beginning your edit is great practice. It allows you to instantly access exactly the shots you need, exactly when you need them.

Remember that good cutting requires that you keep a sense of rhythm and stay engaged in the detailed nuance of a scene. If, in the middle of editing, you have to stop and audition a number of clips to look for the right shot, or manually shuttle through a long piece of media to find the correct section, you can lose the momentum and excitement of the moment.

Part of what makes Final Cut Pro unique, and part of what makes it so popular, is the attention it pays to the subtle but critical need to sustain focus while editing. By taking advantage of features designed to speed your work and remove obstacles and extraneous steps in the process, you can remain focused on the heat and passion of the edit, and groove to the rhythm of the scene.

Begin with the Master Shot

The easiest and most sensible way to begin editing a typical scene is to start with the master shot. The master shot by definition includes the entire scene and, while it may not be the optimal framing for every moment, it provides a framework for you to lean on as you experiment with other shots.

Beginning with the master doesn't mean the sequence ultimately needs to open with it. Precocious young editors automatically frown at the idea of beginning so traditionally, preferring to open a scene on an insert or a close-up. You'll have plenty of time to change the opening shot of the sequence; but to untangle the various shots and weave the story together, it helps to understand the original structure put forth on the set.

1   Double-click Sequence 1 to open it into the Canvas and Timeline.

2   Open clip 1-2.

3   Set an In point after the director calls "action" and before Ann enters the diner (around 01:00:36:00). Set an Out point at the end of the scene, after she pushes the coffee away and before the director calls "cut" (approximately 03:15:15).

4   Edit the clip into the sequence.

▶ **Watch for Performance**

Remember that the most important things an editor should be observing are the actors' performances. Even a brief moment of less-than-optimum performance can destroy a scene's illusion of truth. It is your responsibility to the director, to the actors, and to the project to find the best performances for each line, each moment, and each beat of the scene and try to incorporate them. Inevitably, there will be trade-offs; there might be a camera error that undermines a great moment, or a car horn that might spoil an otherwise perfect shot.

Sometimes the compromises will be more editorial. A change of screen direction or a bit of business might not match from one shot to the next, so you have to use a less-than-perfect take in which the action does match. In another situation, a scene could be too long and you need to trim a few lines of dialogue, or just pull out some of the "air" between lines, thereby changing the nature of the performance.

Don't worry, there are tricks: using those cutaways and inserts, stealing the audio from an alternate take, trimming out a word or a whole line by going to the OTS where you can't see the actor's lips, and so on. In some ways, maintaining the performance quality is the single most important part of your job.

A New Shot Means New Information

If the performances are flawless in the master shot, and no technical elements require cutting, there may be absolutely no reason to even touch a scene. Just drop it in and move on to the next scene. Unfortunately, this is rarely the case, and it is not the case in this scene.

But how do you know when to change the angle? And what to change it to? These are perhaps the most fundamental questions an editor faces. The answer to both is that you should cut to a new shot when doing so will provide new information that will propel the story forward. Every new cut *must provide new information*.

A new shot must answer another of the six basic questions. The shot could be a CU of an actor's reaction that reveals an inner conflict or emotion *(why or what)*. It could be a wider shot that gives context to the events in the previous shot *(where or when)*. Or it could be a new shot that shows a simple mechanical detail such as a loaded gun *(how)*. No matter what, the new shot must provide new information that will propel the story forward.

So you've answered what the new shot must be, but you haven't answered when the new shot must occur. That is revealed by constantly asking yourself, "What is the audience's point of focus?" If the point of focus moves offscreen, or becomes unclear due to staging or a camera movement, you had better cut to a new shot where the point of focus is clear, and serves the story.

That's exactly what happens around 16 seconds into the diner scene.

When Ann reaches the booth, you can see the top of Asteroth's hat, but you don't know who is wearing the hat. Even if you add a shot to the beginning of the sequence identifying him, this moment is still ambiguous in terms of point of focus. Ann speaks to some man, specifically guiding the viewer's focus to him, but this particular angle doesn't allow us to see him.

Remember those basic rules of storytelling. If the audience is dying to know something, you'd better give it to them or risk losing their interest. In this case, the scene is begging for a shot of Asteroth.

1   In the sequence, set an In point after Ann says "Mr. Roth?" at 01:00:16:10.

2   Double-click shot **1E-1** and in the Viewer set an In point right before he says, "Yeah" (around 01:16:42:00). Set an Out point just as Ann crosses into the frame as she sits down (around 01:16:46:15).

Always try to make edits while action is happening in the frame: someone sitting down, lifting an arm, banging on a wall, opening a door, and so on. You'll focus on this concept in more detail in a later lesson but it applies in any type of sequence.

Setting the Out point as Ann is sitting down allows you to "hide" the edit underneath the movement going on in the frame. That movement in the frame pulls the viewer's attention, and when you continue the action on the other side of the cut, the audience is so focused on that movement that they completely ignore the disruption that the cut might otherwise cause.

3 Perform an Overwrite edit to add **1E-1** to the sequence.

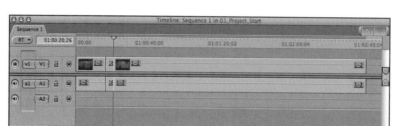

4 Press \ (backslash) to play around the edit.

The In point works fine, but the Out point doesn't match up properly. She sits down in the medium close-up (MCU) and then sits down again in the master.

This happened because the pacing was different in the two shots, and also because when choosing the In point you eliminated an unnecessary pause between her question and his reply.

This is not a mistake. It's a natural part of the editing process. Every new shot potentially messes up the sync or timing of the scene. Finish the job by cleaning up the edit.

5 In the sequence, set an In point at the end of the second clip and play forward until Ann is halfway seated in the master (approximately 01:00:22:25). Set an Out point there.

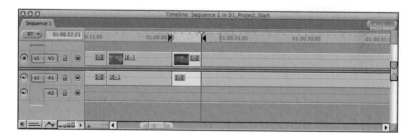

NOTE ► The timecode numbers here refer to sequence time, not the burned-in timecode visible in the Canvas.

6 Press Command-Shift-A to deselect all, and press Shift-Delete to ripple delete the marked section and correct the edit.

7 Press \ to play around the edit again.

Don't worry if the timing of the edit isn't perfect. You'll come back and finesse it later—if you even need to.

The truth is, once you move from a wide master into a tighter shot, it's fairly jarring to jump back out unless you've got a good reason to do so. The general rule is that once you go in, stay in.

Also, since there's no new information in the master at this point, there's no reason to go back to it. The idea of ending the MCU of Asteroth as Ann sits down is a good one, since there is something new going on (she sits), and that angle wasn't the best place to see it, but neither is the master. The best place to see the action is in the MCU of Ann.

8 Open **1B-2** and set an In point just as Ann is sitting down (01:08:36:00).

▶ **Whose Scene Is It?**

Just as all of your edit choices must be informed by the show's overall theme, for each scene you must also keep track of which character dominates the focus: whose scene it is. Inevitably, one character or another is going to be more important than the others. That character demands control of the point of focus. If you shift the focus somewhere else, the scene, and ultimately the whole show, may become muddled and boring.

The dominant character is not always obvious. Often, a scene does not feature the main character. If you're ever in doubt, ask yourself this simple question: Who has the main action in this scene? Does the main action belong to Asteroth, who is providing some crucial information? Does it belong to the waitress, who is actually a spy? Or does it belong to Ann making her request? If you know who's got the main action, you know which character's actions and reactions are going to be essential for the scene to work. Remember, this doesn't only apply to dramatic scenes. Every scene in every show must have a clear point of focus. It must have a single dominant element or character whose actions command the audience's attention.

9   In the Viewer, play the **1B-2** clip forward until something happens that inspires you to cut. That will be the Out point you set for this new clip.

You might have been tempted to cut when Asteroth lifts his head and responds to Ann, but since he immediately looks back down—and you already know that in his MCU his face is completely in shadow—there wouldn't be very much new information. Plus, you would lose her reaction, which is also important. However, if you play forward a few more seconds, something happens that again begs for a new shot.

The waitress walks up and Ann suddenly looks up and offscreen. Doesn't this compel you to show what it is she's looking at?

10 Set your Out point there (around 01:08:52:25).

11 In the sequence, position the playhead on the edit between **1E-1** and **1-2**.

12 Perform an Overwrite edit to add the MCU of Ann to the sequence.

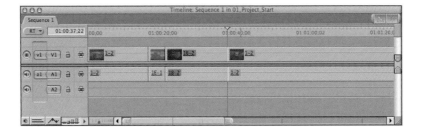

What comes next? If you look through your coverage, there are only two shots you could choose that would provide new information about what Ann is looking at. There's the master shot, where you can see the back of

the waitress and see Ann looking up at her as she arrives, or there's the CU
of the waitress.

Remember that there are no wrong answers. You could justify either shot,
since both have strengths and weaknesses. Of course, you could lament
that you really want a shot that shows the waitress over Ann's shoulder, or
just a CU on the coffeepot. Sometimes you can make such requests and
the production crew will go and pick them up. More often you've got to
live with the shots you're handed, and here you've got to choose between
the master and the CU. Or do you?

13 Open **1J-1**.

In and Out marks have already been set around the line "Need a menu?"

14 Press Shift-\ to play from In to Out points.

15 In the sequence, set an In point just after the waitress says, "Evening," and
Ann looks up. Set the point before she says, "Need a menu?" (01:00:37:03).

16 Overwrite **1J-1** into the sequence and play the whole sequence.

Although some of your edits may need finessing, the scene should be taking shape. When **1J** ends, it cuts back to the master, and both shots work
fine *together*!

This is the best of both worlds, because the CU of the waitress satisfies the audience's longing to know what Ann is looking at, and the master reveals the physical relationship of the waitress to the couple (which is the one important detail absent in the CU).

Furthermore, if you stay on the long shot until after the waitress leaves, you are left with a great two-shot of Ann and Asteroth.

This shot is perfect because it provides more new information. It illustrates the nature of their relationship in a way we haven't yet seen. We see the contrast between his darkness and her lightness. (You don't know the rest of the story, but he is a devil and she is an angel.) It also reveals that, perhaps surprisingly, they are on equal footing. He is not towering over her, or crowding her out of the frame. This subtle detail of their relationship (which becomes very important in a later scene) is only made visible in this long shot.

Remember the rule that once you move in, you shouldn't move back out? Well, here's an exception. You can move back out if something in the shot *provokes* the cut. In this case, the waitress's entrance and exit provides an opportunity to step back from the MCUs. Without the waitress's action, cutting back to this long shot would be very jarring and could have pulled the viewer out of the story. In fact, when you back out from tighter shots to wider ones, it usually signifies that the scene is over. The audience unconsciously disengages from the scene and prepares for a change to the next scene.

Instead, with the waitress to guide us, backing out to the master happens subtly, without activating the audience's "end of scene" trigger. So now, you're free to move back in. And if you play the scene forward another few seconds, the motivation for the next cut should be obvious. Ann takes out the picture, and every single person watching the scene is going to be wondering the same thing: What is she holding in her hand?

17 Open **1C-1** and play it.

In all the **1B** shots, you can't see the picture. The director realized that on set, and so he did this *pickup* of just this one part of the scene to make sure you could see the picture.

This is a case when the editor sends flowers and a thank-you note to the director. Without this pickup, it would have been very difficult to cut this moment of the scene and, since it's such an important moment, the whole scene would have suffered. But fortunately, you have **1C**.

18 Set the In point in both the sequence and the Viewer to the frame where Ann is turning the picture around to show to Asteroth. (See the timecode numbers in the illustration.)

Again, you are using action within the frame to hide the edit. The viewers' eyes will be riveted to the picture in the long shot and, when the cut happens, they will follow the movement of the picture across the cut, never noticing that an edit even took place.

19 Set an Out point in the Viewer after Ann says, "Six years old next week" (at approximately 01:14:52:00).

20 Perform an Overwrite edit and press \ to play around the edit.

You may have to finesse the edit to smooth the movement of the picture turn, but don't worry about it now. You'll have time to go back and trim every edit once the rough cut is assembled.

NOTE ▶ In this case, the director specifically instructed the actor to move the picture out of frame after she turns it around. This was his way of controlling the point of focus within the shot. Sure, the picture pulled us in from the wide shot back to the MCU, but once we get there, it turns out that the picture is not important, Ann is. The audience grasps that it's a Polaroid, but quickly learns that it's not the image on the photo that's significant. In this case, you must follow the director's lead.

Matching Angles

Once you get to the heart of a two-person dialogue scene, it is usually a back-and-forth exchange between the two characters. How and when you choose to cut between shots defines the tone and style of the scene. One thing to keep in mind is that to keep the edits as invisible as possible, you must cut between angles that match one another as much as possible. MCUs should be cut against MCUs, CUs against CUs, and so on.

But not all matching shots are created equal. If one was shot with a long lens and the reverse shot made with a wide-angle lens, they will have different visual qualities and won't cut together very well. Similarly, if one shot is perfectly centered and another is dramatically off-center, cutting between them will draw unwanted attention to the difference between them, and highlight the edit, rather than the content.

Also, in the case of the singles commonly employed in a simple dialogue scene like this one, you ideally want to match *dirty* shots to dirty and *clean* to clean.

Dirty Single Shot

Clean Single Shot

Part of the reason this is important is aesthetic. The closer the geometry of the two shots is, the gentler their juxtaposition. The other important reason for shot matching involves the content. When you deliberately cut a clean single against a dirty one, or a slightly wider shot of one person with a closer shot of the other, it changes the relationship between the characters. This can be a great tool when used deliberately, but otherwise, it is an unwanted distraction.

You can hope that your production crew understood the importance of this, and designed all their shots in matching pairs, but it is still up to you to use them.

21 Open **1E-2** and set an In point just before Asteroth says, "What am I supposed to do? Bake a cake?" (at approximately 01:19:36:00).

22 Set the Out point a bit farther into the clip, around 20:07:00.

23 Edit the clip into the sequence directly after **1C-1**.

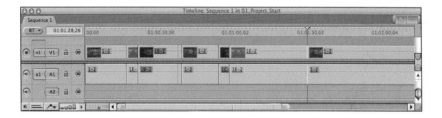

It should be pretty obvious that you'll want to cut back to Ann during the middle of this shot—not just because she has lines, but because her delivery of those lines is compelling and tells much more of the story than Asteroth's reaction does.

TIP ▶ Don't assume that you should always cut to show whomever happens to be talking. In many cases, the reaction of the other person is where the story is really happening.

24 Set an In point in the sequence just after the sound of Ann putting down the creamer (01:01:05:25) and set an Out point in the middle of the movement when Asteroth sits back and before he speaks (14:05).

NOTE ▶ Throughout this book, timecode numbers will be abbreviated to only the relevant digits. If no hours or minutes values are given, they are identical to the hours or minutes of the previous timecode citing.

25 Open **1B-4** and set an Out point in the middle of Asteroth's movement as he sits back (01:12:58:20).

26 Press Option-I to clear the In point, if one exists.

In this case, you can use the movement of Asteroth's hat to hide the edit. By matching the two Out points to occur in the middle of that action, the In point is back-timed.

27 Overwrite the clip into the sequence and play it.

The ending of the edit, hidden by the movement of Asteroth's hat, is fairly well placed; but the beginning feels a little random, or worse, it feels like you deliberately cut to see Ann because you knew she was about to speak.

Anticipating an action like this is a perfect example of a terrible edit. You should never cut to something just *before* it happens. This indicates to the audience that something is about to happen. Rather than feeling immersed in the story, they've suddenly been warned to look out for something.

It is generally preferable to cut just after someone begins talking rather than just before. This gives the viewer the experience that they "turned their head" because they heard the person begin to speak. The same is true for any action or reaction. Let the action motivate the cut, not the other way around.

This can be easily remedied by rolling the edit slightly to the right so the cut happens a moment later.

28 Option-click the edit at the head of **1B-4** on track V1. Be sure to select only the Video track.

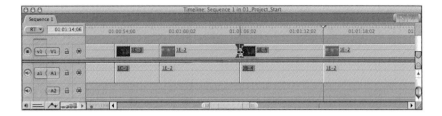

29 Press R to select the Roll tool and type *+10*.

The edit is rolled ten frames to the right.

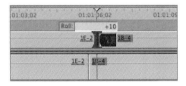

30 Press \ to play around the edit.

That improves the edit dramatically. Later, you will go through every edit in the sequence and perform a similar adjustment to split the video and audio in a similar manner.

Use Gang Sync

Because dialogue sequences like this are so common, Final Cut Pro provides a number of tools that are specifically designed for these cases. One of those tools is the Gang Sync mode.

Ganging the Viewer and sequence together means that whenever you move the playhead in either, the other follows along for the ride. This means that if the clip in the Viewer is in sync with the sequence at one point, you can move the playhead to a different point and the clip in the Viewer will remain in sync.

1 Position the sequence playhead anywhere over the **1B-4** clip.

2 Press F or choose View > Match Frame > Master Clip.

The original clip is loaded into the Viewer, cued up to the same frame, as the sequence shows.

3 Click the Playhead Sync pop-up menu button and choose Gang.

Now the playheads are locked together.

4 Play the sequence forward until just after Asteroth says, "A social worker or something?" but before he says, "Why do you care?" (01:01:26:00).

This is an appropriate edit point because the audience is likely to want to see Ann's reaction to Asteroth's accusation. It also allows you to cut to her for her next action (her confession) without appearing to anticipate that action.

5 In the Viewer, set an In point. Don't bother setting an Out point.

6   Perform an Overwrite edit and play the sequence.

Asteroth's audio gets cut off by the new edit, but that is easily remedied.

7   Option-click to select just the audio of **1E-2** and Shift-drag it to track **A2**.

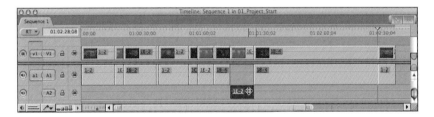

8   Zoom in, then Option-click to select the right edge of just the audio clip and extend it about 1 second.

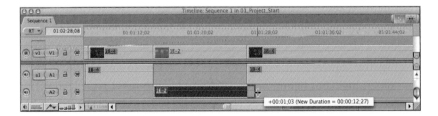

NOTE ▶ This will be much easier if you don't skip the "zoom in" instruction. Also, you may need to turn off Snapping in order to resize the clip to the desired length.

▶ **Eliminating Pauses**

It is generally frowned upon for an editor to modify the timing of an actor's line readings by adding or eliminating the natural pauses that are part of their performance. Sometimes such changes are unavoidable, but you should be careful of distorting the natural pacing of the reading.

However, this warning does not apply to controlling the pacing of the back and forth between characters during a conversation. Onscreen, everything seems slower than it does in reality, so ironically, in order to make dialogue sound more natural, you will almost always need to tighten the pacing of the lines, and often overlap lines that were performed with gaps between them.

In fact, in a scene where dialogue does naturally overlap, when shooting the singles, it is common practice to instruct the actors to deliberately not overlap. This allows the editor to control the pacing of the conversation, just as you did in this last edit.

9 Press \ to play around the edit.

The two tracks are now overlapping, which is perfect because Ann is hemming and hawing while Asteroth is still berating her. This eliminates the awkward pause between their lines.

Delaying the Close-up

The standard coverage provides five basic shots, but so far you've only used three of them. In addition to the OTS MCUs, you have a pair of close-ups, but don't rush to use them too soon. While you can move in at almost any point, once you do, you can't easily move back out without some sort of motivation (such as the waitress appearing).

While close-ups provide the most emotional power, OTS shots have the added benefit of reinforcing the posture and physical relationship between the characters. For example, think about how different this scene would play if the two were sitting side by side at barstools facing forward instead of facing off in the booth. In that case, the OTS shots would show that they weren't looking at each other, but the close-up singles would omit that information.

Save your close-ups for the emotional heart of the scene. It may have been tempting to use Asteroth's close-up for the speech he gave asking Ann about her relation to the child, or her subsequent confession, though at that point you'd be stuck in close-ups for the remainder of the scene. Still, this is one possible editorial interpretation of the scene.

You'll need to determine for yourself what is the essence of each scene. One helpful technique is to identify the "hinge," or turning point, of a scene. Every scene should have a purpose (or it doesn't belong in the show), and that purpose can usually be recognized as a moment where something happens that changes the dynamic of the story, a point from which the story cannot go back. This is the essence of what it means to "move the story forward." In this scene, is the turning point Ann's confession, or is it Asteroth's decision to take on the case? Your answer tells you the moment you should probably save for your close-ups.

Another seemingly practical reason to stay on the MCUs a bit longer is that the action of Asteroth snatching the picture would barely be visible in the tighter close-ups. That action is the hinge of the scene and is the perfect time to move from MCU to CU.

1   Find the frame in the sequence where Asteroth grabs the picture and set an In point in the middle of the action (01:01:49:26).

2 Open **1G-1** (Asteroth's CU) and find the matching frame in the middle of the action as he grabs the picture (01:20:29:23). Set an In point there.

There's not much reason to set an Out point because, as you move toward the end of the scene, you're going to replace all the shots.

3 Perform an Overwrite edit and play around the edit to see how well the action matches.

You should always try to match angles. So now that you've introduced Asteroth's CU, you should support it with Ann's CU.

4 Open **1D-1** and play the whole clip.

One of the great secrets of selecting nonverbal reaction shots is that there's no reason you can't choose a shot that might have happened at a different point in the scene. Many directors will set up a close-up reaction shot and then just direct the actor through a variety of different nonverbal reactions, one after another. This gives the editor a wide range of choices that can be used anywhere in the scene.

There is a moment in this shot where Ann slowly looks up at Asteroth, presumably gauging his reaction to the picture. Since this is exactly what the audience is doing (wondering what he's going to do), it's a perfect choice for the next edit.

5   Set an In and Out point around Ann's look (In: 01:15:51:15, Out: 54:15).

6   In the sequence, watch the **1G-1** shot, and make a determination about how long you should let it play before cutting to Ann's reaction.

Technically, there's no right or wrong answer, but the more accurately you can judge your typical viewer's attention span, the better an editor you will be. Of course, this time will vary depending on the audience you are serving. A good editor should intuitively gauge this sort of timing.

7   Position the playhead where you want Ann's reaction to begin and perform an Overwrite edit. (In the illustration, the edit was made at 01:01:56:25.)

There is still a long pause before Asteroth makes his decision and says his line. This is another subtle timing decision to determine just how long you can string the audience along without losing their attention. In this case, there are probably a few seconds of suspense that can be extracted.

8   In the sequence, set an In point at the edit at the end of Ann's reaction shot and set an Out point just before Asteroth purses his lips and looks up (01:02:02:14).

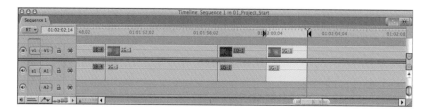

9 Press Command-Shift-A to deselect all (as a safety precaution), and press Shift-Delete to ripple delete those 2 and a half seconds.

One more reaction shot from Ann is required in response to his line, "I'll ask some questions."

If you watch Ann's CU, she makes a subtle nod when he says his line, but makes a more pronounced expression of hope a moment later when he says, "Be here tomorrow." There's no reason not to use the second expression, even though it will go in the place of the first.

10 In the Viewer, find Ann's second reaction and set it (In: 01:16:01:17, Out: 03:26).

11 In the sequence, place the playhead just after Asteroth says, "Nothing more."

12 Disable the target for track **A1**, so only the **V1** track will be used.

13 Perform an Overwrite edit to put the second reaction in the sequence.

End the Scene Quickly

You might expect that the hinge of a scene would naturally fall in the middle, but that's rarely the case. Once the key moment of a scene has occurred, that scene has served its purpose and should be ended. Often, writers will overwrite scenes, extending them long after their purpose has been accomplished. It's your job as editor to recognize this and find an elegant way to exit the scene once it has done its job.

In this case, the scene has been well crafted in that regard, and the physical action of the actor getting up gives you a perfect excuse to cut back out to the wide shot.

1   Place the playhead anywhere over the last clip in the sequence (**1-2**) and press F to load that clip in the Viewer.

There's many ways to open this clip in the Viewer. This just happens to be a quick and easy one.

2   In the Viewer, find the frame midway through the action of Asteroth getting up from the booth and set an In point there (01:03:02:10).

3   Set an Out point after Ann turns back around, and looks at her coffee, and begins to push it away (13:18).

4   Find the frame in the sequence midway through the action of Asteroth standing up (01:02:11:15).

5   Leave **A1** untargeted, and perform an Overwrite edit.

Now all the remains to complete the rough cut is to add the ending shot of the coffee.

6   Open **1M-SER** into the Viewer.

This clip is labeled SER for "series" instead of an ordinary take number. This sort of shot is common when there is a short shot, usually *MOS* (without sound), that the director wants to run several times quickly without starting and stopping the camera each time. Technically there are three takes of this shot, but they are all grouped together. As expected, this shot is MOS so you don't need to worry about the audio tracks.

While notes about numbered takes are usually reported on the camera log, in the case of a series like this one, you may not have any information to indicate which was the best version. You'll have to watch them all and choose for yourself. Here's a tip for that situation. Start at the end and go backwards. This only makes sense since once they got it right, they likely stopped repeating the shot.

7   Set an In point at the beginning of the third take, just before Ann pushes the coffee cup away (around 01:33:59:05), and set the Out point at the end of the take (around 34:11:00).

8   In the sequence, place the playhead at the end of shot **1-2**.

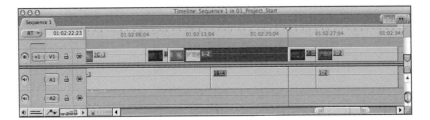

9   Perform an Overwrite edit.

There are still two extraneous audio clips left over at the end of the sequence from earlier edits that you need to get rid of.

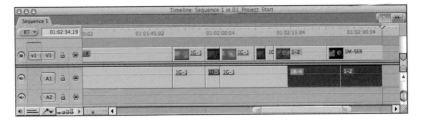

10 Select the audio from **1-2** at the end, as well as from **1B-4**, and press Delete.

11 Press Home and play the whole sequence.

Refining the Cut

Great work. You've successfully assembled the scene, thought long and hard about each of the edits, and created a version of the scene that stays true to the script. Now, you're going to start all over again and make it your own.

First, remember that regardless of how important the script may have been in getting through production, by the time you are editing the show, it really doesn't matter anymore. That doesn't mean you can't use the script as a guide, but if the footage is pulling you in a different direction, you are wise to heed its call.

Many great films are rewritten in the editing room. This is especially true for documentaries, but it can prove equally true for any type of show. It's far more important to create a sequence that makes sense and serves a deliberate purpose than to stubbornly stick to a structure that isn't working, or to insist on including passages or lines of dialogue that are redundant or irrelevant, or that confuse the scene. Don't be afraid to cut, even if it changes the script.

For example in this scene, the coffee gag (where the milk becomes curdled) is fairly important. It provides the transition to the next scene, as well as serving as a broader overarching metaphor; the white cream represents Ann (the angel) being corrupted by mixing with the black coffee (underworld). It's a clever metaphor, subtly integrated into the plot, but there's a minor technical problem. We never see Ann pour the cream into the coffee.

Fortunately, the director realized this and included an insert of Ann pouring the cream (shot **1H**). However, you have to decide how to include this shot in the scene, if at all. If you watch the scene, she does pour the cream, right around minute one. It's just that it happens mostly off-camera.

It would be relatively painless to drop in the insert shot, thereby clarifying how the cream got there, but there is a bigger problem. That long moment when she pours the cream is one of the longest *dead spots* in the scene. When you watch the sequence, it's when the viewer's focus is most likely to stray from the story. We don't know the characters, we don't even know why Ann is here yet, and now we're supposed to sit around and watch while she pours cream in her coffee? What do we care?

Dropping in the insert puts a lot of emphasis on that moment. At best, it spoils the subtlety of the metaphor and, at worst, it pulls the focus in the wrong direction. So what to do?

There's a more radical solution—but it requires some courage (at least when it comes time to explain it to the director). Cut the whole beat. Is this moment necessary? How is that moment propelling the story forward? In this case, since it appears to be harming the scene, you at least owe it to yourself to give it a try.

1   In the sequence, set an In point right after Asteroth says, "Bake a cake" (around 01:01:00:00), and set an Out point at the end of that shot.

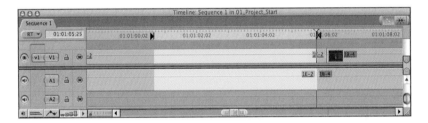

Because you previously split this edit, the audio and video edits don't line up. Since you don't want to cut off the beginning of Ann's line (which starts before the picture cut), be sure to set the Out point at the end of the audio edit instead of the video edit.

2   Deselect all and Shift-Delete the section.

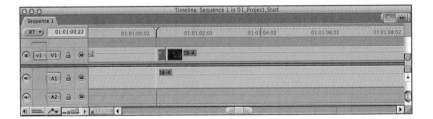

Before you can view the edit you must clean up that bit of the clip left over from the split.

3   Press R to select the Roll tool and select the edit (**V1** track only).

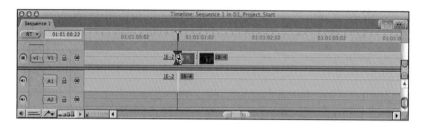

4   Drag the edit to the right to roll over the old piece of the clip.

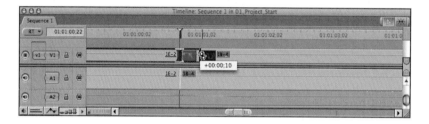

NOTE ▶ In earlier versions of Final Cut Pro you are not able to roll an edit past an adjacent edit.

5   Back up and play this section of the sequence.

Is this an improvement? If you're unsure, play the whole sequence and see how it flows. Do you miss the frames you cut? Does the scene still work? Are you perplexed at the end as to how the cream got in the coffee? Not likely.

Does that feel good? Hopefully it does. Now it's time to attack the rest of the scene with the same ruthless fervor.

If you remember from reviewing the footage in the bin, there's a shot specifically designed to open the scene. Shot **1K** is a slow boom down showing Asteroth sitting alone in the booth. The vertical move parallels the ending shot, providing nice bookends to the scene and, since this is a story about heaven and hell, showing the scene moving down toward the earth is another reference to the broader theme. Perhaps most importantly (though very subtly), it signifies Ann's descent from heaven, which is really the opening event of the scene. With the right sound design, that concept could be enhanced or downplayed. No matter what, it's a satisfying way to introduce this dark, mysterious character without revealing his face, not to mention a fun, fancy camera move that looks cool.

6   Load **1K-SER** into the Viewer.

     Knowing this is a series, you should automatically jump to the end of the clip and watch the takes in reverse.

7   Mark the last take, beginning just after the camera move begins and ending when the coffee cup on the left just reaches the edge of the frame (In: 01:32:20:15, Out: 32:30:00).

8   In the sequence, press Home to move the playhead to the head of the scene.

9   Perform an Insert edit.

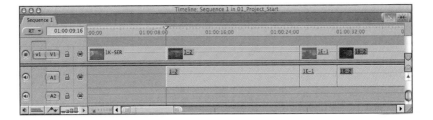

Making It Shorter

Next, look for more places where the scene can be tightened. Are there any lines that are redundant or extraneous? Are there actions that can be simplified or eliminated? Scenes need to play out in their own time, but shorter is almost always better. If a scene plays well at 2 minutes, it will play even better at 1:45. You can go too far, but you are so much more likely to err in the other direction that you shouldn't worry too much about making a scene too short.

Start at the beginning and look for places to trim the overall length of the scene.

1   Play the scene from the beginning.

Assuming the opening shot is going to have a sound effect tied to the camera move, you can leave it alone, but the second clip (**1-2**) does feel a little slow. Does Ann have to pause so long at the door?

It might pay to take a look at the other takes and see if they're shorter. You don't want to trade a better performance for a merely faster one, but it's worth a look. To assist in judging the length, it will help to know exactly how long the current shot is.

2   Position the playhead anywhere over the **1-2** shot and press X to mark the clip.

The Duration field in the Canvas indicates how long that In to Out is (16:10 in this case).

3   Load shot **1-4** and watch it for performance quality.

Unfortunately, even though the actors did fine in this take, the camera operator fumbled the end of the move. He panned too far, so when Ann stops at the booth, she is almost off the edge of the frame.

What else have you got?

4   Load shot **1A-2** and watch it.

This one is more promising. It looks as if it was shot with a different lens. Ann appears smaller at the top of the shot, but the ending frame is almost exactly the same as in **1-2**. This actually is a more dynamic shot, since she appears to make a more dramatic move. The performance is equally good, and the framing at the end of the shot is even better than 1-2 was. But is it shorter?

5   Set an In point just before Ann enters the diner and set the Out just after she says, "Mr. Roth?" (at approximately In: 01:07:15:08, Out: 29:05).

The Duration field says it all: 13:28. That's more than 3 seconds shorter than 1-2. It looks like you've got a winner. Just to be safe, watch both shots one more time to see if there's anything you're overlooking. Once you're satisfied it's the right thing to do, make the switch.

6   In the sequence, press Option-O to clear the Out point. Be sure that track A1 is targeted, and perform an Overwrite edit.

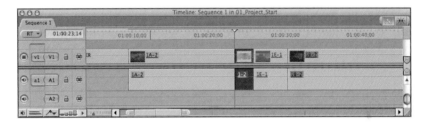

7   Select the little piece of 1-2 still in the Timeline and press Shift-Delete to ripple delete it.

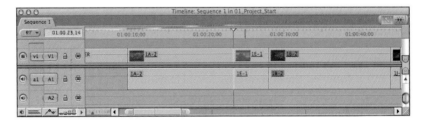

It's looking good! On to the next trouble spot.

8   Play the sequence, looking specifically for shots that seem too long.

What did you find? Perhaps you wondered about the length of the master shot after the CU of the waitress. While all the reasons for including that shot still apply, there's no reason it has to be so long!

Previously, you waited for Ann to pull out the picture to motivate the cut, but this time around, that seems to take an awfully long time. Is there any way to cut out of this shot earlier?

Not really. You could investigate using Ann's movement when she goes for the picture, but for that to match the action in shot **1C**, it would take even longer, and you would be leading the audience to the picture before they knew they cared.

But what about the head of the shot? It takes almost 10 seconds before the waitress leaves the frame. There must be a way to shorten that! The trouble is that Ann has a line ("Just coffee, please") that takes up a lot of that time. However, you can't see her face while she says the line. That means you can move the line forward and shorten the shot.

9   Zoom well into this part of the Timeline and press Command-Option-W to turn on audio waveforms.

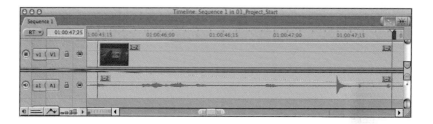

10   Stretch the audio track to make it large enough that you can see the audio waveforms clearly.

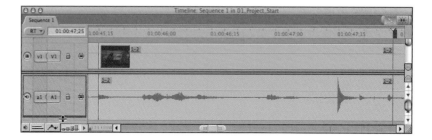

Despite the earlier warning not to mess with the pacing of line readings, all rules are meant to be broken. You need to find a way to tighten this beat. Begin by cutting out the pauses.

11 Press B to select the Razor Blade tool and, pressing Option (to only affect the audio track), add edits on both sides of the words.

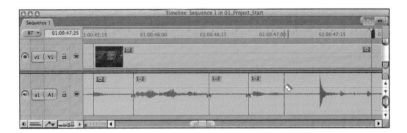

12 Delete the sections that don't contain the words. (Option-click to select just the audio.)

Don't forget about the great sound effect of the coffee cup, but don't think you have to keep it where it is.

13 Cut out the coffee cup sound too.

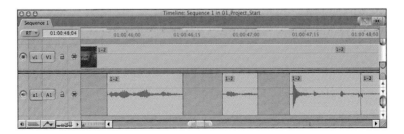

14 Play the sequence and find the last frame before you can see Ann's face (approximately 01:00:48:20).

15 Zoom out in the Timeline and press A to return to the Arrow tool.

16 Drag the coffee cup sound to track A2 to get it out of the way.

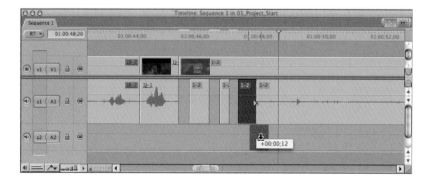

17 Drag the "Please" audio so it ends at the frame before Ann's face.

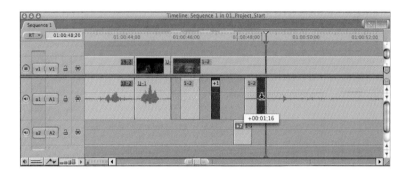

18 Drag the "Just coffee" audio so it occurs right before the "Please."

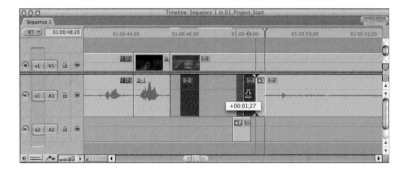

19 Set an Out point at the beginning of the "Just coffee" audio (01:00:47:22).

20 Set an In point at the beginning of the **1-2** clip.

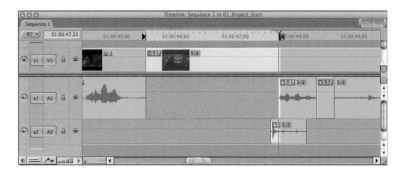

This marked area is the portion of the clip you will remove to shorten the clip. You've cut more than 2 seconds. Not bad!

21 Make sure that the coffee cup sound is to the right of the marked area.

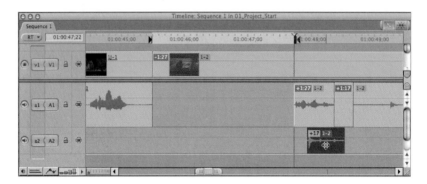

22 Press Command-Shift-A to deselect all, then press Shift-Delete to ripple delete the unwanted portion of the clip.

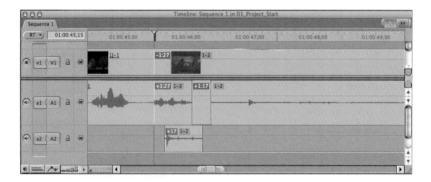

23 Press Home and play the entire sequence.

Amazing, huh? You'd hardly know it wasn't shot that way! This is a trick you can employ in a variety of circumstances.

Split Every Edit

One of the best ways to make your edits invisible is to separate the audio and video edits so they happen at different times. When both audio and video change on the same frame, the audience is twice as likely to notice the edit and be pulled out of the narrative. Scenes of all types benefit from splitting the edits this way, but it's essential for dialogue.

Final Cut Pro has a variety of features designed to accelerate or ease the creation of split edits. One of these is the Extend Edit command.

1   Press Shift-Z to zoom your Timeline to fit the whole sequence.

2   Zoom back in on the second edit, between **1A-2** and **1E-1**.

3   Option-click to select just the video edit.

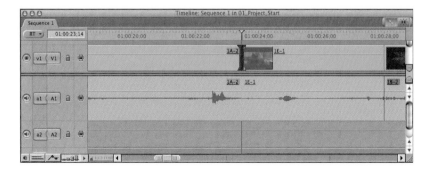

4   Position the playhead about halfway through Ann's line (visible in the audio waveform).

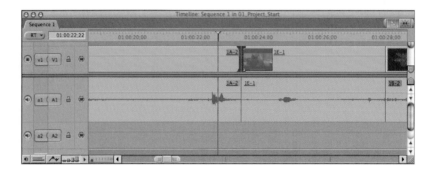

5   Press E to perform an Extend Edit.

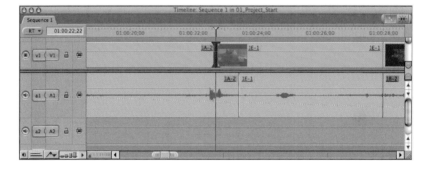

Extend Edit is a quick way to perform a roll edit. It automatically moves the selected edit to the current playhead position. It can work to the right or to the left of the edit point.

6   Play around the edit (\) to see how the split improved the edit.

The next edit to address is between **1C-1** and **1E-2** at 01:01:02:21.

7   Play around this edit, and think about how it could be improved.

For starters, there's a pause between the end of Ann's line and the beginning of Asteroth's line. Tightening that space, so that his response appears as more of a snap, is consistent with his character.

8 Zoom in on that edit and, using the audio waveforms as a guide, set In and Out points around the quiet section at the end of the first clip and the beginning of the second.

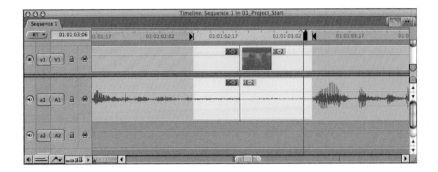

TIP If you're ever in doubt that the area you marked contains the end of a word or something you don't want to delete, press Shift-\ to play from In to Out.

9 Deselect all and press Shift-Delete to remove the gaps.

That improves the timing, but now the edit is begging to be split, since the cut happens just as the other character begins talking.

There are two kinds of split edits. If the video leads the audio, it's called an L-cut and if the audio leads the video, it's called a J-cut. J-cuts are far more common than L-cuts because they support the sound triggering the picture cut. Remember the audience members "turning their heads" because they heard something? Using a J-cut is a very natural and effective way to hide an edit.

10 Press R to select the Roll tool and Option-click to select the edit on track V1.

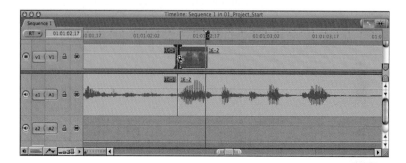

11 Roll the edit to the right by about 10 frames until it's located just past Asteroth's first couple of words.

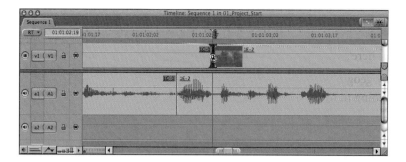

12 Play around the edit.

The next edit is already split as the result of work you did earlier in the lesson. You should repeat steps 8 through 11 on the edit between clips **1B-4** and **1E-2** at 01:01:13:00.

Watch Out for Screen Direction Errors

If you play back the whole scene, it's mostly working very well. However, there is one more edit that still needs adjusting.

13 Play across the third edit (between **1E-1** and **1B-2**) when Ann sits down in the booth.

Does anything about this edit bother you? Something should. There's a screen direction error in it. In the outgoing shot, she's moving from left to right, but in the incoming shot she's moving right to left.

There will be more time spent on screen direction errors in later lessons, but here's a quick preview of one way to solve them.

The geography of the diner isn't in doubt, so it's not a huge error. No one is going to be confused about where she is sitting, but it is a jarring edit and there's no reason to live with it. The easiest way to solve a problem like this is to find another shot where the screen direction is correct. If you can find a shot where she is moving directly on axis with the camera, rather than moving either right to left or left to right, it could easily cut with either shot.

Fortunately, you have that shot in the master.

14 Load **1A-2** into the Viewer.

15 Find and mark the area when Ann begins to sit down, but before she completely settles in her seat (In: 01:07:35:00 Out: 36:00).

16 In the sequence, position the playhead directly on the edit. Untarget the audio track and perform an Overwrite edit.

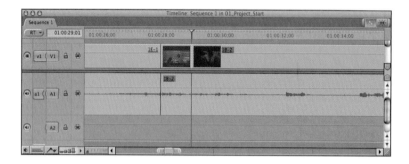

17 Play across the new edit.

While not as smooth as a simple two-shot cut, the screen direction problem is solved and her movement successfully hides both edits.

18 Save and close project **01_Project_Start**.

The Basis for All Editing

The tools and techniques covered in this first lesson are not limited to dialogue scenes. They are the same basic rules you will use (and sometimes deliberately break) in every scene you cut. Everything is built on these fundamentals.

Dialogue scenes are especially good practice. Because the standard editing pattern is fairly rigid, it's like writing haiku: You must learn to be creative and identify the specific details of the scene that make it strong and unique despite the formal rules that constrict you.

Lesson Review

1. What are the three components of story?
2. What question does a long shot frequently answer?
3. What must editors be aware of above all else?

4. What command can be used to clean up an edit point?

5. What are the five basic shots common to most dialogue scenes?

6. What are three other shot categories common to dialogue scenes?

7. How should you begin editing a scene?

8. How can you create a split edit?

9. How do you label and color-code clips?

10. Describe an Extend Edit.

11. What does Gang Sync do?

Answers

1. First, the six questions; (who, what, where, when, why and how) second, the order and pacing of how they are conveyed and third, the theme or purpose.

2. A long shot typically identifies *where* an event is taking place.

3. The theme or main idea of the show they're cutting.

4. Ripple delete.

5. Master shot, OTS of person 1, OTS of person 2, CU of person 1, CU of person 2.

6. Inserts, cutaways, and specials.

7. Review and organize your footage in Final Cut Pro bins; then begin editing with a master shot that covers the whole duration of the scene.

8. Use the Roll tool to make the picture and sound edits occur at different times.

9. Select the clips, then Control-click and choose Label.

10. An Extend Edit is a roll edit that moves the selected edit to the current position of the playhead.

11. Click the Playhead Sync pop-up and choose Gang. Gang Sync locks the playhead in the Viewer with the playhead in the sequence.

2

Lesson Files	Lesson Project Files > Lesson_02 > 01a_Project_Start
Media	Media > FBI Guys Dialogue
Time	This lesson takes approximately 90 minutes to complete.
Goals	Edit complex dialogue scenes with more than two people
	Tackle scenes that combine dialogue and action
	Manage dialogue scenes that occur in more than one location within a single scene
	Use head turns and eyelines to clarify room geometry
	Control scene pacing

Editing Complex Dialogue

By this point, you should feel confident to tackle another dialogue scene similar to the diner scene, but what happens when there are more than two people in the scene? Also, what happens when the subjects move to new positions during the scene? These elements complicate the scene, and require modifications to your editing practices.

Editing Complex Scenes

As with any scene, you are dependent on the wit and competence of the director and the crew. Complex scenes require well-thought-out coverage. In a scene where the actors move during the scene, a crew will often shoot standard coverage for each of the blocking positions. Additionally, transitional elements and little moments that require special attention will receive their own shots, or series of shots. This can quickly add up to a giant slough of footage that you must wade through and make sense of.

1   Open project **01a_Project_Start**.

2   Double-click the Unorganized Clips bin to open it in its own window.

This scene from the film "FBI Guys" is a simple boardroom scene, in which the two desk agents must face their boss after overstepping their jobs and cracking a field case. Although it is a simple scene, it contains several sections. The agents enter the room and sit down; they have a brief exchange with a jealous co-worker; the boss enters and chews them out; another agent explains how their work was helpful; and finally, after they get up to leave, they get up the nerve to ask for a promotion.

The scene contains 25 clips, labeled **43A** through **43Y**.

NOTE ▶ When naming and numbering scenes, the letters I and O are always skipped as they can too easily be confused with 1 (one) and 0 (zero).

Although the scenes are labeled in the order they were shot, that doesn't mean that they are arranged in a way that is useful to the editor. It's up to you to group and organize them so you have a solid understanding of the available options for each section of the scene.

In fact, because different parts of this scene take place in slightly different locations in the conference room, you have to keep track at all times of where the people are in the room. Even though you might have a close-up of Phil sitting at the table performing a perfect reaction, you can't use it during a part of the scene where he's supposed to be standing at the door.

3 Close the Unorganized Clips bin.

4 Click the disclosure triangle to expand the Organized Clips bin.

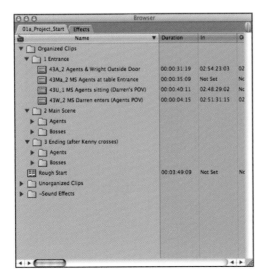

This bin already has been organized into three sections in which the main characters are in different positions. Additionally, two of the sections have been subdivided into shots of the agents and shots of the bosses. Since the majority of the scene is a dialogue between the two agents and the three bosses, this allows you to think of those two parties as two individuals (like Ann and Asteroth) instead of five different people.

5   Click the disclosure triangle to expand the Agents bin in the 2 Main Scene bin and double-click shot **43Y_4 LS Master OTS Blithers**.

6   Watch the clip to get a sense of the scene.

Due to the size of the room, and the complexity of the scene, there is not one single master that gives a sense of the whole sequence. This shot gives a good sense of half of the room, and runs almost to the end of the scene.

7   Expand the Bosses bin in the 2 Main Scene bin and double-click shot **43B_4 LS Blithers OTS Phil&Bob**.

8   Press Shift-\ to play In to Out.

This clip shows the other half of the room.

Both of these long shots are helpful to get a sense of the scene and, because they are staged as OTS shots, they might prove useful during the edit. But because they are so wide, you should already be thinking that they're likely to get only minimal usage in the final scene. Still, they can be helpful as a foundation to the scene, upon which you can build using the tighter coverage.

Finding the First Event

The way to approach a large, multiple-event scene like this is to lay out the overall structure of the scene, and then tackle each event individually.

9 Double-click the Rough Start sequence to open it into the Canvas and Timeline. Home the playhead, then resave the project.

10 Play the scene.

The structure of the scene has already been assembled for you. With a complex scene like this, it's very helpful to lay out a rough assembly of the whole sequence using your masters, even though almost all of it will eventually be replaced with tighter shots. This helps you keep the big picture of the scene in focus as you work on building out the beats one by one.

The first event you'll address is Darren's entrance. When Darren (in the dark red shirt) enters the conference room, he has a brief exchange with the two agents. This is covered in two matching medium shots, **43U** and **43W**.

11 Open **43W_2 MS Darren enters (Agents POV)** and play it.

Darren enters, says his line, then sits down and makes a series of mocking gestures. Obviously, the intention was not to use all these gestures; the actor was providing a series of choices for you.

12 Set an In on the first frame just as Darren enters the shot (around 02:51:31:18) and set an Out after he sits down (approximately 38:00).

By now you're probably thinking that you're going to want a reaction from the agents before Darren sits down, so why are you keeping this shot so long? It's still a good idea to lay in Darren's whole action so you will have a consistent sound track covering his sitting.

13 In the sequence, look for a frame to approximate Darren's position at the beginning of **43W**.

Because **43W** is from the agents' POV, the correct matching frame should be just as Darren passes where they're sitting. Fortunately, due to the master shot's compressed geometry, it's very hard to tell exactly when he passes them. (It could be anywhere from 45:15 to 47:10.) This gives you plenty of flexibility in choosing where to drop in the MS.

14 Set an In point in the sequence at approximately 46:00.

15 Overwrite **43W** into the sequence.

16 Open **43U_1 MS Agents sitting (Darren's POV)** and play it.

You are looking for a moment that sells the idea that they're reacting to Darren. But where is the best place to begin? Always start by looking for a physical movement. Performances are made up of physical actions. Sometimes they are obvious—jumping out of the way or pulling a trigger—but other times they are subtle—a shift in the eyes or a tiny frown. As an editor, you must constantly deconstruct these actions and interpret them. They are your road map to the emotional terrain of a scene. They can also be an indicator of the truth of a performance, and choosing the wrong action can quickly ruin a scene. Regardless of how the actor performed the scene on set, it is in the editing room that their performances are honed.

The action at the cut point carries the most weight because it is juxtaposed against the shot to which it refers. In this scene, there are three distinct actions. First, the agents turn their heads; second, Phil (the dark-haired agent) clenches his fist; and third, they look straight ahead, attempting to ignore Darren. (Yes, sometimes deliberately doing nothing is an action.) You could begin this shot with any of those three actions.

Like every editorial decision, there is no wrong answer, but for this lesson, you'll begin with the head turn.

17 Set an In point two or three frames before the agents turn their heads (02:48:29:02).

18 In the sequence, set an In point just as Darren looks down at his chair (01:00:49:04).

Starting here serves two purposes. Storywise, you're emphasizing Darren's apparent power over the agents by juxtaposing them looking up at him *after* he has looked away from them. Structurally, starting the shot after he looks down means you don't have to cut back to Darren. Since he's already looked away from them, you don't need his reaction to their reaction (which saves you from using any of the hammy "mocking gestures"). Finally, because looking down is the beginning of his sitting down, that tiny gesture plus the sound of the chair sell the idea that he has been seated, without having to show it on screen.

19 Set an Out point in the sequence at the existing edit point between **43Y** and **43B**. Untarget tracks A1 and A2, so Darren's chair audio doesn't get overwritten.

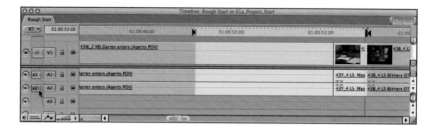

20 Overwrite the clip into the sequence.

21 Play the two new shots and see how they fit.

Not bad. Now the "staring straight ahead" action accidentally serves a new purpose. It looks like the agents are reacting to the entrance of the boss. This can be enhanced further by adding a sound effect of the door opening right before they look forward.

22 In the Sound Effects bin, select **DoorOpenClose** and open it into the Viewer.

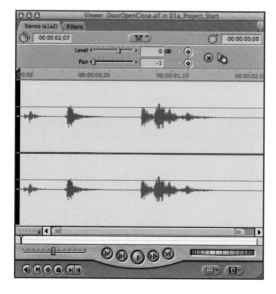

23 Play the clip and set an Out point after the door opens but before it closes.

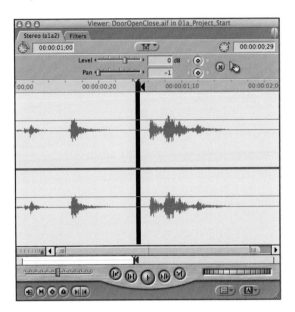

24 In the sequence, find the frame where Phil starts to look toward the front of the room.

He does a sort of double-take, beginning to turn his head the first time around 51:17. Since you want the sound to motivate his look, it should begin shortly before that.

25 Set an In point at 51:12 and target tracks A3 and A4 in the Timeline.

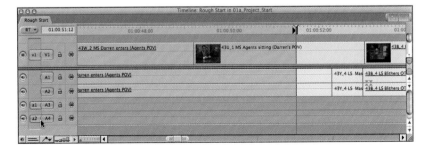

26 Overwrite the door sound into the sequence.

> **TIP** To drag an audio clip from the Viewer, click the drag-target in the upper-right corner of the window.

This sort of sound work is usually done much later in the editing process (for good reasons described in Lesson 10). However, this example shows that you can often use sound in place of (or in conjunction with) pictures in order to best tell the story.

The exchange between the agents and Darren was the first event of the scene and, although you simplified it greatly, its purpose has been served. It is your obligation not just to assemble the events, but also to interpret them and cull only the most essential beats. That finishes the Entrance section of the scene.

27 Click the disclosure triangle next to the 1 Entrance bin to collapse it.

Completing the Second Event

Next, it's time to move to the meat of the scene. Here you're going to encounter the complexities of a dialogue scene with multiple people.

Recall that it's essential to keep track of whose scene it is, since you must pay extra attention to that person (or persons). This is the agents' scene. They are the main characters in the story and, in this scene, the main action is that they are facing the consequences of their prior behavior. Don't be fooled into thinking it's Blithers' scene, just because he does all the talking.

Also, don't forget to look for the turning point of the scene. Without the context of the whole movie, it may be harder for you to spot, but there is a very definite hinge: when Phil corrects the boss's pronunciation of his name. This act of defiance is a major turning point for the character, not just in this scene, but in the film (and it supports the broader themes of the film, self-respect and self-determination).

Unlike the diner scene in "Hope," the hinge here doesn't happen right at the end of the scene, but this is a much larger, more complex scene. In some ways, that action signifies the end of one scene and the start of a new scene in the same location. (That second half has its own turning point when Blithers gives the agents a new assignment.)

Some editors prefer to begin editing a scene by cutting the turning point moment first. While this might challenge your sense of continuity, it's not a bad approach. After all, that's the most important moment, and the stylistic or pacing decisions made there should inform the way you cut the rest of the scene (and not the other way around).

To keep things simple, in this exercise you'll continue to edit the scene in chronological order.

1   Play the sequence from the end of the last edit you made until Blithers (the big bald guy with the moustache) begins talking.

Do you see the need for an edit?

You should only add an edit when it's necessary because some new piece of information is missing. Are the six questions all answered, or is the audience likely to be wondering about something?

Perhaps it occurs to you that what is missing is the reaction of our heroes, the agents. What are they doing while Blithers is getting settled? Are they nervous? Confident? Still sniping with Darren?

2   Open shot **43Mb_3 MS Agents at Table**, and type *1537.* (don't miss the period at the end) to move the playhead to 02:15:37:00.

3   Play the clip from that point.

Here's the agents' reaction to Blithers' entrance. Now, find a section to cut away to while Blithers is getting ready in the long shot. Remember, since it's a cutaway, it can come from anywhere in the shot. As long as they're not talking, nothing will appear out of sync.

4   Set an In point at 02:15:37:20 and an Out point at 39:20.

5   In the sequence, watch the scene until you reach a point that feels like the right moment to lay in the cutaway of the agents. (In the picture below, the edit happens at 01:01:00:10.)

6   Untarget the audio tracks and overwrite the clip into the sequence.

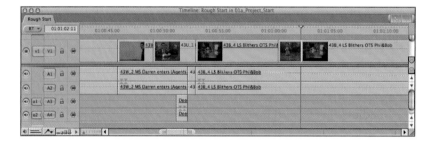

Although in the master there is still a fairly long pause before Blithers says his next line, there's not much reason not to jump right to it.

7   Open **43G_3 MCU Blithers** and set an In point right before he says, "Connolly," at approximately 21:26:41:05.

8   Set an Out point a beat after he says, "Tonto" (approximately 51:20).

9 Target the audio to tracks A1 and A2 and overwrite the clip directly after shot **43Mb_3** and play this section of the sequence.

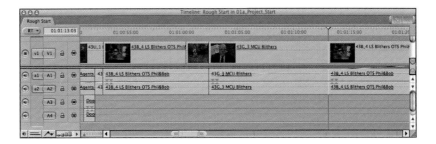

Any ideas coming to mind? You may have thought that edit would be a lot smoother if the audio came in before the picture. Kudos to you if you did think that and, if you didn't, maybe you will the next time.

There's a way to split an edit before you even add it to the sequence.

10 Press Command-Z to undo that last edit.

11 In the Timeline, position the playhead right in the middle of shot **43Mb_3** (approximately 01:01:01:10).

12 Press Command-Option-I or choose Mark > Mark Split > Audio In to set an audio-only In point.

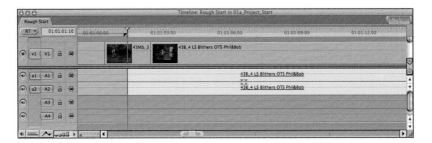

13 Press Down Arrow to move the playhead to the next edit.

14 Press Control-I to add a video-only in point.

You have just defined a split In point in the sequence. Watch what happens when you edit in the shot.

15 Perform an Overwrite edit.

16 View the new edit.

Voilá! Instant split edit. While this practice can be easy in some instances, many times it's just as quick to perform the edit normally and split it afterwards using the Roll and Ripple tools.

At the end of that shot, Blithers looks up to his right, where Kenny is sitting. Any ideas what the next shot should be?

17 Open **43E_2 MCU Kenny** into the Viewer and mark the section where he responds to the Tonto taunt (In: 01:19:36:11, Out: 38:10).

18 Overwrite it into the sequence directly after the Blithers clip.

19 Play around this latest edit.

You can hear the beginning of Kenny's laugh in the Blithers shot, and then again in the single of Kenny. This can easily be cleaned up with a little trimming, creating another split edit.

20 Press R twice to select the Ripple tool and select the Out point of **43G**.

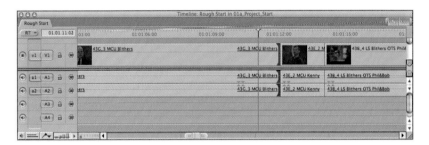

21 Drag the edit to the Left by about 1 second to eliminate the laugh in the outgoing clip.

This eliminates the double laugh, but you still want to see Blithers look up to Kenny.

22 Press Command-Shift-A to deselect the edit. Press R to select the Roll tool and Option-click the video edit.

23 Drag the edit to roll it to the right, watching the Canvas until the frame where Blithers looks up at Kenny is visible.

That four-step process is another common way to create a split edit. It's slower than the previous example, but it allows more precise control over the placement of the split.

Blithers' look motivates the cut to Kenny, but rather than going right back to Blithers, this break gives you the opportunity to take a moment and check out the rest of the room. And guess who the audience is most interested in seeing? The agents. You could go back to the two-shot of the agents, but you've just come off the MCU of Blithers, and another MCU of Kenny. Remember the rule about matching shot sizes? Instead of returning to that two-shot, try going to one of the MCUs of the agents.

24 Open **43P_1 MCU Phil.**

There's a great expression of defeat that would fit perfectly here.

25 Set an In at 02:23:10:16 and an Out at 11:15.

26 Untarget the audio tracks and overwrite **43P** directly after the Kenny shot.

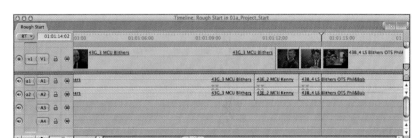

Because you've been trimming seconds from the scene as you've added each of these shots, the audio in the sequence might seem confusing, because the audio from the master shot is repeating the Lone Ranger line while Phil is fretting. However, that's easily fixed with another J-edit.

27 In the Timeline, place the playhead at the start of **43P**. Control-click the ruler and from the shortcut menu, choose Mark Split > Audio In.

28 Move the playhead to the end of **43P**, Control-click the ruler again, and from the shortcut menu, choose Mark Split > Video In.

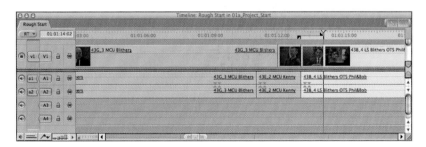

29 Use the Recent Clips menu in the Viewer to access **43G_3 MCU Blithers**.

30 Set In and Out points around the line, "You two ever hear of protocol?" (In: 21:26:56:02, Out: 58:00).

31 Check that the audio tracks are targeted and perform an Overwrite edit, automatically splitting the edit.

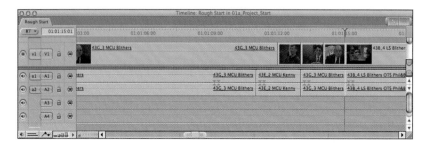

Before you proceed, note that the master clips that were supposed to form the foundation of the scene are getting pretty far out of sync with the edits you've made. If you were close to the end of the scene, you might disregard this, but in this instance, there's quite a bit more to go.

32 In the Timeline, set an In point at the end of the last instance of **43G_3**.

33 Set an Out point after Blithers says, "You two ever hear of protocol?" in the master shot (approximately 01:01:22:15).

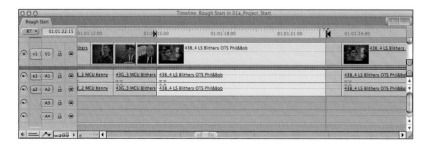

34 Press Command-Shift-A to deselect all, then press Shift-Delete to ripple delete the marked region.

Now the remainder of the scene will remain approximately in sync with the clips you've already edited in. You may have to repeat this occasionally in a scene where you are cutting lines or spaces while laying in the coverage.

Keeping Track of People

The next event in the scene is Bob's rebuttal to Blithers' accusation. You could cut directly to Bob as he begins his line, or you can look for a *bridge*. In this scene, we haven't yet seen a close-up of Wright (the philosopher from the doorway). It would be helpful to incorporate him into the scene and this moment presents the perfect opportunity.

In the story, Wright is Phil and Bob's direct superior, working in between them and Blithers. In this scene, he is (not accidentally) physically sitting between them. Here's an opportunity to reinforce that relationship editorially.

1 Open **43H_1 MS Wright** into the Viewer.

2 Mark the section where Wright wryly looks from Blithers to the agents (In: 01:33:49:20, Out: 51:00).

This shot is perfect because Wright's head turn motivates the next cut. It begs the question: what's he looking at? You can answer that question with the next shot. Head turns are especially useful in complex dialogue scenes because they help clarify the physical relationships between people.

One minor problem however, is that the audio is not good on this shot. (Bob is talking but isn't on mic.) So rather than laying this shot in and then doing another split edit afterwards, this time you can edit in Bob's shot, then go back and drop Wright on top of it. (Yet another way to create a split edit.)

3   Open **43Q_2 MCU Bob** and mark the section where he delivers his line, "Sir, we did present the intel to…" .

On this particular take, Blithers' dialogue nearly overlaps Bob's. Since you don't want to have any double words (or breaths), before editing this shot, you may need to adjust the In and Out points by a frame or two.

4   In the Viewer, press Shift-\ to play In to Out.

If you hear any of Blithers' dialogue on either side, move the In or Out point until Bob's audio is totally clean. The correct In and Out should be In: 02:34:48:00, Out: 50:12.

5   Make sure the audio tracks are targeted and overwrite **43Q** into the sequence directly after **43G**.

6   Use the Recent Clips menu to reopen **43H_1 MS Wright**.

The In and Out points you previously set will still be active.

7 Untarget the audio tracks, position the playhead at the *beginning* of **43Q**, and overwrite the clip into the sequence.

8 Play back this section of the sequence and check that all the edits are working properly.

Before jumping back to Blithers, it might be nice to see what Phil's been doing during all of this.

9 Open **43P_1 MCU Phil**.

If you watch, while Bob is trying to explain, Phil provides one of those invaluable head turns, which will easily motivate (and therefore hide) your cut back to Blithers.

10 Mark the head turn (In: 02:23:24:08, Out: 25:15).

Now you must decide where to put it in the scene. This beat is a mite tricky, since Bob cuts himself off. If you put a video cut at the same moment when Bob stops talking, it will look and sound like a mistake.

That means that **43P** must begin before Bob stops talking, or after it's clear that Blithers has cut him off. Either could work, but momentum and brevity favor starting the shot earlier.

11 Position the sequence playhead right after Bob says the word "intel" (01:01:17:00).

12 Make sure the audio tracks aren't targeted (we don't want to hear the audio from the Phil shot) and overwrite **43P** into the show.

The edit still feels weird, and it's because Blithers' line is starting late. It should begin before Bob stops talking to motivate his silence. If the actors had overlapped their lines on set, you would have a very hard time controlling the edit to make the lines overlap correctly. Fortunately, there are clean versions of their lines that allow you to set the overlap to your liking.

13 Press A to select the Arrow tool and, in the sequence, Option-click the audio tracks for **43Q** (Bob), then Shift-drag them to tracks 3 and 4.

14 Option-drag the left edge of the **43B** (master) audio to the left about 18 frames.

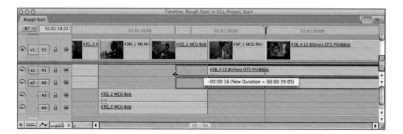

It now makes sense that Bob shuts up (Blithers cuts him off), while the cut to Phil is still sufficiently hidden.

Keeping Track of Location

You've just used a series of six close-ups in a row, featuring five different people. Where are all these people? Are you having trouble keeping track of the geography of the room? If so, the audience is probably having trouble, too.

Fortunately, in this example, the close-ups aren't that close, and you've had three different head turns to reinforce the physical relationships between people in the room. But if you were cutting a scene where the shots were tighter, and you didn't have those head-turn cues, it's very likely that your audience would begin to lose track of the physical space in the room.

Cutting back to the master at this point isn't a terrible choice. It reinforces the geography and could be justified by the natural pause in the conversation following Blithers' action of shutting Bob down. That pause provides an editorial opportunity to reset the stage, so to speak, which is exactly what a cut to the master does.

But this particular master is too wide. While it does have both agents' shoulders, they're really not part of the shot. What this moment really calls for is a shot that you don't have: a slightly tighter master that shows both the agents and Blithers in the same angle.

Since the production is long wrapped, it's not likely anyone's going to go back and pick that shot up for you, so you need to press on without it. And, in this case, the simplest answer is to go back to Blithers' MCU and hope for the best.

1   Use the Recent Clips menu to open **43G_3 MCU Blithers** into the Viewer.

2   Set an In point right before the word "down" (in the line "Stand down") and set an Out point after "superiors" (In: 21:27:01:18, Out: 14:05).

3   In the sequence, position the playhead at the end of Phil's CU (**43P**).

4   Make sure the audio tracks are targeted to A1 and A2, and overwrite the
clip into the sequence.

There is one minor problem with this shot. A distracting camera move in
the middle of this take would be best hidden. Remember that your job is
about controlling the viewer's focus. That camera move pulls attention away
from the content of the scene and puts the attention on the camera instead.

5   Play the sequence until just before the camera move as Blithers says,
"Answer." Set an In point there (01:01:21:07).

Do you have any idea of what to use to cover it up? One idea would be to put
a shot of Darren here. It's been an awfully long time since you've shown him,
and it would be nice to be reminded that he's in the room. Alternatively, you
could show Bob and Phil's reaction to Blithers' attack.

Both of those are valid solutions, but here's one more. Always pay attention
to both sides of an edit. Think about when you're going to come back to
Blithers. If you play forward a few seconds, Blithers is looking up at Kenny.

6   Set an Out point there in the sequence, right around 01:01:22:20, just before Blithers says, "As to why my top field agents…"

7   Open **43E_2 MCU Kenny** and scan through it to find an appropriate reaction.

Remember that Kenny is being reprimanded here, so you should be looking for an expression of guilt. The closest shot is right after his "Tonto" line. He has a sort of embarrassed expression.

Since the Out point is what's going to match Blithers' withering glare, you should focus more on finding the right Out point in the Kenny clip.

8   Set an Out point in the Viewer at 01:19:39:20. Press Option-I to clear the In point.

9   Make sure the audio is untargeted and perform an Overwrite edit.

10   Play around the edit to see how well the cutaway works.

Build Up to the Climax

Throughout this scene, you have pretty aggressively cut out pauses and even whole lines of dialogue. Part of the reason is to make the scene shorter, but it's not quite that simple. First and foremost, your purpose is to pay attention to performance and eliminate any expendable beats where you feel the performance isn't working.

Second, you must be watching for redundancy. Scripts are often full of redundancy. It's redundant when Blithers says, "Now I have to explain to the brass…" and then a moment later says, "How do I look to my superiors…" Both lines serve the same purpose, in terms of explaining the story and explaining the character's motivations. Are both needed? No, not unless some other new information is being conveyed.

Third, you adjust the timing of a sequence as a way to control its pacing. That means that you not only tighten bits of a scene, you might also deliberately pad a moment to allow suspense to build or to draw attention to the action that follows.

At this point in the scene, Phil is finally going to own up to having hatched the whole scheme and at the same time, he is going to stand up for himself against Blithers. It's the turning point and so it deserves a little special attention. You already know how to take extra seconds out of a scene; now you'll learn how to put some back.

1   Position the sequence playhead at the end of **43G_3** and set an In point.

2   Open **43P_1 MCU Phil.**

Rather than going straight to his line, look at the section in Phil's close-up where Blithers is saying, "How do you think that makes me look?" Phil has a great expression of total despair. The audience doesn't yet know what he's going to do, and that's exactly what you want. You want to hold that suspense as long as possible.

3   Set an In point at 02:23:36:00 and an Out point 2 seconds later at 38:00. Be sure not to include any frames at the end of the shot where he begins to look back up, as that begins his next action.

4   Make sure the audio is untargeted, and perform an Insert edit.

NOTE ▸ You can safely ignore the warning that some clips will be moved out of sync.

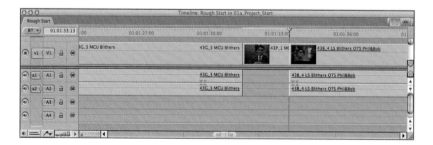

This creates a gap in the audio track, but don't worry. You can easily fill that gap later with room tone and other ambient elements. For now, just get the timing of the moment right.

5   Open **43Q_2 MCU Bob** and find the same section, where Blithers is blathering about his superiors.

Although these two looks happened at the same time in the scene, there's no reason you can't stack them one after the other to stretch out the moment.

6   Set an In point at 02:35:02:00 and an Out point at 03:10.

Be sure not to include any of Bob nodding as he does at the end of this bit. The idea is that they are both defeated and the physical gesture of looking down conveys a different meaning than the nodding.

This is an example where you are completely changing the actor's performance, transforming "complicity" to "despair." Don't worry, he won't mind as long as it makes the film better (and as long as you give him all the credit).

7   Insert this clip into the sequence directly after **43P**. (Again, respond Yes to the Out of Sync warning.)

But that's not enough! It's not just Phil and Bob who are disappointed here. Their mentor, Wright, is also distraught.

8   Open **43H_1 MS Wright** and find the same moment in the scene.

9   Set an In point at 01:34:10:20 and an Out point at 13:13.

This shot ends with Wright looking down to Phil, presumably motivated by Phil speaking.

10 Insert this clip into the sequence following **43H**.

11 Play over the three clips you just inserted and find the frame where you should begin to hear Phil's line (approximately 01:01:36:00).

12 Press Command-Option-I to set an audio In point.

13 Press Down Arrow to move the playhead to the end of Wright's shot and press Control-I to set the video In point.

14 Use the Recent Clips menu to open **43P_1 MCU Phil** into the Viewer.

15 Set an In point just before Phil's sigh at 02:23:40:00. Set the Out point after he says, "Angelino…Sir" at 52:05.

16 Make sure the audio tracks are targeted and overwrite the clip into the sequence.

To further heighten this moment, rather than rushing back to Blithers, you can take this opportunity to show some of the other people's reactions to Phil's confession.

17 In the sequence, set an In point after Phil says, "Responsible" at 01:01:40:00.

18 Load **43Q_2 MCU Bob** into the Viewer and find the moment where Bob turns his head to look at Phil (In: 02:35:06:10, Out: 07:09).

19 Untarget the audio tracks and overwrite the clip into the sequence.

20 In the sequence, set an In point at the end of Bob's shot and set an Out point right before Phil's brooding look, as he decides to stand up for himself (Out: 01:01:42:15).

21 Load **43G_3 MCU Blithers** into the Viewer. Find where Blithers says, "Oh really, Angelina" and set an Out just afterwards, at 21:27:19:06. Press Option-I to clear the In point.

22 Retarget the audio tracks and overwrite the clip into the sequence.

23 Play around the new edit.

The edit mostly works, but Blithers' audio has a double "oh" on both sides of the edit.

24 Select the audio-only edit between **43P** and **43G** (press Option to select only the audio).

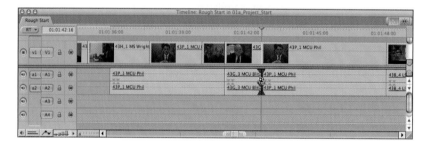

25 Press R to select the Roll tool and type *-10* to roll the edit to the left.

26 Play the whole sequence up to this point and admire all the work you've done.

You might want to cut one more exchange between Blithers' and Phil's close-ups instead of using the master for the last part of this section, but for the sake of the lesson, you can stop here and skip to the next edit.

Mixing Doing and Talking

So far, in all of the dialogue examples, the subjects haven't been doing anything except talking. But in many instances, a scene mixes dialogue and action.

The next section of this scene, beginning with Kenny crossing behind Blithers, is a good, simple example of this.

1 In the Browser, collapse the 2 Main Scene bin and expand the Agents and Bosses bins in the "3 Ending (after Kenny crosses)" bin.

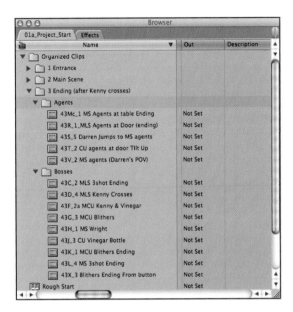

2   In the Timeline, skip to the next edit in the sequence, which begins with
    Kenny walking behind Blithers. Set an In point at the beginning of that shot.

3   Open **43D_4 MLS Kenny Crosses** from the Bosses bin inside the 3
    Ending bin.

    This is a somewhat tighter shot that has a clearer point of focus than the
    wider master shot.

4 Set an In point at the beginning of the shot and an Out point as Kenny reaches for the vinegar bottle (around 01:14:37:21).

5 Overwrite the clip into the sequence.

Once Kenny approaches that bottle, the viewer's attention is likely to be focused there. Because of that, the next most logical shot is the insert shot.

6 Open **43J_3 CU Vinegar Bottle.**

7 Set an In point just before Kenny begins to twirl the bottle (01:43:08:00) and set the Out point as he lifts the bottle out of the frame (13:20).

As always, use objects moving in the frame to hide the edit. In this case, the bottle exiting the frame in this shot and entering the frame in the next is one of the simplest, most traditional ways of covering this sort of action.

8 Overwrite the clip into the sequence directly after **43D.**

9 Open **43F_2a MCU Kenny & Vinegar.**

10 Set an In point as the bottle enters the frame (01:20:48:07) and set the Out point after Kenny says, "Now we know their M.O." (approximately 21:00:00).

11 Overwrite the clip into the sequence directly after **43J.**

12 Play this section of the sequence.

A little cleanup is required to eliminate the double audio between the second two clips. This is a procedure you should be very familiar with by now.

13 Select the audio edit between **43J** and **43F** (press Option to override linking).

14 Press R to select the Roll tool and type *-20* to roll the edit to the left.

Despite all this interesting action, never forget who the scene is really about. Kenny gets the limelight for a moment, but you quickly need to bring back the agents.

15 Use the Recent Clips menu to open **43P_1 MCU Phil** into the Viewer.

16 Mark the area where Phil is watching the vinegar gag.

Try to find a moment that includes a specific physical action, such as the way he sits back in his chair between 02:24:23:20 and 26:10.

17 In the sequence, set an In point just as Kenny says, "immersion oil," around 01:02:20:05.

18 Untarget the audio tracks and overwrite the clip into the sequence.

Although the front of this edit works, coming back to Kenny feels a little awkward because it cuts back to him after just one action (his amazement at the trick) but a beat before his next action (commending the agents).

This insert of Phil might work a little better if it was shifted to the right a few frames.

19 Position the playhead just before Kenny says, "Thanks to you two guys" at 01:02:23:08.

20 Press S twice or from the Tool palette select the Slide tool.

21 Click the **43P** clip and drag it to the right until it snaps to the playhead. (Press N to turn snapping on if it is currently disabled.)

Sliding a clip moves it within the clips around it by rolling the edits on either side of the clip simultaneously. The contents of the clip don't change, but the clip's position in the sequence does.

22 In the sequence, set an In point just after Kenny puts the bottle down and right before he says, "Now we know their M.O." (approximately 01:02:25:10).

23 Use the Recent Clips menu to open **43Q_2 MCU Bob** into the Viewer.

24 Mark Bob's great reaction beginning at 02:35:41:15 and ending at 44:10.

25 Overwrite the clip into the sequence.

26 Open **43H_1 MS Wright** and mark just before and after he says, "Not bad" (In: 01:35:02:00 Out: 03:10).

27 Retarget the audio tracks and edit the clip into the sequence directly after **43Q**.

Naturally, by now you know that you are practically obligated to show the agents' reaction to Wright's compliment, but in the vein of laying down the foundation first, it may be helpful to first drop in Blithers' next line, then go back and cover up part of it with Bob and Phil's reactions.

28 Open **43G_3 MCU Blithers** and set an In point right before Blithers says, "So congratulations," and an Out after he says, "Get back to work" (In: 21:28:18:22, Out: 23:10).

29 Edit the clip into the sequence directly after **43H**.

Now you're ready to go back and drop in the agents' reactions.

30 In the sequence, position the playhead at the beginning of **43G** and untarget the audio tracks.

31 Use the Recent Clips menu to open **43Q_2 MCU Bob** into the Viewer.

32 Set a new In point at the previous Out point (before Bob turns smiling to Phil at 02:35:44:10) and set a new Out point after Bob completes his turn at 45:20.

33 Edit the clip into the sequence so it overwrites the first frames of **43G**.

34 Use the Recent Clips menu to open **43P_1 MCU Phil** into the Viewer.

35 Find the moment when Phil is looking over at Bob and turns back to look at Blithers. Set the In point just before he turns (02:24:28:16), and the Out point right after he completes his turn at 29:13.

36 Edit the clip into the sequence directly after **43Q**.

37 Play back this part of the sequence to see the results of your handiwork.

This is a perfect set of shots, as once again, the head turns serve perfectly to motivate (and therefore hide) the cuts. It's as if they hand off the focus from one to another, from Wright to Bob, from Bob to Phil, and from Phil to Blithers. Of course that's not at all what happened in the room, but through the magic of editing, you are able to integrate all of their individual actions into one seamless story.

Finish the Scene on Your Own

As you can see, despite being a relatively simple scene, all in one location with a minimum of movement or action, and with fairly limited, standard coverage, this sequence provides a wide variety of challenges and opportunities for you to experiment and hone your dialogue editing skills.

Many of the edits you made can be finessed further and enhanced using the various methods and techniques described throughout this lesson.

The project contains all of the footage you need to edit the last bit of the scene on your own, and there is a wide variety of choices available to make your version of the scene unique.

Most important, the ideas and concepts you've covered are applicable to all editing situations, whether they are dramatic, nonfiction, or experimental. All edits should be motivated, and you must consciously control the viewer's point of focus with your choices of shots, edit positions, and the specific frames you choose to edit on.

Furthermore, in all your editing projects you'll use all the techniques you used throughout this lesson such as organizing your footage before you begin, starting each sequence with a skeleton of master shots (even if you eventually replace every one of them), finding the point of no return in each scene (the hinge), breaking complex scenes into smaller sections, and so many others.

Lesson Review

1. What are three things that make dialogue scenes more complex?
2. How do you begin editing a complex dialogue scene?
3. What happens when you use too many close-ups in a complex dialogue scene?
4. What are two possible solutions to that problem?
5. What else can easily get lost in the course of editing a dialogue scene with many people?
6. How does mixing action and dialogue complicate the editing of a scene?
7. How do you create an audio-only In point?
8. How do you perform a slide edit, and what is its function?

Answers

1. More than two people, more than one position, combining action and dialogue.
2. Organize the scene into sections, create bins to group the footage accordingly, then lay down a series of master shots to see the whole scene at a glance.
3. The viewer can lose track of the geometry of the room and the actors' physical relationships to one another.
4. This can be alleviated by cutting on characters' head turns (or by following their eyeline shifts) *and* by cutting back to a wider shot that shows the characters' physical relationships.
5. Minor characters can be completely forgotten if all the emphasis is focused on the main players.
6. Controlling the focus of a scene can be tricky when there is detailed action that must be covered. Never forget the importance of characters' reactions to the action occurring.

7.   Press Command-Option-I or choose Mark > Mark Split > Audio In.

8.   Press S twice or from the Tool palette select the Slide tool. A slide edit moves a clip within the clips around it by rolling the edits on either side of the clip simultaneously. The clip's position in the sequence chances but the contents of the clip do not.

3

Lesson Files	Lesson Project Files > Lesson_03 > 03_Project_Start
Media	Media > Friends Of The Family
Time	This lesson takes approximately 120 minutes to complete.
Goals	Learn the basics of editing action sequences
	Understand how to work setups and payoffs into your scenes
	Begin thinking about how footage affects style
	Learn techniques to build tension in a scene
	Get familiar with the Trim Edit window
	Use dynamic trimming to finesse edit points
	Control overall pacing and scene structure

Editing Action

Just as important as learning to cut dialogue is learning to cut basic action sequences. Action scenes come in many shapes and sizes—from something as simple as a demonstration of a coffeemaker to a full-scale laser battle in outer space. But all action scenes have some things in common and once you learn a few concepts and rules, you'll be ready to tackle almost anything.

While all dialogue scenes are nearly identical structurally, action scenes are almost always unique. Some action scenes take place in a large physical space (for example, ballroom dancing), while others focus on tiny details in one location (such as cracking a safe). Some action scenes involve continual movement from one place to another (like delivering milk). In any of these cases the specific details of the action will often call for different types of coverage.

However, while actions scenes are all different, there are common editing patterns you can apply depending on the type of action scene you're cutting. If you can identify your scene as one of a certain type, that can give you clues as to the best way to approach cutting it.

Later, you'll learn to identify common action scene types such as fights, battles, chases, shootouts, and others. But don't think all fights require fisticuffs or that all shootouts require guns. These categories can be applied to all sorts of action scenes, and each has its own set of guidelines and tricks.

Telling a Story in Action

It's helpful to begin by separating simple actions from complex ones.

A *simple* action scene is one where there is one central activity, usually performed by one person (or thing). This could be as simple as someone practicing their golf swing or tying their kid's shoe, or it could be as complicated as someone taking apart a motorcycle engine or painting a house.

A *complex* scene strings together several simple actions, either sequentially (playing a whole round of golf) or simultaneously (a house-painting competition). As you might expect, complex action scenes require greater organizational forethought in order to cut them quickly and effectively.

Don't forget, however, that your basic charge is still just to tell the story. Most of the basic tenets covered in the dialogue lessons still apply to action scenes. It's usually advantageous to start wide and then move in close; most edits benefit from being split; and, of course, you should still always seek to cut on action within the frame. No matter what the content of the scene, you are still going to use pacing and shot selection to guide the audience's focus.

Most important, don't lose track of the six essential questions. Plenty of zillion-dollar action films fail to engage the audience because they get so caught up in the *what* and the *how* of the action that they don't bother to spend enough time answering the *who* or the *why*. This isn't rocket science—it's campfire storytelling.

As the editor, you are limited to the footage that the production team provides, but it is still up to you to find the best dramatic balance. You set the tempo and pacing of each scene, and choose which questions get answered and which get ignored. Invariably, you will have close-ups of faces and inserts of important details. It's how and where and for how long you use them that ultimately determine the impact of the scene.

Another storytelling concept that you must incorporate into your action scenes is the fundamental idea of the beginning, middle, and end. If you ignore this essential notion, an action scene can quickly become a dense mess of disjointed details without a clear sense of progression.

There may be as many shots of the details of an action as there are pieces of a motorcycle engine. Sure, you can begin with a shot of the assembled engine, and end with a shot of the pieces spread out on the floor; but what about all those shots in between? Assuming you're not making an instructional video about motorcycle maintenance, the truth about how to take apart an engine is irrelevant. You need to determine which shots *tell the story* and arrange them in a way that conveys a sense of progress. Just like a good plot, each shot must depend on the one that precedes it, and it must compel the one that follows.

Learning Action Fundamentals

There are a few critical concepts you should learn to improve your action cutting skills. These are general principles that can be applied in almost any situation. All of these concepts are based on consciously manipulating the audience's anxiety level to induce an emotional response.

The more you understand how to control that anxiety, the more successful you will be as an editor. While this may sound clinical (or perhaps insidious), it is exactly what makes editing effective. It's no secret that certain images and certain editing techniques have a physical effect on viewers. Whether you are evoking terror or catharsis, the goal is to use that power in the service of your theme.

Creating a Setup and Payoff

Setup and payoff are broad storytelling concepts that can be applied very concretely in action scenes. Payoff is another word for satisfaction, and the only way to provide satisfaction is to set up an expectation and then deliver it. In terms of editing, this is done with specific shots. A shot of someone picking up a ripe peach is a setup that reaches payoff when she takes a big, juicy bite. Similarly, a shot of a mail truck is a setup that pays off with a shot of a letter being opened.

The peach-biting or letter-opening shots may have significance on their own, but they provide much more satisfaction for the audience when the editor builds up an expectation prior to fulfilling it.

The further you separate the setup from the payoff, the more effectively you hold hostage a part of an audience's brain. This is commonly called *suspense* because you are in effect *suspending* their attention. Providing a setup shot that establishes an expectation raises a sort of tension in the viewer. When you pay it off, you release the tension. The longer you wait to show the pay-off, the more the tension builds… but only to a point. If you wait too long, you lose the audience. They either forget about the setup or, worse, they start wondering, "Gee, what was that mail truck shot about?" That means they've stepped out of the story—and the next thing you know they're checking their voicemail.

Establishing Cause and Effect

This is a subset of the setup and payoff. If you show a shot of a hand grenade, you compel a later shot of an explosion. The longer you wait to show the explosion, the more tension you create. If you never show the explosion at all, you disappoint (or confuse) the audience. If you show the explosion without the shot of the grenade, you miss an opportunity to build tension, and again you might confuse the audience. The grenade/explosion example is very clear cut, but cause and effect is often much more subtle, and you can change the meaning of a scene by rearranging the order of the shots.

For example, a thief is rummaging through a bedroom. You have three shots: an ECU of her picking up a diamond necklace; a MCU where she picks up a framed picture of a happy couple; and a CU of her face looking forlorn.

If she finds the necklace first, looks forlorn, then finds the picture, the necklace appears to *cause* the sadness, and her sadness seems to *cause* her to pick up the picture. On the other hand, if she finds the picture first, feels forlorn, and then steals the necklace anyway, you have a very different story. If you omit some of the shots altogether, you have yet another version.

Cutting an Action Scene

The scene you will cut in this lesson is of moderate complexity. It is a show-down scene that could be categorized as a unique type of action scene. The scene features multiple parties (rival gangs, in this case) preparing for a con-flict. This example is very literal, but the showdown technique is applicable to any scene that leads up to a conflict: two parents on their way to a custody hearing; students preparing their projects for the science fair; or a romantic couple finally meeting for their first kiss.

The nature of a showdown is to have a gradual buildup of tension that is relieved when it explodes into a contest or is miraculously diffused at the last second. Common showdown editing techniques include crosscutting, accelera-tion of cuts, and copious use of reaction shots.

1   Open project **03_Project_Start**.

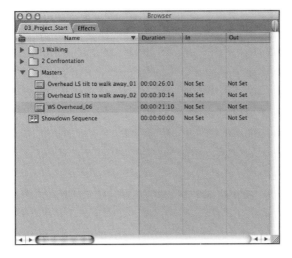

Although the scene is one continuous event, the project has been organ-ized into two primary bins, 1 Walking and 2 Confrontation, as well as a third bin called Masters.

2   Double-click **WS Overhead_06** from the Masters bin and play it from the beginning.

This master shows the main action in the scene: two rival gangs approach each other and, rather than pulling weapons, the leaders pull out baby bottles and they all leave together to tend to their kids.

NOTE ▶ This scene is from a fundraising video for Friends of the Family, a charity that has a program specifically designed to help at-risk teen fathers get out of trouble and responsibly raise their children.

3   Click the disclosure triangle for the 1 Walking bin.

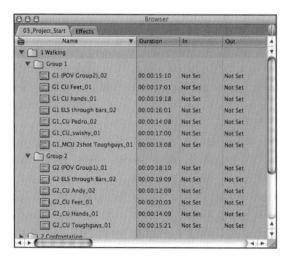

The clips in this bin have been further organized into two sub-bins: Group 1 and Group 2. These will prove to be especially helpful, since many of the shots from the two groups look very similar.

You should notice that the shots for the two groups parallel each other; both groups have "CU_Feet" and "CU_Hands" shots, and both have "ELS through bars" shots. In fact, every single shot is half of a pair—one for each gang.

This may look familiar, because it's the same thing you encountered (and took advantage of) when cutting the basic dialogue scene. These pairs of shots let you *match angles,* one of the hallmarks of effective, invisible editing.

4   Scroll the browser toward the right until the Log Note field is revealed.

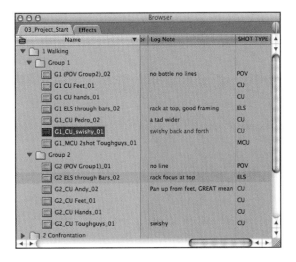

The log notes can provide valuable information about which shots you'll want to use. One repeated word you may notice is "swishy." What does this mean? If you're not sure, you'd best take a look.

5   Double-click **G1_CU_swishy_01** and play it in the Viewer.

The camera continually swish pans between the gang members. While you might be inclined to cut around these messy moves, once you recognize that the footage is full of such movements, an idea should spark in your mind. Rather than avoiding that element, you would be better off to embrace it. In fact, that visual motif provides insight as to how the footage is asking to be cut.

It is always your job as editor to adapt your style to the needs of the footage at hand. Forcing a preconceived editorial style onto footage will just ruin the show. A good editor is one who can be sentimental or gritty, rigid and mathematical, or loose and organic. In this sequence, the director has provided unambiguous cues about how he wanted the scene to look and feel. You'd better respond to it or you'll risk not only the quality of the show, but the opportunity to work with that director again!

6   Double-click the Showdown sequence to open it in the Canvas and Timeline.

Once you've gotten familiar with the footage and its tone and style, it's time to figure out where to start editing. The master shots all begin in the middle of the scene, right before the confrontation, so you need to look for a master-type shot among the walking footage.

7   Open **G1 ELS through bars_02** and play it in the Viewer.

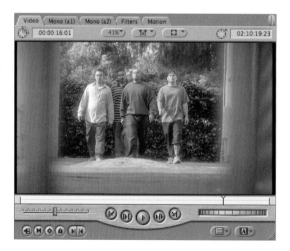

This seems like a great place to start, because it tells you *where* (a playground) and *what* (a gang is on the march). Furthermore, the compositional element of bars in the foreground evokes a prison helping to emphasize the tone of the scene. Also, the rack focus is a great way to introduce the scene, and will work nicely with the swish-pan style you'll incorporate later.

8   Mark an In point just before the first movement is visible from behind the bar (approximately 02:10:09:07) and mark an Out point a few steps after the shot comes into focus (around 14:20).

9   Edit the clip into the sequence.

10   Open **G2 ELS through Bars_02**.

This is the matching angle and, at least for starters, is the obvious shot to follow. Rather than starting on an empty frame like the first shot did, however, you can start these guys a little later in the shot.

11   Set the In point after the second guy becomes visible (around 02:07:10:20) and set an Out point a few steps after the focus has locked (at 15:07).

12   Overwrite the clip directly following the first clip.

Immediately, you've set up the scene. It's clear that there are two groups and, because they're moving toward each other, it's also obvious that they're in conflict. Pretty good work with just two shots.

Building Tension

Since you've so quickly established that there is a conflict brewing, you have an opportunity to heighten the stakes by immediately ratcheting up audience tension.

One effective way to build tension is with the use of close-ups, especially close-ups of details that the audience can't quite put in context. This is pretty easy to understand. Whenever a viewer is watching a movie, he is unconsciously making sense of the shots and trying to understand the story. He is assembling the pieces of the puzzle just as fast as you give them out. When you deliberately withhold information, you make his brain work harder, creating tension.

For example, if you begin a scene with close-ups and withhold the long shot to answer the *where* or *when* questions, the viewer remains in a somewhat unsettled state and doesn't quite know his whereabouts.

Similarly, in this scene, the opening shots set up a conflict. They answer the *what* and *where*, but they don't reveal the *who*. Naturally a viewer is going to crave a close-up or at least a medium shot so he can identify who the participants are. Who is the "good guy" and who is the "bad guy"? By withholding that information, you increase that tension. Of course, you can only stretch tension so far before the viewer loses interest, but you've hooked him with the instant conflict. Let's try to leverage that a bit.

1   Open **G2_CU Feet_01**.

    This is a close-up of feet. It might be even more powerful if they were all wearing army boots (or more funny if they were in flip-flops); but, alas, this is what you've got.

2   Find a frame after they begin walking when the front guy's left foot lands on the ground (02:04:36:10). Set an In point there.

3   Play the clip until the next time the front guy's left foot lands and set an Out point (37:22).

In the Canvas, the guy's feet are mostly obscured by the sand pile, so you can just approximate where his left foot would land.

4   In the Canvas, set an In point at 01:00:09:20.

You now have a subtle but nonetheless useful bit of movement to cut on within the frame. Since the ELS is so far away, and the guys are not exactly all walking in unison, you could probably have gotten away with almost any In point, but why not do everything you can to make as smooth an edit as possible?

5   Overwrite the clip into the sequence.

6   Open **G1 CU Feet_01**.

Naturally, the next shot should be the matching version of the shot from the other gang.

Even though their footsteps are not literally in sync with the guys from Group 2, you can have a bit of editorial fun by doing the same kind of matching action from one feet CU to the next.

7   Find the frame where the front guy's right foot lands and set an In point (02:02:43:00). Let him walk one full stride and mark an Out (44:08).

8   Overwrite the clip directly after **G2_CU Feet_01**.

9   Press \ to play around the edit.

The rhythm lines up nicely but the edit isn't as powerful as it could be. The action is the foot hitting the ground but, once it lands, the action is over (and a new step begins).

The optimal edit would have the foot coming down in the first shot but not landing until after the cut. That way, the viewer's eyes follow the movement across the edit, thereby ignoring it. To make that optimal edit, you would have to guess how far off the ground the foot needs to be (accounting for momentum) in each shot. This is fairly difficult, especially in a situation like this where the two guys aren't even walking at exactly the same speed.

But there's a trick! And it's one of the most useful tricks you can learn to speed up and improve the quality of your action cuts. Make the edit at the moment when the action ends (like you did in Steps 5 through 9) and then roll the edit back slightly to move the cut midway through the action.

10 Press R to select the Roll tool and select the edit between **G2 CU Feet_01** and **G1_CU Feet_01**.

11 Drag to the left to roll the edit, watching the Canvas until the foot is halfway to the ground on both sides of the edit (about 10 frames).

It's kind of fun to watch the canvas as you roll back and forth, seeing how the two shots line up, allowing you to choose the best frame for the cut.

By the way, that trick works on any action cut where you have to guess about how the momentum of a movement will play across an edit. If you have two shots of someone slamming a door, make the cut on the frame when the door is closed in both shots, and then roll the edit back so it cuts in mid-slam.

Crosscutting

From this point in the scene, you will cut back and forth from Group 1 to Group 2 back to Group 1 with nearly every edit. This is called *crosscutting*. Although it is similar to cutting back and forth between characters during a dialogue scene, both groups in this scene are technically still in different locations. Imagine that instead of the groups marching right up to each other in the playground, they were getting ready in separate buildings.

Crosscutting is another technique that builds tension. It asks the audience to keep track of what's going on with Group 1 even as you cut away to Group 2, and vice versa. You're asking them to keep track of twice as much information. This taxes their brains and causes more anxiety. Like other tension-building techniques, you can't keep up that anxiety indefinitely. You have to relieve the stress at some point or risk losing your audience's attention.

Usually in a showdown scenario, the tension is relieved when the two parties finally arrive at the same location. You'll see the same technique employed in Lesson 4 when you cut a chase scene.

1   Open **G2_CU Hands_01**.

2   Watch the Viewer and follow the stride of Andy's left foot. Try to identify the frame where his foot hits the ground and mark an In point (02:04:59:07). Play forward another full footstep and set the Out at 05:00:10.

3   Overwrite the clip into the sequence directly after **G1 CU Feet_01**.

4   Open **G1 CU hands_01**.

It's a little harder to precisely locate the footsteps in this shot, so you'll just have to eyeball it.

5 Set an In point around 02:03:08:06 and an Out point at around 09:12.

6 Overwrite the clip directly after **G2_CU Hands_01**.

Now it's finally time to reveal the gang members' faces. You must decide if you want to show all of the guys' faces or just go straight to the leaders. Since the previous two exchanges focused mainly on the leaders, holding out even longer before showing their faces might try the audience's patience.

7 Open **G2_CU Andy_02**.

Here's your first opportunity to work in one of those swish pans.

8 Set an In just as the camera begins moving up from his feet (approximately 02:05:35:02) and set an Out point after he makes that great scowl around 39:00.

9 Overwrite the clip into the sequence directly after **G1 CU hands_01**.

10 Open the matching single from Group 1: **G1_CU Pedro_02**.

This shot is a nice matching single of Pedro (the Group 1 leader), but it lacks any of that nice swish pan stuff. Perhaps there's something better in one of the other shots.

11 Open **G1_CU_swishy_01**.

This shot contains a great lateral swish onto Pedro that matches the one that introduced Andy, making it a great choice (not to mention that Pedro's performance is better in this take than in his single).

12 Mark an In just after the camera begins its swish toward Pedro and set the Out just before it starts to swish back (In: 02:04:24:04, Out: 26:15).

13 Overwrite the clip into the sequence directly after **G2_CU Andy_02**.

This is the first instance when you are deliberately choosing not to hide the edit as completely as possible. There are several reasons for this. First of all, the swish pans and rack focus shots and handheld camera work all draw attention to the means of production, so you have more incentive to complement those techniques with some similarly self-referential editorial choices. Furthermore, in this specific case, swishing onto the leads (especially if accompanied by a cool sound effect) gives them a much more powerful introduction than a straight cut.

The only problem is that you've moved so quickly into close-ups you need a way to justify stepping back out to a wider shot to show the two gangs coming together in the next section of the scene. Fortunately, you have matching POV shots that can be cut directly from the close-ups since they presumably are what the gang leaders are seeing.

14 Open **G2 (POV Group1)_01**.

15 Mark an In point around 02:01:16:18 and an Out point around 18:17.

16 Overwrite the clip into the sequence directly after **G1_CU_swishy_01**.

17 Open **G1 (POV Group2)_02**.

18 Mark an In point around 02:02:26:02 and an Out point around 28:07.

19 Overwrite the clip into the sequence directly after **G2 (POV Group1)_01**.

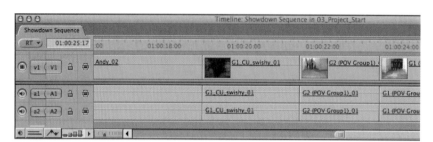

Having moved out from the close-ups to these POV long shots, you've implied that the groups are now in close proximity of each other. It's time to bring the two into the same location.

20 Open **WS_Overhead_06** from the Masters bin.

21 Mark an In just as the two groups cross the frameline threshold (approximately 01:55:35:01) and set an Out just before they come to a complete stop (around 37:00).

22 Overwrite the clip into the sequence directly after **G1 (POV Group2)_02**.

23 Use the Recent Clips menu to open **G2 (POV Group1)_01**.

24 Mark the area just before and after the group comes to a stop (In;
02:01:21:17, Out: 23:06) and overwrite the clip into the sequence
directly after **WS_Overhead_06**.

25 Play back the sequence up to this point.

Ignore the Audio

Now you'll move from the walking part of the scene to the confrontation. To
enhance the suspense during this section, you will need to spread out the dialogue a bit. During production, the guys bantered their few lines so quickly
that it sucked the tension out of the scene; if these were rival gangs squaring
off, they wouldn't speak to each other quite so easily. It's up to you to create
pacing that makes the moment as menacing as possible.

Ordinarily when cutting dialogue, you always get the flow of the audio worked
out before you worry about the picture edit, but in this case you will do the
reverse. Don't worry about all the overlapping or repeated dialogue that happens during these next few edits. You'll go back and clean it up once the picture is in and the pacing feels right.

1 In the Browser, click the disclosure triangle next to the 1 Walking bin to collapse it and click the triangle next to the 2 Confrontation bin to expand it.

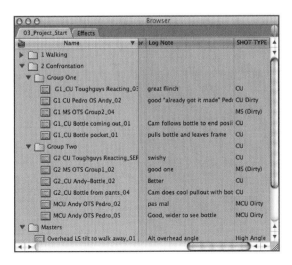

2   Open **G1 MS OTS Group2_04**. Mark the area from before Pedro says, "So what's up?" until after he clasps his hands (In: 01:57:47:04, Out: 48:15).

> **NOTE ▶** Although it's not ideal to back out to a wider shot here, performance trumps matching angles, and this shot had the best performance with the least problems.

3   Overwrite the clip into the sequence directly after **G2 (POV Group1)_01**.

4   Open **MCU Andy OTS Pedro_02**. Set an In point at 02:10:50:04 and an Out point at 51:11.

5   Overwrite the clip into the sequence directly after **G1 MS OTS Group2_04**.

6   Open **G1 CU Pedro OS Andy_02**. Set an In point at 02:17:14:16 and an Out point at 15:11.

7   Overwrite the clip into the sequence directly after **MCU Andy OTS Pedro_02**.

With the main shots for the dialogue section of the scene laid in with approximate timing, you can now clean up the audio.

8   Click the Auto Select icon for V1 to turn it off.

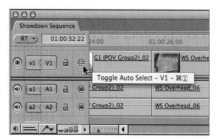

9   Place the playhead at the beginning of **WS_Overhead_06** and begin to play it.

10 Mark an In point before Andy says, "What's up?" around 01:00:26:19. Mark an Out point at the end of the clip.

11 Press Command-Shift-A to deselect all and press Delete to remove that section of the audio tracks.

Because Auto Select is Off for track V1, only the audio tracks are deleted.

Now, instead of Andy saying something as he approaches, you heighten the moment by having him just step up and stare. Although it's a subtle editing difference, you can see it has a dramatic effect on how the scene plays.

Also, although you are leaving a gap of total silence, this can easily be addressed later using *room tone* (an audio ambiance track recording on location) and other sound design elements.

12 Play forward past the next clip into **G1 MS OTS Group2_04**. Set an In right after Pedro says, "'S'up?" but before Andy says anything (around 01:00:29:18).

13 Press Down Arrow to move the playhead to the next edit and set an Out point there.

14 Press Delete to remove the extra dialogue.

15 Play forward and mark an In point just after Andy says, "We gonna do this?"

16 Play over Pedro's "Si mon," and into the next clip. Mark the Out just after Andy (again) says, "We gonna do this?" but before Pedro speaks.

17 Press Delete to remove the repeated lines.

18 Move the playhead back to the beginning of **WS_Overhead_06** and play the section.

Using Dynamic Trimming

The scene is looking okay, but the edits are all occurring right on each guy's lines. I'm sure you've already realized that the scene would feel a little more fluid if the edits were split. This is a great time to become familiar with dynamic trimming.

1 Turn on Auto Select for track V1.

2   Click the Linking icon in the button bar or press Shift-L to disable Linked Selection.

This step isn't necessary to make use of dynamic trimming, but in this instance, you're only going to be trimming the video and this makes it easier to avoid accidentally selecting tracks you don't want to adjust.

3   Double-click the edit point on V1 between **G2 (POV Group1)_01** and **G1 MS OTS Group2_04**.

The edit is selected and the Trim Edit window opens.

Trimming an edit in the Trim Edit window is identical to trimming it in the Timeline. You can roll the edit or ripple either side. The Trim Edit window just provides more detailed information, such as how many frames you have trimmed and how much media is left in each of the clips.

In order to trim effectively, you need to know which audio will be played in the Trim Edit window. This is determined in the User Preferences window.

4   Choose Final Cut Pro > User Preferences and click the Editing tab.

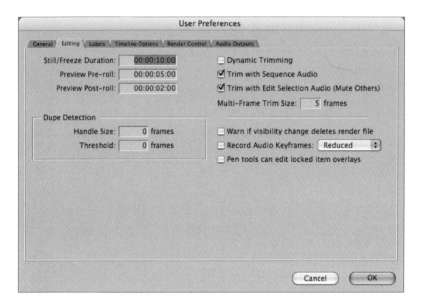

5   Make sure Trim with Sequence Audio is selected and Trim with Edit Selection Audio (Mute Others) is deselected.

For now, leave Dynamic Trimming deselected.

6 Click OK to close the User Preferences window.

7 Make sure the Trim Edit window is active and press the spacebar.

The spacebar works differently in the Trim Edit window than it does elsewhere. Here, it performs a Play Around Edit and it automatically loops. If you want to play forward (or backward) without looping, use the J, K, and L keys.

8 Press the spacebar again to stop the loop.

Before turning on the Dynamic Trimming feature, you should become familiar with how the Trim Edit window works (if you aren't already). The type of edit is indicated by the green bars at the top of the window. A green bar on both sides means roll:

One bar indicates a ripple edit on the side where the bar appears:

If you're ever in doubt, you can also always check the selection in the Timeline.

While you trim in the Timeline by dragging the edit point or typing in numbers, in the Trim Edit window, you can type in numbers or you can click the trim buttons.

9 Make sure the edit is selected as a roll and click the +5 button once and then the +1 button twice.

The edit is rolled forward by seven frames.

10 Press the spacebar to play around the edit and see how the trim improved the edit. Press the spacebar again to stop.

This edit works, but it would have been just as easy, and taken fewer clicks, to just type +7 without ever opening the Trim Edit window.

The real reason the Trim Edit window exists is because it allows you to trim on the fly, also known as dynamic trimming. Dynamic trimming is very simple; when you press the J or L key the sequence plays, moving the edit point with the playhead. When you press K to stop playback, the edit is updated to the new point.

This method of trimming is far more intuitive than typing a number of frames, and it's far more useful than dragging an edit point in the Timeline.

All edit decisions should be made while playing. That's why you should always set Ins, Outs, and markers while the video is moving.

This is a very fundamental and critical point. Editing is about timing. An edit is right when it *feels* right—not when it is adjusted by a specific number of frames. And it's impossible to feel the timing of an edit while dragging an edit point in the Timeline or typing in a number of frames. But it is possible to feel the edit if you are changing it while playing. Enter dynamic trimming.

11 Click the Dynamic checkbox.

12 Press J to move the edit backward.

13 Press K to stop the edit.

14 Press L to move the edit forward.

It takes some getting used to. Don't be afraid. You can go back in the other direction if you go too far, and there's always Undo.

15 Use the J, K, and L keys to move the edit around and get familiar with how it feels.

This is a pretty short shot to practice with, but it's a real world situation. Plenty of times you'll be trimming edits with only a couple of frames to spare.

IMPORTANT ▶ If you have pressed J or L and want to abort the trim operation, press the spacebar instead of K. That will stop playback, and return the edit to its previous location.

16 Once you've got the hang of it, press L and play the edit until just after Pedro begins talking. Then press K to complete the trim.

Aim to put the edit after "So" and just as Pedro says, "What" in "What's up?" You are creating a standard J-edit, beginning Pedro's line while looking at Andy, then cutting to Pedro as if in response. This is the same type of split edit you did again and again in Lessons 1 and 2. The difference now is that you're using a new tool to do it.

17 After you think you've got the edit right, press the spacebar to play around the edit.

Eventually this will become a habit. J… L… K… spacebar… J… K… L… K… spacebar. It will become second nature and you will intuitively begin editing by feel.

18 Once you're satisfied with this edit, press Down Arrow to shift to the next edit point.

The Trim Edit window stays active, but now you're manipulating the edit point between **G1 MS OTS Group2_04** and **MCU Andy OTS Pedro_02**.

19 Again, use the J, K, and L keys to trim the edit dynamically, until you've created a J-cut, where you cut back to Andy just before he says, "Do this."

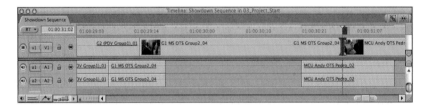

20 Press the spacebar to play around the edit.

21 Once you're satisfied, press Down Arrow again to move to the last edit.

22 Use J, K, L, and the spacebar to adjust this edit to your liking.

You may choose to cut to Pedro before he says, "Si mon," or just after "Si" and before "mon." There is no correct answer; just place the edit where it feels right.

As you can see, it's very easy to adjust one edit, then move on to the next and adjust that one, and so on. This is one of the reasons it makes sense to get your edits approximately right, but wait until most of the clips are in place before doing the final trimming. As you get more comfortable with dynamic trimming, you'll use it all the time.

There is a misperception that dynamic trimming is an "advanced" editing feature. It's not. It's wonderfully easy to do and, once you get the hang of it, it's fun, too! The only obstacle is that you have to know what you are trying to achieve before using it.

Stretch Out the Climax

The next event in the scene is the two leaders pull out their weapons, which turn out to be baby bottles. You could simply show this action in one shot, but to maximize the effect and enhance the surprise, you should stretch out this event as long as possible. Fortunately you have quite a bit of coverage to work with.

1   Open **MCU Andy OTS Pedro_05**. Mark the area where Andy goes for his weapon but don't include any frames where you can see what it is (In: 02:12:03:18, Out: 04:08).

This is a classic setup shot. As soon as the audience sees him going for a weapon, a host of expectations are established. The longer you can wait before paying off on the setup, the more tension you create, and the more comedy when the expectation turns out to be wrong.

2   Overwrite the clip into the sequence directly after **G1 CU Pedro OS Andy_02**.

3   Open **G1_CU Bottle pocket_01**. Set the In on the first frame where his hand moves, and set the Out just before you can identify what it is he's grabbing (In: 02:21:56:19, Out: 57:10).

4   Overwrite the clip into the sequence directly after **MCU Andy OTS Pedro_05**.

5   Open **G2_CU Bottle from pants_04** and mark the In point as he's reaching for the bottle and set the Out point once the bottle is out and held still (In: 03:03:49:00, Out: 50:00).

This is an instance when you can overlap the action slightly to stretch out the moment. This is commonly called double-cutting and you see it done all the time with explosions. In reality, it probably only takes Andy four to five frames to whip out that bottle, but here you've managed to stretch it out to almost 2 seconds!

6   Overwrite the clip into the sequence directly after **G1_CU Bottle pocket_01**.

7   Press \ to play around the last few edits.

Not bad, but you can do better. Sure, you've stretched out the moment when the bottles come out, but you can stretch it even further and make it more suspenseful and funnier.

Bring in the Witness

The idea of a witness is an essential element of successful action scenes. Adding shots of someone in the room watching events unfold provides several benefits. First, it provides an emotional point of view for the viewers to identify with. Typically with most action scenes, the people performing the action are so busy doing that they don't have much time to be feeling or reacting. A witness (especially if it's a character that the audience already knows and relates to) is a perfect solution to this. It's scary to see the hero strapped to a log-cutting machine, moving inch-by-inch toward the spinning blade. But it's twice as moving if you can show that the woman who he was supposed to save tied to a chair nearby watching helplessly. Similarly, even the most mind-numbing corporate speech is made more engaging by cutting to a shot of an audience member in rapt attention.

Furthermore, the witness has another, more technical benefit. It provides a guaranteed cutaway. In the midst of a scene, there may be many reasons why you need to cut away from the action at hand. You might need to change angles or cut around a moment when the make-up artist needed to apply some fake blood. Action scenes are complicated to shoot and they frequently are broken up into many shots. Sometimes you need to divert the audience's attention just for a moment, so you can cut around a hole in the action, or make the scene seem more seamless.

Finally, cutting away to a witness gives you the opportunity to stretch out a moment far longer than it might have been in reality. And this is exactly what you will do at this point in the scene.

8   Open **G1_CU Toughguys Reacting_03**.

A section of the shot is already marked.

9   Move the sequence playhead back to the second-to-last edit.

10   Insert the clip into the sequence.

11 Play this section of the scene.

Seeing the guy's reaction definitely improves the scene and further suspends the payoff. But there's no reason to stop there!

12 Open **G2 CU Toughguys Reacting_SERIES**.

A section of this clip has also been marked.

13 Move the sequence playhead back until it is in between **MCU Andy OTS Pedro_05** and **G1_CU Bottle pocket_01**.

14 Insert the cutaway between those two clips.

15 Play back this section of the scene.

Amazingly you have stretched this tiny moment to almost 4 seconds—and you're not done yet! You've probably stretched the buildup as much as possible, but the event itself, the revealing of the bottles, can be extended a bit as well.

16 Put the sequence playhead midway through the last clip, while Andy's arm is still moving (at about 01:00:36:10).

17 Open **Overhead LS tilt to walk away_02** from the Masters bin.

A section of the clip has already been marked.

18 Overwrite that clip into the sequence.

Because there is a camera move in both shots and because Andy's arm movement begins in shot 1 and finishes in shot 2, this makes for an exciting (maybe even dizzying) edit. Yes, the action is doubled slightly, but this is exactly the place to do it, as it draws added attention to this pivotal moment. How exciting!

However, while all of those elements would likely be the same whether they were pulling out switchblades or bananas, in fact they are pulling out baby bottles. This is an unexpected surprise and will almost certainly elicit a laugh from the audience. You can milk that laugh (sorry for the pun) by adding another shot or two of the bottles. That gives the audience a chance to laugh, plus it emphasizes the silliness of the event.

19 Open **G1_CU Bottle coming out_01**.

An area of the clip has already been marked.

20 Overwrite the clip into the sequence directly after **Overhead LS tilt to walk away_02**.

It would be nice to complement this CU with a matching CU of Andy's bottle, but another option is to go back to the MS of Andy holding the bottle.

21 Open **G2_CU Bottle from pants_04**.

While this breaks the matching angles rule, another CU of a baby bottle
would potentially wear out the joke. It's not like there's any new information learned by seeing a close-up of Andy's bottle. Instead, this angle gives
you the added humor of seeing the tough guys lined up behind this
absurd display (not to mention Andy's delightfully serious expression).

22 Mark an In point at 03:03:51:00 and an Out point at 52:19, and overwrite
the clip into the sequence directly after **G1_CU Bottle coming out_01**.

Before you dismiss this climax, there is one other element that you set up
earlier that has yet to pay off. Any guess what that is? Well, remember the
frightened looks on the part of the witnesses just as the boys were whipping
out their weapons? What happened when they found out it was only milk?

23 Open **G1_CU Toughguys Reacting_04**.

24 Play forward past the witness's frightened reaction to see his smile of relief when he sees the bottles. Mark an In at 02:20:20:23 and an Out at 22:17.

25 Overwrite the clip into the sequence directly after **G2_CU Bottle from pants_04**.

That resolves his story, but what about the other guy?

26 Open **G2 CU Toughguys Reacting_SERIES**. Shuttle through it looking for anything that might work.

Unfortunately, this guy is so stoic that he really has no reaction to the bottle at all. However, there is still hope: At the very end of the shot, unable to keep playing the role, he breaks character and smiles. Guess what? That will work perfectly!

27 Mark an In at 02:13:05:23 and an Out at 07:02 and overwrite the clip onto the end of the sequence.

Finishing the Scene

Just like a dialogue scene, once the turning point has been reached, the right thing to do is get out quickly. This scene has a couple more lines of dialogue and then a final payoff, showing the picnic where the boys' families are all waiting.

1 Open **G2 MS OTS Group1_02**. Mark the area where Andy says, "Hey man, I'm out of formula" (In: 01:58:55:03, Out: 56:07).

2 Overwrite it onto the end of the sequence.

3 Open the reverse, **G1 CU Pedro OS Andy_02**. Mark the area where Pedro says, "I already got it made" (In: 02:17:17:22, Out: 19:06).

4 Overwrite the clip into the sequence.

5 Open **Overhead LS tilt to walk away_01**. A section of the clip has already been marked. Overwrite it onto the end of the sequence.

6 Make sure the Timeline window is active and press Shift-Z to zoom the whole sequence to fit.

You can see that the overall pacing of the show illustrates a natural progression. The early cuts are mostly of a similar length; the cuts then speed up dramatically as you reach the climax, and they slow back down in a denouement. While not all scenes are the same, looking at the big picture like this can give you clues about the pacing. Are your shot lengths generally consistent? Do they vary randomly or is there a visible arc that matches the storyline?

7 Play the whole show and admire your work.

Of course, your work with this scene isn't done. There's loads of audio work to do, to make the scene really come alive. In addition to adding room tone and environmental sounds to fill in the empty gaps you left when you cut the dialogue, you could also add military type marching for the footsteps as the gangs come together, a gasp or two as the bottles come out, and maybe a corresponding sigh of relief once the truth is revealed. Top it all with an urban-flavored rap song that comes to a suspenseful climax at just the right moment and you've got yourself a pretty amazing scene!

Lesson Review

1. What is an action scene?

2. What is a complex action scene?

3. What are setup and payoff shots?

4. What is the advantage of working in the Trim Edit window?

5. What are three common ways to increase tension?

6. What is a quick and effective trick to easily account for momentum when cutting on an action?

7. What is crosscutting?

8. What does the spacebar do in the Trim Edit window?

9. How can you use dynamic trimming?

Answers

1. Any scene where the focus of the scene is an activity.

2. A scene where multiple activities happen, either in sequence, or simultaneously.

3. A setup is a shot that elicits an expectation from the viewer. A payoff is a shot that resolves such an expectation.

4. The Trim Edit window provides detailed information, such as how many frames are trimmed and how much media is left in each clip.

5. Using close-ups without context, crosscutting, and speeding up the edits.

6. By first making the edit on the end of the action, then rolling the edit back to just before it happens.

7. Cutting back and forth between two locations, usually for action that is occurring simultaneously.

8. Play Around Edit Loop. It also aborts a dynamic trim operation.

9. Activate Dynamic Trimming in User preferences by using the Trim Edit window to perform roll or ripple edits while the sequence plays. This enables you to make timing decisions in the ideal context of the flow and pacing of the video.

4

Lesson Files Lesson Project Files > Lesson_04 > 04_Project_Start

Media Media > Slapdash Chase, Hope Fight, Broken Fists

Time This lesson takes approximately 90 minutes to complete.

Goals Control tension and pacing in action scenes

Understand what makes a chase or fight scene effective

Use moving shots to enhance subjectivity

Employ obstacles and setbacks to affect the timing of a scene

Recognize the similarities between fight scenes and
dialogue scenes

Cut on an action, then roll an edit for maximum impact

Utilize sound effects to clarify the action in a scene

Use different coverage to modify the timing of a fight scene

Improve a fight by adding a witness and a second storyline

Chases and Fights

Now that you've got the hang of how to approach a general action scene, it's time to explore some of the more specialized varieties. It's true that all action scenes are unique, but some types have enough consistency that you can employ patterns and techniques that seem to work regardless of the specific content.

For example, nearly all chase scenes have a similar structure. Whether the chase takes place on foot or in spaceships, in a few minutes or over decades, there are two parties; the follower and the followed, and inevitably the follower gains on the followed, suffers a setback, gains again, and ultimately either catches the followed, or does not. For the editor, a chase is an exercise in controlling tension. You can dial up the tension by showing the follower gaining, dial it down a little with a setback, and then ratchet it way up as you race to the final release.

Similarly, fight scenes have patterns that you can manipulate and techniques that you can consistently employ to control the audience's tension level and engage them in the scene.

By recognizing these common structures you can leverage viewers' expectations when you follow the structures, and create audience surprise or humor when you deviate from them.

The beauty of chases and fights is their primal simplicity: A chase is a hunt. The viewer might relate to the hunter or the hunted, but either way it stimulates his caveman-mind, stirring deep unconscious emotions. A fight is nothing short of a battle for survival—you don't get any more primal than that.

Crafting Chilling Chases

Chases are deceptively simple, and depending on the location where it takes place, the coverage is likely to be equally simple. For an editor, chases are a great exercise in skill because they render literal many of the tension-building techniques that you metaphorically explore in almost any type of scene. They reduce all dramatic tension to a single vector: the proximity of pursuer to pursued. By experimenting with that variable, you can learn what works and what doesn't work in terms of guiding your viewer's tension levels.

Keep in mind that not all chase scenes are so easily recognized. Perhaps someone is pursuing a thing instead of another person, or the object of pursuit may not even be known. Often, such scenes are not high-speed adrenaline fests; but even in a slow-burn cat and mouse game, as long as there is pursuer and pursued, the tension is building—or ought to be—and it is up to you as editor to exploit that tension.

1   Open **04_Project_Start**.

The **Slapdash Chase** sequence should already be open in the Canvas and Timeline.

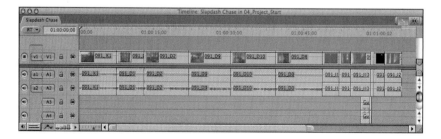

2 Play the scene to get familiar with it.

This scene is very straightforward, and as it is currently cut, it's not very dynamic. Sure, one guy is getting chased and the ending has a little bit of surprise, but the pacing of the scene doesn't vary at all, and the follower never really gains or falls behind the followed.

Determining Distance

An editor controls the flow of tension and improves the chase scene by varying the distance between the parties.

In the current scene, the second shot shows the guys as they get onto the train. First, Mosley (in the blue shirt) gets on in a matching-action cut from the outside of the train, and then, a moment later, Martin (in the white shirt) arrives and begins running after him.

There's no reason you have to stick with the actual timing that occurred during production. Right off the bat, you could increase or decrease the amount of time it takes for Martin to follow Mosley. All you need is a shot of Mosley running through the train that you can cut to before Martin gets on board.

1 Open **091_D2** from the Chase Clips bin.

2 Set an In point on the first frame where you begin to see Mosley (00:24:25:15).

The length of time you allow this shot to play will determine how much of a lead Mosley has on Martin. In this case, you will start by giving Mosley a fairly long lead time.

3 Play the clip until Mosley is almost entirely down the length of the train car and set an Out point around 29:24.

4 In the sequence, find the frame in the second shot in which Mosley is halfway out of the frame (around 01:00:10:15) and set an In point.

This will make a smooth match cut with the In point you set in **091_D2**.

5 Insert **091_D2** into the sequence.

Before you can check the edit, you need to clean up the second half of clip **091_D1** in the sequence.

6 In the sequence, mark an In point on the first frame of the second half of **091_D1** (Step 5 should have left your playhead parked on that frame).

7 Play forward until you see Martin get onto the train, then back up to the frame just before he enters (around 15:19) and set an Out point.

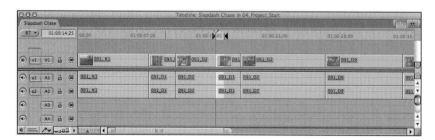

8 Press Shift-Command-A to deselect all (as a safety precaution), then press Shift-Delete to ripple delete that section of the clip.

9 Play these first few clips in the sequence.

You have given Mosley a bit of a lead on Martin, but how much lead? Figure it out exactly.

10 Set an In on the frame in which Mosley first steps onto the train (around 01:00:07:20) and set an Out on the frame in which Martin first steps aboard (around 15:00).

11 Look at the Duration field in the Canvas.

This shows you exactly how far ahead Mosley is: about 7 and a half seconds.

12 Press Option-X to clear the In and Out frames.

13 Play ahead to the next clip (**091_D2A**).

14 Set an In point as Mosley exits the frame around 01:00:20:20 and set an Out point when Martin exits, around 25:12.

15 Look at the duration field again.

Now they're less than 5 seconds apart. Already Martin is gaining on Mosley. Is this desirable? It's up to you. While your audience won't be counting seconds, they will have an implicit sense of timing and will feel that the pursuer is gaining ground.

If you're careless about these measurements, you might have Martin bounce around, being 7 seconds behind in one shot, then 4 seconds behind in another, then 8 seconds behind a moment later. Your audience won't be taking out their stopwatches, but they will very likely sense that the continuity of the scene is off. That might get them looking at their wristwatches, which is a very bad sign.

If you want to hold Martin off a little, you can do so by adding another shot into the scene.

16 Shot **091_D2** should still be loaded in the Viewer; set an In on the first frame where Martin enters the shot (around 00:24:31:20).

Since you know you want to keep Martin about 2 or 3 seconds behind, you know exactly how long you want this shot to be.

17 Press Tab to access the Duration field. Type *2.15* and press Enter.

An Out point is automatically set to ensure this duration.

18 Make the Timeline or Canvas window active and press Option-X to clear the In and Out points you set earlier.

19 Move the playhead to the edit between the second instance of **091_D1** and **091_D2A** and insert **091_D2** into the sequence.

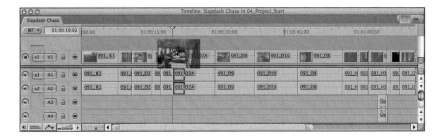

20 Play around the section.

By creating consistent timing across two shot sequences, you reinforce a sense of the reality of the scene. Now, when you show Martin gaining on Mosley in the next section, there will be a concrete sense of tension.

Using Subjective Shots

Another way to get your audience engaged in the chase is to use shots that put the viewer in the shoes of the characters. The *lockdown* shots you used in the first section are essential for conveying the relative distance between the parties (just the way a 2-shot provides a sense of relationship in a dialogue scene); but once that pacing is established, you can heighten tension by using tracking shots.

1   From the Chase Clips bin, open and play **091_D4**.

This is a tracking shot, showing Mosley's face as he runs. Even though a chase scene sustains your audience's attention by raising their adrenaline, to keep them fully engaged, you must answer all of the story questions. This shot adds a little *who* to the *what* and *where* you've already provided.

Because this shot doesn't give you a natural entrance and exit (like the lockdown shots did), you must find another element within the scene that can serve as a beginning and an ending.

2   Set an In point as Mosley crosses the first threshold into the train car (at 00:26:02:17) and set an Out as he enters the next threshold (at 00:26:06:06).

3   Overwrite this clip into the sequence directly after **091_D2A** (at around 28:02).

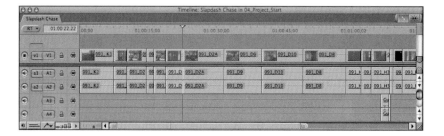

4   Open and play **091_B5**.

This is a similar shot, but featuring Martin. Just as in other scenes, matching angles (MCU tracking shots, in this case) is a good way to hide edits and keep your audience focused on the story instead of the construction.

5   Set an In point just as Martin crosses into the car at 00:15:14:08.

Here, you can further use the train car thresholds to provide a sense of continuity, even though you are actually shifting from one character to another.

This is just like syncing up the footfalls between Andy and Pedro in Lesson 3. Even though neither example is actually a *continuity cut* (where an onscreen action carries you across the edit), you are using the similar composition and movement in each frame to hide the edit.

6   In the sequence, set an In point on the first frame following **091_D4**, and play forward until Martin enters the frame in **091_D9** (around 01:00:33:18) and set an Out point here.

7   Overwrite **091_B5** into the sequence.

Cutting back to the static shot here reminds the audience of the context, and gives you another chance to check in on the distance between the two participants.

8   Play across the next few shots.

9   Set an In just as Mosley gets to the middle of the round bar (around 01:00:38:21).

10 Set an Out when Martin reaches the same point in the car (around 43:25).

11 Look at the Duration field.

Now they are only 5 seconds apart. This is perfect, as it shows Martin gaining on Mosley and thus ratchets up the tension level. Now it's time to give Martin a little setback.

12 Press Option-X to clear the In and Out points.

Creating a Setback

The specifics and the severity of the setback are determined by the events in the script and the way the scene was shot, but it's up to you to determine where and how to use them. In this scene, there really isn't a setback to work with, at least not an intentional one, so you have to be extra creative to construct one out of the footage you have.

Why is it important to include this moment? To maximize tension and make the most of the scene, you need to create punctuation. You must take a single minute-long event with a constant level of tension, and turn it into a series of moments in which the tension ebbs and flows. This is how you keep your viewers on the edges of their seats.

1 Open **091_C4** and press Shift-\ to play from In to Out.

This clip shows Martin struggling to get around a doorway. It's not much, but it's all you have, and you can employ it to signify the moment when Mosley begins to gets ahead of him.

The trick is figuring out how to work it into the sequence. It's obviously a different part of the train, so you need something that will get you from this well-lit area into the darker part of the train where Martin hits his obstacle.

2 Open **091_D4**.

You've already used part of this clip, but there is a section near the end that could help you transition into **C4**.

3 Play the section of the clip past the section you previously marked.

At around 00:26:11:00, Mosley enters another threshold, and this one seems very dark. Even though this isn't actually the part of the train where Martin's obstacle is located, no one will ever know the difference.

4   Set an Out point at the darkest point in the frame, before the camera pans away from Mosley (around 11:23). Moving backwards, set an In point just as he recovers from his near-stumble, around 09:20.

5   In the sequence, position the playhead at the edit between **D10** and **D8** (around 45:12).

6   Insert **091_D4** into the sequence.

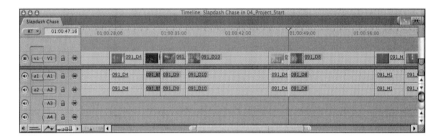

7   Open and play **091_E3.**

This is the section of the train beyond Martin's obstacle. By showing Mosley getting here in a hurry, it will accentuate the delay when Martin gets stuck. In reality, Mosley had to go around the same bulkhead, but you don't have to show it!

8   Insert **091_E3** directly after **D4**.

Now you're ready to put in Martin's setback.

9   From the Recent Clips pop-up menu in the lower-right corner of the Viewer, choose **091_C4**.

The section of the clip is already marked.

10   Insert the clip directly after **E3** and play around this whole part of the sequence.

Doesn't seem like a setback yet, does it? That's because **E3** is just the setup. You still have to show the payoff that results.

11 In the sequence, play across clip **D8** and stop after Mosley clears the frame, but before you can see Martin appearing in the distance (around 55:20). Set an In point here.

12 Press Down Arrow to move the playhead to the next edit, and set an Out point there.

13 Press Shift-Command-A to deselect all, and press Shift-Delete to ripple delete this part of the shot.

By cutting here, and showing the empty hallway behind Mosley, you sell the idea that Mosley has gained some distance from Martin. This is the payoff to the setup in **E3**. Until you show another shot in which you can see both guys in the same frame (or show both of them pass a recognizable landmark in close succession), the audience will assume that Mosley has a substantial lead on Martin.

This is perfect, because in this particular scene, the surprise ending is the thug waiting in the last car. The more we think Mosley is getting away, the bigger the surprise when "the thug" appears.

In another chase, you might use this technique to show the hunted party appearing to get away; but then something else happens that sets *him* back, and brings the hunter back into the game.

14 Open and play **091_B12**.

Here is a tight CU on Martin. Cutting to this close-up after the setback appears to raise the stakes. The audience has seen that he's losing the race, and now they want to see how he feels about that. Showing the close-up here and now gives them a glimpse of that feeling, *even though the shot was not intended for that purpose!* The meaning of this shot is derived from the shots around it.

15 Insert **091_B12** into the sequence, directly after **D8**.

16 Press Shift-Z to fit the entire sequence into view.

Notice anything about the pattern of shots? They get shorter toward the end of the sequence, right up until the denouement at the very end. This is virtually the same pattern as the Friends of the Family scene, and that's not a coincidence. This is another classic technique for building tension. Speeding up the edits as the scene builds adds intensity. This is especially applicable to cross-cutting scenes (which chases almost always are) because there is a natural climax when the two parties come together in the end.

To appreciate the scene in its final form, you can add some music.

17 Drag **Bodo.aiff** directly from the Browser into the Timeline, onto tracks A5 and A6.

18 Play the whole scene.

This is fairly standard chase music, but it still undeniably adds to the scene.

Creating Compelling Combat

To an editor, a fight scene is really nothing more than a dialogue scene in which the parties exchange physical actions instead of exchanging words. To this end, you can expect good fight coverage to parallel standard dialogue coverage with establishing masters, OTS singles, CU singles, inserts, cutaways, and so on.

In contrast to dialogue scenes, fights will likely have more wide shots so the physical action is visible in the frame, and you will have more opportunities to cut back out to them. You will also likely have more inserts or specials that cover details of the action. Perhaps the most significant difference from a dialogue scene is that fight coverage is most often broken up into many more individual shots. Fighters frequently move during the course of the fight. Each time they move from one part of a room to another, a new angle must be shot. Also, fights often incorporate special effects or make-up changes that require frequently stopping and starting the action on set. The result of this is that you have far more shots to manage in your bins, but the resulting editing pattern remains very similar to that of a dialogue scene.

Fights are not always fisticuffs or swordplay. Often the "blows" in a fight are more symbolic or subtle. In fact, many times the line between fight and dialogue becomes blurred. Picture a courtroom scene in which a lawyer grills a defendant on the stand, or a verbal fight between separating spouses. And even in physical fights the combatants might alternate their corporal blows with verbal ones. In essence, a fight is any action in which two parties are in opposition.

1   Double-click the **Broken Fists** sequence.

2   Click the disclosure triangles to collapse the Chase Clips bin and expand the Broken Fists Clips bin.

   This bin contains the first few shots of a martial arts fight from the film "Broken Fists."

3   Open and play **A-16_A-4 Master.**

This shot will serve as your master shot. In addition to the opening camera move that sets up the scene and introduces the character, it contains the whole first episode in a long shot.

4   Set an In just before the camera starts moving and an Out when the actors stumble forward and stop (In: 07:06:37:00, Out: 57:00).

5   Edit the clip into the sequence.

Cutting fights requires being able to break them down, blow-by-blow (literally). You must identify each individual action, so you can identify the best cut points and avoid skipping or overlapping the action of the scene.

This scene is especially challenging because there are nine actions in about 7 seconds. Here is a rundown: Hope (the woman in black) begins with three quick kicks to the left, and then does a roundhouse kick to the right. That is followed by a lateral move with her left arm, then an overhand move with her right. Then Ruby (in blue) grabs Hope's right arm and twists it around. Next, both women block each other with their forearms, and, finally, Hope connects with an elbow to the face. This fight (like all fights) was carefully choreographed and it's part of your job to deconstruct the choreography to bring it to life editorially.

You need to understand how each blow affects the story. As in the chase scene, you want to manipulate the audience's anxiety level by deliberately increasing and decreasing the tension. Each time one of the fighters gains or loses advantage, the stakes change and the tension is impacted. You can emphasize certain moments with close-ups, or tone down other moments by covering them long, or even cutting them out altogether.

6   Open and play **A_16_FB-1 MS Favor Hope.**

This is a reverse, covering the exact same action, but from the other side, and a bit tighter. Because the fight is so active, you could almost cut on any of the nine actions. How do you choose?

Remember the ideas put forth in Lesson 1? You should only cut when there is new information to show, and you should cut to the shot that shows that new information. In this clip, you can see that on Hope's third kick to the left, Ruby blocks with her arm. That information was completely absent in the master shot, so it provides a good reason and opportunity to cut.

7   In the Viewer, set an In on the frame when Hope's foot hits Ruby's arm (at: 07:11:50:13) and let it play all the way until they exit the frame (around 57:20) and set an Out point there.

8   Find the frame in the sequence when Hope's foot reaches its full extension (on her third kick) at 01:00:13:00.

9   Overwrite the clip into the sequence.

10 Play around the edit.

    By cutting directly on the action of the foot block, you actually miss seeing it happen.

11 Press R to select the Roll tool and roll the edit to the left about 6 frames.

NOTE ▸ You may need to zoom in and/or turn off snapping (press N) in order to perform Step 11.

Now the edit happens as her leg is going up, and that movement hides the cut. You slip into the closer shot without drawing attention to it, and show that the kick was blocked. Perfect! But you may be wondering why you didn't cut on this frame in the first place?

It's much easier to match the action across edits by finding the end of the action in both clips. If you guessed, and made the edit "about halfway" through the movement, you would have to judge the momentum in both shots, which may be difficult. This is especially true when working with differing angles and different takes in which the action may have occurred at different speeds. By first making the edit on the clear ending of the action in both shots, you can then confidently roll the edit freely in either direction and maintain sync.

12 Press A to deselect the Roll tool and play the sequence.

The problem with that medium shot is that you can "feel" the choreography; the actors pause slightly after each exchange, almost like they are counting time (which is frequently how fights are staged). But you don't want the audience to see those pauses, so you need to find a way to cut around them.

The first egregious pause comes right before Hope's overhand right blow (at around 15:00). It looks like this is your next place to cut.

13 Open and play **A_16_FA-2 MS Favor Ruby**.

This is a matching reverse of **FB-1**; a medium favoring Ruby.

14 Set an In just before Hope grabs Ruby's arm at 07:10:50:00 and set the Out after they run off screen, around 56:00.

15 In the sequence, look for the action that matches the In point you just set, and set an In there, at 15:05.

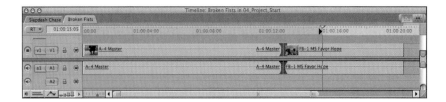

16 Overwrite the clip into the sequence.

Hopefully, you can see the parallels to a dialogue scene: Begin on a wide master, and cut back and forth between matching OTS shots for the bulk of the scene. The last step is to move into close-up for the climax.

17 Open and play **B_16_A-2 MCU Favor Ruby**.

Toward the end of the shot, it becomes a tighter angle on Ruby, which will be perfect for the elbow to the face.

Another thing you need to keep in mind when cutting fights, especially hand-to-hand combat, is that you have to choose the angles that look like actual contact was made.

18 In the Viewer, step through the shot, especially in the section where Hope makes her final blow (01:14:28:14).

Because the camera is directly on axis with the action it's fairly difficult to tell whether or not she actually made contact. (Actually, in this take, Ruby reacts a frame late, but that tiny difference will easily be overlooked when played at full speed.)

19 Open **B_16_FB-1 Profile MCU**.

This shot is already parked on the frame of "impact" and it's very clear that Hope's elbow never touches Ruby. This profile shot may be perfectly useful for other parts of the scene, but to convey the illusion of a solid blow, it's a terrible choice.

20 Reopen **B_16_A-2 MCU Favor Ruby**.

21 Set an In point on the previous action, where both women use both arms to block each other (around 01:14:28:00).

22 Find the matching frame in the sequence (01:00:17:14).

23 Overwrite the clip.

For the sake of the exercise, don't worry about the Out point or the end of the sequence.

24 Press R to select the Roll tool and roll the edit to the left about 10 frames.

25 Press A to deselect the Roll tool, press Home to return to the head of the sequence, and play through the whole sequence.

This is a very simple sequence but it works. You could choose to make a cut for every one of the nine actions. That might seem more exciting, although it would primarily serve to severely disorient your audience (which may or may not be desirable).

In general, you should avoid overcutting. Let the action unfold without interfering any more than is required. Like dance or comedy (see Lesson 5) fights are choreographed to have a specific style and character. If you cut too aggressively, you risk losing that delicate artistry that was chosen for deliberate reasons.

Of course, if the choreography isn't working to tell the story, then by all means do what you can to save it. Your primary obligation is to your audience and if they are confused or bored or distracted, you've failed at your job as storyteller.

Using Sound Effects

There is one more tiny thing you can do to bring the scene (or at least that final blow) to life. It's difficult to feel the impact of the scene without hearing the sound effects of the various hits and blows. You would never expect any audience to buy the scene without the sound in place, and while the show will certainly go through an extensive sound design once you're finished cutting, it can't hurt to drop in a sound effect when it's really essential.

1   In the sequence, position your playhead on the precise frame where Hope's elbow is supposed to connect with Ruby's face (at 01:00:18:05).

2   Drag **Body Hit 11.aiff** directly from the Browser into the Timeline onto track A2 and A3, lining it up to begin at the playhead and overwrite it into the sequence.

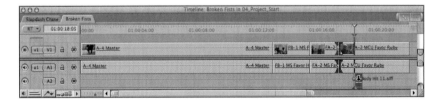

3   Play around that section of the scene.

It's amazing what a difference that sound makes! You don't want to spend much time with sound effects this early in the process, but every so often a little cue like that can have a significant impact on the way the scene plays.

Fights with Weapons

Your editing style must take into account the type of weapons your combatants wield. In a gunfight, the parties will be physically separated. This means that, in many ways, tying the two parties together is an exercise in cross-cutting between separate locations, and you will have to pay special attention to clarifying the geography of the scene. Also, the pacing of a scene is directly affected by the means of battle.

1   Open and play the **Hope Fight** sequence.

This is another scene from "Hope," in which Anne, the angel, fights the arch devil Temeluchus. Notice that this scene, too, has elements of the traditional dialogue structure, using masters, over-the-shoulders, and close-ups.

The two combatants fight with large weapons, giving the scene a very different feel than the hand-to-hand combat of the scene from "Broken Fists." For one thing, swinging a broad sword takes a few seconds, while throwing a punch takes only a few frames. This significantly slows the pacing of the scene.

You have other similar issues, however, and even though the overall scene is slower, the pacing still needs to be consistent within its own rhythm.

2   Play the sequence from about 15 seconds in.

There is an unnatural pause that occurs before Ann thrusts away Temeluchus' spear. The director presumably wanted this moment to play as a moment of struggle, but in this wide shot, it just looks like a mistake.

3   Collapse the Broken Fists Clips bin and expand the hope Fight Clips bin.

4   Open and play **15AV-2z**.

This CU of the same action provides you an opportunity to tighten the timing of the scene, while adding emphasis to the struggle of that moment.

5 Set an In point just before Anne pushes his spear away (around 06:11:01:00).

6 Set an Out point just as she escapes him and spins out of the way (around 02:15).

7 In the sequence, set an In where you want to insert the close-up. You could put it immediately after Temeluchus lands his spear, or you could wait a bit to add to the sense of struggle. In the image, the In point is set at 01:00:18:00:

8 Overwrite the clip into the sequence.

9 Play around the edit.

The timing feels great for the beginning of her action, but now Anne does the whole pushing-away action twice.

10 In the sequence, set an In point on the frame after **15AV-2z** ends, and set an Out after the second pushing away. Attempt to match Anne's position from the end of **15AV-2z**. In both shots, she should just be crossing the second post behind her (around 01:00:20:02).

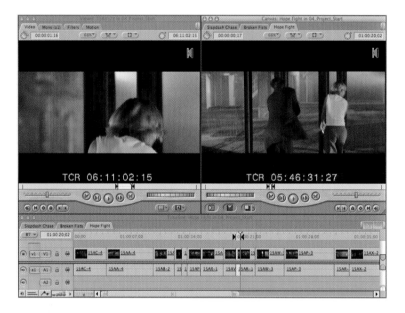

11 Press Shift-Delete to ripple delete the duplicated action.

12 Play around the new edit.

Incorporate a Witness

One of the editor's secret weapons for improving a fight scene is the *witness*. Cutting away to a third party who is observing the fight serves multiple significant purposes. Story-wise, it gives perspective and point of view. It gives the audience an ally, someone within the story to watch the fight with. Typically it's someone who is invested in the story: the boxer's trainer, the victim who is being saved, the child whose custody is being fought over. This witness illuminates the stakes of the fight. Even the most elaborately choreographed and spectacularly violent fights can still seem impotent without this crucial element.

The other reason for the witness is more technical. Filming a fight requires stopping and starting between almost every exchange. To give the editor a consistent and convincing series of cutaways, you need more than a shot of a clock on the wall. You need a separate but connected action.

1   In the sequence, press Down Arrow once or twice until your playhead is at the edit point between **15AW-3** and **15AP-3**.

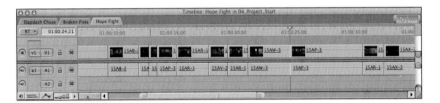

2   From the Hope Fight Clips bin, open **15AF-4**.

3   Press Shift-\ to play from In to Out.

Earlier in this scene, before he began the fight with Anne, Temeluchus knocked out Asteroth. Although you're watching this fight out of context, the audience won't be. And they're sure to be wondering what happened to Asteroth. Now is your opportunity to answer that question, along with using him as the witness for all the great reasons just described.

4   Insert **15AF-4** into the sequence directly before **15AP-3**.

To make this shot feel like it's a part of the scene, you need to hear the fight going on in the background. Due to the production track having the fight choreographer counting throughout, there is no useful track for you to use at this point. You'll just have to use your imagination until the final sound mix.

5   In the sequence, play across the edit between **15AX-2** and **15BA-2**.

This is a sort of jump cut. The two are still battling, but apparently some time has passed because they are in a new part of the room. This is a spot where adding another bit of Asteroth would link the two sections of the scene.

6   In the Viewer, play the rest of the scene after the marked Out point.

7   Set an In point just as Asteroth begins to get up (around 05:05:01:05) and set an Out after the door opens (around 16:12).

8   In the sequence, position the playhead between **15AX-2** and **15BA-2**.

9   Insert the shot into the sequence.

10   Play the whole sequence back.

Intercutting Asteroth's story with the fight scene adds a significant level of complexity and excitement. Now, in addition to the tension created by the fight itself, the audience is following Asteroth's story at the same time. This scene actually continues, with Asteroth bringing the little girl out of the cell, just as the fight comes to a draw.

The footage for this whole scene is in the Hope Raw Clips bin. Experiment with cutting the scene your own way, with and without the witness and using different choices of shots.

Lesson Review

1.   What is the main vector of tension in a chase scene?

2.   How can you measure the time/distance between characters?

3.   How does a close-up inform a chase scene?

4. How do you use an action within the frame to make a good edit?

5. What kind of shots are best for hiding stage fighting?

6. How do the weapons used in a fight impact the editing style?

7. What does a "witness" provide in a fight scene?

Answers

1. The distance between hunter and hunted.

2. Set an In point when the first character passes the edge of frame, set an Out point when the second character passes the same spot, and observe the Duration field in the Canvas.

3. The close-up reminds the viewer of the feelings of the characters involved in the chase.

4. Make the edit on the hard ending of the action, then roll the edit point forward or back slightly.

5. Shots that are on-axis with the action best disguise stage fighting.

6. The larger the weapons, the slower the pacing of the scene.

7. A witness provides a point of view as well as a consistent and compelling cutaway.

5

Lesson Files	Lesson Project Files > Lesson_05 > 05_Project_Start
Media	Media > FBI Guys Pencil Scene
	Media > FBI Guys Pepper Spray
Time	This lesson takes approximately 90 minutes to complete.
Goals	Construct the funniest scene from the available footage
	Find and exploit expectations to maximize surprise
	Increase humor with repetition
	Use reactions to make the audience laugh
	Understand comic timing versus action timing
	Use the axis to control the seriousness of a scene
	Use wide shots instead of close-ups to keep it light

Lesson 5

Editing Comedy

Comedy is serious business, especially for an editor. Nothing stings more than comedy that isn't funny. You already know how critical it is for an editor to be a good storyteller. If you want to cut comic sequences, you must also learn to tell jokes well.

It's very difficult to describe what makes something funny, and humor is notoriously subjective and fleeting. But the structure of comedy can be learned, and techniques can be applied to maximize the potential humor in a scene.

Finding the Laughs

It's unlikely that an editor can successfully wring laughs from bland writing or from performances that aren't funny, but it's easy to squander hilarious material by treating a comedy scene as if it were drama. Similarly, great comic performances can be ruined by a zealous editor working too hard to make it funny.

What makes something funny? Almost always, it can be traced to one of two parallel categories: Someone reacts to a situation in an inappropriate or unusual way, or someone does something predictable and the result is unexpected or unsuitable. The more out-of-place the reaction is, or the more outrageous the result is, the funnier the gag is. Both of these concepts rely on a very simple and familiar concept that is particularly useful to the editor.

Surprise.

Surprise is the lifeblood of comedy. At its simplest, surprise is the result of contradiction. The more surprised a viewer is by the unexpected elements of a scene, the more the potential there is for humor. This theory can be translated to editing in a very tangible way. You already know how to recognize "setup" and "payoff" shots. The editor can control how funny something is by choosing the right setup and payoff shots, and though the precise placement of those shots.

Cutting Comic Dialogue

For the most part, dialogue is dialogue, whether it's intended to be funny or tragic or somewhere in the middle. However, there are decisions you can make that will tilt a scene toward the dramatic or toward the comic.

1   Open project **05_Project_Start**.

2   Double-click **Scene 29 Edit** to open it into the Canvas and Timeline.

3   Play the sequence to get familiar with it.

   This is a scene from "FBI Guys," in which the two desk agents are going through "cold" files looking for a case that they might be able to revive.

The humor comes primarily from a gag in which Bob throws a pencil into the wall behind Phil every time a case is no good.

There are several elements that can be highlighted to enhance the humor. The first is repetition. This can be funny because the audience expects that something different should happen but, instead, the same thing happens again and again.

In this case, two elements are repeated. The first gag is that all of the cases relate to Teamsters. The second is the pencil. Each time a case turns out to be related to the Teamsters and Bob throws the pencil, the scene gets funnier.

One way to enhance the humor is to see if you can squeeze any more repetition out of the scene, perhaps by using different takes of the same action.

4   From the Scene 29 Clips bin, open **A19-29A_1**.

5   Set an In point just before Bob picks up the pencil (19:23:39:09) and set an Out point before he grimaces (41:00).

6   Place the sequence playhead at the fifth edit, between **29B** and **29C**.

7   Insert the new clip into the sequence.

This shot resolves the exchange that previously ended in the shot on V2. This provides the room to add a new back and forth. Now you can insert another shot of Phil.

8 Open **A19-29C_3** and set an In just as Phil says, "Teamsters" (03:22:30:00) and an Out as Bob raises his arm (31:13).

9 Insert this clip after **29A**.

10 Use the Recent Clips menu to reopen **A19-29A_1**.

11 Set an In just as Bob throws the pencil (19:23:43:02) and an Out just before he grabs for the next one (43:18).

12 Insert this clip immediately after **29C_3**.

This adds one complete exchange: Phil says "Teamsters" and Bob throws a pencil. However, you can't cut from Phil saying "Teamsters" right to Phil saying "wait a minute" without creating a sort of jump cut. So you need to add one more "Teamsters", this time from Bob.

13 Open **A19-29C_1** and set an In before the pencil strikes the wall (19:19:58:10) and an Out as Bob picks up the next pencil (20:01:10).

14 Insert this clip right after **29A**.

15 Open **A19-29A_1** again and set an In point before Bob closes his folder (19:23:41:10) and the Out point before he reaches for the pencil again (43:12).

16 Insert this clip right after **29C**.

To end this exchange, rather than adding another clip, you can extend **29C**. Because the clip on V2 will move along as you ripple **29C,** it will remain a good edit and lead right into the remainder of **29C**.

17 Choose the Ripple tool from the Tool palette or press R twice and click the right side of the edit you just made, between **29A_1** and **29C_3**.

18 Drag the edit to the left to extend **29C_3** about 3 seconds until just before the pencil hits, at 03:22:41:20. (Watch the display in the Canvas.)

19 Play the sequence from the beginning to this point.

You may need to finesse some of the edit points, but you have successfully added another round of Teamster reports and two more pencil throws—all fabricated entirely from the existing footage. Each time Bob throws the pencil, it's likely to get at least a giggle from the audience, and the more it happens without Phil doing anything, the funnier it gets.

Using Replace Edit

There is one problem with the edits you just made. You actually used the same portion of **29A_1** twice. It's not obvious, but it might appear strange to see Bob furrow his brow twice in exactly the same way. This can be easily remedied; plus, it gives you an opportunity to use the Replace edit feature.

While most edits are performed by lining up an In or an Out point (or both), Replace is a way of performing an edit by choosing a frame within the body of the clip.

1   Press A to choose the Arrow tool.

2   In the sequence, position the Playhead in **A19_29A_1** just where the pencil leaves Bob's hand (at approximately 01:00:27:20).

3   Open **A19_29A_2** and find the frame where the pencil leaves Bob's hand (at 19:12:58:20).

You do not need to set any In or Out points. The points would be ignored in the Viewer, and they would limit the effect of the Replace edit in the sequence.

4   Untarget audio tracks A1 and A2. Drag the clip from the Viewer onto the Canvas and pause until the Edit Overlay appears, then drop the clip on the Replace edit target.

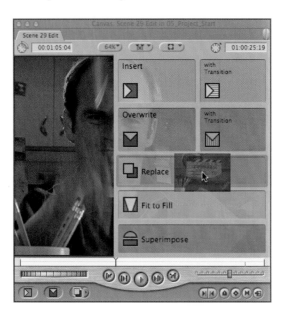

Take 2 replaces take 1, giving a slightly different performance; but because you precisely lined up the action with the Replace edit, the timing should match perfectly.

5   Play the sequence to check your work.

Using Reaction Shots

Comedy is all about surprise and upsetting expectations, but something can be very funny even if it's not a surprise to the audience—as long as it's a surprise to someone. Think of the classic banana peel. There is a setup shot, warning the audience that danger lies in the path ahead. When the hapless victim inevitably slips, it can still be funny, as long as the actor appears convincingly surprised.

You can enhance the humor of a scene by showing how the participant's expectations are confounded.

This theory can be applied to this scene at the point when Phil finally catches the pencil. The audience is surprised and it's a little funny, but what about Bob? Bob is surprised too, and it's his reaction that makes the unexpected action not just surprising, but funny.

1   Find the moment in the sequence when Phil catches the pencil and holds it up beside his head. Set an In point at 01:00:52:23.

2   Open **A19-29Ap_SER** and find the moment when Bob reacts to Phil catching the pencil in the last take in the series. Set an In at approximately 20:16:13:15 and an Out at approximately 14:20.

3   Overwrite the clip into the sequence.

4   Play that part of the sequence back.

    You'll probably agree that the scene is funnier when Bob's reaction is included.

Choosing the Right Performance

In any scene, it's important to find the best performance for each line; but "best" is subjective, and what's best for drama or suspense might not be best for comedy. Also, every time you make an adjustment to a scene, you may change the impact of the other shots in the scene.

In this scene, adding Bob's reaction shot improved the scene, but now his performance in the following line assumes a shift in tone. When Phil catches the pencil, the new reaction shot indicates that it briefly befuddles Bob, but he gets over it less than 2 seconds later in the next shot.

This can be remedied by finding another version of Bob's "force equals mass times acceleration" line in which he still appears somewhat shaken. This not only makes the performance seem more consistent but also makes the scene funnier, since Bob's reaction is unexpected.

1   In the Timeline, position the playhead anywhere over **A19-29Ap_SER** and press X to mark the clip.

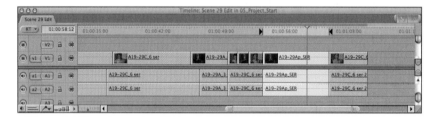

2   Press F to load the master clip **A19-29Ap_SER** into the Viewer.

3   Play through the first take in the series. Set an In point at 20:14:59:06 and an Out point at 15:08:07.

4   In the Timeline, press Command-Shift-A to deselect all, and press Shift-
Delete to ripple delete the marked clip.

5   Re-target A1 and A2 then insert the clip in the Viewer into the sequence.

6   Play the entire sequence to check your work.

The old performance is replaced with the new one. The new performance
is more consistent with the earlier shots, and his embarrassment is funnier
to boot.

Cutting Comic Action

Great physical comedy is an art in itself. In many situations, it should be photographed and edited more like dance than like dramatic action. In general,
you should let the action unfold without editorial interference, as the essence
of comedy is often dependent on the subtle timing and physical actions of the
performers. The magic of a performance can evaporate when those precisely
executed actions are used to carry edits or are broken across multiple shots.

Unfortunately, there is no simple formula for achieving great comic timing, or for acquiring the equally important ability to recognize when the timing is hurting the comedy. Often, a sequence waits too long to reveal the payoff, allowing the tension of the setup to dissipate. Other times, the pacing is too fast and doesn't give the viewer enough time to enjoy the joke.

This next scene from "FBI Guys" is excerpted from a later scene when Bob and Phil bumble their way into the villain's lair and engage in a fight with her lieutenants and henchmen. Just as in scene 29, this situation has solid comic moments, but the editing is not realizing its full comic impact.

1   Double-click **Scene 41 Edit** to open it into the Canvas and Timeline.

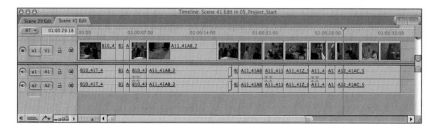

2   Play the first 10 or 15 seconds of the sequence.

Bob screams, "Freeze!" (a classic "setup" shot). Then the henchmen react (functioning in the witness role), then Bob pulls out his pepper spray, which turns out not to work (the payoff). If you analyze the shots, everything seems right, but it's just not as funny as it could be.

In this edit, the joke happens when the pepper spray doesn't work so well, but there's a joke that has been skipped right over: the fact that he's using pepper spray instead of a gun.

This situation contains the short-term humor of undercutting the audience expectation that he's got a firearm. It also serves the story at large by reminding the audience that these desk-bound agents are trying to solve a real-world case. It adds to the humor to show that they don't even have real weapons.

This scene can be much funnier if you split this gag into two separate jokes: first, the reveal of the pepper spray and, second, its ineffectiveness.

First, use dynamic trimming to expand the "Freeze" beat in an organic way.

3 Press R twice to select the Ripple tool and double-click the right edge of **B10_41X_2**.

The Trim Edit window opens with the left window selected (Ripple outgoing).

4   Make sure Dynamic Trimming is enabled.

5   Press J to back up the edit to before Bob says, "Freeze," and press the spacebar to stop playback.

> **NOTE ▶** If you stop playback by pressing K instead of the spacebar, you may get a warning that you can't set an Out point earlier than a disabled In point. If this happens, no harm is caused; just click OK and proceed with the following steps.

6   Press L to play the clip. After Bob says, "Freeze!" wait a short beat, and press K to set a new Out point (approximately 20 frames later).

Indicates how many frames have been trimmed.

7   Press the spacebar to play around the edit.

If you aren't happy with the timing, repeat Steps 6 through 8 until you are satisfied.

8   Press Down Arrow to move the selection to the next edit without closing the Trim Edit window.

The edit will still be selected as an outgoing ripple. This will allow you to add frames to the end of the henchmen shot.

9   Press J to back up the edit to before Bob says, "Freeze," and press the spacebar to stop playback without trimming.

10 Press L to play the clip. When the guys begin laughing, press K to set a new Out point (approximately 2 seconds).

11 Press the spacebar to play around the edit.

Next, you will split the edit so the video leads the audio.

12 Press U twice to switch the edit selection to an incoming Ripple edit.

13 Drag the jog wheel to the right until Bob is midway through his movement of revealing the spray.

14 Press I or click the set In button to set a new In point.

15 In the Timeline, Command-click the two selected audio edits to deselect them.

16 Click the title bar of the Trim Edit window to make that window active again.

17 Press U twice to change the edit selection to a roll.

18 Press J to roll the edit to the left until just before Bob begins his movement (about 13 frames).

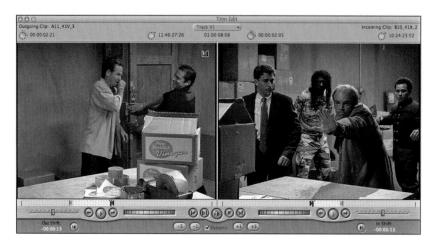

19 Press the spacebar to play around the edit.

Hopefully, you feel that the scene is improved. If you don't, continue trimming the edits until you find the humor is most apparent.

Using the Axis

One key to enhancing humor is to stay away from techniques that emphasize drama. For example, it's a fact that the closer an actor's eyelines are located to the axis of the camera, the more likely the viewer is to be engaged emotionally. This is why OTS shots are so popular in dialogue scenes.

Therefore, the further off-axis a shot, the more objective is the audience's reaction. This is helpful for comedy. You don't want your audience emotionally involved with your characters, especially when they're supposed to be laughing at them.

You can apply this technique here by adding an objective shot of Bob spraying the pepper.

1   In the sequence, set an In point before the camera begins tilting up from the spray on the floor (around 01:00:11:20) and an Out point after the camera move is complete, but before the henchmen look at each other (around 14:00).

2   From the Scene 41 Clips bin, open **A11_41X_4**.

3   Set an Out point after Bob looks up at the henchmen (around 11:51:50:10).

4   Untarget tracks A1 and A2 and overwrite the clip into the sequence.

5   Press \ (backslash) to play around the edit.

You could also choose to replace the first shot of the pepper spray with this profile angle, but in some ways the performance is preferable in the existing shot. However, using this shot at this point provides an additional opportunity to laugh at poor Bob and does so in the less personal off-axis shot.

Additionally, this shot has the benefit of providing an angle on Phil, showing his reaction to Bob's failure. This serves the traditional witness purpose (giving the audience someone onscreen to relate to) and it serves as a subtle setup for Phil's next action when he pulls out his gun.

Using Wider Shots

You can also maximize comic potential by choosing wider shots instead of close-ups. This is one of the most useful general rules for comedy scenes, though like all of these techniques, its impact is subtle.

Close-ups tend to bring the audience into a more intimate, subjective relationship with the actors, similar to the effect of on-axis shots. This effect is magical in drama but it can be deadly in comedy. Additionally, comedy is often physical and, just like dance, cutting in too close can suck some of the energy out of the scene.

You can see this in most cinema or television. Dramas tend to use tighter close-ups than comedies. A tight close-up puts the viewer inside the character's head and, most of the time, that just isn't very funny. There are exceptions, but this is another of those subtle visual cues that audiences have been conditioned to perceive.

In this scene, there is a sudden close-up on Phil when he pulls his gun (around 01:00:24:00).

This works wonderfully, because it's not supposed to be comic (except that he calls the villains "cheese sticks"). It's a surprise, but not a funny one.

However, what follows is a series of three MCUs during the exchange between Bob and Phil. This moment is supposed to be funny, and it *is*. Both actors' performances are terrific; but, the moment still feels too much like drama because the camera is in close and the editing falls into the traditional matching MCU angles. The scene can be funnier by stepping out to a wider shot instead.

6   Place the sequence playhead just after Phil's CU at 01:00:25:17.

7   Open **B10_41V_4**. A section of the clip has already been marked.

Interestingly, this angle, which was too on-axis for the exchange between Bob and the henchmen, is actually perfectly off-axis for the exchange between Bob and Phil. Unlike the close-ups, this shot is ideally suited for maximum comic effect.

8   Retarget tracks A1 and A2 and overwrite the clip into the sequence.

9   Play the whole sequence.

The comedy editor faces a unique dilemma in that it's very difficult to laugh at footage that you've watched hundreds of times, and deconstructed and reconstructed in multiple ways. It's not uncommon for an editor to lose track of how humorous a scene will appear to a fresh audience and, in the worst case, reedit the "funny" right out of it.

Always bring in a fresh eye, a second person, to provide objective feedback. This is advisable for all projects, but especially for comedy. It's also important for your test viewer to be similar to the target audience. Don't expect your teenage son to be an adequate surrogate for a target audience of retired military brass. He might just talk you into cutting a scene inappropriate for the latter's awards dinner.

Now that's a funny scene.

Lesson Review

1. What is the nature of humor?
2. What are the two most common comic structures?
3. When does repetition make something funnier?
4. What tool can be used to adjust the start and end points of clips?
5. How do you perform a Replace edit?
6. How do close-ups affect humor?

Answers

1. Humor arises from the contradiction of expectations.
2. A person reacting in an inappropriate or unexpected way or a predictable action resulting in unexpected outcome.
3. Repetition is funny when it is unexpected. The more times something repeats when the audience expects a change, the funnier it will be.
4. The Ripple tool.
5. Drop a clip on Replace edit in the Edit Overlay window.
6. Close-up shots tend to illicit a more intimate connection with a character, which are usually less comic.

Cutting Nonfiction Material

6

Lesson Files	Lesson Project Files > Lesson_06 > 06_Project_Start
Media	Media > Artistic License BTS
Time	This lesson takes approximately 150 minutes to complete.
Goals	Isolate and "pull" selects and sound bites using subclips or markers
	Organize interviews to tell a story
	Edit an interview to remove pauses and flubs
	"Spot" a sequence for B-roll elements
	Incorporate B-roll to enhance and supplement interviews
	Smooth overall pacing with split-type edits
	Create complex audio integration between interviews and B-roll
	Insert new segments and alter the show's original structure

Lesson 6
Editing Documentaries

Documentary film includes everything from educational nature shows and concert films to scientific polemics and political tirades. There are as many interpretations of the documentary form as there are variants of dramatic film.

From reality television to concert films, there are endless shapes and sizes that fit in the documentary category and innovative filmmakers are continually blurring the lines between traditionally discrete genres. Like all art forms, the documentary is continually evolving, but no matter what technique is in use, your goal as an editor remains the same: Control the viewer's point of focus through shot choice and pacing in order to convey information in the form of a story.

Defining Documentary

In general, documentary film is synonymous with nonfiction film, though that connection is by no means required. The "truth" of the subject is less relevant than the technique used to convey it. Whereas dramatic films tend to bury their themes in the intricacies of relationships and plot, documentaries wear their themes more blatantly on their sleeve. Instead of featuring characters who speak dialogue, documentaries are more often populated with interviews or scripted narration. Still, both categories always have an underlying theme or purpose, and fiction or not, both categories are still storytelling.

While it may be easy to identify the story underlying most dramatic footage, the elements of story in documentary footage may be more subtle. The beginning, middle, and end may not be inherent in the material, but don't be fooled into thinking they aren't essential. You must find a way to create such a structure. You must also answer those who, what, where, when, why, and how questions and weave them into a logical, engaging story. Whether working with documentary or dramatic material, your editorial job is always the same: Control the viewer's point of focus and tell a story to convey a theme.

Cutting Interviews

One of the most common and basic components of documentary footage is the interview. Just as dialogue is the heart of most dramatic material, interviews are the heart of most documentaries. Even though both are essentially shots of people talking, they require decidedly different editing skills and techniques.

The purpose of interviews generally is to provide supporting evidence for a hypothesis. Sometimes the hypothesis is stated explicitly by one speaker and corroborated by others. Other times the theory emerges from what is said by a combination of speakers. A film occasionally might focus entirely on a single interviewee (such as director Errol Morris's fascinating Robert McNamara documentary, *Fog of War*). More often, though, several interview subjects are used. This serves an obvious purpose; the more voices that support a theory, the more credibility that the documentary has.

Unfortunately, nothing is more mind-numbing than watching a series of talking heads—no matter what they are saying. So, documentary editors must come up with ways of making the content engaging. You can flesh out the story using *B-roll* footage or graphics or other supplemental materials, but the interviews are the show's spine. Unless they construct a lean, coherent (and entertaining) story, no amount of flash techniques will keep the audience from changing the channel.

Too often, documentaries get bogged down by long-winded or convoluted interviews. Beginning documentary editors are often timid about cutting aggressively, concerned that cutting will compromise the integrity of the interview. Such fear is folly. If you can't make a documentary engaging, no one will see it anyway.

Once you get over this concern, you'll find there are limitless possibilities for manipulating footage to make a point in a clear, concise, and engaging. This often means combining phrases from different speakers to make a single point. Sometimes you must rearrange a speaker's phrases, or even take phrases or words out of context.

While there is always a danger in rearranging footage to the point of contradicting the intended meaning of what was said, you generally can leave moral questions to the director or producer. They are not likely to allow you to defeat the purpose of the interview, and they're the ones who will have to answer to the interviewee's objections. Your job is to illustrate the script points in the best way the footage permits.

1   Open **06_Project_Start**

This project contains select footage from a "Making of" featurette from the DVD of the film "Artistic License."

2 Click the disclosure triangle to open the Interviews bin.

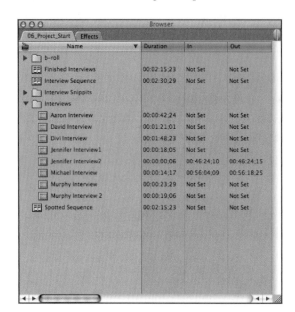

Like any project you should begin by becoming familiar with the footage.

3 Open and play each of the interviews.

Regardless of what other materials you will incorporate into the sequence, the first step is to pull together the interviews into a rough assembly that makes sense and has a good rhythm.

Conceiving the Script

Many documentary directors will provide a script that will identify the intended structure of the show. Just as often, that structure will be determined in the editing room, based on the interview content. In the latter case, you must seek out themes and consistent elements in the interviews that you can combine to create the show. If the interviewer was good, some of those sections will be obvious. She may have asked the same question of every subject, or elicited answers that are narrow enough to group easily.

At first glance, you may feel that there is no useful footage. The interviews all stink; no one spoke in clear, simple sound bites; and the purpose of the documentary seems utterly absent from the hours of talking heads. Relax. That feeling is entirely normal.

In fact, if you don't feel that way, you should worry. If the speakers simply parrot what the director wanted them to say, it will seem inauthentic or staged. The nature of good interviews is that they are subtle. Just as in a dramatic piece the theme is best conveyed in the subtext of dialogue and action, the essence of a documentary is best conveyed through the *combinations* of what people say. The theses and ideas should be inferred by the audience. Your job is to craft the show in such a way that the viewer feels as if he came up with the ideas on his own. And if your show requires that specific words be spoken, you can script a narration.

Sometimes the interviews don't support the hypothesis. In that case, you need to rethink what the movie is about or scrap the footage and start over again. You must find a way to tell the best story you can with the footage you have available.

In the footage used in this lesson, one of the consistent themes is the good vibe on the set and how much everyone liked working together. Other elements that are mentioned in more than one interview are discussions of the cast, and descriptions of the story.

By identifying these three elements you have the beginning of a framework to build around. In some cases, you can literally break up the interviews into segments with title cards (for example, The Crew, The Cast, The Story) or you can subtly weave the sections together by finding transition points in the interviews.

Pulling Selects

Once you've sketched out the overall structure, you begin the editing process by identifying sections of the interviews you are likely to use. Remember, when cutting interviews, you must ruthlessly search for the essence of what is being said. Look for redundancy. People love to repeat themselves when they speak, clarifying their point or trying out different phrasings; but no one wants to hear that repetition. You must find the simplest, shortest segment possible and discard the rest.

Typically, this honing process requires several passes. At each stage you'll shave a word or two off the beginning or end of a sound bite, or even eliminate a whole sentence until you've whittled the material down to its most indispensable elements.

4   Open **Michael Interview**. Set an In point just before the first words he speaks, "The cast and crew…," at 00:54:38:03, and set an Out just after he says, "I feel completely blessed," around 42:13.

5   Press Shift-\ (backslash) to play from In to Out.

You may hear a little bit of his next line at the end of the clip.

6   Make sure your playhead is at the Out point, and press Back Arrow once, then press O to set a new Out point.

7   Press Shift-\ again.

Can you still hear any of his next line? If so, repeat Steps 6 and 7 until you just have the clean line.

8   Choose Modify > Make Subclip or press Command-U.

A subclip is created in the Interviews bin.

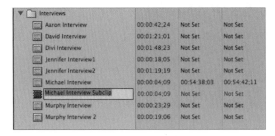

9   Name the subclip with the text of what it contains. Type *MW: The cast and crew are amazing…*

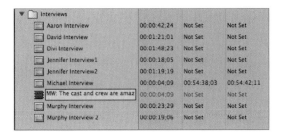

10 In the Viewer, skip ahead to where Michael says, "Carlos, the A.D.," around 00:55:09:08. Set an In point there, being careful not to include any of the preceding word.

11 Play forward until after he talks about Seamus the D.P. and set an Out point after he says, "This has been a great experience so far" (approximately 29:05).

12 Press Shift-\ to play In to Out.

Make sure you don't hear any extraneous words at the head or the tail of the clip. If you do, adjust the In or Out point until the section you want is clearly marked.

13 Press Command-U to make a subclip and in the Browser, name the new subclip *MW: Carlos and Seamus...*

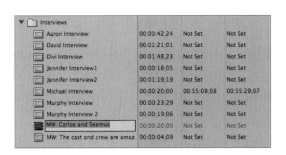

14 In the Viewer, play forward to where Michael says, "And Divi and Nate producing this thing," (around 36:18).

Notice that he says, "And, uh… And Divi and Nate…"

There's no reason for you to include that first false start. Interviews are full of these extraneous "uhs" and "ums" and flubbed words and other minor mistakes. You must make it a habit to mark exactly the words you need and nothing else. You may think it's impossible to cut around some of these—perhaps two words are slurred together into one sound—but you almost always can. Final Cut Pro can make audio edits down to 1/100th of a frame. There's no excuse for leaving in extra words or sounds. Great interview editing is all about making tiny subtle edits. Just start moving frame by frame, setting a new In or Out point and playing from the In to the Out (Shift-\) until you get it right. For those rare cases when you can't make a successful edit, just get it close and later you can make subframe-level keyframes in the Timeline.

Unlike editing dramatic dialogue in which you generally avoid manipulating the nuances and pacing of speech, good interview editing requires precisely this ability.

15 Find the frame right before the second "And" (37:04)

This time, instead of making a subclip by setting an In and Out, you will use an extended marker.

16 Press ` (backquote) to set a marker on that frame.

17 Play forward until just after he says, "Blown away," at 42:08.

18 Press Option-~ (tilde) to extend the marker.

The marker now lasts the duration of that section of the interview. You will see that the clip in the Browser also now has a disclosure triangle next to it.

19 Click the disclosure triangle.

20 Name the marker *MW: Divi and Nate...*

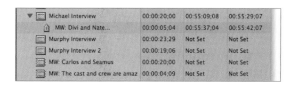

You can use extended markers and subclips interchangeably in Final Cut Pro. There is just one more section to mark in this clip.

21 Find the section in which Michael says, "And the actors," and set a marker that begins on frame 00:56:04:09.

22 Play until just after he says, "It's been really good," at 18:25 and press Option-~ (tilde) to extend the marker.

23 In the Browser, name the marker *MW: The Actors...*

24 In the Browser, Command-click the two markers and the two subclips and drag all four items into the Interview Snippits bin.

25 Click the disclosure triangle next to the Interview Snippits bin to expand it.

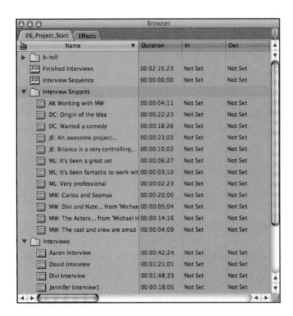

Notice that the two markers you just dragged now appear as ordinary subclips. Most of the other sound bites have been selected already and are collected in this bin.

Pulling Selects in the Timeline

The process just described is efficient and allows you to go through all of your interviews and identify which sections you will be using. You can further categorize them in the Browser, assigning labels or grouping them in different bins according to where they're likely to fit in the show.

However, sometimes it can be easier to do some selecting in the Timeline. This can be especially useful if you think you may want to rearrange the order of some of the clips.

1   Double-click **Interview Sequence** to open it into the Canvas and Timeline.

2   Drag the **David Interview** clip from the Browser into the Canvas.

The entire clip will be edited into the sequence. Obviously you won't be using the entire thing, so the first thing to do is eliminate the sections of the clip you know you don't want.

3 Play the sequence until just after David says, "He's extremely passionate," and set an In point there (around 01:00:13:00).

This mark indicates the beginning of the section you will be deleting.

4 Play forward until just before David says, "His obstacle is," (at around 28:00) and set an Out point there.

5 Press Shift-Delete to ripple delete the unwanted section.

6 Play forward and stop just after he says, "Brianca," at 17:24. Set an In point there.

7 Set the Out point just before David says, "He's kinda eccentric," at 35:06.

8 Press Shift-Delete to ripple delete this section.

9 Set a new In just after he says, "In his head," at 28:16.

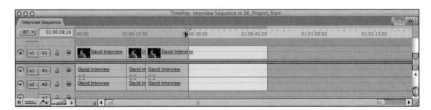

Since you'll be deleting the remainder of the clip, no Out point is necessary.

10 Press Delete to eliminate the marked area.

You have whittled the clip down to three sections that you may want to use. However, the clips can be rearranged so they make better sense. In the first and third clips, David is talking about his character, but in the second clip, he's talking about his boss, Brianca. It is a bit more logical to move the third clip before the second one.

11 Select the third clip and drag it to a position between the first two clips. Make sure snapping is on (by pressing N), then press Option to perform a Swap edit.

The Swap edit (indicated by a curved arrow) rearranges the clips in the Timeline without leaving any gaps.

NOTE ▶ Don't press the Option key before you begin dragging or you will copy the clip instead of moving it. Also be sure to release the mouse button before releasing the Option key, or else you will just move the clip.

12 Play the whole sequence.

The edit between the first two clips is a little rough, mainly because of the extra "He's" at the beginning of the second clip.

13 Play the sequence and park the playhead just before he says, "Kinda eccentric," (at 14:05).

14 Press R twice to select the Ripple tool and drag the right edge of the edit until it snaps to the playhead position.

> **TIP** ▶ This technique of positioning the playhead at the desired place and then drag-trimming to that point is a great way to trim in the Timeline without the guesswork that dragging usually entails.

15 Press A to release the Ripple tool.

16 Press \ (backslash) to play around the new edit.

Don't worry about the obvious visual jump cut. In fact, while putting together the framework of interviews, you generally should ignore the picture entirely. In many cases, you're better off just closing your eyes and listening to the audio. You can always fix jump cuts later using *B-roll* (discussed later in this lesson) or, in the worst case, using *soft cuts* (short-duration cross-dissolves).

Assembling the Clips

Once you've collected your sound bites, you're ready to assemble them. Because there's no inherent order to the clips and because it's easy to rearrange things in the Timeline, one way to start is to drag several clips into the Timeline at once, rearrange them, and trim them there. You probably wouldn't want to do this with an hour's worth of interviews, but for shorter sequences it's sort of fun.

1   Drag the Interview Snippits bin from the browser directly into the Timeline, performing an Insert edit at the head of the sequence.

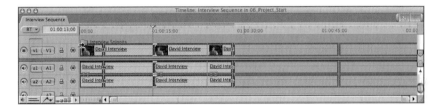

Be sure not to release the mouse until you see the Insert arrow, and the clips appearing as outlines and not solid blocks.

2   Press Shift-Z to zoom the Timeline to fit all the clips.

All of the clips are now in one place, but they are in random order. If you think back to the organizational plan you made earlier, there were three main sections: the crew, the cast, and the story. So, continue by grouping the clips into those categories.

The first clip features Aaron talking about working with the director. That clip would fall into the crew section, so leave it where it is for now. The second and third clips show Divi talking about the origin of the story and wanting to make a comedy. These probably fit in the story section, which is going to go to the end of the sequence.

3 Drag **DC: Origin of the idea** and **DC: Wanted a comedy** to the end of the sequence.

There's no harm in leaving a little gap between these two clips and the clips of David.

4 Press Shift-Z to zoom the Timeline to fit.

5 Select the gap left by the two missing clips and press Delete.

The next clip shows Jennifer talking about how great the crew is, so it stays at the front. The clip after that, **JE: Brianca is a very controlling**, is clearly about her role, which is part of the cast section.

6 Drag **JE: Brianca is a very controlling** to just after David's last clip. Be sure to line up the front of the clip with the end of the David clip, then press Option and release the mouse to perform a Swap edit.

The next clips feature Michael talking about the crew, so you can leave them alone; but **MW: The Actors** needs to be moved to the cast section. Since this is a great introduction to that section, it's only logical to place it at the head of that section.

7   Drag **MW: The Actors** to just before David's first clip. Be sure to line up the beginning of the MW clip with the beginning of the **David Interview** clip, then press Option and release the mouse to perform a Swap edit.

The remaining three clips are all featuring Murphy, and are about the crew. Since these three clips are fairly redundant, it's very likely that at least one of them will get cut before the sequence is finalized. For now, there's no harm in leaving them there.

To clarify the three sections, you can create a gap between the crew and the cast sections.

8   Deselect **MW: The Actors**. From the Tool pallet, select the Track Forward Select tool (or press T) and click the **MW: The Actors** clip.

All the clips are selected from that point forward in time.

9   Drag the clips to the right about 3 seconds.

You may want to turn off snapping (by pressing N) to make dragging easier. Next, you will arrange the clips in the first section.

10 Drag a marquee around the first section and press Option-Shift-Z to zoom into the selection.

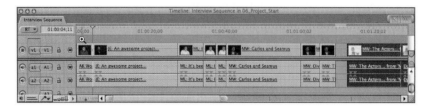

11 Press Command-Shift-A to deselect all.

You need to identify a good clip to begin the sequence. Fortunately, this footage provides a pretty obvious choice: **MW: The cast and crew**

12 Drag **MW: The cast and crew** to the head of the sequence, and perform a Swap edit.

While the Aaron clip is not a bad choice to follow, it talks about the specific role (director), and there are some general crew comments that fit best at this point.

13 Drag **JE: An awesome project...** to the left until it lines up with the edit between **MW: The cast and crew** (clip 1) and **AK: Working with MW** (clip 2). Press Option to perform a Swap edit.

If you previously turned off snapping, you should turn it back on to make sure this edit lines up precisely.

Beginning the Edit

Now that the clips are organized into rough categories, you need to think about the specific order of individual clips. Creating a flow across the edits requires continuity to hide the edits, just the way physical gestures provide continuity to hide edits in an action sequence. With talking heads, there aren't many physical gestures to work with, so you must find continuity in the thoughts conveyed.

1   Play the first two clips.

   While their contents are similar, it's a pretty awkward edit. Part of the problem is that Michael begins a thought and then Jennifer expresses the same thought all over again. You have to trim down the Jennifer quote to its essence, trusting that the setup from the first shot will provide the necessary context.

   When you play her clip, you may recognize the heart of what she's saying. Don't get stuck looking for phrases that start at the beginning of sentences. In the middle of one sentence she says, "All these people come together and donate their time, their talent, their craft." This is a perfect quote. It continues naturally from the first clip, adds several new pieces of information without being redundant, and even has a nice, natural rhythm. The whole quote felt a bit long-winded and rambling, but by reducing it to that 5-second sound bite, she sounds succinct and focused.

2   Set an In point at the beginning of the Jennifer clip and set an Out point just before she says, "All these people," at 01:00:07:18.

3   Press Command-Shift-A to deselect all, then press Shift-Delete to ripple delete that section of the clip.

4   Play forward and set a new In point just after Jennifer says, "Their craft," at 9:24.

5   Press Down Arrow to move the playhead to the next edit, set an Out point
there, and ripple delete that section as well.

Great job! Are there any other clips that would naturally follow? Perhaps
there is something to finish the thought begun by Michael and elaborated
by Jennifer. Aaron's quote starts a new thought, so that won't work, though
it would be nice to bring in a new face. How about Murphy?

6   Play the three Murphy quotes.

Voilá! His third quote is a perfect follow-up to those opening shots.

7   Drag **ML: Very professional** to the end of **JE: An awesome project**, carefully lining up the edit. Press Option to perform a Swap edit.

Next, you'll introduce some of the individual crew members. This will be
great fodder for a B-roll later on, as it will be very easy to show a shot of
Carlos or Seamus as they're being described.

8   Drag **MW: Carlos and Seamus** to the spot after **ML: Very professional** and
press Option to perform a Swap edit.

This is the perfect place for Aaron's quote about Michael's directing. You are
building a very natural structure, talking about the whole crew at the beginning, and then moving into the specifics and talking about individuals. This

is akin to starting a dramatic scene on a wide shot and moving into the close-ups. Coincidence? Not really. It's the same basic storytelling technique. First you tell the *what* and *where*, and just as the audience begins to wonder about the *who*, you provide that information, too.

9 Back up and play through **MW: Carlos and Seamus**. Stop the playhead just after he finishes talking about Carlos and before he mentions Seamus (around 01:00:20:20).

This is a long section and seems like it could be broken up right here. Are there any other clips that might fit? Perhaps something that relates to Carlos or Seamus? There's not a lot left to choose from, but there is one perfect choice.

10 Drag **ML: It's been a great set** to that spot in the middle of the MW clip and press Option to perform a Swap edit.

TIP As this edit illustrates, you can perform a Swap edit anywhere, not just at the head or tail of a clip.

To finish this section you need to think about how this section is going to bridge into the next one, which is about the actors. This might be a good time to step back and take a look at the big picture.

11 Press Shift-Z to zoom the Timeline out to show the whole sequence.

It would be nice to fit in one of those Divi quotes a little earlier. Since Michael mentions her in the second-to-last clip in the first section, that might be a nice transitional element. Try it out.

12 Drag the **DC: Wanted a comedy** clip to the end of section 1 and press Option to perform a Swap edit.

13 Play the whole sequence.

Transitioning between Sections

It's mostly working very well. The only awkward transition seems to be between Murphy's last line, "It's been fantastic" and Michael's introduction of Divi and Nate. If only there was a clip that could bridge that gap; something that was one of the cast or crew following up Murphy's sentiment, but also introducing that next section (about Divi and Nate).

Well, there was a part of Jennifer's quote that you deleted earlier in which she said how great it was to work with Michael and Divi and Nate. That might just do the trick.

1 Place the playhead anywhere over the second clip (**JE: An awesome project**) and press F to perform a match frame.

2 In the Viewer, play the Jennifer quote to see if there's a section that might work here.

3 Set an In just before, "I've enjoyed working," at 00:45:32:05 and an Out just after, "Nate," (but before her next word) at 35:23.

4 In the sequence, place the playhead right before **MW: Divi and Nate** (around 47:00) and perform an Insert edit.

This works wonderfully well. It's a slightly overused but nonetheless effective interview editing technique to repeat exact words across an edit to add emphasis. This is similar to the action scene technique of *double-cutting* a dramatic action for emphasis (described in Lesson 3).

Now, when the audience hears, "Divi and Nate," twice, they're going to be anticipating some information about Divi and Nate. Unfortunately, you don't have any Nate clips to work with, but you do have a clip of Divi, and it's one that explains why everyone's talking about her. She's the producer and the film was her idea.

Now you have to get from her clip into the next section about the actors.

5 Select the gap between **DC: Wanted a comedy** and **MW: The Actors** and press Delete.

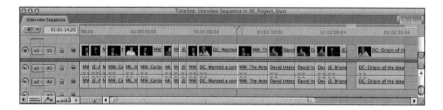

6 Play around that edit.

The edit doesn't work as it is. This is another case in which the second clip introduces a new thought rather than continuing a thought that would carry the viewer across the edit. However, if you trim the first few words of that clip, it suddenly appears that Michael is following up on her thought about the development of the project.

7 Set an In at the beginning of **MW: The Actors** and set an Out just before he says, "We spent a long time casting," around 01:01:16:10.

8 Ripple delete that section and play around the edit.

Much better! Now it makes an organic segue.

This is an important lesson. Pay great attention to the intonations and phrasing of your interviewees. Often, the key to a good edit lies in matching the beginning of a sentence in one edit to the middle of a sentence in another, and the ending of a sentence in a third.

Butchering an Interview

There's no way around it; sometimes you simply have to roll up your sleeves and chop up an interview to make it work. In fact, the more interviews you cut, the more you'll realize it's not a rare occurrence at all. Even brilliant speakers often pause, go off on tangents, hem and haw, or repeat themselves—basically doing everything possible to make it impossible to cull a great sound bite. But if you're good, you can squeeze blood from those stones. And the more comfortable you get slicing and dicing, moving words and syllables, the easier it gets. That's good because you can salvage a great piece of interview that says something critical to your story but in an awkward or convoluted way.

1   Zoom in on the last clip, **DC: Origin of the Idea**.

2   Play across the clip.

>   The sentiment of the clip is wonderful, but there are several problems. The first sentence about "sitting outside smoking and talking" paints a nice picture, but it doesn't make any sense out of context. We don't know who she's talking about or how it relates to the rest of the story.

>   One great test to see if you can cut a word or phrase from an interview is this: Listen to the quote without it. Does it still make sense? Is some essential piece of information missing? If the answers are yes and no, respectively, there's only one thing to do: Cut it.

3   Position the playhead just after she says, "You know," and before she says, "What would be a really funny concept" (around 01:02:15:00).

4   Make sure you have the Arrow tool selected and drag the clip's left edge to the right until it snaps to the playhead.

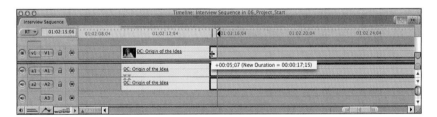

Next, you need to tackle the tangent about whether the person in her story is a "kid" or a "guy." This one is tricky. Obviously, it was important enough to her to stop and correct herself. You don't want to ignore that and disrespect your interview subject. But the way she interrupts herself really ruins the flow of the quote. How can you trim this section to eliminate this unwanted sentence?

5   First, play across the clip and try to set an In just before she says, "a kid."

This is a very difficult edit, because the words "about a" are basically one indivisible sound.

6   Instead, try to set the In after the word "a" but before "kid".

This is a little easier, at around 01:02:18:10.

NOTE ▸ The timecode numbers in this section might not match yours exactly because earlier when you moved this clip to the end of the sequence, you were not instructed to place it at a precise location. Try to perform the edits based on the nuances of the audio rather than the timecode numbers, since that's what you'd have to do in a real world case.

7   Set an Out point just after the "a" and before the "guy" in her phrase, "A guy who works at the DMV" (at around 22:28).

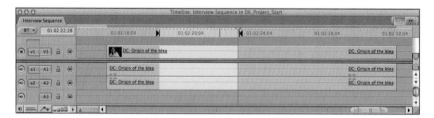

8   Ripple delete the marked section and play across the edit.

Even if you got the timing just right, her intonation of the word "guy" doesn't match the phrase leading up to it.

9 Press Command-Option-W to display audio waveforms and click the Track Height Selector to increase the tracks to the second-largest preset.

It's pretty obvious from the waveforms that the word "guy" is much too loud. Fortunately, you happen to have another instance of that word from a few seconds earlier in the clip.

10 Press F to perform a match frame and load the source clip in the Viewer.

11 Switch to the Audio tab and find the section where she says, "Or a guy, I shouldn't even say kid" (around 00:19:38:03).

12 Zoom in, if necessary, and set an In and Out around the word "guy" in the Viewer.

13 In the sequence, untarget track V1, place the playhead one frame before the edit point, and overwrite the new "guy" into the sequence.

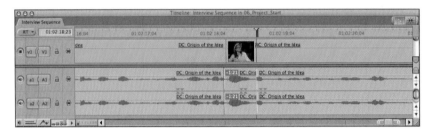

14 Play across the new edit.

Depending on exactly how you made your edits, you will probably need to further finesse this edit to make it work naturally.

15 Select the Ripple tool and drag to the left two or three frames the right edge of the edit between "Guy" and "who works".

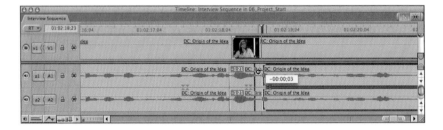

Getting this right may be very difficult, but it is possible. Just be patient and add frames one at a time. Be sure to listen to the edit with your eyes closed. Seeing the jump cut will always distract you.

With that edit fixed you can still improve one more piece of this quote. A few seconds later, Divi says, "And he wants to take a picture... every picture that he wants to take." In natural speech most people would understand what she is trying to say, but for the sake of getting things perfect, why not eliminate that double phrasing?

Again, this is not a simple fix because, for the phrasing to sound natural, she should say, "*And* every picture," but the "and" must come from the first phrase and the "every" from the second.

16 Set an In point just after she says "and" but before "he wants" (around 22:01) and set an Out *about four frames before* she says "every picture".

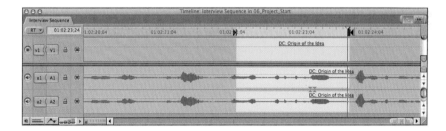

17 Ripple delete the marked area and play back over the edit.

Those few frames of space are critical to getting a natural-sounding edit. If you don't like the sound of your edit, use the Ripple tool to adjust each side of the edit until it sounds natural.

Editing Subframe Audio

Often, to make each edit sound right, you will want to perform little fade-ins or fade-outs at each edit point. Professional audio editors never let any piece of audio begin or end "hard." Such hard Ins and Outs can generate pops or subtle but abrupt changes in sound quality.

Final Cut Pro allows you to create as many as 100 audio keyframes within the duration of a single video frame. So in this case you can create a tiny sub-frame fade to smooth the edit.

1 Zoom in the sequence all the way, centered on the edit point between "And" and "Every".

The dark gray area in the ruler indicates the duration of one video frame.

2 Press Option-W to turn on Keyframe Overlays.

3 Option-click the audio level envelope for the outgoing clip to add a keyframe about half a frame before the edit point.

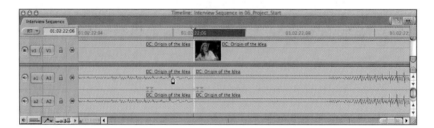

4 Add a second keyframe very close to the edit point and drag it down to the bottom of the clip to create a fade-out effect.

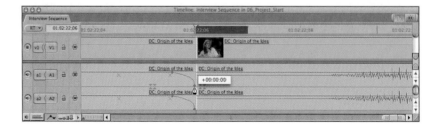

That tiny, half-frame fade out will be barely audible, but it will help to hide the edit ever so subtly.

Finishing the Sequence

When you've completed the surgery on this clip, you still need to choose its place in the project. There is one obvious natural place for it to go, and that's mixed with David's description of his character.

1   Press Shift-Z to zoom the Timeline to fit all the clips.

2   Find the place in the sequence when David says, "He's the photographer that takes the pictures at the DMV" (around 01:01:37:20). Park the playhead there.

3   Select the whole group of clips that comprise the last Divi quote and drag them until they line up with the playhead. Press Option to perform an Insert edit and release the mouse.

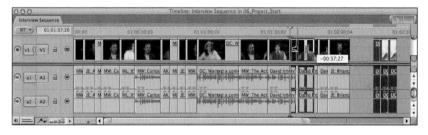

Before

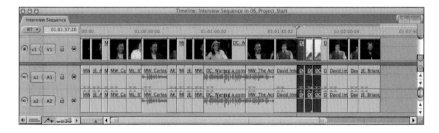

After

4   Play the entire sequence.

The only remaining problem is that there is no ending beat. The sequence just ends with Jennifer's last line. One easy solution is to split in half Michael's last comment about the actors.

This is another common tactic: taking one sound bite and breaking it in half to bookend a section.

5   Play through the **MW: The Actors** clip and park the playhead right after he says, "Bring something to this" (around 23:05).

6   Select all the clips to the right of that clip, beginning with the first **David Interview** clip.

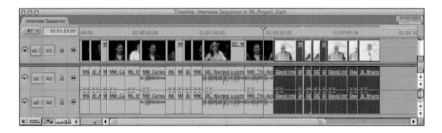

7   Drag left the group of clips until the group snaps to the playhead position. Press Option to perform an Insert edit and release the mouse.

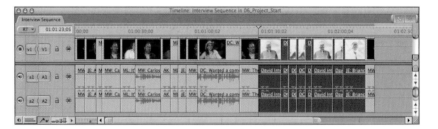

8   Play the entire sequence again.

That bookending helped, but didn't give the ending punch that the sequence ought to have. Perhaps there's something else in the raw clips that can serve as a final shot.

9 Go back to the Interviews bin and open **Jennifer Interview2**.

10 Set an In point just before she says, "And everyone's been really sweet," (00:46:07:22) and an Out point just after she says, "Because we love to work" (22:22).

11 Make sure track V1 is targeted and overwrite this clip onto the very end of the sequence.

Awesome! A great last sentiment, but there's one last nagging thing. At the end of her line, she flubs the word "love" making it sound like "larve." Is this fixable? Is it worth fixing? You've come so far; why not try?

12 Go back to the Viewer and play past the Out point.

In the very next sentence, she says the word "love" clearly.

13 Set an In and Out around that word in the Viewer (In: 00:46:24:10, Out: 00:46:24:15).

14 Press Shift-\ to play In to Out a few times to make sure you cleanly marked only that word (without any of the previous or next words included) and adjust the edit one frame at a time if necessary.

15 In the sequence, zoom in on that last section of the Timeline and set an In point just before the word "love" (01:02:29:28).

16 Untarget track V1 and overwrite the "love" into the sequence.

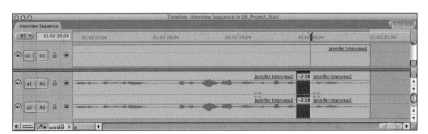

17 Play the whole sequence once again.

There are probably some edits that still need trimming. Tiny fade-ins and fade-outs may improve or smooth out some of the edits, and as with dialogue scenes, splitting the picture and audio edits often helps to improve the overall flow.

You might get ambitious and further tighten things by removing more pauses or "um's." However, your goal should be to create a sequence that sounds like a natural flow of conversation. Remember, it's very important that you close your eyes or get used to listening for the rhythm without being distracted by untidy picture edits. Those jump cuts can be fixed once you begin the second phase: adding B-roll.

Adding B-Roll

By the time you finish editing your interviews, you should have a tight, coherent sequence that smoothly moves from one subject to the next, and tells some kind of a story. But the interviews are just the skeleton. Next you must flesh out the sequence by adding shots to illustrate or expand upon what is being said. Talking heads are notoriously boring to watch, but supplemented with the right B-roll footage you can create a captivating and engaging scene.

B-roll is an old television news term that originated when editing was performed on reels of film. While the primary "A" roll contained the interviews, whenever an edit was necessary, the editor would cut to the secondary "B" footage. Although today nearly all editing is done digitally, that cutaway and supplemental footage is still referred to as B-roll.

In some cases, the B-roll isn't shot until after the interviews have been edited. This ensures that you have cutaways that correspond precisely to what is being said. This usually is the case for shows based on written narration instead of unscripted interviews.

However, documentary editors more often are handed a huge pile of footage that may or may not relate specifically to the contents of the interviews. The editor must wade through all of this B-roll looking for images that will match what is being said.

In many ways, choosing and placing these shots is where great documentary editors show their prowess. The best editors look past the obvious contents of the footage, and find the symbolic or inferred meaning that will illustrate what is being said, and expand upon it. This requires looking at the footage with a very open mind and thinking about how it might be used beyond its most obvious purpose.

1   Double-click the b-roll bin to open it in its own window.

As in all projects, the first step is to get very familiar with your footage. These clips have been culled from several hours of behind-the-scenes footage from the "Artistic License" shoot.

2   Watch all the clips.

The behind the scenes videographer had no idea what would be said in the interviews, so he just gathered random bits of activity over the course of two days. Matching that footage to the interviews is typical of the challenge you will face in many documentary situations.

The more thoroughly you organize your B-roll shots, the easier it will be to find what you're looking for. You can do this organization in any of the common ways, such as creating a hierarchy of bins and sub-bins, using labels, or typing descriptive comments in the various comment fields. Entering specific and descriptive information helps you search for the shots you need by using Final Cut Pro's Find feature.

At the very least, you can group these clips into a couple of sub-bins.

3   If necessary, scroll the Browser until you can see the column labeled Cast or Crew.

4   Click that column header to sort the bin by that data.

5   Press Command-B twice to create two new bins.

6   Label one of the bins *Cast* and the other *Crew*.

7   Select all of the clips marked Cast (in the Cast or Crew column) and drag them into the Cast bin, and drag all off the Crew clips into the Crew bin.

Since the other four clips have both cast and crew in them, they are labeled as *crew + cast*. Rather than choosing which bin to put them in, there's no reason not to put them in both.

8   Select the remaining clips that are labeled *crew + cast* and Option-drag them into the Cast bin.

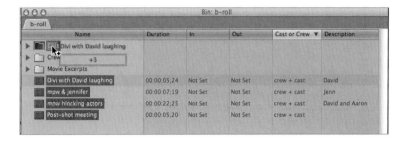

This puts a copy of each of those clips in the Cast bin, but leaves a copy loose in the b-roll bin.

9   Select the clips again and drag them into the Crew bin.

10 Close the b-roll bin.

Spotting the Sequence

Once you are familiar with the B-roll available to you, you should begin thinking about how and where you can use it in your sequence. *Spotting* is the term for watching a program and marking all of the "spots" where something must be done. You might spot a show for moments that need sound effects or for edits that need finessing. In this case, you will look for spots where you think B-roll should be used. This includes long sections of one person talking, jump cuts that require covering, or content that seems to beg for a cutaway to the subject.

Your project contains a version of the interview sequence that has been finessed and is ready for this next step.

11 Double-click the **Finished Interviews** sequence and play through it, specifically thinking about B-roll.

You will immediately realize that you'll want to cut away to a shot of the crew that the interviewees are lauding.

You can use markers to identify the spots you want to address.

12 Press M to add a marker where you want to add your first cutaway.

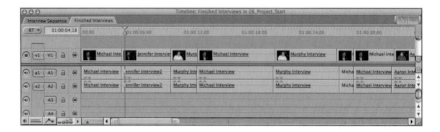

It's not important that the marker go on a specific frame, but it will be helpful if you label the marker something useful.

13 While the playhead is parked on the marked frame, press M again to open the Edit Marker window.

14 In the marker Name field, type *Production Crew* and click OK.

15 Play the sequence until Michael says, "Carlos, the A.D.," and add another marker there.

16 Press M to open the Edit Marker window and name this one *Carlos*. Click OK to close the window.

17 Play forward until the next shot of Murphy.

As he says, "There's a whole lot of production going on," he's looking off screen, which is very distracting. This is a perfect example of a section that ought to be covered by B-roll. But what should the content of the B-roll be? He's talking about "a whole lot of production going on" which could be almost anything. It might be nice to see a shot of him on set, or it might be okay to use generic shots of the crew working. Since his first sentence is about how relaxed the set is, perhaps you can show a shot of people having fun, and then follow it up with people working hard. Either way, another marker should go here.

18 Press M to add another marker, and press M again to open the Edit Marker window. Name this one *Relaxed -> Working hard*.

Because it's important here that the B-roll cover the entire section when Murphy is looking off camera, you can indicate that by extending the marker to the end of his shot.

19 Play forward to the end of the shot and press Option-~ (tilde) to extend the marker.

20 Play forward into the next quote.

At this point where Michael is talking about Seamus the D.P. a gap was removed, resulting in a jump cut. This is another place where a shot of B-roll is all but required to hide the jump cut and illustrate what's so "stellar and crazy" about Seamus. Perhaps you've got something in the B-roll to communicate that idea.

And so on. Rather than spotting the whole show step by step, you can skip ahead to a sequence that has already been spotted.

Adding the B-Roll

As you add the B-roll shots to the interviews, you need to consider what kind of overall balance you want between the two components (talking heads and B-roll). Depending on the nature of the film, and the intended audience, you may favor one or the other. This also may be influenced by how compelling the interviews are on their own, as well as how exciting or engaging the B-roll shots are.

Serious subjects tend to favor more heads and fewer cutaways. Likewise, if the interviews are particularly emotional, cutting away may seem to cheapen or undermine the intensity of what is being said. For lighter material, such as the behind-the-scenes sequence at hand, the more B-roll, the better. Similarly, if you were cutting a piece about athletes or musicians performing amazing feats, you would want to show as little interview as possible to maximize exposure of the (presumably) impressive B-roll footage.

However, you rarely want to completely omit the talking heads. Seeing the face of a speaker provides context and a grounding that gives the piece its structure. When you have several people speaking, as in this sample project, it's important to show their faces, at least the first time they speak. Like all rules, this one can be broken, often to dramatic effect, by withholding the face of a well-known interview subject until after you've heard her speak. By delaying the reveal, you can increase the surprise and enhance the significance of her testimony.

1 Open the **Spotted Sequence**.

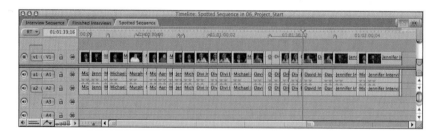

This version of the sequence has already been filled with markers. Each one indicates a place or a section where B-roll ought to go and each is labeled with a suggestion of the type of footage that might fit.

2   In the Canvas, Control-click the Current Timecode field.

The shortcut menu that appears contains a list of all the markers in the sequence. (This list can also be found by Control-clicking anywhere on the Timeline ruler.) Selecting one of the names automatically jumps the playhead to that marker.

3   Choose Seamus from the shortcut menu.

The playhead moves to Michael's quote about Seamus the cinematographer.

4   Click the Browser window to give it focus, and press Command-F to open the Find window.

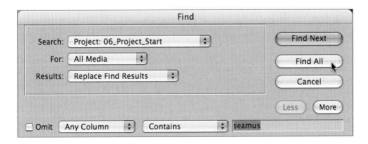

5   Type *Seamus* in the search field and click Find All.

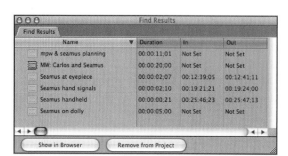

The Find Results bin appears, containing several shots featuring Seamus. The green ones are B-roll and the remaining clip contains the interview.

You must first determine how much time you need to cover in the sequence.

6   In the Timeline, press Up Arrow to move the playhead to the beginning of the clip, and set an In point.

7   Press Down Arrow twice (first to go to the jump cut, then to go to the end of the second half of the quote) and set an Out point.

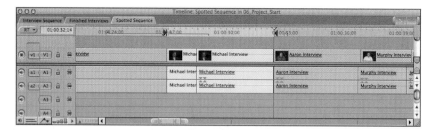

The Canvas Duration field shows you how long this quote is: 5:16. You don't need to cover that entire quote, although you can if you want to, since you've already seen Michael's face in the opening quote.

8   Go back to the Find Results bin and play the first clip: `mpw & seamus planning`.

This clip shows Michael doing all the talking, and Seamus is just listening. It's a nice shot to show their relationship, but doesn't exactly complement the quote.

9   Audition the rest of the clips in the Find Results bin.

Unfortunately, none of them show Seamus doing anything particularly "stellar" or "crazy." The closest is the hand signals shot, where at least he's doing something physical.

10   Open **Seamus hand signals**. Set an In point just as the camera pans over to him (00:19:21:20) and set an Out after his hand signals end and he looks down to the camera (24:00).

11   Press Shift-\ to play In to Out.

This is a nice active shot, but it's only 2 seconds long. You can keep hunting for a longer shot that will fill the space in the sequence, or you can use more than one B-roll shot. In this instance, try the latter approach.

12   Make the Timeline active and press Option-O to clear the Out point.

13   Target the audio to tracks A3 and A4 and perform an Overwrite edit.

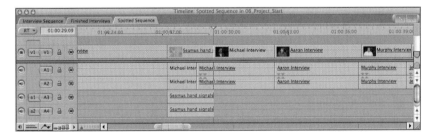

14   Press \ (backslash) to play around the edit.

Not too bad; it covers the jump cut but, predictably, it feels a little brief. This might be improved by adding a second shot, but which one should you use? Ideally, you should pick something that builds on the content of the first shot. This could be a shot with a matching camera move (the hand signals shot featured an aggressive pan), or it could be a shot featuring a similar or complementary angle. Or perhaps there is something else that can speak to the idea of the quote.

15 Open **Seamus handheld**.

Near the end, he does some weird gesture with his fingers. This could be exactly what you're looking for! The two hand gestures are unrelated, and neither one is all that "crazy" by itself; but combining the two just might elicit the right feeling.

16 Set an In point just before the "finger-talking" at 00:25:46:23 and an Out point when he finishes at 47:13.

17 Overwrite this clip directly after **Seamus hand signals** and play the section.

Is it working? Well, you are probably distracted by the audio from the B-roll. While it's unlikely you'll want to hear much of that background noise over the interview, you may later want to include some portion of the B-roll audio in the mix. For that reason, it's good to include it in the sequence, but there's no reason you need to listen to it while you edit.

18 Disable the audio for tracks A3 and A4.

19 Play this section of the sequence again.

The two shots are improving the portrait, but so quickly that they're a little confusing. Adding a third shot might do the trick. Identify where you'd like it to go in the sequence. Think about where you'd like to come back to the interview. One good idea is to return just for Michael's last phrase, "And I love that".

20 Set an Out point just before that line (around 31:20) and, moving backward, set the In point at the edit point with **Seamus handheld**.

21 Open **Seamus at eyepiece**. Set an In just before he leans toward the camera (around 00:12:39:05). The Out will be calculated automatically.

22 Overwrite the clip into the sequence.

23 Close the Find Results bin window.

24 Play around the entire area.

Now that's starting to feel much better. If you had a single shot of him dancing or swinging from the rafters, that might have worked, too. But this is a great example of making do with what you've got. Rather than a single piece of B-roll, you're using three snippits to convey much more information. Seeing Seamus in three different settings, always with the camera and always moving, does give a sense that this is an energetic person, and lends credence to the point about him that you're trying to support.

Splitting the Edit

As it stands, cutting to the shots of Seamus at the exact moment that Michael starts talking about him feels a little stiff. Just like edits in dramatic sequences, this edit can benefit from splitting the audio and video so they happen at separate times. However, this is not a typical edit in which the audio and video are from the same clip, and the video isn't even a single shot, but a mini-montage of three shots. Regardless, the edit will be improved if you create an L-cut, so you see the shots of Seamus a moment before you hear about him.

The Slide tool moves a clip earlier or later in the sequence by changing the durations of the clips on either side without modifying the length of the clip itself.

Before

After

Slide is not very widely used in dramatic editing, but it can be invaluable in cases like this where you want to move around a piece of B-roll. There's only one catch: Final Cut Pro can slide only one clip at a time. In this case, you would need to slide each of the three clips individually. This is tedious and you could accidentally change their individual durations unless you were careful and slid them all the exact same number of frames, which defeats the purpose of using this handy tool.

However, there is a workaround. You can slide multiple clips at once if you do it numerically. Slide works just like Ripple, Roll, and Slip: If you have the tool selected, typing a number automatically performs that type of edit on the Timeline selection.

1   Select the three clips you want to slide.

2   Choose the Slide tool from the Tool palette or press S twice.

3   Type -*10* and press Enter.

The three clips are slid together.

4   Press A to release the Slide tool.

5   Play around the edit.

Now, the clips of Seamus lead the interview audio, creating a sort of split edit. This eases the viewer into the subject change, creating a more sophisticated, organic editorial sensibility. Naturally, this is a stylistic choice and might not be appropriate in every instance.

Integrating B-Roll Audio

Frequently, you will want to mix the audio from the B-roll with the main interview audio. While the content of the interview is obviously paramount, adding a little bit of the sound from the B-roll shot can greatly enhance the overall mix, bringing both components to life in a unique way.

1   Control-click the Timeline ruler and choose the David's Character marker.

The playhead is moved to the section where David and Divi are describing the main character in the movie: a photographer who takes outrageous driver's license photos.

This section of the sequence contains quite a few jump cuts and will need an extended section of B-roll to cover the whole section.

2   Set an In point before the first jump cut (right after David says, "David is the photographer," at 01:01:19:00). Play through the entire Divi interview and set an Out point after the last jump cut, just after David says, "Kinda eccentric," at 34:00).

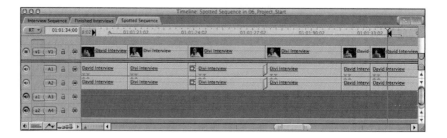

3   Locate the Movie Excerpts bin inside the b-roll bin and open **PhotoMontage**.

This is a montage of the wacky license photos David takes during the film. Since you'll use this clip from the first frame, you don't need to set In or Out points.

4   Overwrite the clip into the sequence.

5   Enable the A3 and A4 audio tracks.

6   Play across this section of the sequence.

This clip has music and the sound of the camera flashes. At full volume it competes too much with the interviews.

7   Press Option-W to turn on Clip Overlays.

8   Drag the level envelope for the **PhotoMontage** audio to –15dB.

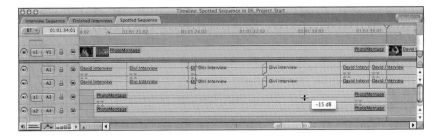

9   Option-click the level envelope near the beginning of the clip to add two keyframes and create a fade-in effect.

NOTE ▶ You may need to zoom in on this section of the Timeline to effectively build the fade-in effect.

10   Option-drag the right edge of the **PhotoMontage** audio clip to extend it as far as it will go.

11   Option-click the level envelope to add a keyframe just before the end of the video of the **PhotoMontage** clip.

12   Option-click to add another keyframe at the far right edge of the clip.

13 Drag down that keyframe to create a slow fade-out effect as illustrated below.

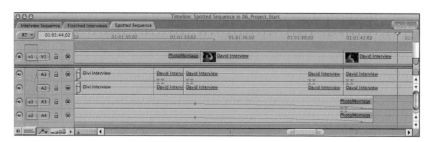

14 Play across this entire section of the sequence.

The music and sound effects from the movie clip nicely complement the interviews. While this is a fairly easy example, using some of the ambient sounds or practical sound effects from any typical B-roll clip can enhance the integration between interviews and B-roll in an organic and subtle way.

Inserting Clips

Sometimes a piece of B-roll requires the audiences' full attention. You want them to listen to the full-volume audio and watch the clip by itself without any interview over it. This technique has many merits. It changes the pacing of the sequence, breaks up the monotony of the interviews, and can suggest an engaging call-and-response feeling.

But beware of losing track of the structure of your show. Don't forget that you are telling a story. Each section of your show must lead to the next; each event must propel the story forward. The edited interviews serve this purpose (assuming you crafted them well). B-roll elements typically illuminate the story, but don't advance it.

Furthermore, these "stand-alone" B-roll pieces must be fully integrated into the shots around them. This can be accomplished by splitting the edits going in and out of them, or interweaving them with the interviews, where the audio goes back and forth in a seemingly seamless way.

1 Control-click the Timeline ruler and choose Brianca.

The playhead jumps to the next edit, when David introduces "his obstacle" Brianca. This time, instead of laying the B-roll over the existing interview, you will cut to a shot of her delivering a line of dialogue that illustrates their relationship.

2   In the Cast bin, open **brianca into cam**. Play the clip and set an In right before she says, "You have 75 seconds per person," at 00:49:32:15 and set an Out just after she says "Snappin'!" at 38:20.

3   Perform an Insert edit.

The clip is inserted into the sequence between David's and Jennifer's interviews. This succeeds in describing what David is saying in a way that would have been nearly impossible without hearing her line.

However, the clip can be integrated into the sequence much more smoothly if you turn it into an L-edit, where the picture begins while David is talking.

4   Press R to select the Roll tool, then Option-click only the video edit at the head of that clip, where **David Interview** ends and **brianca into cam** begins.

5 Drag the edit to the left until it snaps to the previous edit point.

6 Press A to release the Roll tool.

7 Play around this part of the sequence.

The B-roll is seamlessly integrated into the sequence.

There are no rules about how to mix the audio from the B-roll and the interviews; you can completely insert it, or just fit it between the words or phrases without any inserting required.

8 In the sequence, play forward into the interview with Jennifer. Set an In point just after she says "Controlling" (01:01:55:05) and an Out before she says "Manager" (56:08).

9 Open **Jenn Bunny rip** from the Cast bin. Set an In point just before she rips the head off the stuffed bunny (00:26:45:15).

10 Overwrite the clip into the sequence.

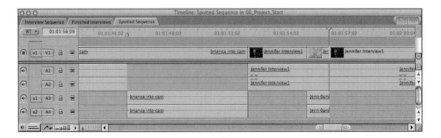

11 Press R to select the Roll tool and Option-click the video edit at the head of the **Jenn Bunny rip** clip.

12 Roll the edit to the left about 10 frames to create a slight L-edit.

13 Press \ to play around the edit.

To perfect the edit, you might want to add a quick fade-in and fade-out on the B-roll audio.

The goal is to marry the B-roll and the interviews together so they feel intimately linked. Indeed, regardless of whether the production team intended for certain images to go with certain lines spoken in the interviews, your job is to make the viewer feel that they were conceived and created for no other purpose.

Having Fun with B-Roll

In addition to supplementing the narration created by the interviews, your B-roll also provides material that can be used to create montages. Such montages can serve as an interstitial or transitional element connecting multiple interview-structured scenes, or it could serve as an introductory or concluding element.

1 Open Media > **ArtLic_BTS.mov**.

2 Study the opening and closing montages.

Building such montages is beyond the scope of this lesson, but some broad guidelines include paying special attention to juxtapositions in composition, isolating action within the frame, matching camera movement across edits, and controlling pacing.

Expanding the Documentary Form

Although the majority of documentary programs are structured around interviews or narration as illustrated in this chapter, such projects frequently contain additional scenes that may take a wide variety of forms. Often a film will include dramatic scenes featuring dialogue or action elements that can be cut based on the principles described in Section 1, "Cutting Dramatic Material." Such scenes range from fully scripted reenactments featuring actors, to fly-on-the-wall observations of real events as they transpire. While these scenes may not have coverage as carefully crafted as you would expect from scripted material, good directors will always provide you with some coverage to allow for editorial options.

Another common format employed by documentaries is a different type of interview, where one subject is interviewed extensively and the interviewer is part of the scene. In such a scene you would typically have shots of both interviewer and interviewee, and possibly even a master-type 2-shot. These scenes can be cut just as if they were a simple dialogue scene.

One type of scene that does have its own unique editing guidelines is a scene that documents an event such as a wedding or a spelling bee. This type of scene is described in detail in the next lesson.

Lesson Review

1. What is the documentary editor's main goal?
2. Name three ways of pulling selects from interviews.
3. How do you perform a Swap edit?
4. How do you create a script from interviews?
5. What is the first step in editing a documentary scene?
6. How can you slide multiple clips simultaneously?
7. What must each section of a documentary accomplish?
8. What does "spot" mean?
9. What makes for good B-roll?
10. How can B-roll audio improve a scene?

Answers

1. To support a hypothesis using storytelling techniques.

2. Using subclips, extended markers, and In and Out points in the Timeline.

3. Drag a clip to a new timeline position and press the Option key until the Swap cursor appears.

4. Using the same familiar components of storytelling.

5. Create a fluid audio track, regardless of jump cuts or other visual errors.

6. Numerically, with the Slide tool selected.

7. It must propel the story forward.

8. It means identifying moments or sections of a show that require further attention.

9. It not only corresponds to the audio that accompanies it, but it also enhances or expands upon it.

10. You can use B-roll audio to split edits and to integrate the B-roll more tightly with the primary footage.

7

Documenting an Event

Aside from interviews and B-roll, documenting an event is probably the most common type of nonfiction film you're likely to encounter. The event could be a wedding, a corporate press event, or a live performance. It could be a road trip to Niagara Falls or a political protest rally.

In each of these cases, you must whittle multiple hours of footage into a concise film that captures the spirit of the event, chronicles the important episodes, and engages your audience.

For starters, it's pretty obvious that you can eliminate an hour of wasted footage shot between speakers at the protest rally, or trim the 20 minutes a bride and groom waited before cutting the cake while someone retrieved Grandma from the dance floor. But once you've pulled the selects—the important moments that must be included—how do you assemble them? How do you tie the moments into a *story*?

By now, the answer should be familiar to you. Just as with narrative films, you need to identify the beginning, middle, and end; to assemble events from a series of moments, each of which depends upon the one it follows and compels the one it precedes.

Construct Your Own Reality

Don't fall into the trap of maintaining the "reality" of the event at the expense of a clear, concise story. For example, at a corporate press event, the flamboyant CEO may have spent 10 minutes demonstrating obsolete technology as a buildup to unveiling the new product. In the video version, you would have 10 minutes screen time when the story isn't progressing. Those minutes might undermine the momentum of the piece and even confuse your viewers. Cut them.

Even the actual order of events is usually not very important to documenting an event. What's far more critical is to assemble scenes so they progress in a natural flow. Of course, you don't want the groom to kiss the bride before the vows; but in your road trip movie, you can relocate the funny moment that happened on the way home right up front, especially if ties together two other shots or moves the story forward.

Don't get caught up in objectivity when the very nature of shooting and editing an event dictates a subjectivity that you simply cannot escape. Inevitably you are abridging the story, and that requires a degree of interpretation. Don't shy away from that fact—embrace it. If you understand the underlying essence of your event, you'll stay true to your theme without becoming a slave to the chronology or other "realities" that will make a boring or confusing video.

Organize Creatively

Whenever you begin a project you examine all of the available footage. This is especially true with an event documentary in which you'll probably have a huge amount of footage covering a wide range of subjects. As always, the process of reviewing the footage is invaluable for familiarization; but, additionally, it helps you find ways to organize and categorize the footage.

For example, the wedding might be divided chronologically into the arrival, the ceremony, toasts, dancing, cutting the cake, tossing the bouquet, and receiving gifts. But you could also identify the footage using different criteria.

You might group all the shots of the bride's family, shots of the groom's family, and shots of friends.

You might additionally call out shots featuring outrageous dancing, laughing, kisses, babies. or celebrating. While these shots won't make up a single scene, they could be perfect for a montage or as a thematic element. You might end each segment with a shot of someone hugging the happy couple. Finding such a motif provides a unifying framework that ties your show together.

Thinking about your program this way opens your mind to new ways of telling the story. Events are chronological, yes, but they also have thematic and content-based structure. There's no reason your video of the political rally couldn't group the three speeches about the environment, even though speeches discussing other issues were delivered between them. You could even go a step further and *intercut* the three speeches into a single segment featuring highlights from each.

Examine Your Footage

This lesson features footage from a travel show called "Destinations." While the show is very structured overall, individual sections are shot in a documentary style, and a wide range of footage is assembled into a story in the edit room. This particular section features the show's host visiting a public market on the Caribbean island of St. Lucia.

The current segment is much simpler than a typical "documenting an event" project, but it provides a sort of micro-event that allows you to explore the same techniques you would employ on a larger show.

1   Open **07_Project_Start**.

The footage already has been grouped into two main bins, Inside and Outside, plus a bin labeled "Intro & transition". This organization defines the overarching structure of the piece. There is an Intro, then you'll move Inside, then there is some sort of transition and you'll move outside.

2   Click the disclosure triangle to open the Inside bin.

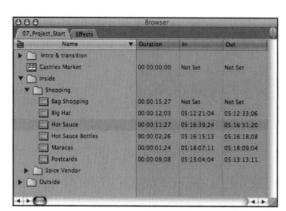

The Inside bin has been subdivided into two sections: Shopping and Spice Vendor.

3   Watch each of the clips in the Shopping bin.

These clips have no obvious or relevant chronological order. They are merely a variety of shots of two women as they wander around the market. They could just as easily be walking around a tradeshow floor in your corporate communications piece, or exploring the lookouts and other sights at Niagara Falls State Park.

4   Open the Spice Vendor bin.

This bin contains clips that take place at the spice vendor's stall. There are several elements, each of which could be edited into a mini-dramatic sequence, and the whole visit to this stall could be arranged as a scene with its own beginning, middle, and end.

5   Open the "Intro & transition" bin and open **Establishing – market**.

This is a typical establishing shot. Although the zoom into the sign is a little clumsy, the shot succeeds in identifying the location.

Just as in dramatic scenes, you answer the *where* and *what* questions by beginning with an establishing shot, thereby providing a context for the scene to follow. This is a great place to begin your sequence.

6   Set an In point before the child crosses the road (around 05:06:31:12) and set an Out after the sign has been on screen long enough to read (around 40:00).

7   Double-click the **Castries Market** sequence to open it into the Canvas and Timeline.

8   Edit the **Establishing – market** shot into the sequence.

9   Close the "Intro & transition" bin.

Constructing a Montage

Next, you will assemble a montage composed of the shots from the Inside bin. Just like assembling the interview sequence, you can begin by pulling selects and throwing them all into the Timeline. At the outset, don't worry about getting everything in the right order. You can rearrange and fine-tune things as the feel of the montage emerges.

1   Open **Bag Shopping** into the Viewer.

The camera operator built some coverage of this event right into the shot. He begins on a wide shot, zooms into a CU on the bag, and then zooms back out as the women move on. You can cut out the zooms to condense the shot, speed up the scene, and better control the focus.

While you could set three sets of In and Out points and perform three edits in the Viewer, it is quicker to add the whole clip and just remove the zooms in the Timeline.

2   Set an In point after the women begin walking (around 05:11:49:18) and use the end of the media as an Out.

3   Edit the clip into the sequence following **Establishing – market**.

4   In the sequence, set an In after Sandi (in the blue shirt) lifts the bag, but before she moves it to the right (around 01:00:11:00).

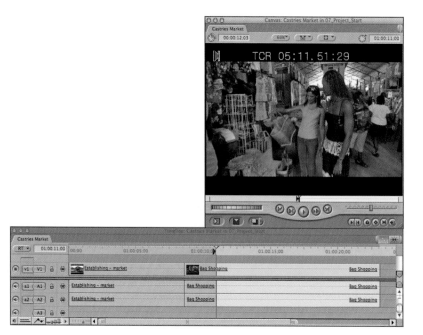

NOTE ▶ When referring to sequence time, be sure to look at the sequence current frame field, and not the burned-in timecode in the Canvas window.

5 Set an Out after the camera has zoomed in, just before Sandi begins twirling the bag (around 16:24).

This will make a nice edit because the beginning of her arm movement will naturally turn into the twirling motion she makes in the CU. This is the sort of serendipitous continuity you should always be on the lookout for.

6 Deselect all and press Shift-Delete to extract the zoom.

7   Play around the edit (\).

How does it look? One minor problem is a sort of audio jump cut. Sandi's line in the close-up cuts off her own line in the long shot. This can easily be remedied by rolling the audio from the CU back to cover over the line from the LS.

8   Press R to select the Roll tool, then Option-click the audio edit and drag it left about 10 frames.

9   Press A to release the Roll tool and play around the edit again.

Cutting out that first zoom succeeds in directing focus to the colorful bag and manages to squeeze out 5 seconds. Now direct your attention to the second zoom. This one happens very quickly and actually achieves exactly what you want: a smooth transition of focus from the bag back to Sandi. So there is no reason to make another edit.

The rest of the clips in the Shopping bin have already been trimmed, so you can edit them all in as a group.

10   Select the rest of the clips in the Shopping bin and drag them into the Timeline, directly following the last clip in the sequence.

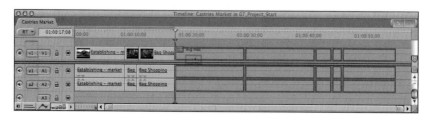

11 Press Shift-Z to see the whole sequence in the Timeline.

Now, you should choose a shot that could be used first in the sequence. This is the same dilemma you face with every new scene, no matter what the content. The most traditional approach is to move gradually from wider shots to closer ones, which, in this case, would mean looking for the widest shot of the inside of the market.

If you look at the footage available to you, both the **Bag Shopping** and the **Big Hat** shots provide a wide angle that could naturally lead you into the scene, but how can you choose between them?

If you examine them further, the background of **Bag Shopping** shows the middle of the market, while the background of **Big Hat** shows what looks like the edge of the market. The second shot is much more sparse, and you can see light coming in from the outside doorway.

Bag Shopping　　　　　　　　　　　Big Hat

It could be argued that **Big Hat** implies that the women have just arrived in the market, while **Bag Shopping** looks like they've been shopping for a while. In reality, none of this may be true, but you must create (and stick to) a logic for the scene that will give the viewer subtle clues about the structure of events.

12 Drag **Big Hat** to line up with the edit between **Establishing – market** and **Bag Shopping**. Before letting go of the mouse, press the Option key to perform a Swap edit.

This sequence provides a great opportunity to use a dissolve effect. The dissolve will further identify this shot as the beginning of the sequence, and will create an organic transition from outside the building to inside.

13 Control-click the edit point between **Establishing – market** and **Big Hat** and choose Add Transition 'Cross Dissolve'.

14 Play the sequence.

It should be obvious that the close-up of the hot sauce bottles would fit naturally as an insert in the preceding shot. Rather than spend time lining it up before editing it in, you can drop it in just about anywhere and use the Slide tool to fine-tune its placement.

15 Option-click only the video of **Hot Sauce Bottles**.

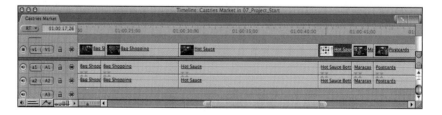

16 Release the Option key and drag the clip to the middle of the **Hot Sauce** shot.

17 Press S twice to select the Slide tool.

While you can drag the clip with the Slide tool, and reposition it in the **Hot Sauce** clip, it's far more effective to play the sequence and make a decision, while experimenting with where the cutaway should begin or end.

18 Play the **Hot Sauce** clip in the sequence, looking for a good place for the insert.

You don't want to begin the insert after you see Jasmin (in the black dress) reach for the bottles, because if you did, her hand logically should be visible in the insert.

This is an important concept. Even though this is a documentary, continuity errors or apparent jump cuts will still be distracting and pull viewers out of the "story." When editing this type of scene you should strive to make it feel like a dramatic scene in which all the coverage was carefully planned, and each cut was provoked and justified.

To that end, note that Sandi looks up and sees the sauces that Jasmin is pointing out at around 01:00:31:15. This look is a perfect cut point, making the insert serve as Sandi's POV.

19 Position the playhead at 01:00:31:15 and Option-drag **Hot Sauce Bottles** with the Slide tool until it snaps to the playhead. (If snapping isn't on, press N).

20 Press A to release the Slide tool and press Command-Shift-A to deselect all.

Now the insert is in the right place, but the audio from that clip is still sitting there after the **Hot Sauce** clip.

21 Option-click the audio for **Hot Sauce Bottles** and press Shift-Delete to ripple delete it from the sequence.

Creating Effective Jump Cuts

The montage is beginning to take shape, but each shot of the two women appears like a jump cut as they move around the market. This style of editing is acceptable in this context, and might play pretty well with some Caribbean music tying the scene together, but you can do better. Instead of cutting from two-shot to two-shot, you can use cutaways or different angles to smooth the edits.

Cutting montages is its own art and often you must use the composition of shots to create effective edits. That means matching physical similarities across edits (linking two shots because they both feature strong vertical lines, for example) or deliberately juxtaposing compositional elements to emphasize the change. A jump cut is when two shots are very similar, but not exactly the same. If the shots are sufficiently different, it no longer reads as a jump cut, but as a scene change. This is why montages frequently employ techniques such as alternating close-ups and wide shots, the more extreme the better.

In this sequence, the edit from **Bag Shopping** to **Hot Sauce** is a perfect example of this problem.

This jump cut can be alleviated by inserting a different shot of the women, such as the **Maracas** shot, between the two shots.

1   Select **Maracas** and drag it to the left until it snaps to the edit between **Bag Shopping** and **Hot Sauce**. Then press Option to perform a Swap edit.

2   Play across the new edit.

Technically, this is still a jump cut; it's a two-shot of the women cut against another two-shot of the women. But not only is the **Maracas** shot a little tighter, it's more on-axis, and the activity of shaking the maracas makes it very clear that this is not an accidental edit but a deliberate choice.

This edit can be greatly enhanced by using another tactic that should be old-hand by now: splitting the edit. If we begin hearing those maracas before we see them, it softens the transition and improves the edit. In fact, you can split both sides of the edit, so the sound not only leads the edit but trails into the next shot as well.

3   Press R to select the Roll tool, then Option-click the audio edit between **Bag Shopping** and **Maracas** and drag it to the left about 10 frames.

4   Option-click the audio edit between **Maracas** and **Hot Sauce** and drag right about 10 frames.

NOTE ▶ You may need to zoom in and/or turn off snapping to roll the edit effectively.

Unfortunately, the sound of those maracas is pretty loud, and the audio edits are now drawing undue attention to themselves. Both sides would benefit from audio dissolves.

5   Press A to select the Arrow tool, then in the Timeline button bar, click the Link button to turn off Linked Selection.

6   Control-click the audio edit between **Bag Shopping** and **Maracas** and choose Add Transition 'Cross Fade (+3dB)'.

7   Control-click the audio edit between **Maracas** and **Hot Sauce** and choose Add Transition 'Cross Fade (+3dB)'.

8   Click the Link button again to turn on Linked Selection.

9   Press Shift-Z to zoom your Timeline out and watch the sequence again, looking for other possible jump cuts that need addressing.

Note that the next edit between **Hot Sauce** and **Postcards** works acceptably well because the people change screen direction across the cut. Changing screen direction is another classic way to accentuate a jump cut.

Building a Scene

Within the bigger context of your event there will be many little episodes that you can edit into scenes. However, editing such material can be challenging. Typically, you will have footage from only one camera, and events aren't repeated, so there's no coverage to work with. You could let the episode play out in real time, but it's unlikely that will make for good cinema, unless the event was utterly captivating and the camera operator was extremely gifted. More likely, you'll have to find ways to abridge the scene, locating key moments and inventing a beginning, middle, and end. You will have to search for visual or content-related links to tie essential bits into a coherent whole. You may have to live with some jump cuts or awkward edits, but when done well, the content of the scene will stand out and have a flow of its own. Any subtle editorial imperfections will be overlooked.

The Spice Vendor bin contains a collection of shots from just such an episode in the Castries Market video.

1   Close the Shopping bin.

2   From the Spice Vendor bin, open **Spices Scene.**

   This is a long clip that shows the bulk of the scene at the spice vendor.

   The shot is very repetitive and not very entertaining. Sandi and Jasmin ask about various spices and the vendor explains what they are. There is no beginning and no ending. How on Earth can you turn this into a scene worth watching? Well, before you panic, look at all the footage you've got to work with.

3   Play **For the Men.**

   This clip is more promising. It contains a humorous exchange about an aphrodisiac. It also starts on a nice close-up on the wood and pulls out to reveal the three women. This could prove to be a good opening for the scene.

4   Set an In point before Jasmin says, "I heard there's a myth," at 05:30:48:28 and set an Out after Sandi says, "An extra mile... Okay," around 31:09:15.

5   Overwrite this into the sequence after **Postcards.**

6 Use the Recent Clips menu to open **Spices Scene** again.

Now that the scene has been opened, you can grab a section of this clip to fill out the middle of the scene. The opening exchange about honey is clearly not good. The beginning of the conversation is cut off, and Sandi is playing with her tongue, which is distracting.

7 Set an In point on the clean close up of Sandi around 05:26:53:20 just before she reaches forward and the camera pulls out.

Don't bother setting an Out point. You can clean up the shot in the Timeline.

8 Overwrite the clip after **For the Men**. Press Shift-Z to zoom your Timeline to fit the entire sequence.

This shot is long and repetitive, but you need to find an effective way to shorten it. The beginning is nice and the bit about the laxative at the end is also funny, but all the spices in the middle seem virtually interchangeable.

You need to start looking for possible edit points. How can you trim a section of this clip without making a glaring jump cut? Look for physical actions within the shot that are repeated. Around 01:01:49:20 Sandi reaches offscreen for the first of several times. This reaching action could provide a cut point.

9 Set an In point at 01:01:49:20.

10 Play forward, looking for a matching action.

By 02:31:00, the camera has moved into a closer shot, and once again Sandi reaches offscreen. Because one shot is a LS and the other an MCU, and because the action is so similar, this will make a transparent edit that will succeed in eliminating a whopping 43 seconds from the scene!

11 Set an Out point at 01:02:31:00 and Shift-Delete to extract the marked section.

Naturally the audio needs to be cleaned up, but that's easy.

12 Press R to select the Roll tool, Option-click the audio edit and drag it to the left about 2 seconds.

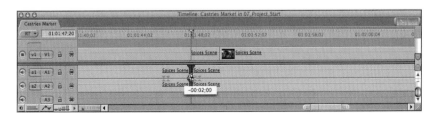

13 Press A to release the Roll tool and play this whole section of the scene.

14 Open **Spices OUT**.

This is a staged shot, but it provides an ending to this scene: The women say goodbye, walk away, and even allude to the produce market outside, making for a perfect segue to the next segment.

The clip already has an In and Out point set.

15 Overwrite **Spices OUT** directly after **Spices Scene**.

16 Play around the edit (\).

Unfortunately, the edit is terrible. The new shot cuts off the action in **Spices Scene**, creating an abrupt and unpleasant transition, but it is salvageable. What you need is a cutaway to bridge the edit.

17 Open **Panning Spices**.

This is a simple cutaway shot panning across all the spices on the table. It's a perfect neutral shot that will cover up the awkward edit you just made. A section of the clip is already marked.

18 Untarget audio tracks A1 and A2, and put the sequence playhead at the beginning of the **Spices OUT** shot.

19 Overwrite **Panning Spices** into the sequence.

20 Play around the edit (\).

The cutaway helps but something still looks awry. The screen direction of the pan contradicts the movement of Sandi's arm in the end of the spices shot. It's a subtle problem, but one that's easily fixable.

21 In the Timeline select the **Panning Spices** shot and choose Effects > Video Filters > Perspective > Flop.

This changes the screen direction of the pan and the cutaway is better integrated into the scene.

Defining a Pattern

While each scene you build has its own structure, you must also pay attention to its place in the framework of the whole show. It's ideal if you can find an editing pattern to repeat for each of the scenes. This gives the show an overall cohesion that makes the end product more professional and makes the story easier to follow.

For example, in this show, each section begins with a brief montage and is followed by a short dialogue scene with one of the locals. As the show progresses, viewers become increasingly familiar with the pattern, allowing them to better understand the story.

Equally important is creating a consistent technique for transitioning between sections. Such transitions can be as complex as animated title sequences or mini-montages, or they can be as simple as differently shaped wipes. The overall tone of the film is often defined by these brief interstitial moments. This is your opportunity to get really creative and incorporate multilayered motion graphics compositions or special effects.

The show in this lesson plays things safe and the transitions between scenes are just simple cross-dissolves.

1 In the Browser, collapse the Inside bin and expand the Outside bin.

2 Open **WS Produce Market.** Set an In point after the camera begins panning at 05:34:45:00 and set an Out point as the camera stops panning around 48:00.

3 Retarget audio tracks A1 and A2, position the sequence playhead at the end of the last clip, and drag **WS Produce Market** to the Overwrite with Transition target in the Canvas Edit Overlay (or press Shift-F10).

This is a one-step method for adding a clip to the sequence and automatically adding a cross-dissolve at the head.

This clip introduces a new location: the outdoor produce market. For this sequence, the montage will be a collection of shots showing the market, followed by a short scene in which Sandi and Jasmin meet a friend who invites them to dinner. This parallels the shopping montage followed by the short scene with the spice vendor.

4   Open **CU Tracking Produce**. Play from In to Out (Shift-\).

This is a close-up tracking shot of the local fruits. An In and Out point have already been marked.

5   Overwrite the clip into the sequence directly following **WS Produce Market**.

It's important to note that these two shots cut together well because they are both moving shots. If you let the **WS Produce Market** shot come to a standstill before cutting to **CU Tracking Produce**, you would undermine the momentum of the scene.

When a moving shot comes to a stop on screen, it draws the viewers' focus to the stopping point. For example, if the produce shot tracked along and then came to a stop on a particular pile of bananas, the audience would assume that something important was going to happen with those bananas. If you end on the bananas, even though they hold no significance, your audience will be distracted, waiting for a "payoff" that never comes. By cutting out of these shots while they are moving you keep the focus of the scene on the overall market rather than on one detail.

6   Open **Produce Vendor CU**. Play from In to Out (Shift-\).

The clip features a CU shot of one of the produce vendors. This is a nice transition from the broader images of the market to the specific people working there.

7   Overwrite the clip into the sequence directly following **CU Tracking Produce**.

8   Play around the edit (\).

This shot fits nicely, but that moment when someone walks past the camera can be put to much better use by moving it to the head of the clip so it helps to hide the edit. Since the clip is already in the sequence, this can be done with the Slip tool.

The Slip tool changes the In and Out points of a clip without changing the duration of that clip. So, for example, in this case it allows you to make the passerby occur earlier in the shot without disturbing the length of the shot or its position in the sequence.

9   Press S to select the Slip tool.

10   Click the **Produce Vendor CU** shot and drag it to the left. Watch the Canvas until the frame containing the passerby is just entering the left frame (about 24 frames).

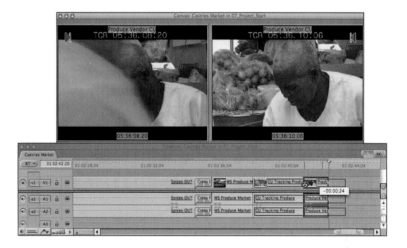

NOTE ▶ You may need to zoom in on the sequence and/or disable snapping to have enough resolution to slip effectively,

Now the passerby appears right on the cut, effectively wiping the Produce Vendor shot onto the screen. Alternatively, you could have slipped the shot in the other direction and used the passer-by to motivate the next edit.

11   Press A to release the Slip tool.

12   Open **Cutting Tuber**. Play from In to Out (Shift-\).

Again, a section of the shot has already been marked. In this case, the shot opens with the action of the vegetable being cut, then the camera tilts up to the woman doing the cutting.

13 Overwrite the clip into the sequence directly following **Produce Vendor CU.**

14 Play across this entire section.

This completes this brief montage. Remember that it may seem easy to find good shots like these, but in the real world you would likely have to scour through several hours of footage to find these 3-second nuggets— and they're easy to miss. Always be on the lookout for movement within the frame or brief moments where the camera comes upon a nice framing of the subject at hand.

Although you don't need to edit the entire next section, it will be helpful to add one more clip to introduce it.

15 Expand the Friend bin and open **Encountering Friend**. Overwrite the clip into the sequence directly following **Cutting Tuber.**

16 Press Shift-Z to view the entire sequence in the Timeline.

17 Play the entire sequence.

Incorporating Narration

You can see how the entire sequence is coming together, and it makes even more sense in the context of the rest of the show. But event documentaries like this frequently can benefit from a bit of narration to tie the story together and provide additional background or context. When a 30-hour event is compressed into a 30-minute show, it often helps to have someone explain what had to be cut out. Narration also allows you to provide a tour guide for the event being documented. The narrator gives a point of entry for the viewer: someone to trust and provide a personal perspective on the film.

Narrations don't always help a show. A narration that just says aloud what is obvious in the images only distracts the audience with unnecessary redundancy. Furthermore, a narration is a performance. A poor or inappropriate performance can hurt a documentary just as much as bad acting can ruin a drama.

Narrations are done in two ways. In one approach, the narration is written first like a script and the show is edited to fit the words and phrases it contains. In the second, the show is cut first, and the narrator watches the final cut and provides commentary to supplement the edit. From an editor's standpoint, the former is handled much like the interviews described in the previous chapter. For the latter, it's just a matter of dropping in the narration and perhaps making minor editorial adjustments to integrate it into the edit.

1   In the Browser, expand the "Intro & transition" bin and inside that, expand the Narration bin.

2   Open and play **Jasmin's Friend VO.aif**.

3   In the Viewer, press Shift-Z to fit the entire audio clip into view.

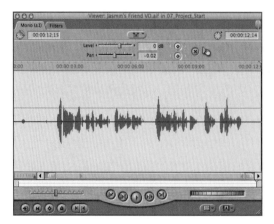

4   Set an In right before her first word and an Out right after her last word. You can use the visual waveforms as a guide.

5   In the sequence, find the place in the last clip when Jasmin says, "Hey Allison." Set an Out point before she starts speaking (around 01:02:47:20).

6   Target the audio track to A3 and overwrite the voiceover (VO) clip into the sequence.

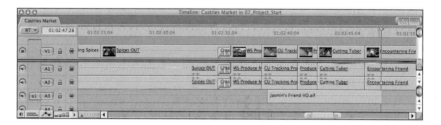

You certainly will want to spend more time finessing the audio levels later and the whole sequence will likely have music mixed in. For now, you at least need to lower the level on the montage clips to hear the VO.

You can turn on clip overlays and use the rubberbands to lower the levels, but there is a quicker, more efficient way to change audio levels on multiple clips at once.

7   Select the four clips from the second montage.

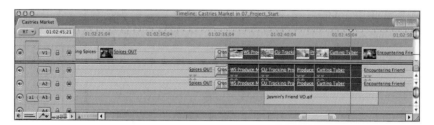

8   Choose Modify > Levels or press Command-Option-L.

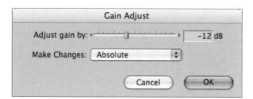

The Gain Adjust window opens.

9 Set the slider to *-12* and in the Make Changes pop-up menu, choose Absolute.

10 Press OK to close the window.

The selected clips all have their audio levels reduced to -12dB.

11 Play across the section to hear how well the narration complements the scene.

This gives you a sense of how narration can improve the overall feel of your sequence. There are two other VO clips in the narration folder. You can experiment with working them into the earlier part of the sequence.

Experiment with Additional Footage

There are additional clips in the "Intro & transition" bin that provide options for opening the sequence and transitioning from inside to outside. Experiment with ways you can construct this sequence and tell different versions of the same story.

More than most other types of shows, event documentaries are very flexible and can be edited in almost unlimited ways. This chapter illustrates just a few of the important characteristics that make event documentaries successful.

Lesson Review

1.   What are three ways of organizing footage from an event documentary?
2.   What makes a jump cut work?
3.   How do you create the beginning of a scene?
4.   How do you create a dissolve between clips?
5.   How do inserts and cutaways figure into documentary editing?
6.   What is an editorial pattern?
7.   What is the advantage of the Slip tool?

8. Describe a one-step method for inserting a clip with a transition.

9. What is the purpose of interstitial elements?

10. How can you simultaneously change audio levels on multiple clips?

11. How can narration improve an event documentary?

Answers

1. Chronologically, by subject, or by theme.

2. Juxtaposing compositional elements in the frame.

3. Show people entering a location or a frame, use wide shots that introduce a setting, or use doors opening or other metaphorical images.

4. Control-click the edit point between clips and choose Add Transition 'Cross Dissolve'.

5. Inserts and cutaways are essential for covering jump cuts and making scenes feel more narrative.

6. Repeating certain structures in every segment of your show, such as montages, consistent uses of wide shots or close-ups, moving cameras, music, or recognizable pacing.

7. The Slip tool changes the In and Out points of a clip without changing the duration of that clip, which allows you to change the contents of a shot without disturbing its length or its position in the sequence.

8. Drag a clip to the Overwrite with Transition or Insert with Transition targets in the Canvas Edit Overlay.

9. The connective tissue between main segments gives you an opportunity to incorporate stylistic elements to add flavor and flair.

10. Select the clips, then choose Modify > Levels or press Command-Option-L. Gain adjustment is applied to the selected clips.

11. Narration can provide a human voice or point of view for the audience to identify with.

8

Lesson Files   Lesson Project Files > Lesson_08 > 08_Project_Start

Media   Media > Lesson_08_Media

Time   This lesson takes approximately 60 minutes to complete.

Goals   Understand the difference between editing music videos and editing other formats

Sync lip-synced video clips to prerecorded audio

Use Gang Sync to ease editing of time-locked material

Use the Roll tool to adjust positions of clips in a sequence

Incorporate B-roll into a music video context

Line up edits with musical beats using dynamic trimming

Music Videos

The music video format is one of the most flexible and exciting types of shows that an editor gets the opportunity to cut. All the rules described in earlier chapters are "up for grabs" because the goal of cutting a music video is fundamentally different from most other projects. Typically the video component is there to serve and supplement the music, and this means that the usual rules related to continuity, coherence, and plot are supplanted by an emphasis on mood and tone.

This chapter will cover some of the techniques frequently employed in music video editing, specifically focusing on the common scenarios of performers appearing in multiple locations and incorporating seemingly unrelated elements that nonetheless help to emphasize the tone of the song.

Technique and Approach

While on one hand, the freeform creativity of editing a music video means there are fewer ways to make traditional "mistakes," it also means you have less structure to guide you in your editing decisions. We've all seen music videos that work; they are fun to watch, they complement the song and promote the artist, and most important, they are memorable and engaging. You've also probably seen music videos that don't work. They feel gimmicky and trite. Sometimes they try to tell a story halfheartedly, or sometimes they are so promotional that they look and feel like an advertisement.

Like other shows, the problem with a bad music video often isn't the editor's fault, but it's still the editor's job to make the best finished piece she can with what she's given. And the unstructured nature of music videos makes it possible to completely reconceive them in the edit room.

Emphasize Tone

Perhaps the single most important rule to keep in mind is that the key to a successful music video lies in identifying and incorporating the tone and mood of the song and reflecting that in the images and editing style you impart. Bouncy, upbeat songs lend themselves to brighter imagery, rhythmic pacing, and jump cuts. Somber, slower songs typically call for slower cutting, moving camera work, and longer shots. Of course, these are just suggestions. The specific song (and corresponding footage) will determine how you should approach your project.

Serve the Audio

One of the things that makes music video cutting deceptively easy is that there is basically no audio editing to worry about. The soundtrack is prerecorded and not malleable. You can literally lock the music track and focus entirely on picture. Of course, the downside to this is that as discussed in previous lessons, manipulating your track is one of the most powerful secret weapons in the editor's arsenal. Now you have to simply work with (or work around) the existing audio. Remember, the picture is merely a way to enhance and complement the track.

1   Open **08_Project_Start**.

This is the project for a music video called Sweet Sound. In this lesson, you will focus on only one portion of the song at a time.

2   Double-click the **First Verse** sequence to open it into the Canvas and Timeline.

This sequence already contains a short portion of the song.

3   Click the Lock icon for audio tracks 1 and 2.

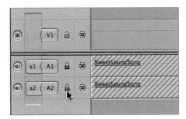

It is pretty much a given that for any music video sequence, you can begin by laying the music track in and locking the tracks.

Examine the Footage

Like any other project, effective music video editing is predicated on a thorough and comprehensive understanding of the source footage. With music videos, you may have the opportunity to juxtapose footage from completely different scenes and even use bits of footage from the heads and tails of shots or "bad" takes that ordinarily would be considered useless footage due to camera errors or light flashes. This makes it all the more essential to meticulously review all of your source footage.

The first thing to check out is the song that you'll be cutting to.

1   Press the spacebar to play the song.

What do you think? Whether or not it's your musical cup of tea is not really relevant. What's important is identifying the sort of feeling it evokes and how you can highlight that feeling editorially.

Of course, there's no right or wrong answer. You might latch on to one particular aspect of the song: the vaguely Latin beat, for instance, or the eerie guitar synth sounds that undermine the otherwise upbeat melody. Or you might pay special attention to the lyrics.

Now, retaining those thoughts and impressions in your head, it's time to check out the video files. This project has two bins of footage. One is labeled B-Roll and the other is labeled Lip-sync.

2   Double-click the Lip-sync bin to open it in its own window.

The production crew recorded the vocalist in a variety of locations. By stitching these locations together, you will create the backbone of the video.

3   Open and shuttle through a couple of the clips to get a sense of the footage you will be working with.

4   Close the Lip-sync bin and double-click the B-Roll bin to open it in its own window.

5   Open and shuttle through a couple of these clips to get a sense of them.

You can see that the overall tone of the footage is rural and rustic. Although the footage maintains a consistent tone and style, there aren't many narrative or continuity-based elements to work with. The painter shots offer an opportunity for a little bit of storytelling, but only in an abstract manner.

6   Close the B-Roll bin.

Syncing the Video
As with most music videos, there is no audio on these video clips. During production, the song was played back on a timecode-capable DAT deck and the camera photographed a smart-slate at the head of each shot. That way it's very easy to precisely sync the clips to the music.

1 Double-click **MCU Static woods** in the Lip-sync bin to open it into the Viewer.

The slate shows the timecode from the DAT player, but the timecode in the Current Frame indicator has a completely different number. That number is the actual timecode on the videotape from which the clip was captured.

In order to take advantage of the timecode information the slate provides, you need to view it in the Current Timecode field.

2   Choose Modify > Timecode.

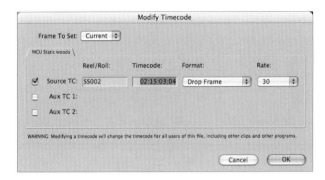

The Modify Timecode window appears. The Source TC fields show the original timecode. It's very important not to alter that, otherwise you may never be able to recapture the clip properly.

To add the slate's timecode to the clip, you must add an auxiliary timecode track. This way you can have two different timecode values for the clip.

3   Click the checkbox next to Aux TC 1.

4   Make sure that the Frame To Set pop-up menu at the top of the window reads "Current".

This indicates that you are setting the new timecode value based on the current frame position, rather than the first frame of the clip.

5   Type *Music TC* in the Reel/Roll field and enter the timecode number visible on the slate. In this case, enter *00010215*.

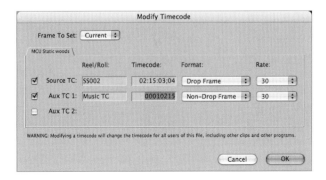

NOTE ▶ You may need to move the Modify Timecode window out of the way to see the image in the Viewer.

6   In the Format pop-up menu, choose Non-Drop Frame and in the Rate pop-up menu, choose 30.

7   Click OK to close the window.

Now the clip has the music timecode stored in the Aux 1 track, but the Viewer is still showing the Source timecode in the Current Timecode field.

8   Control-click the Current Timecode field and choose Aux TC 1 from the pop-up menu.

Now you can view the music timecode for any frame in the clip, which will make it very easy to sync it to the music track.

Preparing to Edit

Once you have made sure all of your clips are properly synced to the music track and your clips are prepared, getting started is simple. For this lesson, the first verse of the song has been isolated in the First Verse sequence.

Although the music clip has the same timecode as your clips, the sequence begins at 01:00:00:00. Editing the video clips in is a lot easier when the sequence timecode matches the music timecode.

If your music timecode begins at or around the sequence timecode, you can simply line it up with the matching number, but in this case it doesn't.

One trick to working around this timecode discrepancy is to temporarily set the sequence timecode to match the music timecode. To do that you need to identify the timecode of the first frame of music used in this sequence.

1   Press the Up Arrow to move the playhead to the first frame of the clip.

2   Choose View > Match Frame > Master Clip or press the F key.

The master clip is loaded into the Viewer at the current frame. The number in the Current Frame field is the number you are looking for.

3   Select the Current Frame field and choose Edit > Copy (Command-C).

4   Click the Canvas or Timeline to give the sequence focus.

5   Choose Sequence > Settings and click the Timeline Options tab.

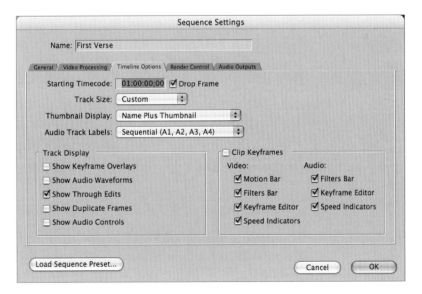

6   Press Command-V to paste the timecode value into the Starting
Timecode field. Press the Tab key to accept the new value.

7   Click the Drop Frame checkbox to deselect it and click OK to close
the window.

Now the music timecode is represented in the Timeline ruler and in the
Current Frame indicators in the Timeline and Canvas.

TIP ▶ Remember that if you plan to output this sequence to tape, you'll
probably want to reset the sequence timecode once you're done editing.

Beginning to Edit

Now that the sequence timecode matches the music timecode, it's time to lay
in some video clips. In many cases you'll have storyboards or other guidance
from the director, but in this case, the director has left all the creative decisions
up to you. With all that freedom, where do you start?

1   Double-click the **MCU Guitar** clip in the Lip-sync bin to open it into the
Viewer.

You'll use this clip as your "base" track. You could have chosen one of the
other shots, but this one seems to capture the essence of the song better
than the others.

2   Click the Canvas window to make it active, then press Home to ensure
that the playhead is on first frame of the sequence.

3   Option-drag the timecode from the Canvas Current Frame field to the
Current Frame field in the Viewer.

This is a quick trick to automatically move a timecode value from one field to another. It works in any timecode field in Final Cut Pro. In this case, it causes the Viewer playhead to move to the frame that matches the audio in the first frame of the sequence.

4   In the Viewer, press the I key to set an In point at the playhead position.

5   Type *2916* in the Viewer Duration field to set an Out point.

6   Drag the clip from Viewer to Canvas to perform a basic Overwrite edit.

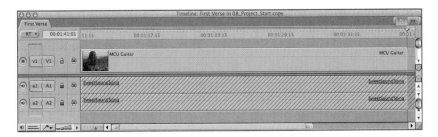

7   Play the sequence to verify that the video and audio are in sync.

8   Double-click **MCU Static woods** in the Lip-sync bin to open it into the Viewer.

Since you've already added matching timecode to this clip, you can edit it into the sequence virtually anywhere and stay in sync, as long as you begin the edit on a matching frame.

9   In the Current Frame field in the Viewer, type *00:01:22:00*.

10 Set an In point on that frame.

11 Option-drag the timecode from the Current Frame field in the Viewer to the Current Frame field in the Canvas.

12 Set an In point on that frame in the sequence.

13 Play the sequence forward about five seconds until just after the vocalist sings the lyrics "learn to unwind" and set an Out point there.

14 Press F10 or drag the Source clip onto the Overwrite target in the Canvas.

15 Play the sequence to see how your new clip fits in.

Using Gang Sync to Simplify Edits

One of the beautiful things about cutting material where the action matches perfectly in every shot is that there are so many shortcuts and tools to aid in editing. One of those tools is the Gang Sync feature, which locks the Viewer and Canvas playheads together so if you move one, the other follows along.

1 Place your sequence playhead anywhere over the **MCU Static woods** clip.

2 Press the F key to perform a Match Frame, thereby opening the master **Static Woods** clip into the Viewer, parked on that frame.

3 In either the Viewer or Canvas, click the Playhead Sync menu button and choose Gang.

With the Viewer and Canvas ganged together, the two windows move in tandem. This makes it very easy to edit another section of this clip into the sequence, ensuring that the new section will automatically be in sync.

4 Play the sequence forward until about 00:01:31:00 (after the vocalist sings the lyric "feeling better than good") and set an In point.

The Viewer is automatically cued to the matching frame.

5 Set an In point in the Viewer.

6 In the Canvas, play forward until the vocalist sings the lyric "enough to go there" (at approximately 00:01:36:00) and set an Out point.

7   Overwrite the clip into the sequence.

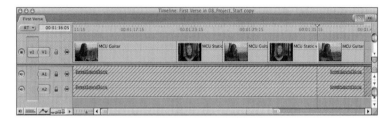

8   Play the sequence to see how your edits look.

Next you'll add one more sync clip to the sequence. This one has been preselected to speed up this lesson.

9   Open **MCU in front of painter** into the Viewer.

This clip already has an In and Out point selected; but before you can edit it into the sequence, you need to make sure that the clip timecode matches the sequence.

10   Option-drag the Current Frame timecode from the Viewer to the Canvas.

The timecode represents the Out point in the Viewer, so in order to make the edit line up properly, set an Out point on that frame in the Canvas.

11 Overwrite the clip into the sequence and play it back to ensure that everything is correctly in sync.

Using Roll Edit to Finesse Edits

Another advantage to knowing that all of your clips will always be in sync, no matter where you put them, is that you can easily roll any edit point without causing problems. In this way, you can even move clips to an entirely new position by rolling the edits on both sides of the clip.

1   From the toolbar, choose the Roll tool or press the R key.

2   Roll the end of the **MCU in front of painter** clip to the right by about two seconds.

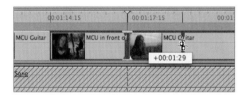

You may agree that the edit is stronger when it occurs mid-phrase, rather than neatly between words or phrases. This is just like splitting edits in dialogue scenes. Moving the picture edits off the natural sound edits (in this case, the phrases of the lyrics) helps to both hide the edit, and to make the juxtaposition more striking.

Another way to roll an edit is to use the Extend Edit command.

3   Select the edit between **MCU Guitar** and **MCU Static woods** midway through the sequence.

4 Play the sequence forward, stopping right in the middle of the word "breath" (at approximately 00:01:22:23).

5 Press the E key to perform an Extend Edit.

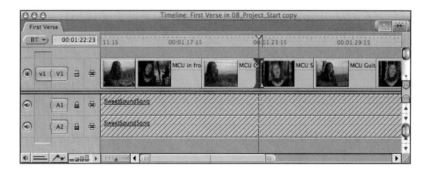

This automatically rolls the edit to the current playhead position. Remember you can extend an edit forward or backwards. So, if you don't like the resulting edit, just move the playhead to a new position and press E again.

6 Experiment with rolling the other edit points in the sequence.

There is no right or wrong edit, and as you'll see, the vocalist is always in perfect sync.

Adding B-roll Elements

Now it's time to add some of the supplemental textural elements to enhance the video. Remember that the purpose of a music video is to entrance the viewer by capturing the mood and tone of the song. This affords you tremendous flexibility. Simply put, you can drop these B-roll elements in nearly anywhere and they'll probably work.

In addition, this is one of the rare cases that I would recommend using a second video track.

1 In the Timeline, Control-click the track header area above Track V1 and choose Add Track.

2   Drag the Source target to V2.

The next clips you edit into the sequence will go onto that new track.

3   From the B-Roll bin, open the **Painter Misc** clip B-roll.

This clip contains a variety of angles of the painter. For this exercise, In and Out points have already been chosen, but feel free to choose your own.

Although you can probably drop this clip anywhere in the sequence without ruining the video, it might be more effective in one place than another. Because the painter is introduced in shot two, it makes sense to add this clip somewhere after that point. In this case, you'll add it midway through that shot.

4   Drag the clip from the Viewer directly to the Timeline, dropping it onto track V2, above the second half of the **MCU in front of painter** shot.

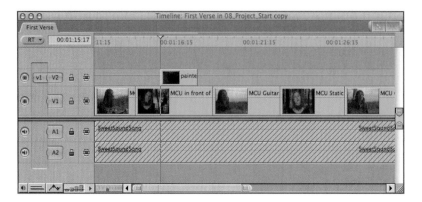

5   Now open **MS Woodswalk** from the B-Roll bin.

6   Press Shift-\ to play In to Out.

Notice that the marked area features the woman coming into focus. In other types of shows, this section might be discarded as junk; but here, that shift from out of focus to in focus articulates the sultry tone of the music and is a perfect part of the shot to use.

Again, choosing where to add this shot to the show is fairly loose, but it seems safe (or at least consistent) to show it after the forest has been introduced in the singing shot.

7   Set an In point in the sequence midway through the first **MCU Static woods** shot (at approximately 00:01:25:00).

8   Drag the source clip to the Canvas to overwrite it into the sequence.

9   In the Viewer, play the clip forward until the section where the vocalist again becomes obscured by a tree due to the camera move.

Entrances and exits always make for good edit points, and this sort of in-camera "exit" is no exception.

10 Set an In and Out point around that section, beginning at approximately 00:02:15:00 and ending about three seconds later.

11 Drop this clip into the sequence about midway through the second MCU **Guitar** shot (around 00:01:29:00).

12 Play your sequence.

It's coming along. You can see that as the B-roll gets added, the show becomes more interesting, and the mood and tone begin to emerge as the thread that ties the pieces together.

You'll add one more piece of B-roll, only this time it will be for a practical reason. Although when editing music videos you often can bend the usually inflexible rules of continuity and storytelling, one thing you can't easily ignore are sync errors.

Despite the fact that the timecode guarantees that the shots should all be in sync, that doesn't take into account the possibility of human error. The vocalist has to lip-sync the song again and again, and occasionally she might flub a line or maybe even just sing it in a slightly different way that doesn't look quite right.

That kind of event occurs at the beginning of the second shot where she sings the lyric "you'll come around." It's not exactly out of sync, but it also doesn't look right. Using a piece of B-roll, you can cover that up, as well as open the section with a shot to emphasize a certain mood, thereby improving the video overall.

13 From the B-Roll bin, open the **Swinging Park** B-roll.

This shot shows yet another location, but it also introduces a bit of playfulness that helps to brighten the overall tone of the video from a somewhat somber palette. In this case, this shot will help you control the tone of the piece, not just reflect it.

14 Drop the **Swinging Park** shot onto track V2, beginning right at the head of the sequence.

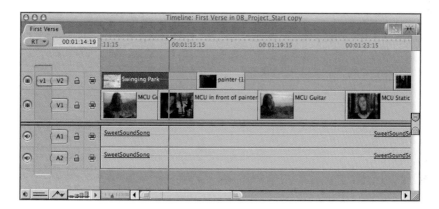

Finding the Beat

This sequence is by no means finished. You could easily add several more B-roll shots, and continue to tweak the edits points. However, one more easy way to make the video feel just a bit more professional is to adjust each edit point to ensure it lands precisely on the musical beats.

To do this, you must, of course, find the beats, and while some music software can automatically detect beats, in Final Cut Pro you must do this manually.

1   Unlock the music tracks.

2   Select the audio clip in the Timeline and press the Home key to move the playhead to the beginning of the sequence.

3   Play the sequence, and as you hear each beat, tap the M key to add a marker on that frame.

This often works best if you close your eyes while listening.

4   After you've completed the sequence, listen to it again, and watch to see if the markers look like they're positioned accurately at each musical beat. You can also see visually if they appear evenly spaced in the track.

If you want to try again, just press Control-` (the backquote key, which is usually located with the ~ character on the upper-left side of the keyboard) to delete all markers and start over. It might take you a few tries to feel confident, but once you get the rhythmic hang of it, it's pretty easy to mark the beats accurately (or at least close enough).

Once you've got the beats marked, you're ready to adjust the edits so they land directly on the beat.

5   Zoom in to the first edit point.

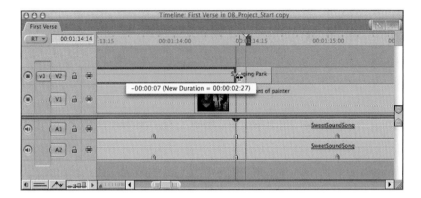

Make sure Snapping is turned on.

6   Drag the edge of the **Swinging Park** clip until it snaps to the nearest marker.

7   Press the Down Arrow to jump to the next edit.

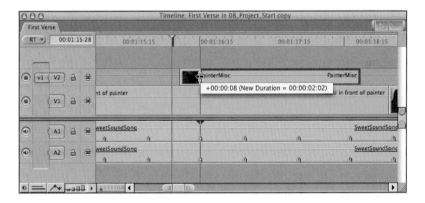

8   Drag the edge of the **Painter Misc** clip to line up with the nearest marker.

9 Press the Down Arrow again, and adjust the Out point of the
Painter Misc clip.

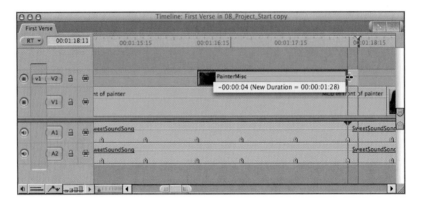

10 Press the Down Arrow again and use the Roll tool to adjust the next edit
so it snaps to the nearest marker.

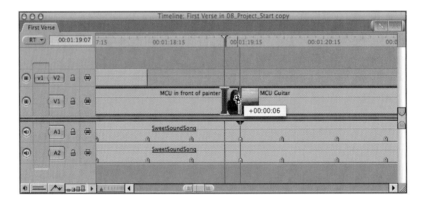

11 Press the Down Arrow again and repeat the same steps for each edit.

In some cases, you may have clips on V2 that are obscuring edit points on V1. In that case, be sure to align the clip on V2 with the marker. The edit on V1 is irrelevant.

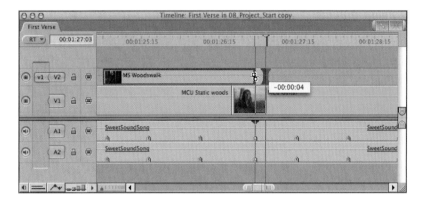

12 When you're done, go back and watch the whole show.

Pretty cool, huh? It's fun to have the video move along with the music so rigidly. You can amplify this effect by making all of the shots the exact same length (for example, exactly one measure, or half a measure).

While editing directly on the beat gives your show a satisfyingly uniform rhythm, remember it's not a requirement. Some music videos beg for more rhythmic cutting, and some work better when cut more irregularly. You might cut a song's chorus on the beat and the verses off beat. Or cut on the beat again and again, and then finally break the pattern to add extra emphasis to one shot. You might consistently cut on the upbeat instead of the downbeat.

Using Effects

Music videos are continually evolving. New ideas and techniques are being introduced all the time. Frequently, a variety of special effects find their way into music videos. Just like editing, these effects should be motivated by the style, tone, and mood of the song. You'll commonly find effects such as step-editing (removing frames), ramp speed effects, and complex color correction effects that can all be accomplished right in your Final Cut Pro sequence. However, learning how to perform those effects is beyond the scope of this book.

Lesson Review

1.   How do you sync slate timecode with Current Frame timecode?
2.   How do you temporarily set sequence timecode to match a clip's timecode?
3.   When are roll edits useful with dealing with music video footage?
4.   How can you quickly move a timecode value from one field to another?
5.   How can you lock the Viewer and sequence playheads together?
6.   Why would you do this?
7.   Describe a method for marking musical beats in Final Cut Pro.
8.   Aside from video content, what other visual devices can be used in music videos?

Answers

1.   Choose Modify > Timecode and and create an auxiliary timecode track and enter the data from the slate.
2.   In Sequence Settings, copy the timecode from the clip's first used field into the Starting Timecode field.
3.   Because the footage has identical timing on both sides of the edit, you can roll with impunity.
4.   Option-drag it.
5.   Use Gang Sync.
6.   When the timing of the clip in the Viewer matches that of the sequence and the two are ganged together, you can line up new edits automatically.

7. While playing a clip (preferably with your eyes closed to improve concentration), press M as you hear each beat to place a marker at that point in the sequence

8. Music videos make frequent use of simple effects and color correction techniques to deliberately abstract the story or draw more attention to the techniques of construction.

9

Lesson Files   Lesson Project Files > Lesson_09 > 09_Project_Start

Media   Media > Turn to Stone, Broken Fists

Time   This lesson takes approximately 60 minutes to complete.

Goals   Create multiclips from multiple camera footage

                Control the view of multiclips in the Viewer

                Edit multiclips on the fly

                Control audio and video of multiclips separately

                Rearrange, add, and delete angles from a multiclip

                Adjust sync of angles within a multiclip

                Apply filters to multiclip angles and move them to another angle

Lesson 9
Multicamera Editing

Although traditional filmmaking is done with a single camera, some types of productions use more than one camera operating at the same time. Most often this is done when documenting a live event, such as a sports match or a musical or theatrical performance. Shooting with multiple cameras is essential in these instances because otherwise there would be no way to edit the footage without automatically jump-cutting. Multiple cameras are also frequently used for complicated stunts or for action that is difficult to stage or repeat, such as improvisational performances.

Of course, sacrifices must be made when shooting with more than one camera. Framing options are severely limited if you are going to avoid showing other cameras in the shots, and lighting must be unnaturally even to ensure that all angles get an acceptable image. This explains the very formulaic and artificial look employed by many television sitcoms and soap operas in which three cameras are operated simultaneously and the show is edited on the fly using a broadcast switcher.

Editing Multicamera Footage

Although there are some limitations for the production team, editing multi-camera source is especially easy. Remember the special tools you employed in the music video lesson because you knew that the matching timecode guaranteed that the lips would stay in sync regardless of where you made your edits? When multiple cameras are capturing the same exact action at the same exact time, you get those same advantages. Not only will the lips be in sync, but any action in the scene happens simultaneously in all the shots. In many ways, multicamera setups are an editor's dream, except that using limited camera angles often means you may not have the exact close-up or insert that would most clearly tell the story.

Because multicamera content is such a special situation, Final Cut Pro 5 has a special feature designed to take advantage of multicam footage and simplify editing.

Using the Multiclip

Final Cut Pro 5 can group multiple clips together into a *multiclip*. A multiclip can hold up to 128 shots in a single clip; when the shots are used in a sequence, you can toggle between each of the shots, called *angles*, that are currently visible.

Although you can create and use multiclips in a variety of ways, this chapter will focus on one recommended workflow that takes advantage of special features in Final Cut Pro and also serves the creative needs of multicam editing. Although this lesson won't focus on the details of when and why specific edits are made, the same creative rules and techniques described in earlier chapters should apply (such as the idea of each cut providing new information, or cutting on moving objects within the frame).

Creating a Multiclip

While you can collect any group of clips into a multiclip, the multiclip is primarily designed for clips that are synchronous, especially clips that were photographed in a multiple-camera situation.

However, though the clips may all contain the same content, you must synchronize them manually in Final Cut Pro. This means that you need some information to link the clips together, such as matching timecode, or a slate clap, or even a flashbulb going off that is visible in all the angles.

1 Open **09_Project_Start**.

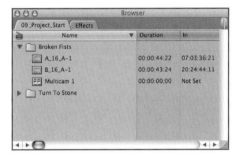

This project contains two sets of clips, each of which was created in a multiple-camera environment.

2 In the Browser, double-click **A_16_A-1** in the Broken Fists bin.

3 In the Viewer, find the frame where the slate closes (07:03:36:21) and set an In point there.

TIP When looking for the frame where a slate closes, you should always step through the frames one at a time, stepping backward and forward until you're sure you have found the first frame where the clap stick has closed.

4 Double-click **B_16_A-1** to open it in the Viewer.

5 Find the frame where the slate closes in this clip (20:24:44:11) and set an In point there.

6 Select both clips in the Browser and choose Modify > Make Multiclip.

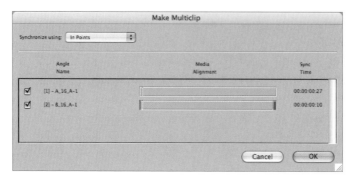

The Make Multiclip window appears. You can see which sections of the clips overlap based on the sync point.

7   Verify that the "Synchronize using" pop-up menu is set to In Points and click OK.

A new clip appears in the Browser named **A_16_A-1 [1]-Multiclip**.

8   Double-click the multiclip to open it in the Viewer.

9   Play the clip.

Both angles play simultaneously.

10 While the clip is playing, click each of the two angles in the Viewer.

The active angle has a blue border around it. Also, notice that the multiclip name changes in the Browser to reflect the currently selected angle.

Editing With a Multiclip

Linking the clips together gets you prepared, but editing the multiclip in a sequence is where the real fun starts.

1   Click Angle 1.

2   Set an In point just before the woman stands up, at approximately 07:03:54:00.

3   Set an Out point after the action ends, at around 07:04:20:10.

4   Double-click the **Multicam 1** sequence to open it in the Canvas and Timeline.

5   Option-drag the clip from the Viewer into the Canvas as an Overwrite edit.

> **NOTE** ▸ Because clicking the Viewer for a multiclip changes the current angle, you can't simply drag a multiclip to edit it into a sequence the way you can with an ordinary clip. Pressing the Option key tells the program that you want to drag the clip as a whole, allowing you to edit it into the Canvas or Timeline.

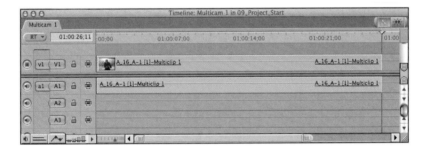

Once the multiclip is edited into the sequence, it appears like any other clip, but don't be fooled. It has special features that allow you to switch angles—even while it's playing back. However, in order for those features to work correctly, you must first set two controls.

6   Set the Playhead Sync mode to Open.

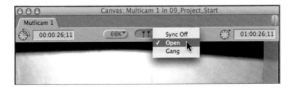

This instructs the Viewer to display the clip currently under the playhead. If this setting is set to another option, you can still change angles in the Viewer, but the video won't play there.

7 In the Timeline, click the RT menu and verify that Multiclip Playback is selected.

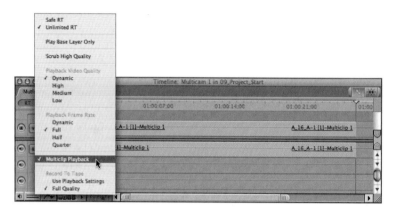

8 Play the sequence and, while it plays, click back and forth between the angles in the Viewer.

Each time you click, you are creating a virtual edit point, indicated temporarily with a blue marker in the Timeline.

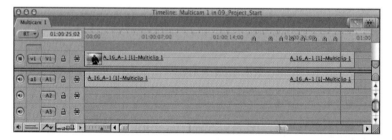

Once you stop playback, the blue markers automatically transform into edit points.

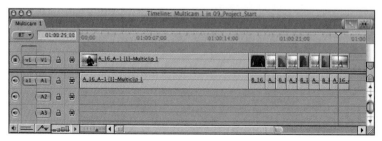

You can continue to improve your sequence by modifying these edits. If you roll any edit point, both clips will remain in sync; but rippling, slipping, or sliding edits or clips will cause the affected clips to be moved out of sync.

NOTE ▶ Be sure that the Canvas or Timeline window is active. If the Viewer window is active, the multiclip edits will not work.

You can continue to improve your sequence by modifying these edits, adding transitions or switching which angle is displayed for any particular clip. (See "Working with Many Angles" in this lesson.)

Collapsing a Multiclip

Once your angles have been selected, you may want to prevent further angle changes by converting the sequence into a simple list of edits. This is called *collapsing* the multiclip. Collapsing causes the original source clips to replace the multiclips in the sequence. This is important if you are generating an Edit Decision List (EDL) or other exported list where the presence of a multiclip might hide the correct timecode values required for recapture. Fortunately, collapsing multiclips isn't permanent.

1   Press Command-A to select all the clips in the sequence.

2   Choose Modify > Collapse Multiclip(s).

The angles are converted into ordinary clips based on the master clips to which they refer.

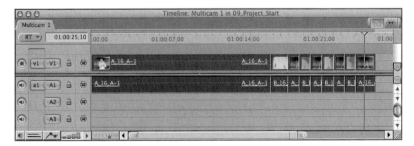

3   To switch a clip back to the multiclip in order to change its angle, select it and choose Modify > Uncollapse Multiclip(s).

Working with Many Angles

The previous example was very simple, involving only two angles; but Final Cut Pro can accommodate many angles in a single multiclip and things quickly can get more complex.

1   Open the Turn To Stone bin and select the nine clips.

2   Control-click any of the selected clips and from the pop-up menu choose Make Multiclip.

The Make Multiclip window appears.

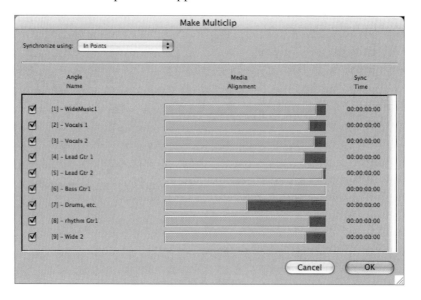

NOTE ▶ You can also Control-click the bin, itself, and choose Make Multiclip to select all of the clips in the bin.

In this case, rather than syncing the clips based on an In point set on a slate clap, all these clips share identical timecode.

3 In the "Synchronize using" pop-up menu, choose Timecode.

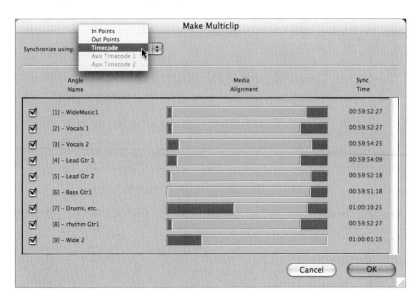

The Make Multiclip window displays the way the various clips
overlap. Some of the clips are significantly shorter than the others.
Selecting one of these angles in an area where there is no media will
just show black.

4 Click OK.

The new multiclip is created in the Turn To Stone bin.

Multiclip names always start with the name of the angle currently
selected, but you can modify the rest of the name, just like changing
any other clip name.

5   Select the multiclip in the Browser, then click it to edit the item name.

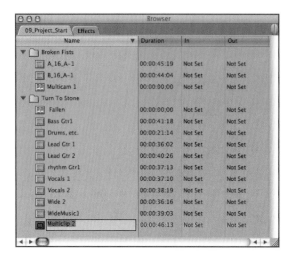

When the clip name appears, only the editable part is visible.

6   Type *Fallen Multi* and press Return.

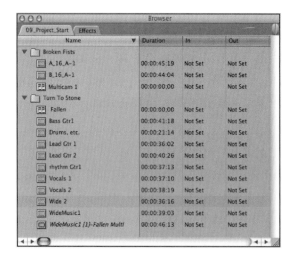

The new name still includes the current angle, but now ends with your customized name.

7 Double-click the multiclip.

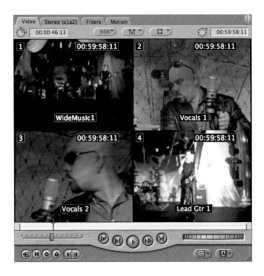

The Viewer displays the **Fallen** multiclip.

8 Shuttle through the clip until you can see video in all four angles.

9 Click the view settings button in the Viewer and choose Multiclip 9-Up.

While this looks impressive, it's a lot of information for you to monitor, and a lot of data for your computer to display at one time. Depending on how powerful your Macintosh is, playback performance may be so reduced that it becomes impossible to edit during playback.

In most cases, working in 4-Up is more manageable, but which of the four clips will you monitor? This choice is controlled by the order of the angles, and you can modify that in a number of ways, as you'll see in the next section.

Setting Angle Order

The order of the clips initially is set based on the value in the Angle field for each clip. The Angle field can be entered when logging clips, or at any time in the Browser or Clip Properties windows.

1   Double-click the Turn To Stone bin.

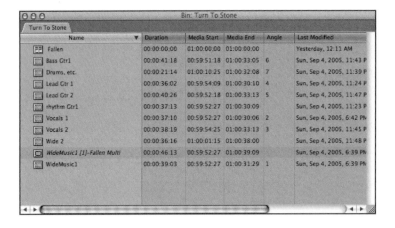

The Angle field is visible to the right of the Media End field.

Final Cut Pro works hard to determine how to arrange clips that don't have a value in that field. If the clip name is identified with an A followed by a number (such as A2 or A11) then that number will be used. If not, the first

number that appears in the clip name will be identified as the angle number. (For example, **CUGuitar_7_01** would be identified as Angle 7.) If no
number is identified, the reel name and, finally, the media file name are
consulted.

If two clips have the same angle number and are included in the same
multiclip, they appear in the order they were sorted in the Browser window at the time the multiclip was made, pushing other angle numbers
down the list (so if there were two Angle 5 clips, Angles 6 and 7 would
become Angles 7 and 8).

2   Close the Turn To Stone bin.

3   In the Viewer window, Command-drag one of the angles to rearrange it in
the 9-Up display.

The other clips move to make room for the new clip.

4   Arrange the clips so that the first four clips are: **Bass Gtr1**, **Lead Gtr 1**, **Vocals 1**, and **WideMusic1**.

5   Choose View > Multiclip Layout > Multiclip 4-Up.

Now, the first four clips are visible, and you can play the sequence and switch among them on the fly.

6   Position your mouse in the lower-right corner of the Viewer window.

A small, boxed arrow appears.

7   Click the arrow to move Angles 5 and 6 into the 4-Up display.

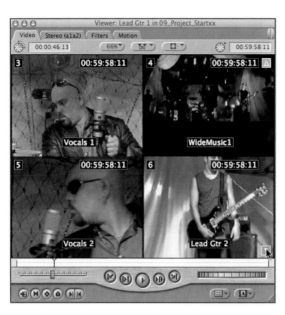

Each time you click that arrow, another row of angles is revealed. You can scroll up through the rows by clicking a similar arrow in the upper-right corner of the display.

Deleting and Adding Angles

You can change the number of angles in a multiclip after it has been created by dragging and dropping into or out of the multiclip view.

1   Scroll the view so that Angles 1 through 4 are visible.

2   Click the **Bass Gtr1** angle to make it active.

3   Command-click the **Vocals 1** angle and drag it out of the Viewer window.

The angle is removed from the multiclip.

NOTE ▶ You cannot delete the active angle.

4   In the Turn To Stone bin, select the **Vocals 1** clip and drag it into the Viewer, then pause until the menu appears.

5   Choose Insert New Angle and release the mouse button.

The angle is added back into the multiclip.

Alternatively, you could have chosen to overwrite one of the existing angles, or added a new angle affiliate, which would add the angle not only to the multi-clip currently in the Viewer but also to any other affiliates to that multiclip. You would do this, for example, if you were adding an angle to a multiclip that was already used in a sequence and that had been divided into multiple edits. Technically, each of those edits is an affiliate to the master multiclip. Choosing Insert New Angle Affiliates adds a new angle to each instance of the multiclip in the sequence.

Offsetting Sync

In the event that one of the angles in your multiclip is out of sync with the remainder of the angles, you can correct it directly in the Viewer window, as long as you have some way of determining how many frames out of sync it is.

This sort of error can occur if the timecode or In points that you used to sync the multiple angles were incorrect at the time you created the multiclip. In this example, the timecode value was set incorrectly on the source clip.

1   Navigate the Viewer to frame 00:59:54:20.

2   Find the **Lead Gtr 1** angle.

Notice that the timecode visible on the DAT player in the video reads 00:59:54:24. Somehow the timecode for this clip was marked four frames too early, making the clip out of sync with the remainder of the angles (not to mention with the accompanying audio).

3   Press Control-Shift and drag your mouse over that angle to the left until the timecode display in the video reads 00:59:54:20.

That angle has now been properly synced with the rest of the multiclip.

Editing the Multiclip

Remember that in order to do any actual editing of a multiclip, you must first put it in a sequence.

1   In the Turn To Stone bin, double-click the **Fallen** sequence.

The sequence opens in the Canvas and Timeline. Make sure the Playhead Sync menu is set to Video + Audio.

2   In the Viewer, click **Bass Gtr1** to make that angle active.

3   Play the clip until the camera pulls out and settles on the opening wide shot for that angle. Set an In point there (at approximately 00:59:54:15).

4   Press the Down Arrow key to advance the playhead to the end of the clip.

5   Set an Out point there.

Since this footage is only used to illustrate the multiclip technique, just the first 30 seconds or so of the song has been included.

6   Option-drag the clip into the Canvas and perform an Overwrite edit.

Preset Multiclip Button Bars

Final Cut Pro provides a preset button bar configuration to assist with multi-clip editing. This provides shortcuts to the most common multiclip controls such as turning on multiclip display, switching the Viewer to 4-Up view, and even switching and cutting between different angles.

You can further customize the button bars to suit your personal multiclip editing style, for example, if you often use the 9-Up display or frequently switch audio and video angles together.

1   Choose Tools > Button Bars > Multiclip.

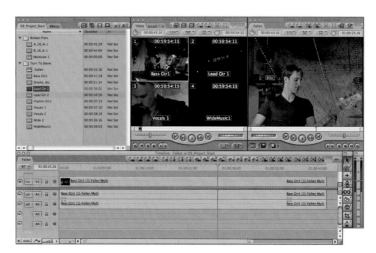

Dozens of buttons are added to the Viewer, Canvas, and Timeline windows. These buttons can be used to configure Final Cut Pro for multiclip editing, and even to perform the edits themselves.

2   Set the Playhead Sync mode to Open.

3   Switch focus to the Timeline or Canvas and play the sequence.

4   Instead of using the Viewer to cut between angles, click the Green buttons in the Timeline button bar to cut between Angles 1 through 4. For this example, just make a few edits.

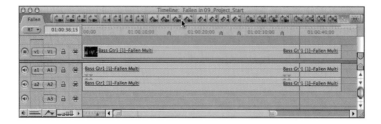

The temporary blue markers appear whenever you click one of the angle buttons and, once playback is stopped, the markers are converted to edits.

As you can see, there are buttons to perform a variety of other actions as well, such as cutting the audio separately from the video (see "Separating Audio and Video" in this lesson) and switching between angles with effects on them (see "Applying Effects to Multiclips").

Switching Angles

Once your multiclip has been divided into the separate clips, you may want to change your mind and choose a different angle for a segment. This is called *switching* angles.

1 Control-click the second clip in the Timeline.

2 Choose Active Angle > Vocals 1.

That segment is changed to display the **Vocal 1** angle. Or, you can use the buttons in the button bar to switch angles.

3 Deselect all clips, then position the playhead over the third clip in the Timeline.

If a clip is selected, the buttons will Switch the angle of that clip. If nothing is selected, they will apply to the clip under the playhead.

4 Click the Switch Video to Angle 2 button in the Timeline button bar.

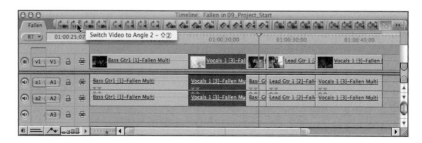

Alternatively, you can step through the different angles in order by clicking the previous and next angle buttons in the Canvas or Viewer button bars.

Using the Keyboard

As usual in Final Cut Pro, you can work with multiclips most efficiently when you program keyboard shortcuts that help you quickly perform tasks at the touch of a key (or two).

Final Cut Pro 5 has a preset keyboard layout specially designed for multiclip editing. This layout transforms the number keys so you can quickly switch and cut between angles.

You can choose this special keyboard layout by choosing Tools > Keyboard Layout > Multi-Camera Editing. Although no obvious changes occur, your keyboard has been transformed into a multiclip editing machine:

▶ Pressing the 1 through 0 keys automatically switches the current video angle to the angle of the number you press (0 serves as angle 10).

▶ Pressing Option with a number key switches the audio to the angle number selected.

▶ Pressing Command with a number key *cuts* the multiclip, switching the new angle to the number chosen. This is equivalent to clicking the different images in the Viewer.

▶ Pressing Shift with a number key switches the video along with any applied effects to the new angle number.

One advantage to using keyboard shortcuts is that you can easily press different keys to perform quick cuts or switches while the video is playing back. Another advantage is that you can cut or switch among up to ten angles at once. You can even switch among more than ten angles if you program additional keys to additional angles.

If you forget what shortcuts are in the Multi-Camera Editing keyboard layout, the tooltips on the button bar will give you a quick reminder.

Separating Audio and Video

So far in this lesson, you've been cutting or switching multiclip angles with audio and video linked, or just changing the video (when using the buttons or keyboard shortcuts). So you've probably realized that you can switch the audio and video angles separately.

This is exactly what you would want to do with the current footage, in which the prerecorded version of the band's song is attached to only one of the clips. All the other video tracks include scratch audio, which is great for ensuring that all the clips are in sync but not ideal for a finished video.

When you edit a multiclip by clicking images in the Viewer, the channels that are affected are controlled by the setting in the Playhead Sync menu.

1   In the Viewer, click the Playhead Sync menu button and choose Audio > All.

This setting can also be found in the View menu in the Multiclip Active
Tracks submenu.

2   Click the WideMusic1 angle in the Viewer.

A green border indicates which angle is providing the audio while a blue border indicates the selected video angle.

3   Make sure that the Sync mode is set to Open and that Multiclip Playback is selected.

4   Make the Timeline or Canvas window active and play the sequence.

5   As it plays, click between the different angles in the Viewer.

This time, only the green box moves and, correspondingly, the edits you make in the sequence only affect the audio tracks.

Switching Audio and Video Separately

In addition to cutting audio tracks independently from the video, you can switch audio and video separately for clips that are already edited in the sequence.

1   In the Timeline, position the playhead over the first clip in the sequence.

2   Click the Switch Audio to Angle 4 button or press Option-4.

The Timeline displays the different names for the audio and video tracks of that clip.

3   Control-Option-click the audio tracks for the second clip. Choose Active Angle > WideMusic1.

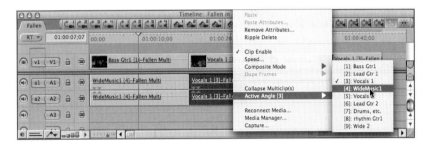

The clip's audio is now set to WideMusic1, although the video is still set to Vocals 1.

4   Choose View > Multiclip Active Tracks > Video and Audio.

This resets the editing mode back to all tracks in preparation for the next exercise.

Applying Effects to Multiclips

You can apply filters, speed changes, and other effects to multiclips, just like ordinary clips, but you must determine whether you want the effect applied to an individual angle or to the whole multiclip, regardless of which angle is currently active.

Once a filter or effect has been applied, you must account for that effect when switching angles on the multiclip.

1   In the Effects tab, open the Video Filters bin and then open the Image Control bin.

2   Drag the Desaturate filter to the last clip in the Timeline. Pause before releasing the mouse.

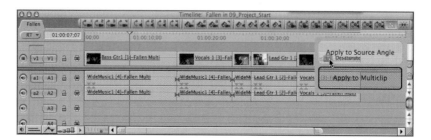

A menu appears, providing two choices: Apply to Source Angle or Apply to Multiclip.

3   Choose Apply to Source Angle.

4   Move the playhead so you can see the effect of the filter in the Canvas.

When a filter is applied to an individual angle, only that angle is affected and changing to a different angle will leave that filter behind, unless you choose the Switch Video with Effects command. In that case, the filter is carried along and applied to the new angle.

5   Click the Switch Video with Effects to Angle 4 button in the Timeline button bar or press Shift-4.

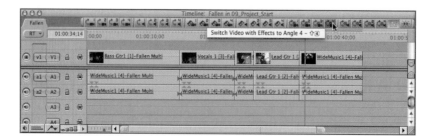

The angle is switched and the filter is applied to the new angle. Other effects, such as speed and motion effects, can also be moved from angle to angle in the same manner.

Lesson Review

1. What is a multiclip?

2. How do you create a multiclip?

3. How do you drag and drop a multiclip from the Viewer into the Timeline or Canvas?

4. What are two settings you must activate before live multiclip editing is possible?

5. What does it mean to collapse a multiclip?

6. How do you rearrange multiclip angles in the Viewer?

7. How do you control which tracks are affected by Multiclip edits?

8. Can filters and effects be applied to multiclips?

Answers

1. A multiclip is a special type of clip that contains between 2 and 128 *angles*, any one of which can be used at one time.

2. Select the clips in the Browser and choose Modify > Make Multiclip.

3. You must hold the Option key in order to drag and drop a multiclip in the Viewer.

4. Turn on the Multiclip Editing setting in the RT menu and set the Playhead Sync mode to Open.

5. Converting a multiclip back into individual clips after it has been edited in a sequence.

6.   Press Command while dragging the angles to rearrange them in the Viewer. Command-dragging an angle out of the Viewer deletes it from the multiclip.

7.   Choose the video and/or the specific audio tracks listed in the Playhead Sync menu.

8.   Filters and effects can either be applied to the active angle or to the whole multiclip. In the latter case, the effect will remain applied even if the angle is changed.

Working with Audio

10

Lesson **10**

Sound Editing

If seeing is believing, then perhaps hearing is feeling. While the visual component of your show contains the information and hard details of the story, it is the subtle combination of voices, sound effects, and music that are stitched together to create a tapestry of emotion and tone.

A film's soundtrack is often the indicator of its level of professionalism and quality. Amateur filmmakers finish cutting their picture and call it done. For professionals, *locking* picture is only the beginning of a new phase of postproduction.

On professional shows, every line of dialogue is organized, balanced, equalized, and filtered; ambiances are constructed for each scene, usually composed of many different sources; sound effects are inserted for every justifiable onscreen activity that might make a sound; and, finally, music is mixed to complement and supplement the other components.

Waiting Until the Picture Is Locked

While you typically do a fair amount of sound editing during the picture editing process, it's wise to save the bulk of the sound editing for the last step. For example, take a simple case in which a shot has audio that fades in at the beginning and fades out at the end.

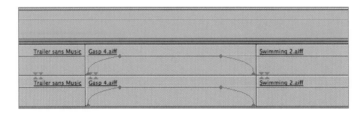

If later in the editing process you wind up tweaking that edit and shortening the clip by five frames, you will have to completely rebuild your fade out.

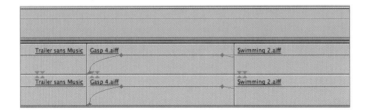

If it only happens occasionally, this isn't a big deal, but it can amount to a lot of duplicated effort over the course of an entire show. This is especially true, because by the time your show is complete, every single audio clip in your sequence should have a tiny fade at the beginning and end.

Furthermore, during the sound editing process you will add hundreds of tiny sound effects files. Keeping track of these and making sure they remain in sync with every edit is a headache you can easily avoid by waiting until picture is locked before beginning your sound editing.

Last, as you get serious about your sound, you will begin to add a large number of audio tracks to your project. Professional sound editors will put each character's dialogue on a separate track, in addition to allocating a few tracks for ambiances, a few more for specific sound effects, and a few more for music. These quickly add up and editing a scene while carrying around dozens or even scores of audio tracks really slows you down.

Traditionally, sound editing is done by a different person and on a different system than picture editing. This has many inherent benefits. Sound editing is a specialized art and, in many ways, a totally different type of skill. This may sound surprising. Picture editors are constantly making changes to the sound tracks, so aren't they inherently good sound editors? While picture editing is about taking things away—"eliminating the bad bits," as famed film and sound editor Walter Murch calls it—sound editing is all about adding things back in.

Sound editors layer dozens of discrete sounds to create a single effect, and they do this for every moment of every scene. Effectively matching sounds to pictures is not always an obvious process. It takes a special talent to look at a shot of a person getting stabbed and think of the sound of slicing watermelons, or to match images of tornadoes with slowed-down lion roars. Sound editors are constantly recording things, adding to their libraries. In fact, in the sound world, editors boast about the size of their effects collections, or about the most bizarre sounds they've recorded. Picture editors are storytellers. Sound editors are designers.

Sound editing is usually broken into six stages. First, the dialogue is cleaned up and optimized; then ambiances are made for each scene; sound effects are then added; sound design elements are built and added; music is added; and finally, all of the elements are pulled together in a final mix.

Editing Dialogue

Almost all movies contain human voices. The voice communicates information, emotion, and can elicit an almost unlimited variety of responses in the listener. Our ears are specially tuned to hear and understand human speech and we are very susceptible to miniscule changes in pacing, timbre, or volume. This incredible sensitivity translates into a special challenge for editors seeking to keep viewers caught up in the story and not be distracted by tiny audio mistakes created by poor sound recording or editing.

Fortunately, there are many tools designed to improve the quality of recorded voices. Final Cut Pro includes one audio filter designed to remove unwanted pops that can occur when a microphone is placed too close to the speaker's mouth (Vocal DePopper), and another to remove excessive sibilance (the Sssss-sound) that can occur during recording (Vocal DeEsser).

Soundtrack Pro features a variety of other dialogue-oriented tools, including a variety of reverbs to help match a voice to an environment and a filter that can speed up or slow down the delivery of a line without generating a give-away pitch change. Countless third-party audio tools are available that can improve the quality of recorded voices depending on the problem you are facing.

Even so, don't rely on your ability to "fix it in post." If the microphone was too far away from the subject, or the background noise level was too high during recording, there is often nothing you can do to salvage the audio. In those cases (and they happen all the time, even on professional shows), the audio has to be re-recorded in a studio.

Like other lessons in this book, this one uses a dramatic scene as an example, but the concepts and techniques are just as applicable to nonfiction works. Documentaries need just as much sound design and finessing as narrative films.

1   Open **10_Project_Start**.

A sequence called **Showdown Sequence** is already open that contains a completed edit of the Friends of the Family project.

2   Play through the sequence.

When you finished Lesson 3, you left this sequence in need of some serious sound work. Now you'll have the chance to finish that job.

Organizing Your Tracks

Dialogue editors make a point of isolating each character's voice onto its own track. This is because traditional sound mixing equipment can give each track its own equalization and filters. So, all of a character's lines can have the same sound settings and, if you want to modify those settings, you only need to make adjustments once. Final Cut Pro doesn't have this ability, so there isn't as much advantage to separating characters' lines onto discrete tracks, but it does help for organizational purposes.

Fortunately, in this project, you previously chopped up most of the dialogue lines into their own clips, so separating them will be easy. Since Pedro has more lines than Andy, you can leave Pedro's lines on tracks 1 and 2 and put Andy's on tracks 3 and 4.

At around 28 seconds, Pedro says his first line, "So what's up?" At 29:18 Andy says, "We gonna do this?"

3   Zoom into that section of the Timeline.

4   Option-click the audio for **MCU Andy OTS Pedro_02** to select it.

5   Shift-drag the clips to tracks 3 and 4.

Pressing Shift constrains the horizontal movement so the clips will remain in sync with the picture.

6   Skip to the next lines at around 42 seconds.

The first line is Andy's so you'll move it to tracks 3 and 4.

7 Option-click the audio for **G2 MS OTS Group1_02** to select it.

8 Shift-drag the clips to tracks 3 and 4.

NOTE ▶ Be sure to release the Option key or you might accidentally copy the clip instead of moving it.

The next line is Pedro's so you can leave it alone. After that, they each have a line, but those lines are part of the same clip.

9 Press B to select the Blade tool.

10 Press Option and click to add an audio-only edit after Andy says "All right, let's go," at about 45:23.

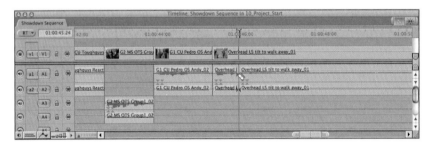

11 Option-click again to add another audio-only edit after Pedro says, "Let's go" at 46:15.

12 Press A to select the Arrow tool and Option-click the audio of Andy's line (the first part) and drag it to tracks 3 and 4.

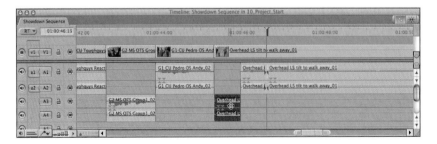

You've successfully separated Andy's lines and moved them to tracks 3 and 4; but it's hard to locate Pedro's lines because all the other audio clips are still on tracks 1 and 2.

13 Press Shift-Z to fit the whole sequence into the window and Option-drag a marquee around the audio for all the clips from the head of the sequence up until the first shot containing Pedro's line.

It's easy to find Pedro's first line, because it's the first clip before Andy's line on tracks 3 and 4.

14 Shift-drag the selected audio clips down to the space below tracks 3 and 4.

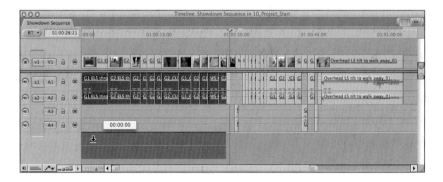

New tracks automatically appear to accommodate the clips.

15 Option-drag a marquee around the audio for all the clips between "Si, mon" at 31:21 and "Hey, man, I'm out of formula" at 42:11.

16 Shift-drag the selected audio clips down to tracks 5 and 6.

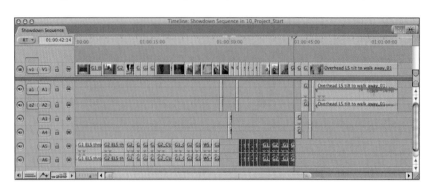

17 Option-click the audio from the end of the last clip (**Overhead LS tilt to walk away_01**).

18 Shift-drag the clip to tracks 5 and 6.

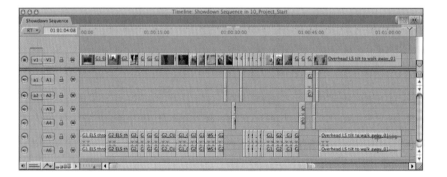

Softening the Edges

Audio clips with abrupt beginnings or endings are undesirable. At worst, they can cause pops or distortions. At best, they create subtle shifts in the tone of the soundtrack that are potentially distracting and unwanted.

Every single piece of audio should be faded in and faded out, even if the fades are short in duration. As part of your sound-editing pass, you should apply fades to your audio clips.

1   Zoom all the way in on the first line of dialogue in clip **G1 MS OTS
    Group2_04**—Pedro's "So what's up?"—at around 28 seconds.

2   Press Option-W to turn on clip overlays.

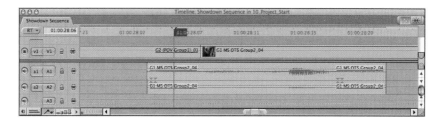

3   Option-click the level envelope just as the "s" from "So" becomes audible
    at around 28:06.

4   Option-click to add another keyframe near the head of the clip and drag it
    down to –inf dB to create a fade-in.

5   Press Down Arrow twice to move your playhead to the end of the clip.

6   Use the same technique of adding keyframes to create a fade-out.

7 Press Down Arrow again to move to the beginning of the next audio clip (**MCU Andy OTS Pedro_02** on tracks A3 and A4).

8 Repeat the process to create a fade-in and fade-out on this clip.

9 Walk through all of the remaining clips on tracks A1 through A4 and apply similar fade effects to the head and tail of each clip.

Pay special attention not to cut off any words. For the last two clips be especially sure to set the last keyframe at the very right edge of the clip.

TIP Sometimes when adding or adjusting keyframes near the edges of clips your cursor may accidentally select the edge of the clip instead of the keyframe. This can be overcome by zooming in further or by using the Pen tool (P).

Filtering Dialogue

No matter how well the dialogue was recorded, a little bit of equalization, compression, or noise reduction can do wonders to make it sound punchier and clearer. This is sometimes called *sweetening*.

1 Navigate to Pedro's first line in **G1 MS OTS Group2_04** at 28 seconds and park the playhead anywhere within the clip.

2 Turn off Auto Select for track V1 and press X to set the audio clip.

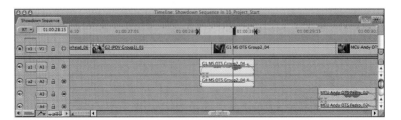

3   Choose View > Loop Playback or press Control-L.

Now, when you play from In to Out, the sequence will loop continuously around this clip. This is perfect for adjusting audio filters.

4   Choose Effects > Audio Filters > Final Cut Pro > Parametric Equalizer.

5   Double-click the audio clip to open it into the Viewer, then click the Filters tab to access the controls for the Equalizer filter.

Equalizers are filters that allow you change the level of specific *bands* (frequencies or frequency ranges). For example, you can turn up the volume on the high-pitched sounds without changing the level of the rest of the audio track. The result doesn't sound louder, but it changes the overall tone of the clip.

In general, you should use equalizing filters to attenuate (lower) the bands you want to eliminate rather than *boost* (raise) the parts you want to accentuate. Raising levels, even of specific bands, can cause distortion or clipping.

6   Press Shift-\ (backslash) to begin the looping In to Out playback.

Listen to the clip and try to identify how it might be improved. As is typical of dialogue recording, the mids are pretty strong, but there is very little strength in the low frequencies, and not much crispness to the highs. The right way to address this is to lower the mids so that the highs and lows stand out more clearly.

The parametric equalizer works by selecting a frequency, identifying "softness" using the Q slider to control how many nearby frequencies are included in the effect (the effective bandwidth), and then adjusting the gain for that frequency range.

7 While the clip continues to loop, drag the Gain slider all the way to its maximum.

This will allow you to hear which frequencies you are selecting.

8 Drag the Frequency slider down to about 100 Hz and then very slowly drag it up to about 3000 Hz and back down again.

This is the range (100 Hz–3 KHz) that contains most of the frequencies common in human speech. Male voices typically contain more of the lower frequencies, and females more of the higher frequencies, though there is wide variation among individual speakers. Also, human voices, like most sounds, simultaneously exist at many frequencies.

As you adjust the Frequency slider, you are listening for the frequency where the maximum effect is heard. This is the area where the bulk of the voice resides. In this clip, it's around 535 Hz. When the slider is set there, the voice is almost entirely unintelligible. Of course, your goal is to make the voice more intelligible, not less; so now that you've found the spot, you need to lower the Gain slider.

9 Drag the Gain slider down all the way to -20 dB.

Now you have attenuated the mid range of the voice dramatically.

10 Drag the Gain slider back toward 0 dB, listening carefully until the voice sounds both warm (meaning there is enough upper bass) and crisp (meaning there is enough treble).

In this case, a setting of about -7 should work.

You should try to limit most audio adjustments to a maximum of 5–10 dB in either direction. Adjustments beyond that range usually distort the sound in an entirely unnatural way.

Last, you can adjust the Q slider to affect how wide a range of frequencies is affected by the filter.

11 Drag the Q slider all the way to 20.

This limits the effect of the Gain slider to a very narrow range of frequencies around 535 Hz.

12 Slowly drag the Q slider to the left to about 5.

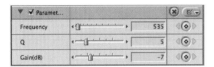

The lower the number, the wider is the bandwidth of frequencies. A higher number will create a more focused, dramatic effect. A lower number will create softer, more subtle effects because it affects a wider range of bands, tapering off the effect as it moves away from the target frequency.

13 Turn the Gain slider all the way up or down, and then adjust the Q again if you want to hear a more dramatic example of the effect of the Q slider.

Be sure to return the Gain to -5 to -10 and the Q to 5 once you've finished experimenting.

14 Deselect the checkbox next to the filter name to hear what your clip sounds like without the filter.

This will automatically stop playback.

15 Press Shift-\ to begin the loop again.

16 Select the checkbox again to turn the filter back on and play from In to Out.

You may want to add additional parametric EQ filters to isolate and attenuate other frequencies. The overall effect of the EQ process should be subtle, but attenuating the mids results in an apparent boosting of the lows and highs, which makes the clip appear both warmer and brighter without getting muddy.

There are other common EQ filters such as High- or Low-Pass filters that can further enhance your audio. A Low-Pass filter eliminates bands above a designated frequency, letting the lows "pass" through the filter. A High-Pass filter "passes" frequencies higher than a designated frequency. Frequently, there are unwanted rumblings in the low frequencies and unwanted hissing in the highs that can be eliminated with these filters.

Compressing Dialogue Dynamics

Next, you will apply a Compression filter. Human speech typically has a fairly wide *dynamic range*, meaning there is a big difference between the very quiet sounds and very loud sounds. The problem is that if you raise the overall level so the quiet parts can be heard, the loud parts can be too loud, which is undesirable as it may lead to distortion or *clipping* (chopping off the top part of the waveform).

Compressors reduce the dynamic range of a clip by lowering the loud parts (anything above a certain *threshold* dB). This allows you to increase the overall audio level. Typically, compressors permit you to optionally "preserve the volume," maintaining the impact of the loud parts while keeping the quiet parts well within an audible range.

Compressing the dynamic range results in an audio track that seems to have more "presence." Because the relative volume is more uniform, it seems to stand out more from other elements in the audio mix. Of course, you don't want to compress too much, or the voice may seem unnaturally disconnected from the rest of the sound environment. Typically, sound editors apply just a tiny bit of compression to dramatic dialogue, and apply compression more generously to interviews and narrations.

1   Choose Effects > Audio Filters > Final Cut Pro > Compressor/Limiter.

This filter is applied to the clip, after the Parametric EQ.

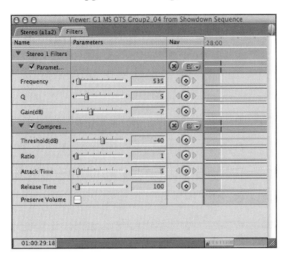

The Threshold slider sets the decibel level above which attenuation is applied, and the ratio determines how much attenuation is applied. At a ratio of 1, the filter has no effect.

2 Press Shift-\ to begin the looping playback.

3 Increase Ratio to 2 and select Preserve Volume.

4 Raise Threshold all the way to 0.

With the threshold that high, the filter has no effect.

5 Slowly lower Threshold until the apparent volume seems to increase, but the *noise floor* doesn't seem to get any louder (around -12).

6 Press the spacebar to stop the looped playback.

The noise floor is the background noise audible beneath the sound level of the words. You want this to remain as quiet as possible. If you compress the clip so much that this noise gets louder, you are probably causing more harm than good.

Once you have the filters the way you want them, you can apply them to the rest of Pedro's lines.

7   Select **G1 MS OTS Group2_04** in the Timeline and press Command-C to copy the clip.

8   Select the rest of the clips on tracks A1 and A2 and press Option-V.

    The Paste Attributes dialog opens.

9   Select the Filters checkbox under Audio Attributes and click OK.

    Both filters are applied to all of Pedro's lines.

10   Press Option-X to clear the In and Out points.

11   You should repeat this entire process for Andy's dialogue.

    Because their voices are different, Andy will need his own unique EQ and compression settings. While the same settings will likely work for each instance of a character's dialogue within a scene, you will probably need to create different settings for each scene, even for the same characters.

Creating Perspective

Although dialogue levels should be consistent across your entire program, it's also important to vary the level of the audio depending on the relative camera position. For example, when cutting from a close-up to a wide shot, there should be a subtle but perceptible attenuation in volume to reflect the new distance between audience and subject. Similarly, when cutting from a facial close-up of an actor to a shot over his shoulder, the volume of that actor's voice should be reduced slightly.

Such changes must be subtle and don't necessarily represent the volume shift that would occur in real life. For example, in a single shot of a couple walking from very far away into a close-up, the level of their dialogue should be gradually increased as they approach the camera. But you don't want the beginning of the shot to sound so quiet you can't hear what they're saying (as it would be in reality), and you don't want the end of the shot to be louder than the overall dialogue in the film. Still, without this slight perspective shift, the sound would feel very flat and disconnected from the images.

Creating Ambiances

Unless you're in outer space, every location has some inherent background noise. An office building's ambient sounds might include air conditioners, elevators, or flickering fluorescent lights. An apartment's ambiance might include creaky floors from upstairs, or water pipes in the walls. A city park's ambiance might contain birds singing, wind in the trees, and light traffic from a nearby road. Public places frequently have low-level talking noise called *walla.* These combinations of sounds define each environment and are just as important to making a scene feel "real" as being sure the camera is focused.

In film, you can use ambiance as a subtle way to communicate information about a scene. When the prodigal son returns to confront his family, the house might have a menacing low rumble recorded inside a deep freezer and, after the reconciliation, that sound may finally dissipate.

Good ambiances are a combination of appropriateness to the environment and appropriateness to the emotional tone of the scene. You probably don't want to hear birds chirping in a prison scene (even if they were doing so in the real prison location), but you can't exclude rain sounds if you can see that it's raining in the scene.

1   Listen to the current sequence from the beginning.

It may help if you close your eyes.

The first few clips seem to have no ambiance whatsoever, and then at
around 20 seconds, as **G2 (POV Group1)_01** begins, some ambiance suddenly can be heard. Then, as the next clip starts, the audio makes an
abrupt level change, and then each subsequent edit comes with a subtle
shift in ambiance level.

You may try to smooth out these edits with cross-fades or by creating
a room tone audio loop that covers the entire scene, but it is even easier
to just delete them. In a moment you'll add your own ambiance tracks,
which will provide the overall background for the scene, so why fuss trying to salvage the production sound? Obviously, you can't throw out the
sections in which the guys are speaking, or any sections in which there is
other useful sound (such as during the ending as they walk to the picnic);
but as for the rest, get rid of it!

2   Option-drag a marquee around the audio tracks from the beginning of
the sequence until the first dialogue clip begins at around 28:00.

3   Press Option (to select just audio) and Shift (to add to the current selection) and drag to select the clips between the two dialogue sections.

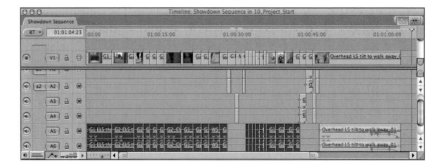

4   Press Delete.

There, wasn't that easy? Now the question is how to handle the dialogue
sections. Because natural ambiance is present between the words, and

before and after the guys speak, you can hear it kicking in and dropping out, which sounds terrible. Adding artificial ambiances will help, but that additional background noise will still be audible, and it will make the dialogue sound funny. So, you need to cover the entire section when they're speaking with a constant level of actual room tone from the location.

Using Room Tone

Most productions will record a track of *room tone* for every location used in the show. This is usually 30–60 seconds of "silence" recorded from the same microphone position used for recording the dialogue. This can be invaluable for filling holes in your track, such as the ones created in this sequence when you eliminated the duplicated lines (in Lesson 3). Even if you're adding a combination of ambiance tracks, the background noise heard while people are speaking will suddenly vanish in those holes and that subtle change may be detectable unless the changes are bridged with bits of room tone.

If you don't have a room tone track, you can usually make one by stitching together segments of "silence" from between words in the current shots.

1   Park the sequence playhead somewhere over clip **G1 MS OTS Group2_04** (between 28:00 and 29:23).

2   Press F to perform a match frame and open the master clip into the Viewer.

3   Click the Mono (a1) tab, and press Shift-Z to zoom the whole clip to fit.

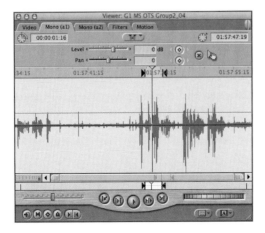

You want to find a relatively long section of "silence" that you can use to create a loop of room tone. It doesn't have to be literally silent (in fact, it probably won't be), but you want to make sure that there are no distinctive sounds, such as footsteps or a dog bark or anything else that might be identifiable in a loop.

This clip has a section between when the director calls "Action!" and the first line of dialogue that should work perfectly.

4   Set an In about 1 second after the director calls "Action!" (around 01:57:39:00) and an Out about 1 second before the first line of dialogue (at 45:00).

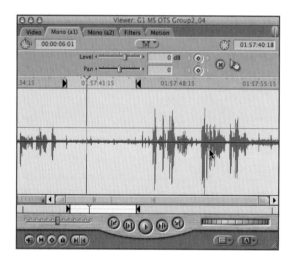

You should always leave some extra "clean" space before the In and after the Out because, in order to make a loop, you may need to create crossfades that will require additional frames and you don't want to hear any of the dialogue during them.

5   Play from In to Out.

There are some distracting noises in this section: voices and some foot-steps. It's not ideal, but the level of those distracting elements is pretty low, and it's all you've got, so you need to make it work.

6   Make the Timeline active and choose Sequence > Insert Tracks.

The Insert Tracks dialog appears.

7   Enter *4* in the Audio Tracks field and click OK.

Four new tracks are added to the Timeline.

8   Untarget track V1 and set a1 and a2 to tracks A7 and A8.

9 Set an In point in the sequence a few seconds before the first line of dialogue (around 26:00) and overwrite **G1 MS OTS Group2_04** into the sequence.

10 In the Timeline, select the audio clip you just added, and Option-drag it to the right, overlapping a little of the end of the clip.

TIP You must release the Option key before releasing the mouse button, otherwise you will perform an Insert edit instead of an Overwrite.

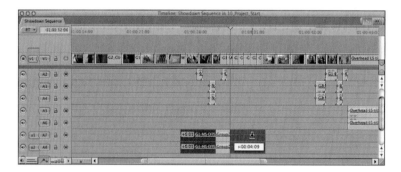

11 Repeat Step 10, dragging copies of the clip to the right a few more times until the gap left by the second section of dialogue is also covered.

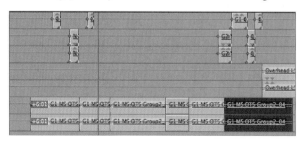

Try to overlap different amounts of the clip each time. This aids in making the room tone sound less like a loop.

12 Control-click the edit between the first two pieces of room tone and choose Add Transition 'Cross Fade (+3dB)'.

13 Repeat Step 12 for each of the edits, including the beginning of the first clip and the end of the last.

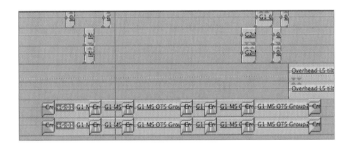

The transitions at the head and tail of the section should actually be 0 dB cross-fades, since they are fading to and from silence.

14 Control-click the first transition, and choose Cross Fade (0db).

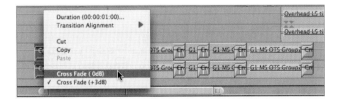

15 Repeat Step 14 for the last transition.

16 Play this entire section of the sequence.

NOTE ▶ Because of the audio filters applied to the dialogue clips, and the number of additional tracks, you may need to render your audio before it can be played.

The room tone should successfully cover the silences left by the dialogue edits.

Increasing Real-Time Audio Tracks

By default, Final Cut Pro is set to mix 8 tracks of audio in real time. If you exceed that number you'll see a red line in the render bar. Filters and audio transitions count as multiple tracks; so, with enough filters or transitions, you can get that red render bar even with fewer than 8 tracks.

However, most modern computers actually can mix quite a few more than 8 tracks in real time, depending on what kind of video is being played and the speed and number of the hard disks containing the files. (Trying to simultaneously access 8 different tracks from the same hard disk is stressful, even for fast hard disks.)

You can set the number of tracks you want Final Cut Pro to attempt to mix in real time in the General tab of the Final Cut Pro User Preferences window.

1   Choose Final Cut Pro > User Preferences.

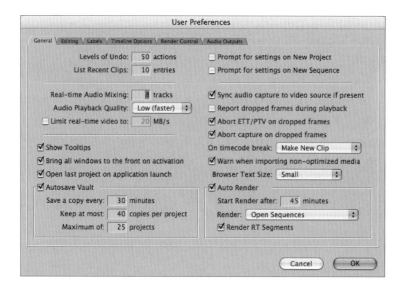

2   Set Real-time Audio Mixing to 24 tracks.

If you set this to a number of tracks higher than your computer can actually manage, Final Cut Pro will stutter or drop frames during playback. Additionally, the Audio Playback Quality setting (in the same window) affects how many tracks can be played in real time. The higher this setting is, the fewer tracks that can be processed in real time.

If during the remainder of this lesson you encounter dropped frames or other playback problems, you can reset the Real-time Audio Mixing setting to a lower number of tracks.

Incorporating Prerecorded Ambiances

Once the room tone is meshing with the dialogue tracks, it's time to add some additional environmental sounds to provide atmosphere.

1   Click the FOF Sound FX bin disclosure triangle to expand it.

2   Open **Quiet Tone.aiff** from the Ambiances bin.

This is a neutral environmental tone with a little bit of distant traffic, and no birds or other natural sounds. It's perfect for the beginning of the sequence.

Now that you're beginning to get an unwieldy number of audio tracks in your sequence, you'll want to simplify the Timeline as much as possible.

3   Click the Timeline Track Height button to set the Timeline tracks to their smallest size, and click the Clip Overlays button to turn off that display. Also, drag up the separator bar between the video and audio tracks as high as it will go.

4   Drag **Quiet Tone.aiff** into the Timeline and add it to tracks A9 and A10, beginning at the very head of the sequence.

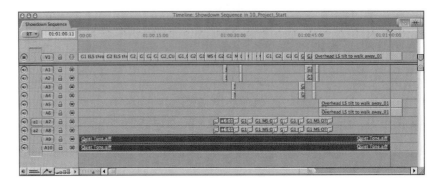

5   Press Control-L to turn off looping and play the sequence from the beginning.

This tone adds some sonic continuity that ties the entire scene together. You may want to lower its level a bit, but you can save that for the final mix stage, when you have a better idea of what other sounds will be present in the scene.

Additionally, when the tone of the scene changes—after we learn that they are not going to rumble, but are going to feed babies—it makes sense to change the ambiance to reflect this. Adding some chirping birds might just do the trick.

6   From the Ambiances bin, open **Birds FX 02.aiff**.

A section of the clip has already been marked and outfitted with a slow fade-in and short fade-out.

7   Drag **Birds FX 02.aiff** to the sequence, into the area below tracks A9 and A10. Line up the clip so its Out point lines up with the end of the last clip in the sequence.

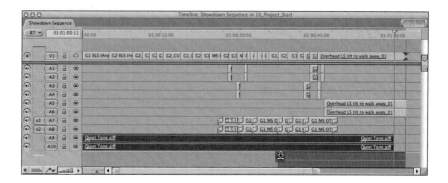

8   Play the whole sequence to hear how the birds fit.

The birds help, but they aren't enough. There needs to be more signs of life, human life, and that means walla.

9   From the Ambiances bin, open **Crowd Walla Children.aiff**.

Again, to shorten the lesson, a section of the clip already has been marked.

10   Drag **Crowd Walla Children.aiff** into the area of the sequence below tracks A11 and A12, lining up the clip so it ends with the birds clip.

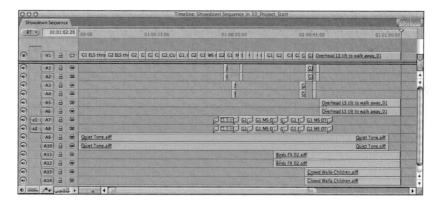

11   Press Home and play the sequence back from the beginning.

You can hear how adding additional elements continues to enhance the texture of the scene.

Adding Sound Effects

The next stage in the sound design process is to add sound effects for every element in the scene that might possibly make noise. Every time someone picks up or puts down an object, takes a step, and rustles their clothes you should add a sound effect to make the show feel full and realistic.

Many sounds are recorded during production and, depending on how well they were recorded and how well the actual sound matches what the audience *expects* something to sound like, you may or may not choose to replace those sounds with prerecorded sound effects, or with sound effects custom-recorded for the show (called *foley*).

Even if there were sound effects recorded during production, diligent sound editors extract those sound effects and put them onto a dedicated sound effects track. This is especially important for shows that might get dubbed into other languages. In that case, the sound editor will be required to turn in an *M and E mix*, which contains the music and effects tracks but doesn't include the dialogue. If the production sound effects are only located on the dialogue tracks, they will disappear when the original dialogue tracks are removed in preparation for dubbing.

If there are sound effects that overlap lines of dialogue, you can't extract them from the dialogue tracks. While this won't be a problem for the native language mix, when creating the M and E mix, you will need to replace those sounds.

Spotting for Sound Effects

The first step in adding your sound effects is to *spot* your sequence to identify all the moments when sound effects are needed. This is identical to the process you used in Lesson 6 to mark the spots that needed B-roll.

1   Play through the show, looking for spots where sound effects are required.

Right away, you probably realize that you're going to need footstep sounds. Even if you don't need them for the opening wide shots, once you cut to a close-up of the feet, the footage is begging for some footsteps sounds.

2   Add a marker somewhere over the first feet shot (around 10:00) and name it *Footsteps*.

In actuality, you will want to add footsteps for the entire opening sequence. Once you introduce the sound, it must continue as long as you can see that the actors are still walking.

3   Continue playing the sequence, looking for areas that need sound effects.

Around 29:00, Pedro claps his hands together. There is a barely audible sound on the production track of the actual clap, but a sound effect here would emphasize the moment.

4   Add a marker there and name it *handclap*.

Then you come to all the business with the bottles coming out. There are a number of sounds that would fit here: pants rustling , the witness gasping, maybe even a tiny splash when you see the close-up of the milk.

5   Add markers for each of these moments.

You might also want to add more footsteps as the gangs walk to the picnic tables, but you can skip that for now to speed the lesson.

Adding Sound Effects

Now that you know what sounds you need, you have to figure out the exact sounds you can use for each of these spots. Soundtrack Pro includes a large library of sound effects, and you can purchase sound effects libraries that contain thousands of variations on every imaginable sound. Auditioning the various sounds can be fun as you listen for the nuances that make one or another sound the perfect match. But very often, professional sound designers will still record their own sounds, either synced directly to the events in the scene (foley recording) or just recorded *wild* for later integration.

1   Click the disclosure triangles to collapse the Ambiances bin and expand the Foley and Sound FX bin.

For this lesson sound effects have been preselected for you, but in reality, you will probably have to search through hundreds of sounds to find the perfect ones for your project.

Now you're ready to begin laying in the sound effects. The footsteps are going to be the most difficult and complex, so skip that and start with the second sound effect.

2   Control-click the Timeline ruler and choose handclap.

The playhead jumps to the moment when Pedro claps his hands.

3   From the Foley and Sound FX bin in the Browser, open **Body Hit 02.aiff**.

4   Zoom into the Timeline and find the exact frame in which Pedro's hands touch (01:00:29:02).

5   Drag **Body Hit 02.aiff** into the Timeline, to the area below the bottom tracks so it begins on that frame and adds two new tracks to the sequence.

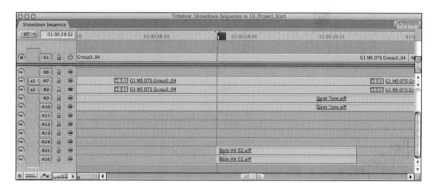

NOTE ▶ Even though there is plenty of room to put the sound effect on tracks that already exist, it is wiser to keep your ambiances on their own tracks and your sound effects on their own tracks. This makes it easier during mixing to turn off all the sound effects, or all the ambiances, at one time.

6   Press \ to play around the edit.

The sound effect lines up perfectly, but it's a little too loud.

7   Select **Body Hit 02.aiff** in the Timeline and press Command-Option-L to open the Gain Adjust dialog.

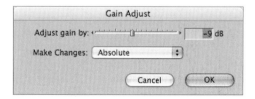

8   In the Make Changes pop-up menu, choose Absolute, and set the Gain to -9 dB. Click OK to close the dialog.

9   Play around the edit again.

Now the hand slap is present in the scene, but not overwhelming. If you wanted to make Pedro seem more menacing, you could choose to make the hand sound even louder.

Move on to the next effect, which is the clothes rustle when the guys pull the bottles out.

10   Press Shift-M to move to the next marker.

TIP ▶ To move to the previous marker, press Option-M.

This should show Andy lifting his shirt as he grabs for his bottle.

What's needed is a nonspecific sound of clothes rustling.

11 Open **Clothes 1.aiff**.

12 In the Viewer, press Shift-Z to view the entire clip.

You can see in the waveform that there are two different takes in this clip. The first one is longer and more constant, and the second is shorter with a clear peak. Even without listening, you can guess which one will be better in this case.

13 Just to be sure, play the clip.

The sound is fine, but the level is too high.

14 Lower the level to -10.

15 Set an In point before the second sound begins (around 04:15) and set an Out after it winds down (around 07:15).

16 Drag the sound effect into the Timeline, onto tracks 15 and 16, so it begins just as Andy begins reaching for his bottle (around 01:00:32:03).

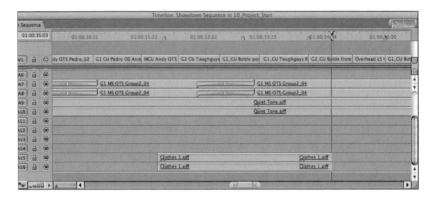

17 Play around the edit.

That works great. Now you need to add a sound for Pedro reaching into his pocket.

18 Open **Clothes 2.aiff**.

19 In the Viewer, press Shift-Z to fit the entire waveform into view and listen to the clip.

This clip has five different takes of different lengths.

20 Mark the moment when the third rustle happens (In: 04:00, Out: 5:10).

21 Lower the level to -8.

22 Find the frame in the sequence when Pedro begins to pull the bottle out of his pocket (around 33:20).

23 Drag **Clothes 2.aiff** into the Timeline and to the area below the last track, adding two new tracks to the sequence.

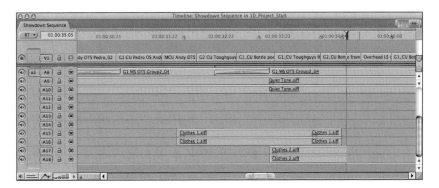

24 Play around the edit.

The rustling does a great job of bringing that moment to life, except that now, when Andy finally gets the bottle out, there is no accompanying sound.

25 In the Viewer, mark the area of **Clothes 2.aiff** when the second rustle happens (In: 2:03, Out: 3:03).

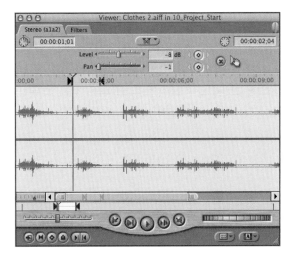

26 Find the frame in the sequence when Andy actually pulls out the bottle (around 34:22) and drag **Clothes 2.aiff** onto tracks A15 and A16.

It's okay if it covers up the end of **Clothes 1.aiff**.

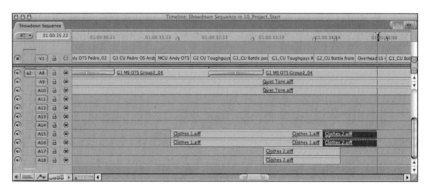

27 Play around the whole section.

It may be hard to hear just the sound effects with the other tracks playing at the same time. It would be ideal if you could temporarily *solo* the track you're working on, silencing everything else.

28 In the lower-left corner of the Timeline, click the Show Audio Controls button.

Mute and Solo buttons appear for each track. The Mute button (the speaker icon on the left) temporarily silences playback of that track, and the Solo button (the headphone icon) turns off the other tracks.

29 Click the solo button for track A15. Then click the solo button for track A16.

Now, only those two tracks will play.

30 Play around the section with the rustling.

You can hear the sound effects clearly now and judge them for timing, level, and appropriateness without the other tracks to distract you.

31 Deselect the Solo buttons for tracks 15 and 16 to turn off soloing.

There are a few more sound effects to add, but beyond this point you are beginning to venture out of ordinary sound effects editing and into *sound design*.

Designing the Sound

Sound design is a general term for the entire sound editing and mixing process; but it is also specifically used to refer to sound elements that are not naturally present in the scene but are used to enhance the scene. For example, you might add the sound of a heartbeat to a scene to convey someone under increasing stress. Often, these sounds might be construed by the audience to be in the character's head, or they might be sounds that evoke a certain emotional response. This is where sound designers contribute their creative interpretation of the scene.

Of course, you don't want to go too far. As with all editing, the goal is rarely to draw attention to the process. You might pat yourself on the back for foreshadowing a character's downfall with an ominous thunder rumble just as he shakes hands with a villain, but if the scene is taking place under sunny blue skies, it's likely to draw attention away from the scene and onto the "clever" filmmaking.

1 Open the **Sound Design** sequence.

2   If you have red areas in your render bar press Option-R to render the sequence.

3   Play the entire sequence, paying special attention to the sound.

First of all, you can hear that the footsteps have been laid into this sequence. Footsteps are among the trickiest sound elements for a number of reasons. For one thing, different shoes sound different on different surfaces, and everyone walks with a unique gait. Second, footsteps are percussive, so they are very audible in real life. Even though we don't typically notice them, when they're absent from a scene, the scene feels strangely empty. And third, because production crews use very directional mics focused primarily on people's mouths, footsteps are rarely present in the production tracks. For all these reasons, footsteps are a sound designer's nightmare.

If footsteps are hard to work with in general, this scene might be a worst-case scenario: two parties that need to sound different from each other, and each party consisting of multiple people. To add insult to injury, the close-up shots of the feet emphasize the importance of the footsteps and, at least for that section, require that they appear in near-perfect sync with the picture.

In most cases, rather than trying to match prerecorded footfall sounds to the picture, footsteps are recorded on a *foley stage*, where a *foley artist* watches the movie playback, and mimics the onscreen steps using the appropriate shoe and surface type.

This example shows that you can use prerecorded footstep sounds if you have to, taken here from Soundtrack Pro's extensive library. If you want to give yourself a bonus lesson, use the clips in the Footsteps bin and try to re-create the edit by yourself.

Footsteps aside, what else can you do to enhance the sequence? With all of the *practical* sounds placed (sounds that match specific actions seen on screen), you can now turn to more metaphorical or abstract elements.

First, think about the ambiance. While the quiet tone track is sufficient background, you can do more to convey the tone of the scene.

4   Close the Foley and Sound FX bin and expand the Sound Design
     Elements bin.

5   Open **Wind 2.aiff.**

     Adding wind noise will introduce a subtle sense of danger to the scene. If
     this is present at the beginning and fades out as the birds begin, it will fur-
     ther underscore the dramatic transition at that point.

6   Set an In at the head of the sequence and set an Out a few seconds after
     Birds FX 02.aiff begins (around 40:00).

7   Control-click the track header for track A13 and choose a1 from the
     shortcut menu. Control-click A14 and choose a2.

8   Overwrite **Wind 2.aiff** into the sequence.

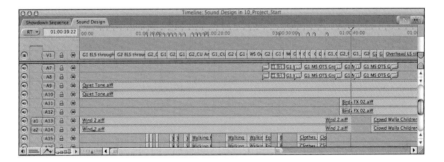

9   Control-click the ending edit of **Wind 2.aiff** and choose Add Transition
     'Cross Fade (0dB)'.

10   Press Home to return to the head of the sequence and play the sequence to
     hear how the wind influences the scene.

     The impact is subtle but effective. Wind noise is a classic sound design
     tool that can be used in a wide range of situations.

     If you're willing to get a little more abstract, you can have some fun with
     sound design elements.

11 Play the part of the sequence when the guys pull out the milk bottles (starting around 34:00).

Waving a bottle in the air doesn't actually make a sound, but that doesn't mean you can't pretend it does! This is an important moment in the scene, and you have an opportunity to add dramatic tension with a sound effect.

12 Open and play **Swish 1.aiff.**

This will add emphasis to the bottle move, and as long as you keep the level relatively low, it won't sound unnatural.

13 Place the sequence playhead at 35:03 just as Andy pulls out his bottle.

14 Drag the sound effect to tracks A19 and A20, and line it up so it begins at the playhead.

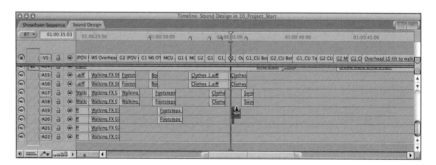

15 Play around the edit to hear the effect.

You may need to adjust the timing slightly so the sound occurs in sync with Andy's arm movement. It sounds a little funny, but mainly because it's too loud.

16 Double-click the clip, and in the Viewer, set the level to -7.

17 Play around the edit again.

By lowering the volume, the sound effect works to enhance the action in a subtle way rather than drawing attention to itself.

Alternatively, you could go over the top and use a more dramatic sound effect to play up the dueling storyline.

18 Open and play **Sword 4.aiff.**

19 Lower the level to -10.

20 Drag the clip into the sequence, lining it up with the beginning of **Swish 1.aiff** and placing it on tracks A21 and A22.

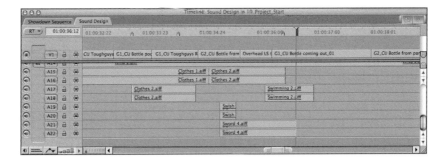

21 Play around the edit.

The unsheathing sword sound is metaphorically accurate, although obviously there's no way the bottle would make that sound, right? Well, the truth is there's no way the bottle would make the swish sound either. Depending on the overall style of your show, you may or may not be able to get away with these sorts of choices, and like all sound design, the volume of the effect determines how pronounced it is. You might be able to keep the sword sound by just lowering the level to the point where it's still audible but not drawing attention to itself.

At this point, you are also combining the sound of the swish and the sound of the sword. This may be making the overall effect too loud, but by balancing the levels of the two sounds, you may be able to create an effect that is greater than the sum of the parts.

Combining Sounds

What is the sound of a car crash? It's actually a combination of dozens of distinct sounds all happening together. There is the screeching of tires, the impact of metal on metal, the crumbling of fiberglass, the shattering of a brake light, the debris falling to the ground, and so on. Many, many distinct sounds go into that one "sound effect." And that is not the exception—it is the norm. For every sound effect you create, you will typically combine several sounds to make a full, complex, realistic-sounding effect.

But how do you combine so many sounds without creating a muddy blob of sound in which none of the elements are heard? This is the delicate art of mixing. Good sound mixing requires paying careful attention to the levels of each element, as well as to the frequencies (pitch) of the sounds you are mixing. You can easily combine the high-frequency shattering of glass with the low-frequency thud of metal colliding with metal. Also, by adjusting the timing of your sound effects so as not to precisely overlap their *attack* and *decay* periods (the build-up and wind-down of the sound), you can mix several sounds that appear to happen at the same time but each element can be detected.

1   Open and play **Low Frequency Hit FX.aiff**.

This is a very generic bass note that could be used musically or used to add some gusto to a higher-pitched sound effect.

2   Find the moment in the sequence when Pedro slaps his hands together (around 29:00).

Because at this point in the story the audience still thinks the guys are going to fight each other, using the bass note to add weight to this gesture makes it more threatening. But, you don't want it to be so loud that it draws attention to itself.

3   Lower the level to -8 dB.

4   Drag **Low Frequency Hit FX.aiff** to the sequence onto tracks A21 and A22, and line it up so it begins at the same frame as **Body Hit 02.aiff**.

Professional sound designers rarely use a single sound for any effect. You don't have to use five different clips for every situation, but it is a good idea to think about how you can incorporate this technique to improve your sound design.

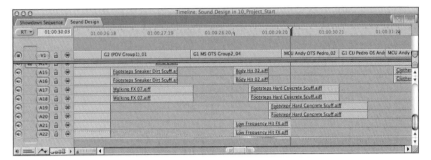

As usual, there's plenty more for you to do if you want to continue working on this project on your own.

5   To see a finished version, open and play **The whole shebang.**

Although the music obscures quite a bit of your sound design, don't be fooled into thinking you can skip over that design work as long as you slather on enough music at the end. The music should supplement, not replace, the sound design elements. Using music as a primary sound design element is cheating, and it cheats your audience as well. If you're relying entirely on someone's musical composition to convey the tone and emotional impact of your scene, you are giving up control of a very crucial and essential part of your job as storyteller.

Sometimes editors lay a "temp track" into a scene to provide a rhythm to cut to, or an emotional tone to reinforce. This can be helpful, but once picture is locked, you should turn off the music and go through the sound-editing process described in this lesson before adding music back in. Who knows, you may find you don't need the music at all!

Editing Music

Musical soundtracks fall into two categories: *practical* or *source music*, which is appears to be coming from a source within the scene, such as a radio or a live band; and *score*, which refers to music added to the film for the purpose of supplementing the scene.

Practical music will be mixed to sound like it is coming from a specific location. So when someone turns off the car, or walks out of the party, the music will end.

Score can be further divided into prerecorded songs, and original music composed to go with the show. If your show contains both, only the latter is referred to as the score. There are other terms commonly used such as *stingers* and *stabs*, which are very short musical elements timed specifically to moments in the show, such as a character's entrance or a moment of suspense.

Often you'll use just the beginning and end of a song, since most songs are at least 3 minutes long and most scenes are less than 2. Those beginnings and endings are wonderful when they reinforce the start and finish of your scene, but cutting out a chunk of the middle of the song requires music editing.

Music editing for film requires a specialized set of skills, somewhat unrelated to the skills used when editing music during its composition. You need to be able to identify the measures, rhythms, and arrangements of a song, and stitch together different sections to create a version that is exactly the right length. Sometimes you will remove a verse or double the length of a bridge. Sometimes you just find one measure and loop it three or four times to make the overall length of the song fit your scene.

▶ Using Commercial Music

It is illegal to use published music in your film or video projects without obtaining rights from both the author and publisher. You may think you can get away with it, but be aware that the music industry lawyers spend all day looking for violators. They patrol film festivals, tradeshows, and even the Internet. If you are caught, you can suffer a fine and a lot of legal hassle.

In addition to libraries of royalty-free music—and all the amazing loops in Soundtrack Pro—there are thousands of musicians who are eager to help you use their music for free. You should consider using these resources

Continues on next page

▶ **Using Commercial Music** *(continued)*

instead of ripping your favorite band's latest single and throwing it into your movie. If you still feel compelled to use commercially published music, do your homework and get the rights.

You typically need two sets of rights to use music in a film. You need the publishing rights (usually held by either BMI or ASCAP), which is the permission to use the composition of the song; and you need the performance rights (sometimes called *sync* rights), which covers the specific recording of the song you want to use. If you can get publishing rights but not sync rights, you can hire a band to *cover* the song (record their own version) and use that version in your film.

For very reasonable prices, music publishers frequently offer limited rights that allow you to show your film in festivals or similar limited engagements. If you want to begin selling your film for profit, you then need to renegotiate those rights.

Some lazy editors steal tracks from the published scores of finished films. This may be tempting, since the music was created as the soundtrack for a film in the first place. It may fit nicely in your film, but beware. Publishers almost never allow a piece of music composed specifically for a film to be reused in another film (for fairly obvious reasons).

1   Close the Friends Of The Family bin and expand the Art Lic Trailer bin.

    This bin contains the trailer for "Artistic License" and the original music that goes along with it.

2   Open and play the **AL Trailer** sequence.

3   Open and play **Farewell to Innocence.aif.**

4   In the Viewer, press Shift-Z to fit the entire waveform into view.

It can be very helpful to look at the waveform for a song you want to use as a potential score. Typically, you will be most interested in the beginning and end of the song. However, when a song has transitions or bridges where the music makes a sudden or dramatic change, this might be a section you can use as well.

Such bridges often can be identified by looking at the waveform. Sections in which the waveform dips indicate a section of relative quiet, which means there is an upcoming ending (leading into the bridge) and beginning (starting the next section) that could be useful in your show. This clip has two such dips midway through the song.

In this case you will use the beginning of the song to begin the trailer.

5   In the Viewer, set an In point just before the music kicks in, at 05:13.

6   Play the sequence and think about the best place to begin the music.

The trailer opens with a J-cut, when the first line of dialogue begins over the title card and then the picture arrives a moment later. This is a fairly strong opening, and adding music might undermine it. Instead, try beginning the music after that beat, on the cut to the next scene.

7 Set an In point in the sequence just before Brianca says, "I'm warning you, Milken!" at 06:24.

8 Target a1 to track A3 and a2 to track A4 and overwrite the music into the sequence.

Because you didn't set an Out point in either Viewer or sequence, the music extended well past the end of the trailer video.

9 Press Shift-Z to fit the entire sequence into the view.

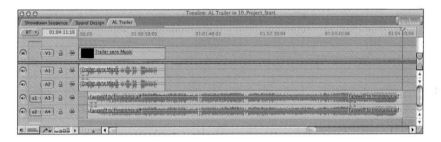

10 Drag the right edge of the music clip to the left until it lines up with the end of the video clip, and press Shift-Z.

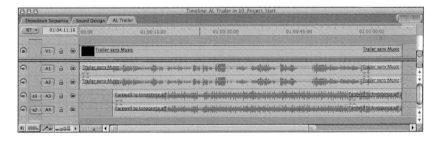

11 Play the sequence.

The music works very well with the trailer. It almost seems like it needs no editing at all, until you get to the end where the music is just cut off. You could simply fade it out, but it would be far superior to use a natural musical ending to add punctuation to the end of the show.

The first, obvious place to look for an ending is at the end of the song.

12 In the Viewer, play the ending of the song.

There is a nice ending, but the song seems to have progressed to a totally different instrumentation by that point and there is no obvious way to integrate that ending with the beginning you're using. What about those bridges you identified earlier?

13 In the Viewer, play across the dip in the waveform at around 00:02:04:00.

This is an interesting section, but it doesn't really work as an ending, since it continues to build until it explodes into the next section.

There is another dip in the waveform a little earlier, around 00:01:30:00.

14 Play across the section starting at 01:30:00.

This section is more promising. The two-beat, pause, two-beat, silence, phrase could easily work as an ending for the song.

15 In the sequence, watch the ending of the trailer, starting around 56:00. Think about how you might tie those ending beats into the picture.

There are two possibilities. One idea is to line the first beats up with the shot of Brianca "crushing" David with her fingers, and the other is to line it up with the beginning of the ending credits. Start by trying out the first approach.

To do this, you can use the Replace edit.

16 In the sequence, set an In point 5 or 10 seconds before the finger-crush and set an Out at the end of the sequence.

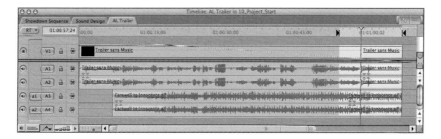

You know you're going to have to clean up the In point edit, so there's no need to make it precise.

17 Place the sequence playhead directly on the frame where the finger-crush happens (approximately 01:00:57:24).

18 In the Viewer, position the playhead precisely on the frame where the first beat (of the four ending beats) occurs (around 00:01:30:00).

It may help to zoom in on the waveform.

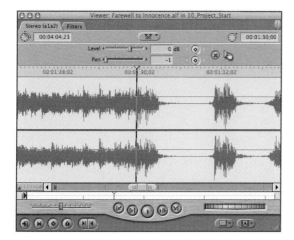

19 Drag **Farewell to Innocence.aif** to the Canvas and when the Canvas Edit Overlay appears, choose Replace.

A Replace edit is unlike all the other edit styles that base their edit timing on the first or last frame of the marked section of the clip (the In or Out point). Instead, a Replace edit lines up the playhead position in the Viewer with the playhead position in the sequence. This allows you to base an edit around a frame that occurs somewhere *between* the In and Out points. The source clip replaces the area between the In and Out markers on the target tracks in the sequence.

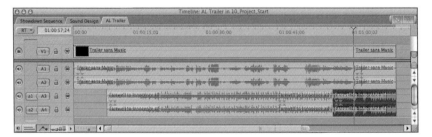

If no In or Out points are specified in the sequence, the boundaries of the current clip are observed instead.

20 Play around the new edit.

The timing works very well, although the music starts again after the four beats, when you really want it to go to silent.

21 Zoom in on the end of the sequence and drag the right edge of the music clip to the left to where the visible gap in the waveform indicates the silence after the four beats (01:01:01:00).

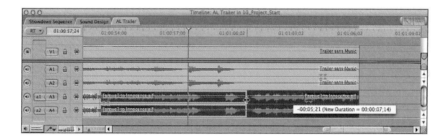

Now you need to tackle the other side of the edit, and find some way of meshing the two parts of the song. Ideally you can find the beginning of a measure in each section and line them up, so the musical rhythm feels continuous. Unfortunately, it is very unlikely that the timing will line up perfectly, so you have to get creative.

Begin by using markers to identify the rhythm in each piece. This is similar to the marking beats exercise you did in Lesson 8; but, rather than adding a marker on every beat, just add markers on the beginning of each measure. Since this music is in 4/4 time, that means a marker every four beats.

22 Zoom back out and click the Show Audio Controls button in the lower-left corner of the Timeline.

23 Click the Solo buttons for tracks A3 and A4.

24 Select the first section of the music track on A3 and A4.

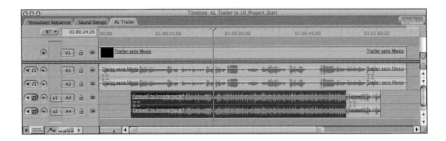

25 Move the sequence playhead to the section where the drum break occurs (around 25:00) and begin to play.

26 Each time a measure begins, press the M key to add a marker. Try to get the markers exactly on the first beat.

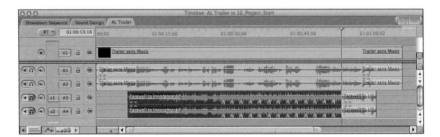

Now you need to add markers in the second piece of the music.

27 Press R to select the Roll tool and select the edit point between the two pieces of music. Drag it to the left about three-quarters of the way toward the beginning of the sequence.

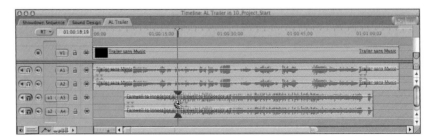

There's no need to be precise, as this is just a temporary edit to expose more of this part of the song. It will be easier to find the beats the longer you listen to the music, so the further you drag it to the left, the easier it will be.

28 Press A to select the Arrow tool and select the second piece of the music.

29 Move the playhead to the beginning of that clip and begin to play.

30 Press the M key at the top of each measure.

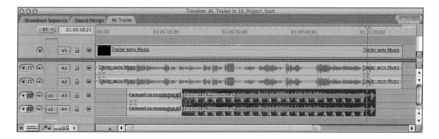

About halfway through the section, it gets a little difficult to find the start of each measure because the music gets a little syncopated. If you find it too difficult to mark each measure, just mark the beginning of each phrase or section when the music changes. Ultimately, you are looking for a good place to switch from the first piece of music to the second, so those beginnings of sections are the most useful sections to spot.

31 Select the Roll tool again and roll the edit back to the right, so the edit falls about midway through the sequence.

32 Press Command-+ several times to zoom into that section of the Timeline.

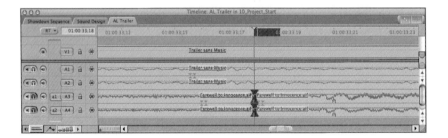

33 Roll the edit so it falls directly onto one of the markers in the first piece of music.

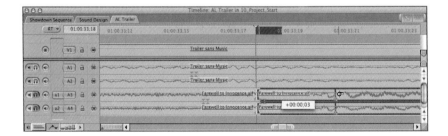

Now you can see how many frames separate the two pieces of music. For the rhythm to sound continuous across the two pieces of music, the marker to the right needs to line up exactly with the edit point.

34 Press R twice to select the Ripple tool and ripple the incoming clip (on the right side) until the marker lines up with the edit point.

35 Play around the edit.

The transition will still sound rough since the musical style changes abruptly, but the rhythm should remain consistent across the edit.

36 Control-click the edit and choose Add Transition 'Cross Fade (+3dB)'.

A cross-fade effect appears on the edit.

37 Control-click the transition icon and choose Duration (00:00:01:00).

A Duration dialog appears.

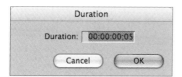

38 Type 5, and press Enter to set the duration to five frames and click OK.

39 Play around the edit again.

Now the transition should sound a little smoother, although depending on the marker you lined up on, it may or may not be an ideal edit. It doesn't matter, as long as the rhythm sounds continuous. You can now move the edit anywhere you want and the rhythm will remain consistent.

The trick is to find a good place to hide the edit. One of the best techniques is to look for a loud section in the main audio track that might serve to cover up the musical edit.

40 Deselect the Solo buttons for A3 and A4 to un-solo the tracks.

41 Zoom back out to show the whole sequence, then select the Roll tool and drag the transition to the right until it is underneath the area in tracks

A1 and A2 where the waveform appears large (indicating a loud area), around 49:15.

Using the Roll tool on a transition moves the transition without affecting its duration or other settings.

Use snapping to line the edit up precisely with the markers, so the transition still occurs at the head of a measure.

42 Press Home and listen to the whole sequence play.

The edit isn't completely invisible, but it isn't drawing too much attention to itself, either. You can experiment with placing it elsewhere in the sequence if you like.

The rippling you did earlier moved the four beats at the end of the scene a little bit to the left. This can be remedied in one of two ways. You can move both pieces of music to the right to make up for the frames you trimmed, which means the music at the head of the show will begin a few frames later, or you can live with the whole piece ending a few frames earlier. It's up to you to select the compromise you prefer.

The bigger remaining problem is that the music level is competing with the dialogue in the first half of the trailer.

Using the Mixer

Although you can use the clip overlays to do simple audio fades, when you want to control an audio track's level over a longer period of time, it's far more efficient to use the Audio Mixer. Lesson 11 will cover the Audio Mixer in more detail, but this exercise will give you a short preview.

1   Choose Tools > Audio Mixer or press Option-6.

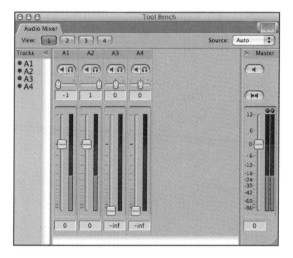

The Audio Mixer window appears.

2   Press Home to move the playhead to the beginning of the sequence.

3   Play through the sequence once, just watching the Audio Mixer window.

Tracks 3 and 4 begin at -inf, and then jump up to 0dB at the point where the track begins.

You should be thinking about what changes you'd like to make. The music starts off fine, but after the first line of dialogue, it begins to seem too loud. Then, around the time when Brianca screams "Milken!" the volume no longer seems excessive. In fact, it propels the energy of the scene.

4 In the button bar of the Audio Mixer, click the Record Audio Keyframes button.

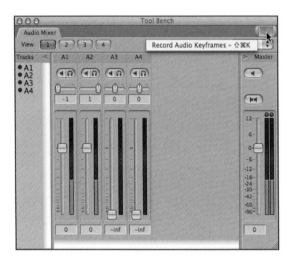

With this setting activated, you can drag the audio sliders and control the clip levels manually while the scene plays. It does take a bit of practice to get good at this, but just like trimming edits, it is preferable to make changes as the sequence is playing and you can hear everything in context, than it is to drag around keyframes when the playhead is stopped.

If you make a mistake, you can always clear the changes you make, and there's always Undo.

5 Press Home to move the playhead to the beginning of the sequence.

You're going to concentrate entirely on tracks 3 and 4, which are linked together (because they are a stereo pair). So, you just need to drag the slider for one of them.

Remember your goal: You want to lower the audio after the first line of dialogue ("I'm warning you, Milken!") and then bring it back up when she screams, "Milken!" That's only two moves; the rest of the time, you can leave the slider alone.

6 Press the spacebar to begin playback.

7   As soon as the sliders for tracks 3 and 4 jump up to 0 dB, grab one of them and smoothly drag it down to about -7.

8   Hold it there until you hear Brianca scream "Milken!" and then smoothly drag it back up to 0 dB. Press the spacebar to stop playback.

That's it! Your level changes appear in the clip as keyframes.

9   Play back the sequence and listen to your work.

If you don't like the results, you can reset the keyframes and try again.

10   Double-click the first instance of **Farewell to Innocence.aif** in the Timeline.

The clip is opened into the Viewer.

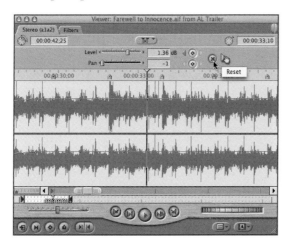

11   In the Viewer, click the Reset button.

All audio keyframes are eliminated.

12   Press Option-6 to bring the Audio Mixer window to the front.

13   Repeat Steps 5 through 9.

If you're still unhappy with the mix you can repeat Steps 10 through 13 ad infinitum.

Lesson Review

1. What are the six stages of sound editing?
2. How should audio filters be applied?
3. What does a compressor filter do?
4. What makes a good ambiance?
5. How do you manually create room tone?
6. What are three ways to control a clip's level?
7. How do you navigate to markers within a sequence?
8. How can you effectively combine sounds?
9. How do you stitch together pieces of music with different timing?
10. What advantage does the Audio Mixer window offer?

Answers

1. Dialogue, ambiances, sound effects, sound design, music, and the final mix.
2. By looping playback and adjusting sliders until satisfied.
3. A compressor reduces a clip's dynamic range by attenuating loud sections of a clip.
4. Appropriateness to location and appropriateness to theme.
5. Select a section of "silence" from a dialogue clip and duplicate it, then stitch the duplicates together with short cross-fades.
6. The level slider in the Viewer, the Clip Overlays in the Timeline, or the Levels dialog.
7. Shift-M moves to the next marker; Option-M moves to the previous marker. Also, you can Control-click on the Timeline ruler or Current Timecode field and choose the name of a marker from the shortcut menu.
8. Choose sounds with differing pitch, timing, and levels.

9. Use markers to identify the beginnings of measures or phrases, roll and ripple to line up the markers in the two clips, and then apply a short cross-fade effect. Finally, roll the edit to a place where it can be well hidden.

10. It allows you to automate clip levels dynamically while playing.

11

Lesson Files   Lesson Project Files > Lesson_11 > 11_Project_Start

Media   Media > FBI Guys Pencil Scene

Time   This lesson takes approximately 60 minutes to complete.

Goals   Explore the difference between peak and average audio levels

Choose an appropriate decibel level for a sequence's dialogue

Explore the Audio Mixer

Use views to create different arrangements of audio tracks in the Audio Mixer

Record level keyframes to automate an audio track in real time, by moving faders in the Audio Mixer

Lesson **11**

Audio Finishing

Have you ever heard the expression "Video is two-thirds audio?" Well, it's true. The ear is more sensitive than the eye, and viewers are much more tolerant of mediocre picture quality than they are of less-than-perfect audio. Look no further than the infamous *Blair Witch Project*. Despite being photographed to deliberately look like it was shot by frightened kids with a $200 camcorder, it was given a million-dollar sound mix before being released into theaters.

Happily, there's no reason why your audio should ever turn a viewer away, because creating a quality audio mix can be a simple process. In this lesson, you will use a reference tone to correctly configure the level of your sequence's audio. Then, you'll learn how to set the level of audio clips, use Final Cut Pro's Audio Mixer, automate audio tracks in real time.

Preparing the Sequence

Movies are all about suspending your disbelief—losing yourself in the magic of the story and forgetting reality, if only for a moment. So in the finest cinematic tradition, suspend your disbelief by pretending you're not a video editor, and put on the hat of an audio engineer.

1   Open **11_Project_Start**.

The **Pencil Scene** sequence should open, with six tracks of audio.

2   Choose Final Cut Pro > User Preferences (Option-Q), and in the Editing tab make sure that the Record Audio Keyframes box is deselected.

3   Click OK.

Muting and Soloing Audio Tracks

The secret to good audio is getting the dialogue right. More than any other sound in your video, it is the dialogue that commands your viewer's attention. In the following exercises, you're going to hop into the viewer's frame of mind by focusing your attention on the sequence's dialogue alone. So you should temporarily disable the audio tracks that do not contain dialogue. In Final Cut Pro, there are three ways to do this:

▶   Disable the audio track by clicking its green Audible button. (These buttons are often called Track Visibility buttons—even on audio tracks—but this book refers to them as the Audible buttons.) If the Audible button is disabled, the audio track's sound does not play.

▶   Mute the audio track. A muted track does not play.

▶   Solo the dialogue audio track. Soloing a track turns off the sound of all the other audio tracks in a sequence (except for other soloed tracks, which continue to play).

1   For the next several steps, it will help to hear the sequence's audio as you turn audio tracks on and off, so in the Timeline, move the playhead to the beginning of the sequence and press the spacebar to begin playback.

2   On track A5 and track A6, click the Audible button to turn the tracks off (disable them).

Clicking the Audible button is a good way to turn off the track's sound, as long as you remember the following: Disabling the Audible button not only turns the track off, but also excludes it from the rendered or output version of your movie—this includes movies exported to QuickTime, Print to Video, Edit to Tape, and so on.

A less permanent way to turn off a track's sound involves using the Mute buttons. Muted tracks are still included in the sequence's sound when you export it to a QuickTime movie or print to tape.

Before you can mute a track, you need to show the audio controls in the Timeline.

3   In the lower-left corner of the Timeline, click the Audio Controls button.

Mute and Solo buttons appear at the far left of each track.

Muting and soloing audio tracks affect the sequence only while you edit it. When it comes time to output the sequence, the Mute and Solo button choices are overridden, so all muted or soloed tracks are included in your final renders.

Disabling audio tracks with the Audible button has one other distinct advantage over using the Mute and Solo buttons: It removes the strain the audio track places on your computer's CPU. Muted tracks, on the other hand, still consume CPU cycles, because you can instantly turn these tracks back on by unmuting them. If your sequence drops frames as it plays, click the Audible button to disable audio tracks you don't need to hear, and save those CPU cycles for more important parts of your project (like adding more effects to the other tracks).

4   On track A3 and track A4, select the Mute button.

The Mute button has a black speaker on it. Selecting it turns the speaker yellow and temporarily turns off a track's sound. Consequently, track A3 and track A4 can no longer be heard.

5   Deselect the Mute buttons to unmute track A3 and track A4, and then reenable track A5 and track A6 by selecting their Audible buttons.

All audio tracks are now playing together.

6   On track A1 and track A2, select the Solo buttons.

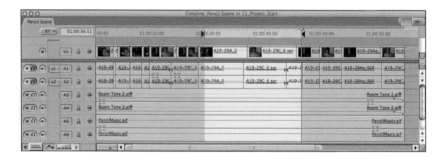

Track A1 and track A2 are soloed. All the sequence's other tracks are automatically muted so you can't hear them. That's great, because for the next few exercises you are going to concentrate on getting your dialogue right, so it's fine to have the other audio tracks temporarily silenced. You'll turn track A1 and track A2 back on a little later, but leave them soloed for now and continue to the next exercises.

Understanding Dialogue Levels

Imagine you're channel surfing in your living room. As you switch through the programs, you pay the most attention to the dialogue, which is the main way a program delivers aural information to you. The music and background sounds all slip into a supporting role, and your ears' attention focuses on the spoken words. You'll also notice that the sound of dialogue across all television channels is more or less uniform, and always reaches your ears at the same volume level. In other words, the average volume of the dialogue purposefully has been configured to be consistent across all broadcast programs. This allows a more pleasant viewing experience, because you can confidently flip between programs without having to jump for the remote control's volume buttons to raise or lower the television's sound.

To keep the level of dialogue constant, broadcast television uses an average level of dialogue that corresponds to approximately -15 dB to -12 dB on Final Cut Pro's digital level meter. For example, if you were to take a video sequence from Final Cut Pro in which the average dialogue level was set to -12 dB, use DVD Studio Pro to turn it into a DVD-Video, and then play that DVD on your TV, your dialogue would sound at exactly the same level as the dialogue on a television broadcast. Consequently, if you want your sequence to play at the same volume as broadcast television programs, it's a good idea to ensure that the average level of your sequence's dialogue is between -15 dB and -12 dB as you edit in Final Cut Pro.

Comparing Peak and Average Levels

One of the most important audio concepts to understand is the difference between peak and average audio levels.

Peak level is represented by spikes in the waveform. These spikes represent short bursts in volume that last only a fraction of a second. In music, the peaks usually correspond to rhythmic elements in the song, such as kick drums and cymbal crashes. In dialogue, peaks typically fall on the "plosive" sounds, or hard consonant sounds such as *p*, *t*, and *k*. In fact, if you say the word *peak*, you can even hear how your own voice sounds louder and more pronounced during the "p" and "k" portions of the word, while it's quieter during the "ea."

A waveform's average volume level is represented by a line that distinguishes the waveform's solid body from its peaks. As you listen to an audio stream, you are much more sensitive to the stream's average level than you are to the peak level, and if the audio sounds too loud or too quiet, it's very likely the average level that you are noticing, not the peak level.

Dialogue: Common Average and Peak Levels in Final Cut Pro

Delivery Format	Average Volume	Peak Volume
Broadcast television	-12 dB	-6 dB
VHS tape	-12 dB	-3 dB
Theatrical Dolby Digital	-20 dB	-3 dB

Let's take a moment to explore peak and average levels using the **PencilMusic.aif** file. This file contains music, not dialogue. Nonetheless, music is very dynamic in nature, with noticeable spikes that provide a good example of the difference between peak and average audio levels.

1   In the Browser, double-click the **PencilMusic.aif** audio file.

2   Press Shift-Z to fit the entire waveform into view.

NOTE ▶ This piece of music was built specifically for this scene, so the silence at the end of the file is intentional.

3   Play the audio file and see if you can hear the differences between the peaks and the average levels.

This Viewer is quite narrow, whereas the audio file itself is fairly long. To get a bit more space to display the file, you can drag the Audio tab out of the Viewer and drop it into the Timeline window.

4   In the Viewer, drag the Audio tab, called Stereo (a1a2), out of the window. Don't release the mouse button.

5   Drop the Audio tab in the tab area of the Timeline window.

The audio waveform fills the Timeline window.

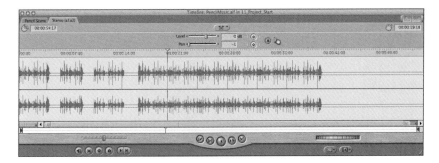

With the waveform spread across the Timeline window, it becomes much easier to see it in detail. Notice the peaks in the waveform, and then look closely at the more solid part of the waveform—its body. Although it takes a bit of practice to identify a file's average level, you can get close by thinking of it this way: If you shaved off the peaks of the waveform, you'd be left with a flat, smooth wave. This smooth wave would come close to representing the waveform's average level.

Exploring Dynamic Range

Dynamic range is the difference between your audio stream's loudest and quietest portions, and it's important to take dynamic range into consideration when you determine how loud your sequence's dialogue should be. For example, film soundtracks are often mixed using a wide dynamic range. They are meant to play on the big screen, with big sound systems that are very efficient and accurately reproduce a wide difference between loud and quiet sounds. In a movie, you want to hear the lovers' whisper, and you want to be shocked by the exploding car. You want to hear the rumble of the low-rider car as it drives by, and you want the thrill of the roar as the low-rider revs its engine. You want big sound, and consequently a big dynamic range is required. For this reason, movies typically mix in dialogue at between -20 dB and -31 dB. At first glance this may seem surprisingly low on the level meter, but it's all relative; add an explosion that peaks at -6 dB, and you've got a very dynamic—and dramatic—soundtrack.

Television, on the other hand, has different concerns. Most televisions today are not equipped with efficient speakers, and the mono 3-inch driver on the front of a typical budget television has a hard time just reproducing sound, let alone blasting the full dynamic range of a film score. Consequently, audio destined for TV uses a severely reduced dynamic range. The following chart lists the dynamic range required for several different types of programs:

Dynamic Range vs. Program Delivery Format

Delivery Format	Dynamic Range
Broadcast television	6 dB
Videotape	12 dB
Theatrical Dolby Digital	20 dB

Using the Audio Meter

In Final Cut Pro, -12 dB is a very significant number because it makes a good reference level to use for video destined for broadcast. When you output your sequence to analog tape formats, such as BetaSP or VHS, you should adjust your tape recorder so that -12 dB on Final Cut Pro's level meter is 0 dB on your tape recorder's analog, or volume unit (VU) level meter. (On an analog audio meter, 0 dB is often referred to as *unity gain*.)

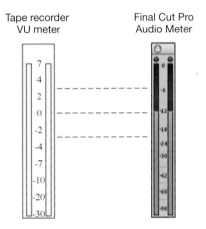

NOTE ► Only professional VHS decks provide audio level controls.

Digital videotape recorders such as DV, HDCAM, DVCPRO, and Digital Betacam receive digital audio straight from Final Cut Pro and will record audio at levels identical to those you see on your Final Cut Pro Audio Meter.

1   In the Timeline window, click the Pencil Scene tab to bring the sequence back into view.

2   Press Shift-\ to play from In to Out.

   Right now, tracks A1 and A2 are soloed, so all you hear is the production sound. This marked section contains a continuous section of talking.

3   Look at Final Cut Pro's Audio Meter, and note the peak levels compared with the average levels.

   As the sequence plays, the Audio Meter pulses between a high and a low value. The high value represents the sequence's peak level, and the low value approximates the average level. The difference between these two levels determines the audio stream's dynamic range.

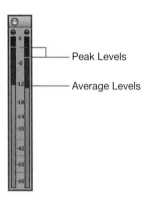

The Audio Meter helps you determine peak values by temporarily holding a yellow line in position at audio peaks. (This is called a peak and hold display.) The average volume level, on the other hand, takes a bit of practice to work out. As you watch the Audio Meter pulse between its high and low levels, notice that some green is almost always displayed in the Audio Meter, and the volume level very rarely drops to silence. Pay careful attention to the lowest level of the green in the display. For all intents and purposes, this is the average level of the audio stream. In this example, the average level of the dialogue is approximately -18 dB.

4   Press the spacebar to stop playback, and look at the Audio Meter.

Even though the sequence has stopped playing, the Audio Meter continues to show the level of the frame the playhead is currently parked on.

Choosing a Reference Level

So, you've examined a lot of the theory involved in audio—now it's time to start mixing! The first step to creating a great mix is calibrating your speakers using a reference tone. A *reference tone* is a steady 1 kHz sine wave that sounds like a long, sustained note. It's important because this reference tone helps you set a comfortable monitoring level and provides a volume reference to use as you set the levels of your sequence's dialogue.

The reference level is used for two purposes. First, if you are outputting your sequence to tape in preparation for broadcast, you should always include one full minute of video bars and audio test tone at the beginning of the sequence. This test tone plays at the same average level as the dialogue in your sequence, and it allows the broadcaster to calibrate her equipment to play your audio at the correct level. The test tone also provides a steady signal you can use to calibrate your audio signals to an appropriate listening level, and that's the purpose you'll put it to in the next few steps.

For the purpose of this exercise, initially assume you want your video to play at the same level as standard broadcast television. To achieve this, you'll use a reference level of -12 dB and then calibrate your speakers to an appropriate listening level for mixing.

1   Press F to perform a match frame wherever you are in the sequence. This will return a Video tab into the Viewer. Click the Viewer's Video tab, and in the lower-right corner of the Viewer, click the Generators button.

The Generators pop-up menu opens.

2   Choose Bars and Tone (NTSC).

The Bars and Tone Generator appears in the Viewer.

3   Click the Viewer's Play button.

A 1 kHz test tone plays. Notice that Final Cut Pro's Audio Meter holds steady at -12 dB while the test tone plays. This is an appropriate reference level for broadcast television.

However, if you intended to mix your sequence with more dynamic range than is required for television, you would need to lower the level of the test tone from its default -12 dB, as demonstrated in the following steps.

4   Click the Viewer's Stereo (a1a2) tab to display the test tone.

Toward the top of the Stereo tab, you'll see Level and Pan sliders. If you look closely, you'll notice the Level slider is set at -12 dB. This, of course, is exactly the same value displayed on Final Cut Pro's Audio Meter.

5   Move the Level slider down to -20, and check out Final Cut Pro's Audio Meter. (If the test tone is not playing, click the Play button to start playback once again.)

The Audio Meter now displays a level of -20 dB.

If you continued with this more dynamic reference level, you would mix in the dialogue at approximately the same volume level as this lower test tone, which, in turn, would give you more *headroom*, or more room above the dialogue level to mix in effects such as those explosions and revving car engines referred to earlier.

6   Set the Level slider back to -12 to ensure that the test tone plays at -12 dB.

▶ **Audio Monitoring**

It is critical that you perform your final mix in an environment that matches the environment of your intended audience. Room acoustics and speaker types have a huge impact on the way your audio sounds. If you create your final mix in a perfectly soundproof environment and you're making a safety video for airplane passengers, or you're mixing in your bedroom with tiny speakers and planning to project the finished film in a cavernous theater, you're in for unpleasant surprises.

If you don't have the flexibility to create your mix in the intended environment, at least make a preliminary cut and schedule a preliminary screening in your target location. Then, having heard the results, go back and tweak your EQ and dynamic range settings to accommodate those acoustical conditions.

Continues on next page

▶ **Audio Monitoring** *(continued)*

Furthermore, if you're fantasizing that your film is going to be screened exclusively in movie theaters and you build a mix with 18–20 dB of dynamic range, but instead the vast majority of viewers watch it on DVDs on their laptop computers, neither you nor the audience are going to be happy with the results. You're far better off planning for a narrower dynamic range, or even making multiple versions like feature film sound engineers commonly do.

7   Play the -12 dB test tone, and adjust your speakers so the tone sounds neither too loud nor too quiet.

The test tone should be loud enough so that you can hear it clearly, but not so loud that it tires your ears. As you mix your audio in Final Cut Pro, don't change the volume of your speakers. Maintaining a consistent playback level lets you get used to the volume you're working at, which, in turn, gives you a good feel for how your audio sounds. When it comes to volume, consistency is the key!

NOTE ▶ Adjusting speaker volume is not the same thing as adjusting the Viewer's Level slider. You can adjust the speaker volume by increasing or decreasing the output volume of your computer using the speaker keys at the top of the keyboard's keypad.

Setting a Dialogue Level

Now that you've decided upon a reference level and have properly configured your speakers, it's time to tackle the sequence's audio. The first step in this process is to set the dialogue so its average level is approximately the same as the level of your reference tone.

If you take care to set your dialogue to the same level as the reference tone, all of your sequence's other sounds fall naturally into place. For the purpose of this lesson, you'll stay with the broadcast-compatible reference tone of -12 dB.

> **NOTE ▶** You also must pay attention to your sequence's peak level. For broadcast, audio that uses a reference level of -12 dB should never peak above -6 dB on Final Cut Pro's Audio Meter. For tape formats such as VHS, -3 dB is an appropriate peak level for sequences that use a reference tone of -12 dB.

1   Play the sequence again and determine the average level of the dialogue.

Right now the average level of the dialogue is approximately -18 dB. Furthermore, this level is consistent across the entire sequence. Your reference tone is at -12 dB, so you need to raise the level of each audio clip by 6 dB. You could progress clip by clip through the sequence, grabbing the pink level overlay line, and raising the level of each clip by hand. But that would be a slow and arduous task. Instead, use the following trick to boost the level of all the clips at once.

2   With the Selection tool, drag a selection range around all of the audio clips in track A1 and track A2.

All of the clips in track A1 and track A2 are selected.

3   Choose Modify > Levels (Command-Option-L).

The Gain Adjust window opens.

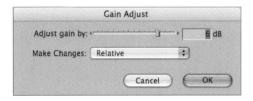

This window lets you simultaneously adjust the level of several audio clips. It's simple to use; just grab the slider and set an amount to adjust the gain by. Positive values increase the level of the selected clips; negative values decrease it.

However, there is one important setting in this window, and that's Make Changes. This setting has two different values: Absolute and Relative.

▶ *Absolute.* All gain adjustments are absolute, which means each selected audio clip is moved to the exact value indicated on the "Adjust gain by" slider. If the clip contains keyframes, the keyframes are erased.

▶ *Relative.* This is the default setting. All gain adjustments look at the current level of each individual clip, and then adjust the clip by the amount specified in the "Adjust gain by" slider. If the clip contains keyframes, each individual keyframe is adjusted by the amount specified in the "Adjust gain by" slider.

4   Leave the Make Changes setting at Relative, set the "Adjust gain by" slider to 6, and click OK.

The level of each clip increases by 6 dB.

5   Play the sequence again and watch the Audio Meter.

Now the average level of the dialogue is approximately -12 dB. Perfect!

With the dialogue set to the correct level, it's time to adjust the level of the sequence's other audio tracks. You'll do that in the following exercises using Final Cut Pro's Audio Mixer.

Exploring the Audio Mixer

Final Cut Pro's Audio Mixer is a great component in your audio editing arsenal. With a fader (level slider), a Pan slider, and Mute and Solo buttons for every audio track in your project, the Audio Mixer mimics the functionality of a hardware audio mixing console.

Using the Audio Mixer

Open the Audio Mixer and take a look around.

1   Choose Tools > Audio Mixer (Option-6).

A Tool Bench window opens containing the Audio Mixer.

This window is dominated by a central section that contains a dedicated level fader for each track in your project. At the top of each track's fader is a Pan slider, a Mute (speaker) button, and a Solo (headphones) button. The Mute and Solo buttons in the Audio Mixer provide exactly the same function as the Mute and Solo buttons in the Timeline when you click the Show Audio Controls button.

A quick glance at these buttons shows that track A1 and track A2 are currently soloed. This means tracks A3 through A6 cannot be heard.

2   On track A1 and track A2, select the Solo button to turn soloing off for those two tracks.

3   Press Home to go to the head of the sequence, then play the sequence.

Watch the track faders. In Final Cut Pro, levels are assigned to the individual clips rather than to the track as a whole. Consequently, as the sequence plays you will often see the level faders jump up and down to reflect the level of each individual clip. Areas of the Timeline that do not have an audio clip are silent, and the track faders obligingly drop to -inf (infinity) when these blank spaces are encountered.

4   While the audio is playing, drag A2's Pan slider to the left.

A2's audio is now heard completely in the left speaker.

5   Option-click A2's Pan slider.

The Pan slider jumps back to the center. Holding Option while clicking a fader is a quick way to reset the fader to its default setting, and it works not only on the Pan slider, but on each track's level fader as well!

TIP ▶ To gear down and make a fader's movement more precise, hold the Command key as you drag the fader. This works with all sliders in Final Cut Pro.

6   Grab the Master fader (on the right side of the window) and drag it down to the bottom.

The Master fader controls the level of the entire mix, so lowering the Master fader causes the entire mix to drop in level.

TIP ▶ If you are using a mouse with a scroll wheel, you can position the pointer over a fader and use the scroll wheel to move it up and down. This is often easier and more precise than dragging.

The scale used for the Master fader can be a bit confusing at first. By default, the Master fader sits at 0, but does not indicate whether the 0 refers to unity gain or -12 dB on the digital scale. In fact, the 0 setting here indicates that no boost or attenuation has been applied to the level of the sequence as a whole. However, should you so desire you can apply up to 12 dB of boost to the entire mix, or attenuate the mix until it is silent.

7   Option-click the Master fader.

The Master fader returns to 0.

8   In the Track Strips pane, raise or lower the faders on tracks A3 through A6 to set the level of these audio tracks.

Listen closely to the dialogue as you adjust these faders, and set the level so that the dialogue in track A1 and track A2 is still clearly present and easily heard above the other elements of the mix.

Working with Views

This sequence has only 6 audio tracks, which is a very manageable number. Indeed, a quick glance shows that all 6 tracks easily fit in the Audio Mixer. But what happens if you have 24 audio tracks, or 64? Or even the maximum number of 99 audio tracks available in Final Cut Pro? In those situations, your Audio Mixer would become very crowded. Happily, the Audio Mixer lets you hide audio tracks, which allow you to focus only on the audio tracks you currently need to adjust.

Even better, Final Cut Pro gives you access to four different views, or custom track configurations, in the Audio Mixer. For example, you can create one view for dialogue tracks, one for ambiances, one for sound effects, and one for music. When it comes time to adjust the dialogue, just enable the view that contains your dialogue tracks, and only those dialogue tracks will appear in the Audio window.

1   In the Track Selection pane on the left edge of the Audio Mixer, deselect track A6.

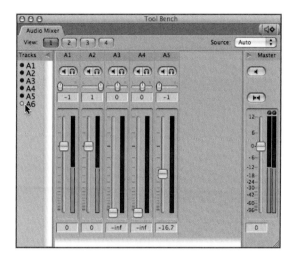

The dot beside track A6 turns from black to an outline. Track A6 is hidden, and its track strip disappears from the Audio Mixer.

2   In the Track Selection pane, deselect tracks A3, A4, and A5 to hide them.

Track strips for A1 and A2 are the only ones that remain visible in the Audio Mixer.

3   If the sequence is not playing, play it now.

Although tracks A3 through A6 are hidden in the Audio Mixer, you can still hear them. This demonstrates an important point: Hidden audio tracks are not turned off—they continue to play.

4   In the top-left corner of the Audio Mixer, click View button 2.

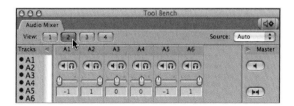

All of the audio tracks are once again visible in the Audio Mixer.

5   Return to the Track Selection pane once again, but this time deselect track A1 and track A2 to hide them.

You've just created a second view that contains only the music and ambiances. Now, if you wish to adjust the dialogue, click View button 1. If you need to adjust the background audio, click View button 2.

6   Switch back and forth between View 1 and View 2 by clicking the View 1 and 2 buttons. When you're done having fun, leave View button 2 selected.

Resizing the Audio Mixer

Views go a long way to helping you deal with sequences that use many audio tracks. There will, however, be times when you need to adjust several audio tracks at the same time. In these situations, it helps to resize the Tool Bench window that holds the Audio Mixer tab so that all the tracks are visible.

Resizing the window with the Audio Mixer has another distinct advantage: If you are attempting to make very subtle level adjustments, the Audio Mixer's faders might seem a bit short, and not exact enough in their movement. You can increase the resolution of these faders by dragging the bottom of the mixer toward the bottom of your screen. This makes the Audio Mixer nice and tall, which gives you more precise control over fader movements.

1   Drag the Tool Bench window to the left (by its title bar).

Notice that the Tool Bench is actually its own window and not part of the Viewer. When you opened the Tool Bench, it completely covered the Viewer, but it's actually an independent window that you can open, resize, and close, as needed.

2   Drag down the bottom-right corner of the Tool Bench window toward the bottom of the screen.

The Tool Bench window becomes taller—and so do its faders! You now have very precise control over your fader settings.

On the other hand, the Audio Mixer is now obstructing a lot of your valuable screen real estate. Final Cut Pro contains a window arrangement that is tailored for audio mixing.

3   Choose Window > Arrange > Audio Mixing.

The Tool Bench window opens in the top-right corner of the screen, displaying the Audio Mixer in a tab.

Using Real-Time Keyframing

Real-time keyframing is arguably the coolest audio feature in Final Cut Pro, because you can record level, pan, and audio effects changes in real time simply by moving a fader or slider. Real-time keyframing really shines if you need to do quick edits like *ducking* (temporarily lowering) background music so it doesn't drown out a section of dialogue, or when creating custom level fades.

1   In the top-right corner of the Audio Mixer, click the Record Audio
    Keyframes button (Shift-Command-K).

    You can now record keyframes in real time, as the sequence plays.

    NOTE ▶ You can also enable and disable audio keyframe recording by
    opening the User Preferences window and selecting the Record Audio
    Keyframes box.

2   Open User Preferences by choosing Final Cut Pro > User Preferences or
    pressing Option-Q. Click the Editing tab.

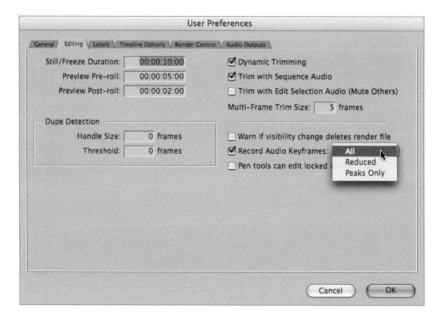

3   In the Record Audio Keyframes pop-up menu, choose All and click OK.

4   In the Timeline, press Option-X to clear the In and Out points.

5   Press Home to move the playhead to the beginning of the sequence, then press the spacebar to start playback.

6   In the Audio Mixer, drag up and down the fader for track A5 as the sequence plays.

Track A5 and track A6 are a stereo pair, so as you move the fader for track A5, the fader for track A6 comes along for the ride.

7   After you've made a few changes to the fade, stop playback.

In the Timeline, notice that your fader movements have been recorded as keyframes in the **PencilMusic.aif** clip overlay.

With the Record Audio Keyframes option set to All, Final Cut Pro records keyframes for every fader movement. This is precise, but it also means that over the course of the sequence, there are many tiny abrupt adjustments. Often a curve will be smoother (and easier to adjust later) if it consists of fewer points.

8   Choose Final Cut Pro > User Preferences and click the Editing tab.

9   Choose Record Audio Keyframes > Peaks Only. Click OK.

10   Press Home to return to the top of the sequence and play it again.

11   While the sequence plays, drag up and down the fader for track A5 in the Audio Mixer.

12   After a few movements, stop playback.

First of all, notice that the keyframes for the tracks have been entirely replaced. Each time you make changes, it erases the previous keyframes.

Because you changed the setting to Peaks Only, far fewer keyframes are recorded this time.

13   Deselect the Record Audio Keyframes button in the Audio Mixer button bar to disable real-time keyframing.

WARNING ▶ When you're done recording real-time keyframes, always disable this option! If you don't, adjustments you make to Level and Pan sliders in the Viewer and Timeline will automatically be recorded as keyframes, which may not be desirable.

Resetting a Clip's Keyframes

If you record keyframes, either intentionally or accidentally, and then decide you don't want them, you can reset the clip and delete all keyframes using the following technique.

1   In the Timeline, double-click the **PencilMusic.aif** audio clip in track A5 to open it in the Viewer.

2   In the Viewer, click the Reset button.

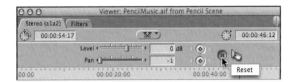

3   All of the clip's Level keyframes are deleted, and its overlay is set back to its default value of 0 dB of boost/attenuation.

Lesson Review

1.   Do peak levels or average levels indicate the apparent volume of a clip?

2.   How is dynamic range measured?

3.   What is a reference tone used for?

4.   How do you limit the number of visible tracks in the Audio Mixer?

5.   Is a muted track included when you export an AIF?

6.   Is a disabled track included when you export an AIF?

7.   How do you reset a slider in the Audio Mixer?

8.   On Final Cut Pro's Master fader what does 0 (zero) mean?

Answers

1.   While peak levels show the absolute highest levels a track reaches, average levels are a better indication of the overall volume of a clip.

2.   In decibels (dB) measuring the difference between the quietest and loudest levels in a program.

3.   A reference tone should indicate the average level of the dialogue in your program. It informs exhibitors, broadcasters, or duplicators at what level they should set their equipment in order to reproduce the sound the way you intended.

4.   The Audio Mixer contains four views, each of which can contain a subset of tracks from your entire program.

5.   Muted tracks are included in all exports and output.

6.   Disabled tracks are not included in any exports or outputs.

7.   Option-click a slider to reset it. You can also Control-click and choose Reset from the shortcut menu.

8.   On Final Cut Pro's Master fader, 0 (zero) means no boost or attenuation. It is not an indication of decibels (dB).

Project Management

12

Lesson Files
Lesson Project Files > Lesson_12 > 12_Project_Start

Media
Media > FBI Guys Pencil Scene, FBI Guys Pepper Spray, Gold Fever, Hooploose Footage, Misc Clips, Sweet Sound Music Video, Turn To Stone

Time
This lesson takes approximately 150 minutes to complete.

Goals
Master the various parameters associated with all clips

Use complex Find commands to locate specific items

Modify clip reel name and timecode

Use Auxiliary Timecode fields

Change reel numbers for a group of clips

Sync up audio and video from separate clips

Create and modify merged clips

Work with 16:9 media and sequences

Understand the special needs and workflows for 24p projects

Lesson 12
Advanced Clip Management

Good editing requires an organized workspace. Nothing is more important than managing the parameters, settings, and data associated with your clips. Even tiny errors can balloon into serious problems, including data loss, if you do not thoroughly understand how data is managed in Final Cut Pro and how to catch and correct problems.

Additionally, a solid understanding of Final Cut Pro's clip architecture can give you more flexibility in your editing decisions and improve your workflow and productivity.

Using the Browser as a Clip Database

Final Cut Pro's Browser is actually an immensely robust database containing more than 75 different parameters for each clip or sequence it contains. The first step to managing that database is to understand what those varied parameters are.

1   Open the Lesson_12 > **12_Project_Start** file.

2   Expand the Browser window to fill your screen. Scroll through all of the columns.

Although you can disregard many of the columns most of the time, it's important to know where to find this information when you need it.

3   Double-click the bin called FBI Guys Clips.

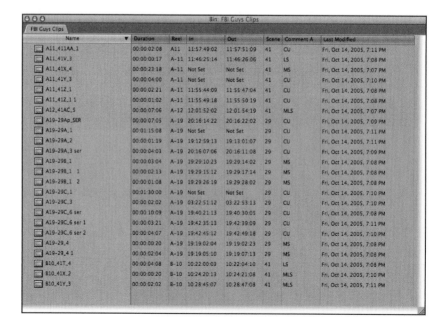

This bin has most of the columns hidden.

4   Control-click the header on the Comment A column to access the shortcut menu.

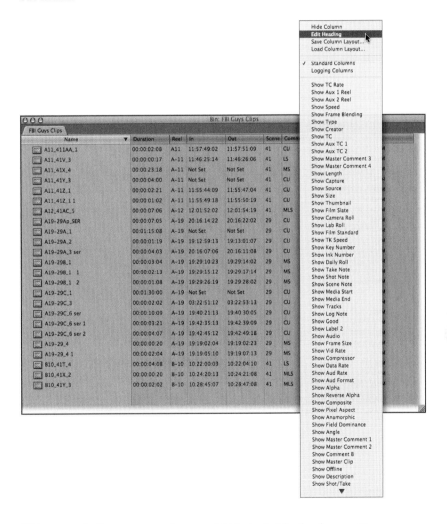

This control allows you to show and hide individual columns. You can see
there are quite a few columns to choose from. For now, do not add any
additional columns.

5 Select Edit Heading.

This allows you to rename the column header. You can only modify the heading name for certain columns.

6 Type *Shot Type* in the header area for the column.

Saving and Sorting Columns

There is no right or wrong way to use the columns in the Browser. Different editing situations require different columns to be visible or hidden at any given time. If you create a set that you would like to reuse, you can save and restore the column layout.

1 Control-click the Browser column header area and choose Save Column Layout.

2 Name the layout and save it in the Column Layouts folder in the Final Cut Pro User Data folder.

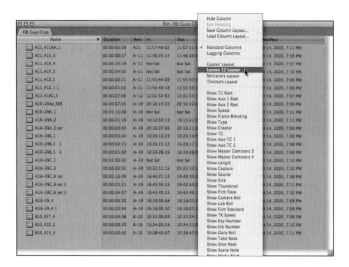

The first 10 layouts stored in this folder will appear in the shortcut menu for every browser or bin window. Choosing one will restore that set to the current window.

You can also control the browser view using sorting and secondary sorting.

3   Click the header of the Scene column.

The clips are sorted by that column. A black sort arrow appears in the header.

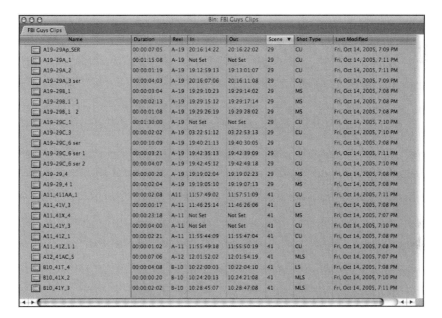

4   Click the header again.

The sort order is inverted.

5   Shift-click the header of the Shot Type column.

Now the clips are sorted by Scene first, and Shot type second. Each additional column you Shift-click will be added to the sort. You can identify the primary sort column because the Sort arrow is black, and secondary sort arrows are gray.

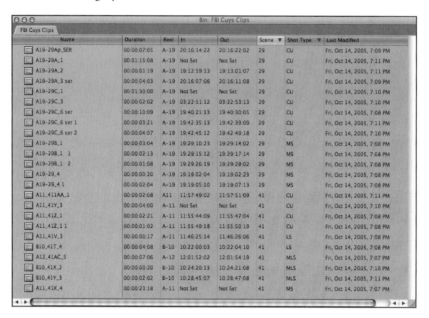

6   Click the header of the name column to reset the sorting.

Final Cut Pro 5 added one more view option in the Browser to address the common complaint that the text in the Browser was painfully small and hard to read. There are now three sizes for the text.

7   Choose View > Text Size > Medium.

The text in the Browser gets bigger. This affects all Browser windows and even changes the clip names in the Timeline.

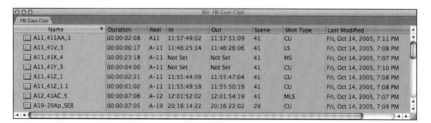

Viewing a Clip's Item Properties

Another way to view the contents of the database is to view the Item Properties window for an individual clip or sequence.

1   Select the clip **A19-29A_1** in the FBI Guys bin and choose Edit > Item Properties or press Command-9.

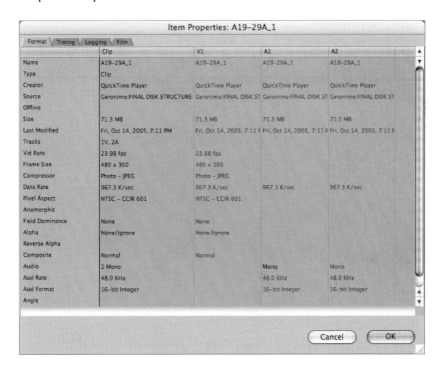

This window has four tabs that contain nearly all of the information found in the Browser columns. Because the data may be different for each of the audio or video tracks, each track is listed as its own column. Changes you make in this window will update the Browser window, and vice versa.

2   Click OK to close the Item Properties window.

Using Complex Find Operations

While you are probably familiar with how to use the Find command to locate a clip based on the text in its name, that's only the tip of the iceberg in terms of Final Cut Pro's Find capabilities. There are many advanced types of Find operations that can prove useful when you're working with a large, complex project.

Finding Unused Media

1   Choose Edit > Find, or, with the Browser active, press Command-F.

The Find window appears.

2   In the For pop-up menu, choose Unused Media.

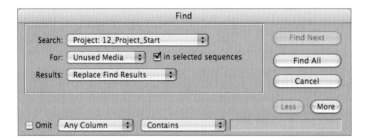

This instructs Final Cut Pro to search for clips that are not used in certain sequences. If you select the "in selected sequences" box, it will only find clips not used in currently selected sequences. If you leave the box deselected, it will find clips not used in any sequences in the active project. With this setting, you do not need to enter anything in the Search field.

3   Deselect the "in selected sequences" box and click Find All.

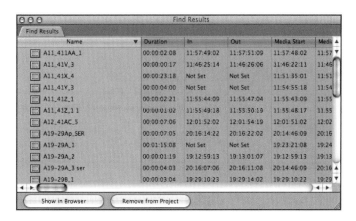

The Find Results bin appears. This is a useful way to assess which clips in your project are not currently used in any sequences. Alternatively, you can search only for Used Media.

Once you've done a Find All search and created a Find Results bin, you can further refine your results by searching within the Find Results project.

4   Leave the Find Results bin open and press Command-F again.

5   From the For pop-up menu, choose All Media.

6   From the Column pop-up menu, choose Media Start and set the middle column to Greater Than.

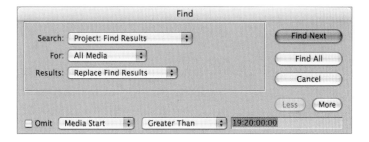

7   Enter *19:20:00:00* in the Search field and click Find All.

Be sure to type all zeros and colons for best results.

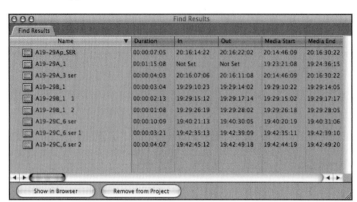

These settings will find clips with a starting timecode above the timecode you entered. This can be very helpful if you know the rough timecode number of a shot you're looking for. You can also search on the Media End column or combine them both to find a specific timecode value.

You could further combine this type of search with more criteria to find clips of a certain name, from a particular reel, or based on any of the comment fields you may have filled out during logging.

You can even omit certain criteria. The example shown in this figure is searching for clips with certain timecode and without the word "CU" in any column.

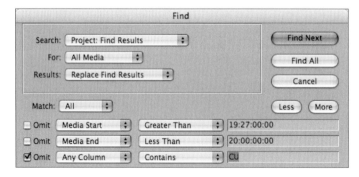

Working with Timecode

One of the most important properties of any clip is its reel and timecode information. This data is the only connection between the digitized clip and the data on the tape from which it was captured. If you modify this information, Final Cut Pro might not be able to recapture the clip. Further, if you wanted to move your sequence into another application (as you might do for color correction or other special effects), you would not be able to accurately reassemble it without the correct reel number and timecode value.

Viewing Timecode

Timecode comes in a variety of formats based primarily on the frame rate and counting method. For example, a 24 fps clip has different timecode values than a clip recorded at 60i. Likewise, clips at 29.97 fps (standard NTSC video) can be represented in two different ways: drop frame and non-drop frame.

1   Close the Find Results bin and close the FBI Guys Clips bin.

2   Choose Window > Arrange > Standard or press Control-U.

3   Double-click Gold Fever Merged to open it into the Viewer.

4   Click the View Settings button in the Viewer and choose Show Timecode Overlays.

Video track timecode ———   ——— Audio track timecode

The Viewer shows the timecode for the video and audio tracks on top of the image. Merged clips based on video and audio from different files show different timecodes for each track.

The overlays disappear when the clip is playing. You can also view a clip's timecode information in the Clip Properties window.

5   Press Command-9 or choose Edit > Item Properties.

6   Click the Timing tab.

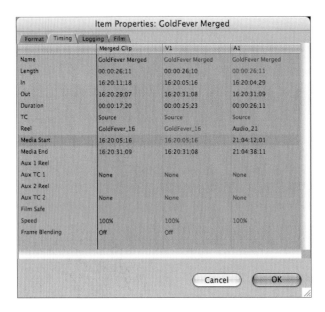

The timecode value for the first frame in the clip is shown in the Media Start row.

7   Click OK to close the Item Properties window.

Fixing a Bad Reel Number

There are occasions when you need to change this vital information. One common mistake is to neglect to change the reel number when logging multiple tapes, resulting in clips with incorrect reel numbers.

1   Double-click the Gold Fever Clips bin to open it into its own window.

2   Scroll the bin window until you can see the Reel column.

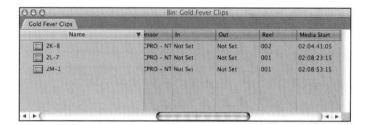

Often, you can identify clips with a faulty reel number based on the hours value in the timecode field. In this bin, the last two clips are marked reel 001, but their timecode starts with hour 02 in the Media Start column. Although this isn't a guarantee of a reel error, it can be a good indicator, since the hour indicator is often used to differentiate sequential tapes, especially those used in field production.

3   Select one of the clips with the incorrect reel number.

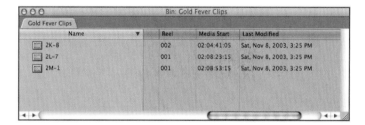

4   In the Reel column for the clip, type *002* and press Return.

> **NOTE ▶** Changes made to a clip's reel number or timecode fields actually change the media file on disk. This means that every other clip that refers to the same media file will be updated to reflect the change you make. Even other applications that can read timecode will see the new information.

5 Click OK to accept Final Cut Pro's warning that you will be changing the file on disk.

6 Select the third clip in the Gold Fever Clips bin.

7 Control-click the Reel column and choose 002 from the shortcut menu.

8 Click OK in the dialog warning you about changing the file on disk.

Modifying Timecode

Occasionally, rather than fixing the reel number, you may need to change the timecode number assigned to the clip. Although you can view the clip's current starting timecode by looking at the Media Start column, this information is not editable in the Browser or Item Properties window. You can only modify one clip's timecode at a time.

1 Open the Timecodes bin.

2 Double-click the clip **1P-1** to open it into the Viewer.

3 Choose Modify > Timecode.

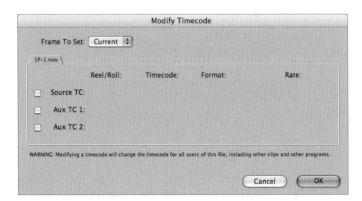

In this example, the clip was somehow erroneously reset to 00:00:00:00. Fortunately, this clip has BITC (Burned-In Time Code) so you can use that to restore the correct timecode value.

4   Select the Source TC checkbox.

5   Make sure the Frame To Set pop-up menu at the top of the window is set to Current.

This ensures that the number you enter in this dialog is assigned to the current playhead position.

6   Move the window so you can see the Viewer and enter the timecode number from the BITC in the Source Timecode field to match the number visible. If you did not adjust the clip in the Viewer, it should read 01:28:05:00.

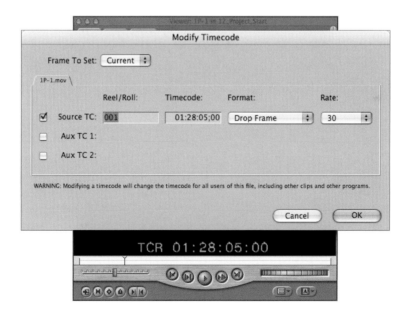

7   Choose Format > Drop Frame and leave Rate set at 30.

8   Click OK to close the dialog.

Now, you can shuttle around the clip in the Viewer and see that the Current Timecode field always accurately matches the number burned into the video.

Using Auxiliary Timecode Tracks

In addition to the primary timecode track, Final Cut Pro allows you to assign two auxiliary reel numbers and timecode tracks. This information is also written into the media file, so once you add such an auxiliary track, it will appear in any other clip that points to the same media file.

This can be essential for clips shot at one frame rate (for example, 24 fps) and then transferred to another (such as 25 fps or 29.97). Another common example is where footage from multiple sources is going to be used in a multiclip. You might have tape from three cameras, each with its own timecode. Additionally, a smart slate used during production indicates the timecode from a music playback device. Each of the clips needs to contain both sets of timecode.

You can keep the video's original timecode in the Source Timecode fields and use an Auxiliary Timecode field to store the version from the music. You can then use the Auxiliary Timecode value to sync up the clips in the multiclip, or if you're not using multiclips, you can compare the timecode values during editing to guarantee that the video is in sync with the prerecorded song.

1   In the Timecodes bin, open the clip **MCU in front of painter** into the Viewer.

2   Park the playhead on one of the first few frames, where you can see the timecode displayed on the smart slate.

3   Choose Modify > Timecode.

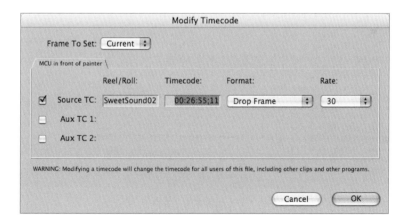

4   Select the Aux TC 1 checkbox to enable the Auxiliary timecode fields.

Type *DAT Playback TC* in the Reel field to indicate the source of this timecode.

5   In the Frame To Set pop-up menu, choose Current and leave Rate set to 30.

6   Type in the timecode number visible on the slate into the Aux TC 1 Timecode field.

7   Click OK.

Now, your clip has two timecode tracks assigned to it. You can choose which one you want to view in the Viewer and Browser windows.

8   In the Viewer, Control-click the Current Timecode field.

9   Choose Aux TC 1.

Now all editing of this clip (including exporting edit decision lists) will reference this alternate timecode value.

Viewing Alternate Timecode Formats

Final Cut Pro includes tools to view timecode in alternate ways to accommodate certain workflows with HD footage or with PAL footage that is going to
be output to film. You can view 60 fps (or 59.94 fps) footage as 30 fps, and you
can view 25 fps PAL footage as 24 fps.

You might want to view 60 fps material at 30 fps to match the display on some
DVCPRO HD decks, or if you're going to be finishing the project on SD (standard definition) video at 30 fps.

1   In the Timecodes bin, double-click **chaseSidewalk** to open it into the Viewer.

    This clip is a 60 fps DVCPRO HD clip. As you step through the clip, you
    can see that the Current Timecode field updates consecutive frames up to
    59 before rolling over to 00.

2   Control-click the Current Timecode field and choose 60 @ 30 from the
    shortcut menu.

    This instructs Final Cut Pro to display each frame number twice with an
    asterisk next to the second instance of each number.

This does not change the file or the timecode associated with the file; it only changes the way the timecode is displayed in the Viewer.

NOTE ▶ The 60 @ 30 option is only visible on clips with 60 fps or 59.94 fps timecode.

Similarly, you can choose to view 24 fps footage at 25 fps. This is commonly employed when 24 fps film material has been transferred onto 25 fps tapes (the standard PAL frame rate). This allows you to edit in a 25 fps sequence but generate a 24 fps EDL. Unlike the 60 @ 30 setting, 24 @ 25 is set in the Modify Timecode window rather than the Current Timecode field view settings.

Recording to Dual Systems

Often, your picture and sound will be recorded on separate media. This might be because the picture was recorded on film (which can't record audio) or because production logistics required recording the audio separately from the video, usually onto a DAT or hard disk recorder. This process is called dual-system recording because two devices are used (one for picture and one for audio).

If your footage was recorded in this way, an additional step is required before you can edit the footage. You must line up the audio and video elements so that lips and voices (and everything else) will play back in sync.

Syncing Clips

In most cases, dual-system media will have been shot using a slate (sometimes called a clapboard) to provide a clear frame in both picture and sound that can be easily synchronized.

1   From the Sync These Clips bin, open the clip **GoldFeverVideo**.

2   Find the exact frame where the clap stick on the slate closes and set an In point at that frame.

    Although this is a timecode slate, in this case the numbers don't correspond with the timecode in your audio clip, so you should disregard them.

3   Open the clip **GoldFeverAudio.**

4   Find the frame where the sound of the clapboard can be heard (at 21:04:13;24).

5 Set an In point at that frame.

You have now identified the same point in time on each clip.

Merging Clips

To combine these two clips into a single item for editing, use the Merge Clips command.

1 Select the two clips in the Browser window.

2 Choose Modify > Merge Clips.

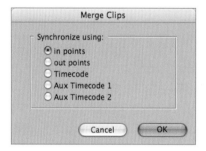

This opens the Merge Clips dialog.

3 Set the clips to synchronize based on the In points you just set.

4 Click OK.

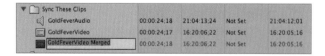

A new clip is created in the Browser in the same bin as the other two clips. This merged clip points to the two separate media files on disk.

You can combine up to 24 mono or 12 stereo audio tracks with a single video track in a merged clip.

5 Double-click the new clip to open it into the Viewer.

Because the audio clip starts before the video clip, there are transparent frames at the beginning of the clip.

From this point on, you can edit with this merged clip, and the audio and video will remain in sync.

In some cases, you will not have a slate to assist you in syncing your audio and video clips. You may, however, have identical timecode in the two clips. This can happen if the DAT player was slaved (synced) to the video camera on set, or if some other device was sending identical timecode to both camera and audio recording device. In these cases you can use Merge Clips to connect the separate audio and video files based on the timecode numbers in the clip, or by enabling one of the auxiliary timecode fields in the Modify Timecode window and entering the synchronized timecode numbers.

Then, set the Merge Clips dialog to merge based on that Aux TC field.

Syncing Clips Manually

If you have no timecode numbers or clapboard sound to help you sync your audio and video, you're going to have to do it by hand. While this may sound daunting, experienced editors frequently face such situations and know how to handle them without fear.

1   From the Browser, open the Sync Me sequence.

    This sequence contains an audio and video clip that need to be aligned.

2   Play the sequence.

    First you must determine whether the audio is early or late. In this case, it's easy to recognize that the audio is considerably early. When you're only a few frames off, it can be very difficult to tell. The best thing to do is to find a section of the clip that features a percussive sound, or at least a plosive vocal sound (such as a p, b, or t).

3   Play the clip until approximately 9 seconds in, when the bottle is put down.

This is a great place to find your sync because the glass makes a sharp sound.

4 Display Audio Waveforms by clicking the Timeline Layout Popup.

5 Locate the large burst in the audio waveform that corresponds to the bottle sound (around 07:00).

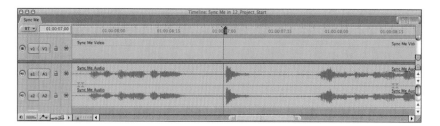

This indicates where the glass sound occurs.

6 Turn off the audio tracks by clicking the Audible button for A1 and A2.

Turning off the audio allows you to find the video frame with which you're going to sync without distraction.

7 Play the sequence until you see the frame when the bottle is put down (at approximately 01:00:09:05).

8   Drag the audio clip so the waveform burst approximately lines up with the video frame you chose. Zoom in on the Timeline if necessary.

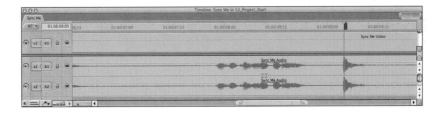

9   Turn the audio tracks back on and play around the area in question by pressing \ (backslash).

Your audio and video should be in close synchronization, but you always want to make sure they're as exact as possible.

10 Select the audio clip and type +3.

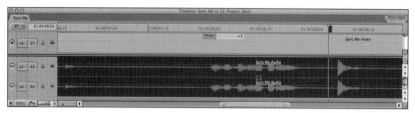

This will move the clip forward by three frames.

11 Play around again.

Does the sync appear better or worse?

12 Type -6 and play around again.

How about now? You've now heard the sync three frames past and three frames before your original position. Which of the three positions sounds most accurate? If you can't tell, you may need to move the audio clip five frames in either direction instead of three, or find a better event to sync on.

Once you find the position you think is most accurate, move the audio clip by +1 frame, and listen, then -2 frames and listen. Eventually you will find the frame that seems in perfect sync.

Before you merge the clips, watch the whole clip and look for other percussive or plosive sounds to make sure it all looks right. The larger the monitor you are using, the easier it usually is to identify correct sync.

13 Once you are happy that the clips are in sync, select the clips, choose Modify > Link, then drag the new linked clip to the Browser.

With time, you will learn to recognize when clips are in or out of sync, and when they're out, you'll be able to guess pretty accurately as to how many frames off they are.

Working with 16:9

Both high-definition video and theatrical motion pictures are almost always screened at a wide *aspect ratio*, such as 16:9 or 1.85:1. These numbers indicate the ratio of the picture's width to its height. Most standard-definition televisions, however, have an aspect ratio of 4:3. To show wide aspect ratio footage on a 4:3 television, you must use a letterbox; otherwise the image will appear stretched vertically.

Stretched (incorrect)

Letterboxed (correct)

Most video cameras give you the option of shooting in either 4:3 or 16:9 ratios, and Final Cut Pro accepts both formats. You can identify 16:9 clips by the setting of the anamorphic checkbox in the Browser columns or Item Properties dialog. If a clip appears abnormally stretched or squeezed on your computer monitor, that checkbox might be set incorrectly.

Many television programs are shot in 16:9 but broadcast in 4:3, cropping off the sides of the image. Why? The main reason is that most viewers are not yet accustomed to watching a letterboxed image on their TV sets. It's ironic that amateurs letterbox 4:3 to make it look "professional," while professionals crop 16:9 to fit the 4:3 aspect ratio.

This creates some challenges when editing a project that needs to work at both 16:9 and 4:3. Take, for example, an actor walking out of the frame—pretty common, right? But as soon as the actor leaves the 4:3 area, he is still within the 16:9 frame, so where do you make the cut? You have to decide which format should be optimized and which compromised.

Editing 16:9 Footage

Capturing and editing 16:9 material can be as simple as selecting the right Capture and Sequence settings.

1   Press the Option key and choose File > New Sequence.

The Sequence Preset editor opens.

2   From the Preset pop-up menu, choose DV NTSC 48 kHz Anamorphic.

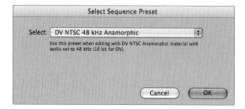

This creates a sequence ready to edit 16:9 footage.

Such a sequence will always appear stretched on a normal TV monitor (unless the monitor has a 16:9 switch). This sequence should only be used to output to a tape format that supports the widescreen format (such as DV or HD) or for output directly to a widescreen DVD.

3   Name the sequence *16:9 Sequence* and double-click it to open it into the Canvas and Timeline.

4   Open the Frame Size bin and double-click **Palm Trees**.

5   Edit the clip into the sequence.

Notice the clip accurately fills the wide aspect ratio Canvas.

6   From the Frame Size bin, drag **Bass Gtr1** into the Canvas.

Bass Gtr1 is a 4:3 clip. Notice what happens when a 4:3 clip is edited into a 16:9 sequence. The clip retains its original size and shape and is centered in the sequence. If you wanted the 4:3 clip to fill the 16:9 sequence, you would need to scale it up, and cut off the top and bottom of the image.

Editing 16:9 Footage in a 4:3 Sequence

You can easily incorporate 16:9 footage in a 4:3 sequence, automatically creating a letterbox.

1   Press the Option key and choose File > New Sequence.

     The Sequence Preset editor opens.

2   Choose DV NTSC 48 kHz.

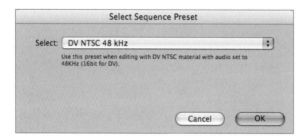

This creates a standard 4:3 sequence.

3   Name the sequence *4:3 Sequence* and double-click it to open it into the Canvas and Timeline.

4   Reload **Palm Trees** into the Viewer, if necessary.

5   Edit the clip into the sequence.

     The 16:9 clip fits into the Canvas, leaving transparent bars at the top and bottom of the screen (commonly called a letterbox).

This can be advantageous if your goal is to deliberately create a 4:3 image with a letterbox matte. You might do this if your final output was VHS or another 4:3 native format, and your source footage was all 16:9, or if you were mixing 16:9 footage into an otherwise 4:3 sequence.

However, if you actually wanted an anamorphic sequence, you cannot simply change the setting after clips have been edited in. These next steps will illustrate why.

6   Choose Sequence > Settings or press Command-0.

The Sequence Settings window opens.

7   Select the Anamorphic 16:9 checkbox and click OK.

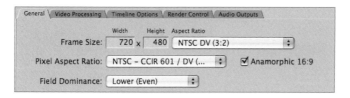

The sequence is now accurately set to 16:9, but the clip already edited in has been double-squeezed.

This can be remedied in one of two ways. Either you can delete all the items from the sequence and reedit them in, or you can reset the Aspect setting in the clip's Motion tab.

8   In the Timeline, double-click the **Palm Trees** clip.

It opens into the Viewer.

9   Switch to the Motion tab and click the Reset button for the Distort parameters.

The clip's settings are reset, and it now appears correctly matched to the 16:9 sequence.

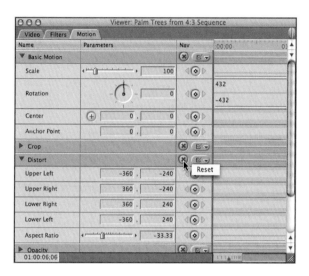

If you had multiple clips that needed to be reset, rather than opening each one individually and resetting the Motion parameters, you could change one, then copy it, select all the others, and choose Paste Attributes.

This will reset the parameters for all the pasted clips in one operation.

Using a native anamorphic sequence for your 16:9 clips allows you to preserve the maximum image quality and delays any cropping or converting until the very end of the process.

If, once your show is complete, you need to create a letterboxed version for any reason, just drop your 16:9 sequence into a new 4:3 timeline and voilá! Best of all, with most codecs, no rendering will be required.

24p Editing Basics

For many years, video makers have strived to simulate the characteristics of film to help lend their low-budget productions high-budget cinematic flair. It's not that film is inherently superior to video, but that elusive "film look" carries with it the cachet and magic of the Hollywood dream factory.

One of the most noticeable and significant differences between film and video is the frame rate at which it is displayed. While video typically runs at 25 or 30 interlaced frames per second, film is projected at 24 full frames per second.

Modern video formats now have the ability to operate at 24 full frames per second (commonly called 24p). However, traditional video equipment—especially the hundreds of millions of televisions in use around the world—still operates at 25 or 30 interlaced frames per second.

Whether you're editing a show that originated on a 24p format (including 35mm film) or one that intends to output onto a 24p format, you should become a little familiar with navigating back and forth between the 24p world and the traditional interlaced worlds of NTSC and PAL.

Converting 24p to 29.97

Unless you have lots of hard drive space and special hardware, you will need to do your editing work at less than full film or high-definition (HD) video resolutions. Most producers have their material transferred to standard-definition video. The process of transferring film to video is known as *telecine*. HD material transferred to standard-definition videotape is called a *downconvert*. In either case, how do you get 24 fps to play at NTSC's 30 fps and not have it look like a Keystone Cops comedy?

Although we often refer to NTSC video as running at 30 fps, it actually runs slightly slower. This became necessary when NTSC color television standards were developed and had to be compatible with black and white television sets. Never mind the actual details; what is important to know is that it runs at $30 \times 1000 \div 1001$, or 29.97 fps.

When film is run through a telecine machine or when 24p video is downconverted to NTSC, it also runs at slightly less than 24 fps. The adjustment or *pulldown* is $24 \times 1000 \div 1001$, or 23.976 (commonly referred to as 23.98) fps. Most 24p video in NTSC countries is shot at this pulled-down speed, so there is no difference between the high-definition and standard-definition running times. Some new 24p DV camcorders also record at 23.98 fps.

To understand how this pulldown works, let's pretend that video runs at 30 fps and film at 24 fps. How do you get one second of film (or 24p video) to equal one second of standard-definition video? It doesn't make sense at first, because it doesn't divide up evenly: 30 divided by 24 equals 1.25.

The trick is that NTSC video is made up of two fields per frame, or 60 fields per second. In the early days of television, a cathode-ray gun was used to project the image onto the phosphorous surface of the screen, but the picture would flicker at 30 fps. The solution was to draw every other line in one pass, known as a *field*, then fill in the remaining lines on the second field. So we can think of NTSC video running at 60 fields per second. Does this help our mathematical dilemma? Not really: 60 divided by 24 equals 2.5, and you wouldn't want to cut frames in half. However, if we alternate between copying each frame of film (or 24p video) to two fields and then three fields of NTSC video, we can successfully compensate for the frame rate/field rate ratio.

This is known as 3:2 pulldown, although it would be more accurate to call it 2:3:2:3 pulldown, because that is what is really going on. The start of this 2:3:2:3 pattern (or *cadence*) is called the A frame, and this is copied to two NTSC video fields. Next comes the B frame, which goes onto the next three video fields. Since at this point we don't have a complete video frame, we need to copy the next, or C, frame to two video fields. Finally, the D frame is copied onto the remaining three video fields. Now we have four frames of film, or 24p video, conformed to five whole frames (that's 10 fields) of NTSC video; 10 divided by 4 equals 2.5.

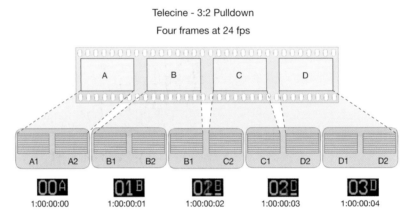

Telecine - 3:2 Pulldown

Four frames at 24 fps

Five video frames at 29.97 fps

Timecode and A Frames

The relationship between 24 fps media and 30 fps video becomes even more important when working with timecode. Telecine and downconverting use 30 fps non-drop-frame timecode. Every A frame—the start of the 2:3:2:3 pattern—must land on a timecode frame that ends with either a 0 or a 5. In other words, an A frame should show up on video frames where the timecode ends on 00, 05, 10, and so on. It is also important to start every clip on an A frame. If you reverse telecine (convert from 30 fps back to 24 fps) a batch of clips with Cinema Tools, it looks for the A frame using timecode, and if any clip doesn't start on an A frame, it trims a few frames off the head so that it does start on an A frame.

The importance of starting every clip on an A frame is maintained through Final Cut Pro when the Film Safe option is selected in the Browser. This way, if the sequences are run through the Media Manager and the clips are trimmed, they will always start on an A frame.

Viewing Edge Code and Timecode

You may have seen clips with numbers all over the image area. These numbers are windows into what is normally invisible—the film edge code, and the video and audio timecodes. Having timecode and edge codes burned onto the image area helps us see that the logs and lists for the offline edit match up to the original media.

Sound for film and for 24p video shot for theatrical release is usually recorded on a separate recorder. This requires tracking yet another set of timecode numbers from the audio recorder.

Working with film requires tracking even more numbers. During the manufacturing process, numbers and bar codes are exposed to the edge of the film. When the film is developed, these become visible and are used to match the negative to the final edit. These numbers are called keynumbers, or keycode. And if a positive workprint for projection is made, it may have another set of numbers applied between the sprocket holes with a special numbering machine. These numbers are known as ink numbers, or Acmade code, named after a popular film numbering machine. Although keynumbers are added by the manufacturer and are arbitrary, ink numbers can represent daily rolls, scenes, or other specific information that helps bring order to the otherwise chaotic mix of codes and numbers used in film editing.

Working with so many numbers on the image might seem distracting, but they are considered essential in film and 24p offline editing. Traditionally, this information is burned into the video image during the telecine or downconvert process, but Final Cut Pro offers another option.

You can enter the information into the Cinema Tools database and view it laid over the video images. This allows you to hide all those codes when you're concentrating on the story, and display them when you need to verify that all the numbers are lining up correctly.

1   Open the Gold Fever Clips bin and double-click **2K-8**.

2   Turn on Video Overlays by choosing View > Show Overlays or pressing Control-Option-W.

3 Turn on the Keycode and Ink Numbers overlays by choosing View > Timecode Overlays > Keycode, and View > Timecode Overlays > Ink Numbers.

Keycode Numbers

NOTE ▶ This clip does not have any embedded ink numbers, so turning this on has no effect.

Now the overlays display all of those crazy numbers so you can verify that your edit lists are accurate.

Editing 24 fps Originals at 29.97

Film and 24p video can be edited in a 29.97 fps NTSC video project. This process is known as matchback. For film, videotape numbers and timecode are matched back to camera rolls and keynumbers. In the case of 24p video, the 30 fps timecode from the downconverted video is matched back to the original 24 fps timecode. Although considered inferior to editing at 24 fps, hundreds of made-for-cable movies as well as theatrically released films have been successfully finished this way.

One problem when editing a matchback project is that the 3:2 cadence is often changed during editing. This means that the predictable AA BB BC CD DD pattern can break. For example, when you make an edit, the outgoing frame of the last shot may be a DD frame and the incoming frame of the next shot might start on a BC frame. This makes it difficult to figure out where the original frames should start and end.

Another problem is that the software must check the running time and make adjustments to keep from drifting out of sync. This is usually noted in the cut list as a one-frame adjustment, but it is not always apparent.

There have been many attempts at improving the process, but the fact that so many matchback projects are finished without major problems attests to its effectiveness. Successful matchback projects can often be credited to the skill of negative cutters and to online editors who faithfully match the offline edit as closely as possible.

Using Film-Safe Editing

The Film-Safe feature is actually used for any 24 fps material when edited in a 30 fps sequence, whether it originated on film or video. For example, footage shot on 24p HD is often dubbed to 30 fps SD NTSC tape for editing. Once you've made your editing decisions, an EDL is created, and the original HD footage is conformed to match the edit, creating a 24p master for broadcast, duplication, or printing to film.

Because there are duplicate frames in the NTSC version (added during the 24-fps-to-30-fps conversion process), it is possible for you to make edits on such new imaginary frames (that don't exist in the 24p original). This would cause problems when trying to conform the HD footage. However, you can prevent this by activating the Film Safe setting for your clips.

1 Select the three clips in the Gold Fever Clips bin.

2 Scroll through the Browser columns horizontally until the Film Safe column is visible (in the last column).

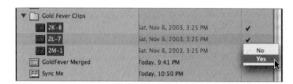

3 Control-click the Film Safe column and choose Yes.

A checkbox will appear in all of the selected clips.

Although Final Cut Pro will let you make edits on these imaginary frames, when you perform a Media Manager trimming operation on your completed sequence, this setting will ensure that the trimmed clips will always begin and end on real frames, not imaginary ones.

Returning 29.97 fps to 24 fps

As you saw, it takes some doing to get film telecined or 24p HD video down-converted to standard-definition NTSC video. Now, in order to work at 24 fps, we need to undo all that.

Final Cut Pro can remove the extra video fields (added during the telecine process) during capture when it is used with special video hardware like the Aurora Film IgniterX and the AJA KONA video cards. It can also capture directly to 23.98 fps from digital video if it was recorded using the advanced 2:3:3:2 pulldown setting found in some Panasonic cameras (see the following section).

Alternatively, Final Cut Pro (with the help of Cinema Tools) can reverse telecine 30 fps clips to their original 24p state, accurately disassembling and reassembling the frames.

1   Select both clips in the Telecined Clips bin.

2   Select Tools > Cinema Tools Reverse Telecine.

That's it. You have now converted both of those 29.97 fps clips into 24 fps clips. You can verify that by looking at the timecode for those clips.

3   Select one of the clips in the Telecined Clips bin.

4   Choose Edit > Item Properties > Format (or press Command-9).

The Vid Rate column now reads 24 fps.

5   Click OK to close the Item Properties window, and choose Modify >
Timecode.

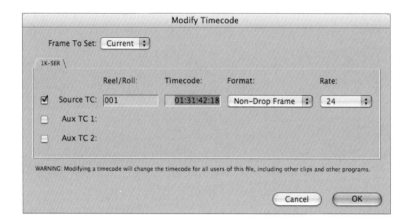

The custom timecode associated with the clip is still there, but has been
converted into 24 fps timecode.

WARNING ▶ This operation is not reversible. It permanently alters the
media files on your disk! This is one of the most potentially destructive
commands in Final Cut Pro, and what's more, there's no confirmation dialog. Also, this command will reverse-telecine files that were never telecined
in the first place. Any 30 fps file will be modified and data will be lost! You
have been warned!

If you want more control over the reverse-telecine process, you can use the
Cinema Tools application. There you can choose to make new clips (instead of
changing the 29.97 originals) and reverse-telecine to 23.98 instead of 24 fps.
For more information on using Cinema Tools, see Chapter 15.

Using 2:3:3:2 Advanced Pulldown (Panasonic 24p)
In order to convert 3:2 pulldown material to 24 fps QuickTime files, you
have to take apart and reassemble video frames to recover the original film
or 24p frames. In the case of DV, this involves uncompressing video frames,
separating the frames into individual video fields, rebuilding new frames, and
finally recompressing the video. All this takes time and there is a chance of

image degradation, although due to the quality of Apple's DV codec, you will probably never notice it.

The 2:3:3:2 pulldown used on Panasonic 24p cameras, also called advanced pull-down, does not straddle the C frame between two video frames. Only the BC video frame needs to be removed during reverse telecine. This avoids the need to reassemble frames to get to the original progressive frames. An added benefit is that Final Cut Pro can capture directly to 24 fps. Even if you need to postprocess the clips in Final Cut Pro or Cinema Tools, it is faster than working with 3:2 pulldown material.

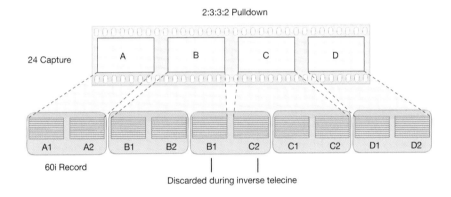

There is one disadvantage to 2:3:3:2 pulldown: a somewhat greater amount of visible motion jitter compared to 3:2 pulldown. However, 3:2 and even film projected in theaters shows motion jitter on certain speeds of camera pans and other camera movement. Furthermore, most people can't see the difference between 3:2 and 2:3:3:2 video.

> **NOTE** ▶ The Cinema Tools Reverse Telecine command will automatically detect 2:3:3:2 files and reverse-telecine them correctly.

Capturing to 24p with Final Cut Pro

Choosing the settings for capturing 2:3:3:2 media is relatively easy. If you don't already have a capture setting, simply modify one of the DV capture settings and check the "Remove Advanced Pulldown (2:3:3:2) From DV-25 and DV-50 Sources" checkbox in the Capture Preset Editor. Final Cut Pro will identify the BC frames and remove them before writing the QuickTime movie at 23.98 fps.

If you have already captured 2:3:3:2 advanced pulldown clips at 29.97, you can use Final Cut Pro to remove the pulldown.

1   Select the clips in the Advanced Pulldown bin.

2   Choose Tools > Remove Advanced Pulldown.

The clips are automatically converted to 23.98 fps. This command will not modify clips that do not contain the 2:3:3:2 advanced pulldown.

WARNING ▶ This command modifies the actual media files on disk and throws away data from the original file. Use with caution!

Audio Issues with Reverse Telecine

Typically, projects that are going to be finished on film are edited at 24 fps, while projects to be finished on 24 fps HD are edited at 23.98. Final Cut Pro and Cinema Tools can accommodate either speed, but special consideration should be given to audio.

When Cinema Tools reverse-telecines the clips to 24 fps, it pulls up the audio to maintain sync. This means that the audio on 24 fps clips that were synced in telecine will have a sampling rate of $48,000 \times 1001 \div 1000$, or 48,048 Hz. However, if the original production audio is synchronized separately from telecine in Final Cut Pro, it must remain at the original 48 kHz sampling rate.

Mixing these sampling rates shouldn't present any problems, though it does add some load to the processor. The playback quality should be set to low or the audio may need to be rendered. Don't worry about low-quality audio on your finished project; Final Cut Pro resamples and mixes down in high quality when outputting to tape or QuickTime files.

Editing 24 fps Footage

It's important to make any changes to your footage's frame rate before beginning your edit. This is so you can ensure that your sequence and source clips have matching frame rates. Once you have converted all of your source clips to 24p, you must create a sequence with the correct settings.

1   Create a new sequence.

2   Choose Sequence > Settings.

3   Click the Load Sequence Preset button at the bottom of the window.

4   Choose DV NTSC 48 kHz - 24 from the pop-up menu and click OK.

    You are now set to edit your reverse-telecined clips.

Watching 24 fps reverse-telecined clips on a computer monitor is just as smooth as viewing NTSC clips. However, achieving smooth playback on an NTSC monitor requires special attention.

When a clip is set to play at 24 fps, it really does play back at 24 fps, but when it is output via FireWire to an NTSC monitor, Final Cut Pro duplicates frames as needed in order to make up the 29.97 fps that the monitor needs. Which frames are duplicated is not always predictable. The result is a jitter that is most apparent on certain speeds of camera pans and movement in the frame. This artifact will not be present when you finish your project at 24 fps on film or HD, but can be distracting when monitoring during the edit.

You can control how Final Cut Pro gets from 24 fps to 29.97 fps by choosing the pulldown setting in the System Preferences window.

1   Choose Final Cut Pro > System Settings.

2   Choose the Playback Control tab.

3   Set the Pulldown Pattern pop-up menu to 2:3:2:3.

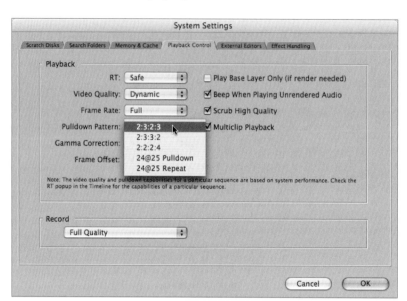

This setting provides the smoothest playback, but is also the most demanding on the processor. If you are playing back material originally captured using the Advanced Pulldown method, you can set this control to 2:3:3:2. Alternatively, for maximum performance, you can set this control to 2:2:2:4, which simply adds one extra frame at the end of each cycle. This setting will cause the most visible stutter on the NTSC monitor, but is the least taxing on the CPU.

Video cards like the Aurora IgnitorX and AJA KONA will reinsert the pull-down on output without requiring any help from the CPU.

What About PAL?

To the user, working in PAL is almost exactly the same as working in NTSC, though the math required is quite different. Also, you must use different settings to account for the other ways that PAL differs from NTSC.

Getting from 24 fps to 25 fps

When 24 fps material such as film is telecined or downconverted to 25 fps PAL video, it is usually done at a pulled-up speed of 25 ÷ 24, which results in everything running approximately 4 percent fast. Although this is barely noticeable visually, it can often be detected by the pitch shift that occurs in the audio. Some telecine machines can automatically compensate for this pitch shifting.

Alternatively, the telecine can maintain the original 24 fps frame rate. It involves inserting an additional video field every 12 frames and is known as a 24&1 transfer. However, cut lists on 24&1 transfers can be accurate to only plus or minus one frame, and you cannot use reverse telecine to get rid of the extra fields. This method is seldom used in editing.

Editing 24 @ 25

If you plan to edit your footage at 25 fps, but at a later time you're going to want to matchback to the 24 fps master (whether it's on film or 24p HD), you must choose the correct sequence preset to edit with.

1   Create a new sequence.

2   Choose Sequence > Settings.

3   Click the Load Sequence Preset button at the bottom of the window.

4   Choose DV PAL 48kHz 24 @ 25 from the pop-up menu and click OK.

    This sequence will appear to have a 24 fps frame rate, but all the timecode windows (and EDLs) will display at 25 fps. This allows you to edit in 24 fps, but the timecode will always match the 25 fps timecode on your PAL source tapes.

Getting from 25 fps to 24 fps

Final Cut Pro and Cinema Tools can convert PAL clips back to 24 fps, although, instead of performing a reverse telecine where the fields are deconstructed and reconstructed, the clips are conformed. Conforming a clip means that each frame is given an equal duration (in fractions of seconds) based on the frame rate you specify. For example, if you conform a clip with 480 frames to 24 fps, each frame is assigned a duration of 1/24th of a second and thus the clip becomes 2 seconds long. This changes the duration of the clip, thereby undoing the 4 percent change that occurred during the telecine.

Outputting 24 fps Footage to a PAL Monitor

Just like outputting your 24fps video to an NTSC monitor, Final Cut Pro must add in extra frames to make the video play back on an external PAL monitor. You can choose quality or performance using the Pulldown setting in the Playback tab of the System Preferences window.

1   Chose Final Cut Pro > System Settings.

2   Choose the Playback Control tab.

3   Set the Pulldown Pattern pop-up menu to 24@25 Pulldown for the smoothest looking playback.

4   Set the Pulldown Pattern pop-up menu to 24@25 Repeat for better performance.

Lesson Review

1.   How do you customize the name of a Browser column?

2.   How do you sort a bin by more than one column?

3.   How many timecode tracks can a clip have?

4.   What is 60 @ 30 Timecode?

5.   How do you sync clips whose video and audio are in different files?

6.   What happens when you edit 16:9 footage into a 4:3 sequence?

7.   How is 24p material converted to 29.97?

8.   How is 29.97 material converted back to 24p?

9.   What is Film Safe editing?

10. What is Advanced Pulldown?

Answers

1. Control-click the column header and choose Edit Heading (only available on Comment fields).

2. Shift-click additional column headers to perform an secondary sort.

3. Three: one Source timecode, and two Auxiliary Timecode tracks.

4. A way of viewing 60 fps timecode at 30 fps. Every frame number is doubled and the doubled frame contains a trailing asterisk.

5. By using the Merge Clips command.

6. It is automatically letterboxed.

7. Each frame is spread across multiple fields in one of several *cadences*.

8. The cadence is identified and the duplicates removed. This is called reverse telecine.

9. Film Safe editing prevents you from making edits on imaginary frames.

10. Advanced Pulldown is specific to Panasonic 24p cameras and is an alternate cadence that is especially easy to reverse, at the expense of a minor quality loss.

13

Lesson Files	Lesson Project Files > Lesson_13 > 13_Project_Start
Media	Media > Friends Of The Family, FOF OfflineRT
Time	This lesson takes approximately 45 minutes to complete.
Goals	Learn when and how to use the Make Offline command
	Use the Reconnect Media command to resolve offline files
	Use the Source column to identify a clip's media file
	Use Reveal in Finder to find a clip in the Finder
	Consolidate media to move a project across computers
	Trim a sequence to delete unneeded media
	Create offline resolution clips
	Replace offline resolution clips with full-resolution clips
	Create an offline sequence to prepare for capturing full-resolution clips

Lesson **13**

Managing Media

One of the most satisfying things about working in a nonlinear editing system like Final Cut Pro is that you almost never have to think about the physical realities of film and tape. Inside Final Cut Pro, you can rename the clips, reuse them, cut them up, even combine and distort them using special effects. Because Final Cut Pro is entirely nondestructive, nothing ever happens to the weighty media files in your Capture Scratch folder. They remain intact and safely backed up on your original source tapes.

But sooner or later you're going to have to face those files, either to make room for a new show, or to move your project from one system to another, or perhaps to take advantage of the offline/online model of editing.

Understanding the Relationship Between Clips and Media

Your media files are usually just QuickTime movies stored on your hard drive. There's nothing to stop you from moving them around or deleting them in the Finder, but it's not a good idea to do so. Your Final Cut Pro project relies on those media files, and if you move them around or manipulate them outside Final Cut Pro, you may be in for a surprise. Whenever Final Cut Pro opens a project (or whenever you return to an open project in Final Cut Pro from another application), it scans your hard drive to check that all of the files referenced by the project are present. It also verifies that they are the same size and shape that they were in the last time you opened the project. If any files are missing or have been changed, you get a warning message:

You are given the choice to ignore the files (by checking the appropriate box in the Forget Files area), reconnect the missing files, or continue with them *offline*. When used in a sequence, the Timeline bars of offline clips are white; in the Browser, offline clips' icons have a slash through them.

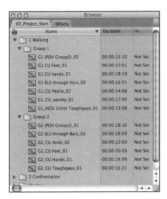

You can continue to edit your project, temporarily ignoring the missing files. This is your only choice if the needed files are on a disk that is temporarily unavailable and you plan to reconnect or recapture them later. However, playing across an offline clip shows the offline screen in the Canvas or Viewer.

Search Folders

Final Cut Pro 5 introduced a new tool to prevent offline clips from occurring in the first place. You can specify folders for Final Cut Pro to search automatically whenever it can't find a file. If you're a mobile editor, frequently working on different systems, this may not be very helpful; but if you mainly work on one Mac, and organize your media intelligently, this can keep you from ever seeing that Offline Files dialog.

1   Choose Final Cut Pro > System Settings.

2   Click the Search Folders tab.

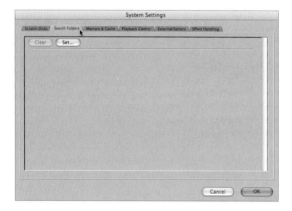

3   Click the Set button.

4   Navigate to the folder where you store all of your media (for example, your Documents folder, or the root of your media drive) and click Choose.

You can add as many search folders as you like. Whenever a project includes files that may be missing, Final Cut Pro will first look in these folders before bothering you with the Offline Files dialog.

5   Click OK to close the System Settings window.

Forcing Clips Offline

There are some occasions when you will want to deliberately place clips offline. For example, if you have an effects shot that is being re-delivered from your compositor, you might want to take the previous version offline.

1   Open **13_Project_Start**.

2   Open the Edit 1 sequence.

3   In the Timeline, select G1 CU Feet_01.

4   Choose Modify > Make Offline.

The Make Offline dialog opens.

You are presented with a choice to leave the media file where it was on the disk, to move it to the Trash, or to delete it.

NOTE ▶ Be very careful with this function! If you delete files this way, they will be gone forever. Also, if there are other affiliate clips in your project that point to the same media file, they will be placed offline as well.

5   Select "Leave Them on the Disk" and click OK.

The offline clip should remain selected in the Timeline, but it now shows as white, and the affiliate clip in the Browser has a red slash through it.

Reconnecting Offline Files

When faced with an offline file, you can repair it at any time (providing that the corresponding media file exists on your disk) using the Reconnect Media command.

1 Select the offline clip **G1 CU Feet_01**in the Browser.

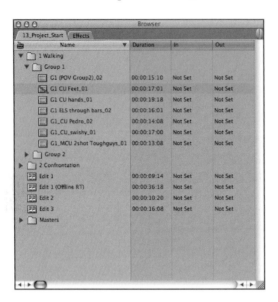

2 Choose File > Reconnect Media.

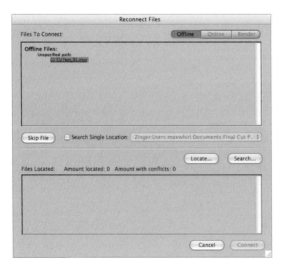

The Reconnect function was completely rebuilt for Final Cut Pro 5 and, although it is more robust than in previous versions, it is also a lot more complicated.

First, notice the three buttons at the top of the dialog. These buttons allow you to reconnect your offline, online, and render files separately. This project doesn't have any online or render files, so those buttons are dimmed.

The upper pane in the dialog lists the missing files, grouped by their last known location. The first file in the list is highlighted, and you can choose to skip, locate, or search for this missing file.

If you click the Search button, Final Cut Pro will scan the disks identified in the Search Location pop-up menu and attempt to locate the missing file.

3   Deselect the Search Single Location checkbox.

> **NOTE ▶** It is easy to forget to deselect this setting, which means the search feature won't find files you are sure are on your disk. Don't fret; just deselect the box and search again.

4   Click the Locate button and click OK.

5   Navigate to Friends Of The Family media folder and find the clip **G1 CU Feet_01**.

In this case, you are going to reconnect to a new version of the clip.

6   Select the file **G1 CU Feet_01** and click Choose, then click Connect.

Ordinarily, you can leave the Matched Name Only box selected, so all files without names identical to the ones you're searching for will be grayed out, preventing you from selecting them by mistake.

The offline clip **G1 CU Feet_01** in the Browser is now reconnected to the original media file of the same name on your hard drive. The red slash is gone, and the affiliate clip in the sequence **Edit 1** is updated as well.

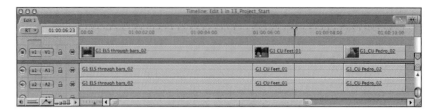

Reconnecting Online Clips

Another way to complete this same procedure would be to simply select the original online clip and choose Reconnect Media without making it offline first. This allows you to replace the media associated with a clip without first making it offline.

You performed the task in two steps here to illustrate all of the available options.

Deleting Media for Unused Clips

Another reason you might choose to make clips offline is to save disk space. If your project includes clips that you are not using, you can delete the media files associated with them to recover storage space or just to tidy up your hard disk. While you can just delete files in the Finder, it may be difficult to determine exactly which files are safe to remove. The following procedure prevents you from accidentally deleting a file that is used in your show.

1   Select the sequences **Edit 1, Edit 2**, and **Edit 3** in the Browser.

2   Perform a Find by pressing Command-F or choosing Edit > Find.

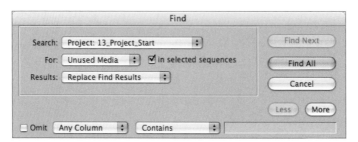

3   In the Find dialog, choose Unused Media and click the option "in selected sequences" to select it. Then click Find All.

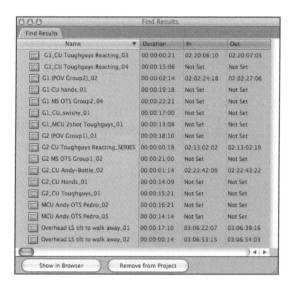

NOTE ▶   If your Find dialog has search criteria still active from any previous search, click Less to disable the additional criteria and return the dialog to its default state.

4   Select all of the clips in the Find Results bin.

5   Choose Make Offline from the shortcut menu or from the Modify menu.

To delete the clips, you could choose either Delete from Disk or Move to Trash. In either case, the timecode information associated with the clips remains so you can recapture them at any time. Just don't delete the offline clips from the Final Cut Pro project.

6   Click Cancel and close the Find Results bin.

Locating a Clip's Media File

The procedures described so far have focused on modifying the relationship between a clip and its media file. Sometimes you may want to simply identify a clip's media file on disk.

This can be useful for both offline and online clips. When you encounter offline clips in your project, you may not know why those files are not available. Sometimes, an external hard drive containing the media might not have mounted; or maybe a file or folder got renamed or moved. When moving a project from one location to another, it is fairly common to encounter some clips that have lost links to their corresponding media files.

One trick that can help you track down the correct media for an offline clip is to check the Source column in the Browser.

1   Control-click the Browser column and choose Show Source from the shortcut menu.

2   This column provides the path to the media file associated with the clip. If the clip is missing, this column provides the path to the last known location of the file. If you manually forced the clip offline, it will simply report that the clip is offline. Still, for missing clips, this might help identify what disk is unmounted or provide other clues to the proper media file.

If you want to find on a disk the file associated with any clip (online or offline), the Reveal in Finder command gets you there in a hurry.

3   Control-click **G1 CU hands_01** in the Browser and choose Reveal in Finder or choose View > Reveal in Finder.

The Finder window containing the selected clip is brought to the front.

This command can be used on offline clips as well, but if the media file is nowhere to be found, nothing happens at all.

NOTE ▸ Reveal in Finder may give unexpected results when used with merged clips or multiclips.

Using the Media Manager

The Media Manager is Final Cut Pro's versatile and comprehensive media manipulation tool.

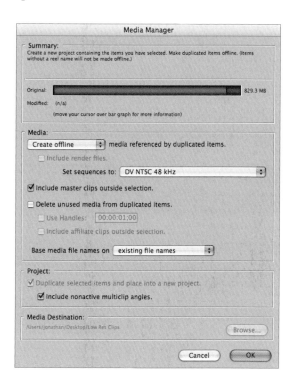

Whether you are moving your project from one computer to another, trying to eliminate clips and files you're not using, preparing a sequence for output, or even recompressing a group of files from one codec to another, the Media Manager is your one-stop shop.

Consolidating Media

When you need to move a project from one computer to another, you may not know where all of your media resides. Although most files are probably in your Capture Scratch folder, there may be a graphic or still file in another location. Sound effects files may be extracted from CD and stored in yet another location. Rather than manually scouring your disk for related files, you can be sure not to miss anything (and avoid grabbing files you don't need) by using the Media Manager tool.

1 Press Command-A to select everything in your Browser.

2 Choose File > Media Manager.

3 In the Media section, choose Copy from the pop-up menu.

This will duplicate all the media associated with the selected items (in this case, the entire project) and place them in a new location.

4 Click the Include Render Files checkbox to select it.

5 At the bottom of the window in the Media Destination section, click the Browse button and select a location on your disk for the copied files. Create a new folder for the copied media.

To move your files from one computer to another, you typically would want to set this destination to a removable or external hard disk that you could move to a new station.

6 In the Media section, deselect the "Delete unused media from duplicated items" checkbox.

In this example, you want the project on the new computer to be identical to the previous version so you do not want to delete anything.

7   Leave the "Base media file names" on pop-up menu set to "existing file names".

8   Be sure the "Duplicate selected items and place into a new project" check-box is selected.

This last setting creates a new project on your destination volume that points to the new versions of the media files. Although this step is not required (you could manually copy your existing project file in the Finder), this ensures that the new project will not have any offline files, and you won't have to reconnect media when the project gets to the new workstation.

The summary at the top of the window details your operation. The size of the bars indicates the relative amount of disk space your media is occupying. The top bar is the current state, and the bottom bar shows what will happen after you complete the Media Manager operation. Because in this example you are not deleting anything, the two bars are identical.

9   Click OK.

Immediately, you are prompted with a Save dialog, asking you to name and save the new project file. Save it on the same disk as the new media.

10   Click Save.

The program will then perform the Media Manager operation and open the new project in the Browser.

11   In the new project, open the sequences and clips to confirm that the new project is an identical copy of the old project. Then close the new project.

Moving Media

If you have limited disk space, or you are consolidating your media onto a single disk (as you might do to prepare for backing up a project to DVD), you can choose Move instead of Copy in the Media Manager.

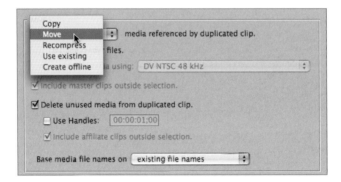

With this setting, your original media files will be consolidated into a single location, and the original files will be deleted. You will not wind up with two copies of your files.

Trimming Sequences in Media Manager

This type of trimming has nothing to do with adjusting edit points, but rather is a way to eliminate excess media after your sequence has been completed. This usually should not be done until you have completely finished making major editorial changes.

1   Select sequences **Edit 2** and **Edit 3**.

   The operation will be applied only to the media referenced in these two sequences.

2   Control-click the selected items and choose Media Manager.

3   In the Media pop-up menu, choose Copy.

NOTE ▶ Although Final Cut Pro will let you choose Move or Use Existing to modify existing media files, doing so when trimming clips is extremely dangerous. If a power failure or crash occurs during the operation, your files could be left in an unusable state, requiring you to recapture all of your media. When trimming, always create new files. Once the operation is complete, you can delete the original media.

4   Select the checkbox marked "Delete unused media from duplicated items".

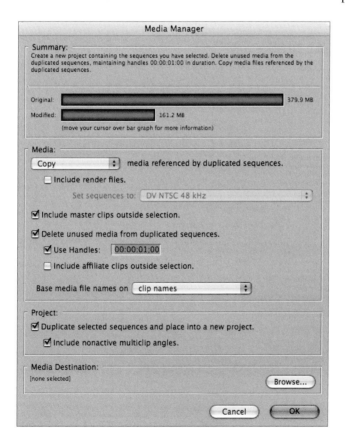

When you select this checkbox, the summary section at the top of the dialog changes dramatically. Now, the modified media bar is much smaller

than the original. This difference reflects the media outside of the In and
Out points of the clips used in the two selected sequences.

5   Select the Use Handles checkbox and set the value to *1:00*.

Although presumably you are completely done editing, there could be an
emergency or problem that might require a tiny adjustment to your edit.
Adding a little bit of wiggle room is a good way to accommodate such an
unforeseen issue if one should arise after this operation is completed.

6   Deselect the "Include affiliate clips outside selection" checkbox.

If this checkbox is selected, the Media Manager will scan the rest of
your project for any other uses of the clips contained in your selected
sequences. If such clips exist, and they have In or Out points set, the
Media Manager will include that section in the newly created clips. This
means that you will not save as much space as you would by ignoring
those clips.

Because you specified Copy for this operation, there is no harm in ignoring
this additional media. If you had specified Move or Use Existing (instead of
Copy), then you would be permanently deleting the media that you might
be planning to use in another sequence.

7   Select the "Duplicate selected Items and place into a new project" checkbox.

This will create a new project containing only the selected sequences and
pointing to the new, trimmed media.

8   Set your destination and click OK.

9   Name the new project file and click Save.

After the files are processed, the new project is automatically opened. If
you do not plan to make any additional changes or use any of the media
from the old project, you can select all the items in the old project and use
the Make Offline command to delete the media files from your disk.

NOTE ▶   In this case, do not delete these files because they will be
required later in this lesson.

Working with Low- vs. High-Resolution Clips

Many times it is impractical to make all of your editing decisions using full-resolution media files. For example, if your original media was HD resolution captured using a PCI card, you may want to do your editing on another station that does not have that card installed.

Alternatively, you may want to save disk space by working in a lower-resolution format. This allows you to store more hours of media on your disk. Also, because lower-resolution files are less taxing on a computer's CPU, you can work on a less powerful workstation and achieve more real-time effects than you could with your full-resolution media.

In this workflow, once you've made all of the editing decisions in the low-res version, you return to the full-resolution media to create the final version for output. Working in the low-resolution mode is sometimes called *offline editing*, and working with the full-resolution clips is called *online editing* (or just *onlining*).

> **NOTE ▶** Do not confuse offline and online editing with the concept of offline and online clips, as described in the section "Understanding the Relationship Between Clips and Media," earlier in this lesson.

Creating Low-Resolution Clips

In order to perform the offline edit, you must have a copy of your clips in a reduced-quality format. If the original format is DV, your offline format is most likely going to be Offline RT (Photo JPEG). If the original is uncompressed SD, you could still use Offline RT, but you might just reduce the resolution to DV, so you could still work with a relatively high-quality image that can be viewed in an external NTSC or PAL monitor. If the original source is HD, you could create an offline clip in uncompressed SD, DV, Offline RT, or even a lower-bandwidth variety of HD such as DVCPRO HD.

If your clips are already captured, you can convert them to your offline version using the Media Manager.

1   In **13_Project_Start**, select the Masters bin.

2 Choose File > Media Manager.

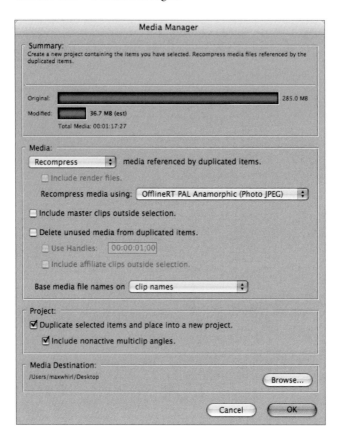

3 In the Media pop-up menu, choose Recompress.

The Recompress Media Using pop-up menu now becomes active. In this menu, you can choose the format for your offline clips.

NOTE ▶ Any sequences selected in the Media Manager operation will be altered so the sequence settings will match the format of the new clips.

4 From the Recompress Media Using pop-up menu, choose OfflineRT PAL Anamorphic (Photo JPEG).

5 Deselect the Delete Unused Media checkbox but be sure to leave Duplicate Selected Clips. Be sure "Include master clips outside selection" is selected.

6 Set your destination and click OK.

7 Name your new project and click Save.

Once the processing is complete, you are ready to edit your offline clips.

8 In your new project, create a new sequence and name it *Low Res Edit.*

9 Select the new sequence in the Browser and choose Sequence > Settings.

10 Click the Load Sequence Preset button in the bottom-left corner.

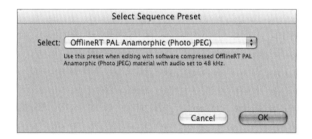

The Select Sequence Preset dialog appears.

11 From the Select pop-up menu, choose OfflineRT PAL Anamorphic (Photo JPEG).

This is the same list that you were choosing from in the Media Manager dialog. It is critical that your sequence settings match your clip settings.

12 Click OK in both the dialogs (first Select Sequence Preset and then Sequence Settings).

Now your sequence is set to match your clips. You can edit your newly compressed clips into this newly created sequence. When your editing decisions are complete, use the Media Manager to perform a Trim operation as previously described. Then, you can recapture the trimmed sequence in full resolution for your final output. So let's do that next.

Returning to Online Editing

Once you've completed your editing with the low-resolution clips, you're ready to return to the high-resolution clips.

If you have the original clips available on a different hard drive or a different system, you can get your project up to full resolution in a few short steps. In this case, the offline files are Offline RT, and the online clips are DV PAL.

1   Close the offline project you created in the previous exercise and click back to the **13_Project_Start** tab in the Browser, or reopen it if you've closed it.

2   Double-click the sequence **Edit 1 (Offline RT)** to open it in the Timeline.

3   Choose Sequence > Settings or Control-click and choose Settings from the shortcut menu.

4   Click the Load Sequence Preset button in the bottom-left corner of the dialog.

5   From the pop-up menu, choose DV PAL 48 kHz Anamorphic and click OK. Then click OK in the Sequence Settings dialog.

Your clips in the sequence will appear to shrink, but what actually happened is that the sequence got larger. The render bar probably also changed from gray to red, or at least to green. That's because your clips no longer match your sequence settings. But this is only temporary.

6   Select the sequence icon for **Edit 1 (Offline RT)** in the Browser and from the File menu or the shortcut menu, choose Reconnect Media.

This will perform a reconnect operation on all of the clips in the sequence.

Now it's important not to use the Search button, because if you do, Final Cut Pro will automatically find the Offline RT version of the clips. Instead you will use the Locate function to find the files manually.

7   Click Locate.

A Reconnect dialog appears, asking you to choose the correct version of the clip to reconnect.

8   Navigate to the Friends Of The Family folder, and select the only clip name that is not dimmed.

9   Click Choose then Connect.

Because the "Reconnect all clips in relative path" checkbox was selected, all of the additional files in the sequence will be reconnected, and your sequence will be ready to go.

Prepare for Recapture

If you captured directly to your offline format, before you can reconnect your clips you need to recapture them at their native resolution. To ease this process, you can use the Media Manager to create an offline sequence at the correct resolution, ready for recapturing.

1   Select the **Edit 3** sequence.

2   Open the Media Manager.

3   From the Media pop-up menu, choose Create Offline.

This forces you to create a duplicate project and dims the Browse button, since that applies only to situations in which you are creating new media.

This setting also causes the Recompress pop-up menu to change function so it becomes a "Set Sequences To" pop-up menu. This automatically does the work of changing your sequence settings (which you did manually in the previous exercise).

4   From the "Set Sequences To" pop-up menu, choose DV PAL 48 kHz Anamorphic and click OK.

5   Name your new project file *New Project for Capture*, designate where to save it, and click OK.

A new project opens, with one sequence and a bin of master clips. At this point, you simply select the sequence and perform a batch capture set to full resolution (in this case DV PAL Anamorphic). Since you don't have the actual source tapes, you will not be able to do this final step now.

Once your clips have been recaptured, you are ready to fine-tune and lay your sequence to tape.

If you had any effects or elements that required rendering, you would need to re-render them in the new sequence. You should also look carefully at those sections to be sure they look correct, especially if they involved any clip motion.

Lesson Review

1.   What are the two most likely causes of an offline clip?

2.   What are two different meanings of offline?

3.   What is the difference between the Locate and Search buttons in the Reconnect Media window?

4.   Why would you choose to use Locate instead of Search?

5.   How can you find the media associated with a clip on your disk?

6.   What does it mean to trim a sequence?

7. Why would you want to trim a sequence?

8. When would you trim a sequence?

9. How do you trim a sequence?

Answers

1. A hard disk that is turned off or not connected to the computer, or the project was created on a different system and you don't have the media files.

2. Offline either means a clip disconnected from its media, or it means a low-resolution version of your clips, used for creating a rough version of the sequence.

3. Locate allows you to manually choose the directory, while Search automatically finds the file for you.

4. If you had more than one version of the file and you wanted to control which version was linked to the clip in your project.

5. Either choose the Reveal in Finder command or look at the Source column in the Browser or Item Properties window.

6. Creating a copy of the sequence where only the media between the clips' In and Out points is kept, and the excess media is discarded.

7. Generally to save disk space, or to create a streamlined backup of your sequence for later recapture.

8. Only after editing was completely finished.

9. Using the Media Manager and selecting the Delete Unused Media setting.

14

Lesson Files	Lesson Project Files > Lesson_14 > 14_Project_Start
Media	Media > Hooploose Footage, Friends Of The Family, Turn to Stone
Time	This lesson takes approximately 150 minutes to complete.
Goals	Create MPEG and H.264 files for DVDs using Compressor
	Convert NTSC to PAL
	Change 29.97fps media to 24p
	Transcode between SD and HD formats
	Create droplets for automatic drag-and-drop encoding
	Export QuickTime reference and self-contained files
	Export audio and OMF audio

Transcoding and Outputting Video

In this lesson, you will output your files to DVD, the Web, and third-party applications. You will use Compressor to encode MPEG-2 files for use in DVD authoring and for MPEG-4 files suitable for the Web. You will also use Compressor to convert between different frame sizes and frame rates. You will export audio via OMF, and export a QuickTime reference file for use in other applications.

Outputting for DVD

Once you have a completed movie, you typically will need to output it to a distribution medium. Currently DVD-Video is the most popular format for distributing high-quality video, but once you choose that format, you still must decide whether to make your DVD in 4:3 or 16:9 aspect ratios, and choose a frame rate. Furthermore, video for DVD must be converted into the MPEG-2 format and MPEG-2 has many different attributes that control quality, encoding speed, and playback versatility.

Compressor is a Final Cut Pro tool designed specifically to ease this encoding process by providing presets and the ability to batch encode to multiple formats and versions.

Exporting to MPEG-2 Using Presets

You can export an MPEG-2 file directly from Final Cut Pro, although you'll be using Compressor to do most of the work. Compressor contains presets that allow you to simplify the enormously complex compression choices to a few relatively easy questions.

1   Open the **14_Project_Start** project and select the **Showdown Sequence** sequence in the Browser.

2   Choose File > Export > Using Compressor.

    Compressor is launched with your sequence added to the batch.

3   In the Batch Name field, name your batch *Showdown1*.

    Leaving the Batch Name untitled will make it difficult for you to track the history.

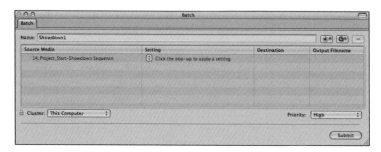

4   In the Batch window, click the Setting pop-up menu.

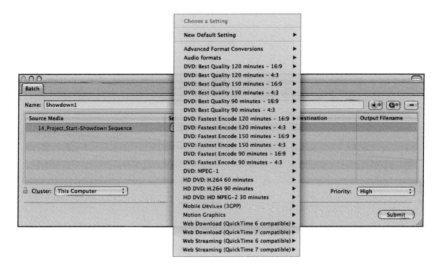

A full menu of presets appears. For now, just look at the ones that begin with "DVD".

The first thing to decide is whether you want Best Quality or Fastest Encode. This is the difference between two-pass encoding and one-pass encoding. Obviously, Best Quality usually will result in better-looking video, with less visible compression artifacts; but it can take much more than twice as long as a comparable Fastest Encode setting. For this lesson, you'll choose from the Fastest Encode section.

Next, you need to consider how much video you will be trying to fit on the disk. The presets give you three options: 90 minutes, 120 minutes, and 150 minutes. This is important because the less video you plan to put on the DVD, the more disk space can be allocated for the video you do use. So, if you have less than 90 minutes of video, choose the 90 minute preset because it will be higher quality. If you want to fit 145 minutes of video on the disk, you will have to use the 150 minute setting, which uses a lower bit rate (to save space) and will have reduced quality.

It's also important to understand that these values refer to the total minutes of video you plan to include on the DVD, not how long the current file is. For example you might have a DVD that includes five movies, each of which is 20 minutes long (for a total of 100 minutes). If you encoded them each at the 90 minute setting, they would likely take up too much space and you couldn't fit all of them on the DVD.

Last, you need to choose whether to make the video in standard (4:3) or widescreen (16:9) format. This largely depends on whether you are exporting from a standard or widescreen sequence in Final Cut Pro. However, it's important that all the video on any one track of your DVD be in either one format or the other.

5 From the "DVD: Fastest Encode 90 minutes – 4:3" submenu, choose the "MPEG-2 6.2Mbps 1-pass 4:3" preset.

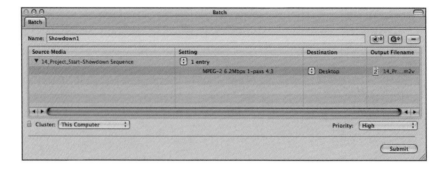

This adds that compression preset to the list in the Batch window.

However, this is just the video. DVDs read their video and audio from separate files (at least while they're being constructed). So you still need to choose an audio compression preset to create an audio file for your DVD.

There are only two types of audio that all DVD players can play: PCM (also known as AIF), which is a standard uncompressed stereo audio file, or Dolby, which is a high-quality, compressed audio format that is commonly used for most motion pictures.

Dolby (also known as AC3) has the added benefit of being a smaller, lower bandwidth file, that means: a) you can fit more stuff on your disk, and b) you can use a higher data rate for your video file without exceeding the playback maximums for most DVD players. The AC3 format also allows you to encode more than two channels into your audio stream, such as 5.1 or Dolby Surround, and so on.

Each of the DVD preset sets includes an AIFF 48/16 and a Dolby 2.0 setting, but don't be fooled; any preset with the same name is identical. Also, there is an option to choose All at the top of each preset set, but there is virtually no need to have both the AIFF and AC3 files created. This is an obsolete legacy setting from previous versions of the software suite in which you needed to use a separate application (A.Pack) to convert the AIFF files into AC3 files.

6 From the Setting pop-up menu, choose Audio formats > Dolby 2.0.

That preset is added to the queue.

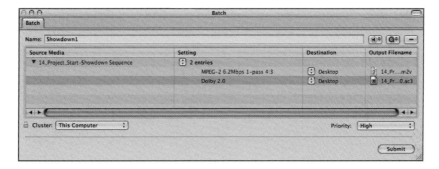

Setting the Destination and File Name

Before submitting the batch, you should check the settings for both the Destination and Output Filename columns.

7 From each of the two Destination pop-up menus (one for each preset), choose Source.

This instructs Compressor to create the new files in the same source folder as the original. In this case, because you are compressing directly from a Final Cut Pro sequence, the new files will be saved in the same directory as the Final Cut Pro project file.

8   Finally, double-click the name listed in the Output Filename column for
the video preset and type *Showdown.m2v*.

9   Double-click the name listed in the Output Filename column for the
audio preset and type *Showdown.ac3*.

It is very useful to name the MPEG file and the AC3 file exactly the same.
DVD Studio Pro will automatically recognize that files with identical
names are linked, saving you a few steps.

This file is now ready to compress. You can continue to add more presets
to this clip, or switch back to Final Cut Pro and export another sequence to
Compressor before beginning the render. This enables you to get everything
ready to go and then perform the compression all at once while you go for a
walk in the park, go home for the weekend, or perhaps take a month abroad,
depending on how many files you are compressing and at what settings.

10   Click the Submit button to begin compressing the files.

The batch is submitted and the Batch Monitor is launched.

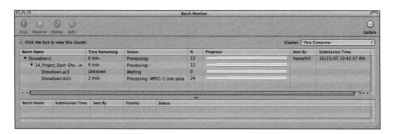

Batch monitor is a separate application from Compressor. You can quit
Compressor and the Batch Monitor will continue to render your files. The
Batch Monitor indicates which file currently is being rendered and approximately how much time remains for the process. Like most progress bars, the
time indications are just estimates.

Customizing Settings

While the presets are a great starting point, video compression is notoriously
fickle. Settings that produce amazing results with one scene might create a

blocky, smeary mess with another. There are many individual parameters that you can adjust individually to optimize your settings for a specific video. Unfortunately, good results almost always require a fair amount of trial and error, and compression can be pretty slow; so, for best results, find a short section of your show that is likely to challenge the compression method (such as fast cutting, fast horizontal pans, grainy images, etc.) and try compressing just that bit under a variety of settings. Fortunately, customizing your settings in Compressor is quite easy.

1   In Compressor, click the Import File button (or choose File > Import File). Navigate to Media > Broken Fists and select **BrokenFistsFight1**.

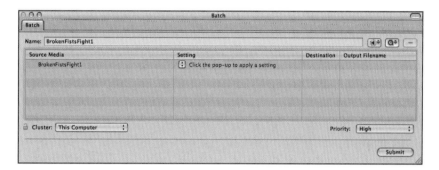

The batch is automatically named **BrokenFistsFight1**.

2   From the Setting pop-up menu, choose New Default Setting > MPEG-2.

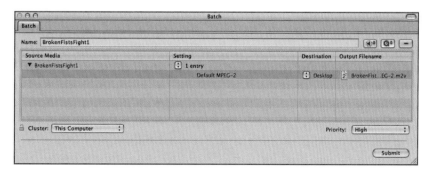

A new item is added to the batch list.

3   Double-click the Default MPEG-2 setting to open the Inspector.

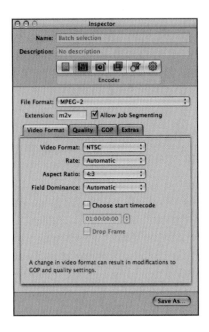

The Inspector shows all of the attributes and parameters for the setting, spread across six categories (the six icons at the top of the window).

NOTE ▶ The Preview window also opens when you double-click a setting. In this case you will not be using the Preview window, so you may choose to close it or move it out of the way.

4   If it is not already active, click the Encoder icon (the second button) to access the encoding settings for the preset.

The Encoder category has four tabs to organize the various controls. The first tab is the Video Format tab.

5   From the Video Format pop-up menu, choose NTSC. Set Rate to
     Automatic, select Aspect Ratio 4:3, and Field Dominance to Automatic.

6   Check the Choose Start Timecode checkbox and set the Timecode value to
     01:00:00:00.

     This ensures that all movies generated with this preset will have a starting
     timecode of 1 hour.

7   Click the Quality tab.

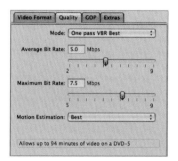

     The Quality tab is where you can set the bit rate of the compressed file, as
     well as what sort of encoding method (or mode) is used.

8   From the Mode pop-up menu, choose Two pass VBR.

VBR (or Variable Bit Rate) is a superior way of encoding MPEG-2 content. It means that complex scenes can be encoded at a higher data rate and simple scenes can be encoded at a lower data rate. This reduces overall file size, allowing you to fit more content on your DVD.

Two pass VBR further improves image quality by performing the encoding twice. The first pass assesses which scenes in the show will need higher data rates and which scenes can be reproduced accurately with a lower data rate. Of course, the downside is that Two pass VBR takes twice as long to compress.

9 Set Average Bit Rate to 3.5 and Maximum Bit Rate to 7.

In general, the higher your average bit rate, the less important it is to use the two-pass method. Typically, two-pass provides significant improvement at data rates below 3.5 Mbps.

10 Set the Motion Estimation to Better, the middle setting.

Motion Estimation detects movement within the frame. The higher the setting here, the better Compressor will be able to accommodate that motion without turning the video into a blocky mess. Of course, the higher the quality setting is, the longer the encode time. A good rule of thumb is to use the Good setting when using One Pass mode, and only use the Best setting when using the one or two pass VBR Best modes.

11 Click the GOP tab.

GOP stands for Group of Pictures and this tab helps you control the size of the chunks in which your MPEG-2 stream will be encoded. This is part of the magic that helps MPEG-2 video look so good. MPEG-2 is far more sophisticated than other keyframe-based compression formats, and Compressor lets you fine-tune the GOP structure to optimize your picture quality.

Without going into all the technical details (you can consult the Compressor Help file for that), suffice it to say that you can use the following settings as a starting point.

12 Set the GOP Structure to IBBP, Closed, with a GOP size of 15 frames (12 for PAL) and a pattern of IBBPBBPBBPBP (the default).

Other GOP Patterns
If your video contains many sections of very fast cutting, or lots of motion within the frame, you may find the quality of your video degrades significantly between keyframes (I-frames). In this case, you can try setting the GOP structure to IBP or IP.

These settings will create many more keyframes, which will make your video look better, but will require significantly higher data rates (and will occupy more space on the DVD). Typically IBP requires at least 6 Mbps and IP requires 8 Mbps for adequate quality.

Similarly, the smaller the size of the GOP, the more groups you'll have and so the more keyframes you'll have. This results in higher-quality video, but at the expense of a higher data rate.

Open GOPs allow P and B frames to reference keyframes from other GOPs. Closed GOPs always begin with their own I-frame and any P- or B-frames in that GOP can only reference keyframes within that GOP. Open GOPs can achieve lower data rates by requiring fewer I-frames; however, Open GOPs cannot be used on mixed-angle or multiple-angle DVDs.

Also, chapter markers must be set on I-frames, so Closed GOPs allow for more accurate placement of chapter markers. (With Open GOPs your marker may be as far as half a second away from the frame in which your scene begins.) In general, stick to Closed GOPs unless you're really hurting for disk space and are not using frequent chapter markers.

1   Click the Extras tab to examine the remaining settings for your custom preset.

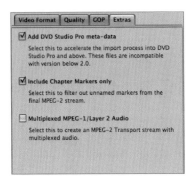

2   Make sure that the "Add DVD Studio Pro meta-data" checkbox is selected.

This setting significantly reduces the time DVD Studio Pro requires to open and parse the video files you create.

3   Select the "Include Chapter Markers only" checkbox.

This will instruct Compressor to ignore any extraneous markers that may be in your Final Cut Pro sequence when the file is encoded.

The last checkbox is only used for special cases when your MPEG stream is intended for direct broadcast instead of DVD.

If you want to save these settings as a new custom preset, you can click the Save As button, but because this preset is already attached to the item in the batch list, you do not need to save it.

4   Close the Inspector.

5   Select a destination in the Batch window and click the Submit button to begin compressing the file.

Creating Video for HD DVDs

DVD Studio Pro 4 can create HD DVDs using the H.264 codec. You can create H.264 video streams directly from Final Cut Pro using Compressor. The process is exactly the same as creating MPEG-2 streams for standard definition DVDs, except you use different presets.

1   In Final Cut Pro, select **hooploose HD.**

    This is a 960 x 720 HD sequence at a frame rate of 60i.

2   Choose File > Export > Using Compressor.

    Compressor comes to the front (or launches) and the sequence is added to the batch.

3   From the Settings pop-up menu, choose HD DVD: H.264 60 Minutes > All.

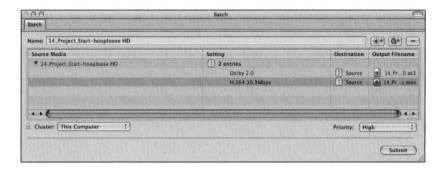

    Two entries are added to the batch list, one for audio and one for video.

4   Set the destination for both items to Source.

    You can click the Submit button now to begin the encoding, but instead, you will create a custom HD compression setting.

Using Custom H.264 Settings

Compressing for HD is very similar to compressing for SD, but some of the settings have different names and slightly different functions. In this exercise, you will customize the preset and save it as a new, custom setting.

1   In the Setting column of the Batch window, double-click the preset H.264 10.3Mbps.

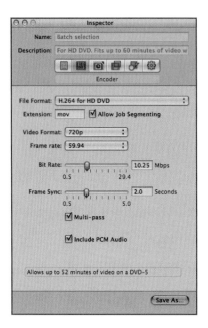

This opens the Inspector window as well as a Preview window in which you can see how the compression will affect your image.

2   In the Inspector window, set the Video Format pop-up menu to Automatic.

This will set the frame size to match the size of your sequence.

The Frame rate pop-up menu automatically will be set to 59.94 (because the existing sequence is an NTSC sequence).

3   Set Bit Rate to 7.20 Mbps.

The H.264 compression algorithm is nearly twice as efficient as the MPEG-2 codec, so you can expect higher quality at a lower bit rate. However, keep in mind that the larger your video frame, the higher the required bit rate.

Because this sequence is the smaller 720p frame size, you can conserve space by lowering the bit rate without compromising on quality.

4   Set the Frame Sync slider to 1 second.

The Frame Sync setting controls how often automatic keyframes are added to your compressed movie. The higher the setting, the less frequently keyframes are added, which aids in controlling file size but may threaten quality. The ideal setting will depend on how dynamic your show is.

5   Make sure the Multi-pass setting is selected.

This is equivalent to using the Two pass VBR mode in the MPEG 2 settings. Multi-pass takes twice as long, but ensures a better distribution of bits and can significantly improve visual quality, especially at lower data rates.

6   Deselect the Include PCM Audio checkbox.

In most cases, such as in this example, you will encode your audio into the Dolby AC3 format as a separate item in the batch list, which makes this setting redundant.

7   Click Save As to save your custom preset.

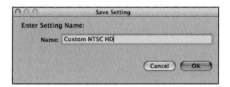

The Save Setting dialog opens.

8   Name the preset *Custom NTSC HD* and click OK.

Although you opened the Inspector by double-clicking the item in your batch list, the custom setting you just created is not automatically applied to the item; instead it is added to the Custom bin in the Presets window.

9   Press Command-2 to open the Presets window.

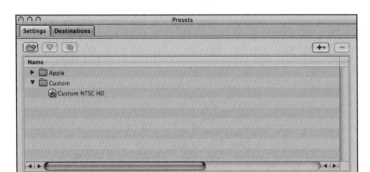

Alternatively, you can create a new preset directly in the Presets window, as described in "Creating Custom Presets" later in this lesson.

10   In the batch list, click the pop-up in the Setting column menu and choose the Custom NTSC HD preset from the bottom of the list.

11   In the batch list, choose the H.264 10.3 Mbps item and press Delete.

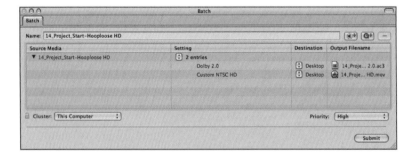

12   Click Submit to begin compressing the HD video file.

Making Video for the Web

There are countless video formats currently in use on the Web. Final Cut Pro Studio provides presets for two popular formats: MPEG-4, a high-quality, low-bandwidth, widely compatible codec; and H.264, which produces excellent results at low bandwidth settings, although it requires QuickTime 7 or higher for playback. Technically, H.264 is a variant of the MPEG-4 codec, but it is not playable on older devices that can play MPEG-4 video, such as cell phones.

After choosing which codec you want to use, you must additionally choose whether your file should be *streaming* or *progressive download*. Typically, shows shorter than 10 minutes are ideal for progressive download while streaming is more appropriate for longer shows. However, streaming files require special streaming software on your Web server while progressive download files can be embedded into any Web page with no special software required.

Exporting for the Web Using Presets

Generating a video file based on one of the Web-ready presets is identical to exporting for DVD or HD DVD.

1   In Final Cut Pro, select **Showdown Sequence.**

2   Choose File > Export > Using Compressor.

    Compressor opens and the sequence is added to the batch list.

3   In the batch list, click the Setting pop-up menu and choose Web Download (QuickTime 7 Compatible) > H.264 100Kbps.

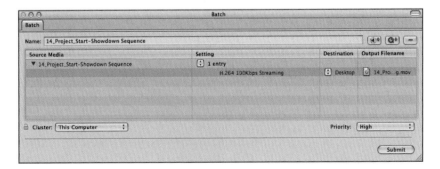

For comparison, the H.264 preset for HD is 10.3 Mbps, more than one thousand times the data rate of this Web preset.

This preset has audio built in, so you don't need to add an audio preset to your batch. If you want to examine the specific settings contained in this preset, you can view them in the Inspector.

4   Double-click the preset name to open the Inspector.

Although this preset uses the same codec as the HD presets, the Inspector has an entirely different set of controls and options.

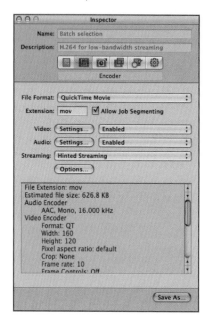

5   Click the Video: Settings button.

The QuickTime settings window opens.

This window has many of the same controls found in the Inspector for the HD DVD preset. By default, the video is set to 10 fps, and the Multi-pass setting is active.

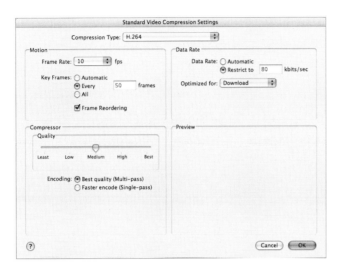

6   Click OK to close the window.

7   In the Inspector click the Geometry Button.

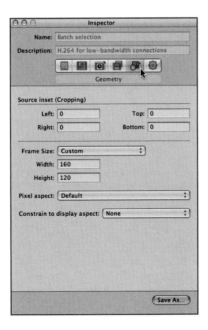

This is where you can control the frame size of the output movie. By default, this setting creates a movie that is 160 x 120 pixels wide.

Remember, if you make changes in the Inspector, those changes will not modify the existing batch (unless you began by choosing a default setting). For now, don't make any changes.

Creating Custom Presets

Obviously, you can create custom Web presets to modify the frame rate, frame size, or other attributes. However, you also can use Compressor to create Web video files using file formats such as AVI, MPEG-1 or Sorenson Video QuickTime files. To export a file in one of these formats you must create a custom preset.

1   In Compressor, open the Presets window by choosing Window > Presets or pressing Command-2.

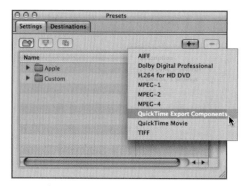

2   From the "Create a new setting" pop-up menu, choose QuickTime Export Components.

This format allows you to create AVI or 3GP files, which are common formats for older Web sites and cell phones respectively.

3   In the Inspector, name the preset *AVI Export Preset*.

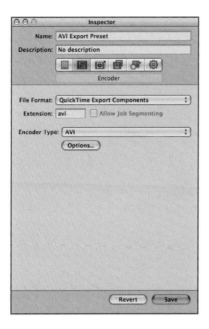

4   Set Encoder Type to AVI.

You can leave all the other settings at their default.

5   Click Save to dismiss the Save Setting dialog.

You can now access this AVI export preset for any item in your batch list.

Using Sorenson Video Presets

Sorenson Video is still a popular Web video format that enjoys wide compatibility and relatively high quality at low data rates. Compressor can generate Sorenson Video QuickTime files. Be aware, however, that Compressor cannot take advantage of the VBR supported by the Sorenson codec.

1   In the Inspector palette, set the File Format pop-up menu to QuickTime Movie.

2   Name the preset *Sorenson 320 300kbps*.

3 Click the Video: Settings button.

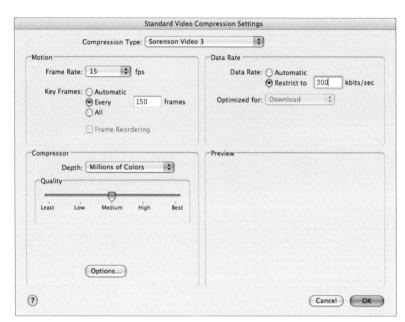

The Standard Video Compression Settings window appears.

4 From the Compression Type pop-up menu at the top of the window, choose Sorenson Video 3.

5 Set Frame Rate to 15 fps and the Keyframes to "Every 150 frames".

6 Set Compressor Quality to Best.

7 Set Date Rate to Restrict to 300 kbits/sec.

NOTE ▶ If you own Sorenson Pro, the Options button at the bottom left of this window provides access to VBR, Watermark, and the other settings unique to the professional version. However, in the current version of Compressor accessing these settings may cause Compressor to unexpectedly quit.

8 Click OK to close the settings window.

9   Click the Audio: Settings button.

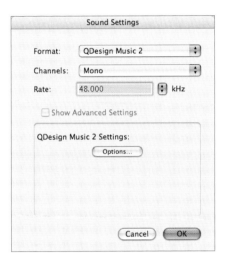

The Sound Settings window appears.

10 Set Format to QDesign Music 2, Channels to Mono, and click OK.

Now the video and sound settings are set.

11 Click the Geometry button in the Inspector.

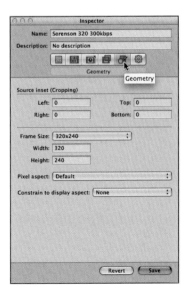

12 Check that Frame Size is set to 320 x 240 and click Save.

Your new preset appears in the Custom folder in the Preset list.

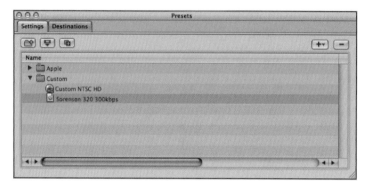

Exporting Audio

Final Cut Pro can export audio in a wide variety of formats, each tailored for a specific workflow. Whether you are finishing your audio mix in Apple's Soundtrack Pro, Digidesign's Pro Tools or another dedicated audio tool; recording multiple channels directly to a multichannel recorder (using special audio I/O hardware); or outputting tracks to be encoded for multi-channel surround sound, Final Cut Pro can accommodate you in nearly every case.

Setting AIFF Options

The simplest type of audio output is a simple stereo mix. This will generate a two-channel AIFF file that can be played back in any stereo-capable software or hardware.

1 In Final Cut Pro, select Showdown Sequence.

2 Choose File > Export > Audio to AIFF(s).

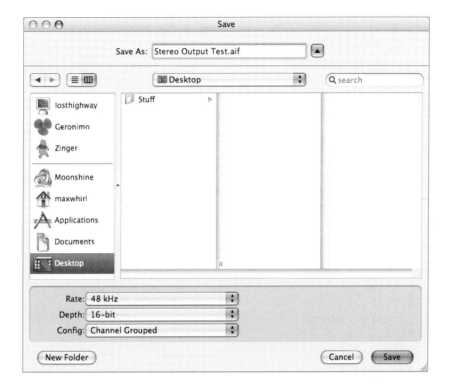

The Save dialog appears.

3 Name the file *Stereo Output Test* and set the destination to your Desktop.

4 Set the Rate pop-up menu to 48 kHz, Depth to 16-bit, and Config to Stereo Mix.

> **NOTE ▶** Final Cut Pro can now output audio up to 24-bit and 96kHz for maximum quality; however, there is no advantage to exporting to a quality setting higher than the source audio.

5 Click Save.

The stereo audio file is saved to your Desktop.

Exporting Channel Groups

In addition to a stereo mix, Final Cut Pro can also export your audio as channel groups. This option will export multiple mono or stereo AIFFs based on the audio channel settings in your sequence.

1   Double-click **Showdown Sequence** to open it.

2   Choose Sequence > Settings to open the Sequence Settings window.

3   Click the Audio Outputs tab.

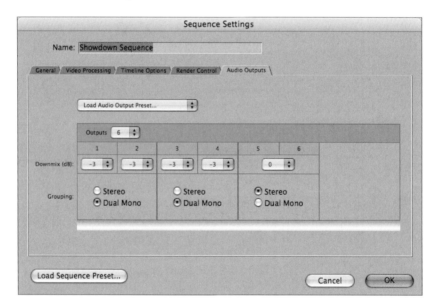

This sequence has six outputs: four mono channels and one stereo pair.

4   Click OK to close the Sequence Settings window.

> **NOTE ▶**   You will probably see a warning dialog indicating that the current audio device doesn't have enough outputs to play the sequence correctly. This sequence requires special audio hardware. In order to complete this exercise, do not select the Downmix checkbox. Click OK to close the Warning message.

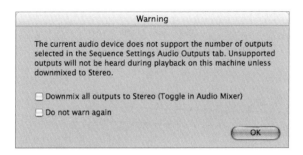

5 Choose File > Export > Audio as AIFF(s).

The AIFF Export dialog opens.

6 From the Config pop-up menu, choose Channel Grouped.

7 Set the desired destination for your output files and click Save.

NOTE ▶ Because the Channel Groups setting will create as many files as you have audio outputs, each file will be based on the name you enter in the AIFF Export dialog with an incrementing digit appended to the end (e.g., xxx-1, xxx-2, xxx-3).

Making a Multichannel QuickTime Movie

It is also possible to export a single QuickTime file with as many audio channels as you have set in your Final Cut Pro sequence.

1 Choose Sequence > Settings or press Command-0.

The Sequence Settings window opens.

2 In the General tab, make sure the Audio Settings: Config pop-up menu is set to Default.

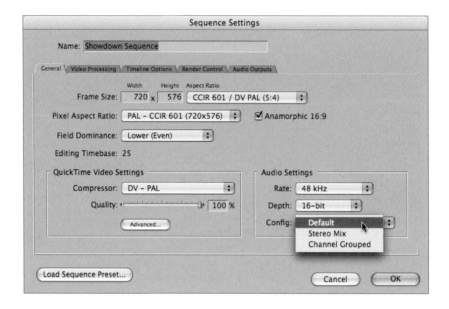

The other two choices in this menu are identical to the Stereo Mix and Channel Groups option discussed earlier in this lesson.

3 Click OK to close the Sequence Settings window.

You can click OK if the Audio Output warning dialog appears again.

4 Choose File > Export > QuickTime Movie.

The Export to QuickTime Movie dialog appears.

5   From the Include pop-up menu, choose Audio Only and select the Make Movie Self-Contained checkbox.

6   Set a destination for your output and click Save.

A QuickTime movie will be created with six audio tracks, corresponding to the six tracks in your Final Cut Pro sequence.

Exporting Audio to OMF

Many filmmakers prefer to perform their final audio mix in ProTools or another dedicated audio workstation. You can export the audio from your Final Cut Pro sequence into an interchange format called Open Media Format (OMF) that can be imported into ProTools and other software. An OMF file contains all of the audio data from all of the tracks in a Final Cut Pro sequence. It maintains the arrangement of individual clips and tracks, so when the OMF file is opened in another program, the audio portion of your Final Cut Pro sequence is faithfully reproduced. Be aware, however, that Final Cut Pro does not export audio track level information (often referred to as *automation*) in its OMF export, so any level adjustments made in Final Cut Pro will be lost. Also, audio filters and effects will not be included in the OMF file.

1   Choose File > Export > Audio to OMF.

The OMF Audio Export dialog opens.

Although you can modify the sample rate and bit depth, it is usually best to leave those settings so they match the audio in your sequence and source footage.

2   Set Handles to 5 seconds (00:00:05:00).

Adding handles is especially important for audio clips. The engineer who will import your OMF will likely be adding fades to the beginning and end of every single audio element in your show. The more extra footage you provide, the more flexibility the audio editor will have.

3   Leave the Include Crossfade Transitions checkbox selected and click OK.

The OMF Save dialog appears.

4   In the bottom-left corner of the window, deselect the Hide Extension checkbox.

The extension .omf is added to the file name. Since the file may be going to a Windows-based workstation, it's best to leave the .omf extension visible.

5   Choose a destination for your OMF file and click Save.

Delivering Corresponding Video

If you're doing your audio mix in a separate application, it's very important to lock your picture before exporting the OMF. If you make editorial changes in Final Cut Pro after handing off the audio to a sound editor, you could create sync problems that will be difficult to fix.

Typically, in addition to the OMF, you will also deliver your sound editor a QuickTime movie of the corresponding picture with BITC (Burned-In Time Code) that matches the timecode in the OMF (which is based on the timecode in the exported sequence).

It's essential that the picture and sound are exactly the same length. It's also a good habit to provide a sync beep at the head and tail of your show.

You can see an example of such sync beeps at the head and tail of Showdown Sequence (note that they appear in every track). Also notice that the timecode for the sequence begins at 00:59:58:30 and the first frame of picture begins at exactly 01:00:00:00.

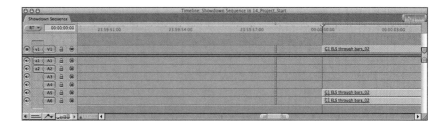

Exporting to Dolby AC3 Format

If you are preparing your audio for DVD, the best format to use is Dolby AC3. This format is compressed, so it takes less space and less bandwidth on the DVD, plus it has the added benefit of being able to store multiple channels for use in surround sound. You can encode AC3 in a wide variety of formats from a single mono channel all the way up to 5.1 (Left, Center, Right, Left Surround, Right Surround, and Low Frequency Effects).

To create surround sound AC3 files, you must already have prepared your audio into separate tracks for the multiple channels. This could be one QuickTime movie with multiple tracks, or separate files for each channel.

> **NOTE** ▸ All audio to be compressed to AC3 needs to be sampled at 48 kHz and all files need to be the same length, or Compressor will add silence to the end of shorter tracks to make them all the same duration.

1   In the Batch window, click the Import Surround Sound Group button.

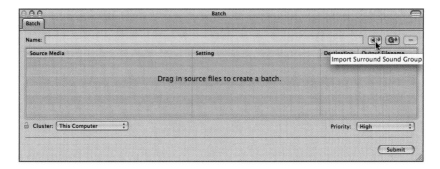

The Surround Sound Mapping sheet appears.

2   Click the L icon in the upper left corner.

3   Navigate to Media > Surround Mix and open FinalMix.L.

   This opens the audio file that will go into the front left channel.

4   Click the Center box, and open FinalMix.C.

5   Follow the same process to assign the Right, Left Surround, Right Surround, and Low Frequency Effects channels. This example does not have a Center Surround channel.

   FinalMix.R is the right channel, FinalMix.Ls is the Left Surround, FinalMix.Rs is the Right Surround, and FinalMix.LFE is the Low Frequency Effects channel.

6   When all the channels are assigned, click OK to add the group to the batch list.

7   From the Setting pop-up menu, choose New Default Setting > Dolby Digital Professional.

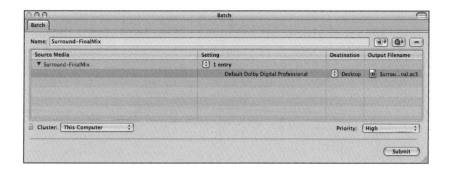

8 Double-click the new setting to open the Inspector window.

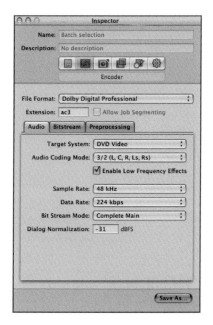

9 Set Audio Coding mode to 3/2 and select the Enable Low Frequency Effects checkbox (if it's not already selected).

10 You can adjust the data rate for higher or lower compression quality, but the default 224 kbps is sufficient for most 5.1 streams.

The Audio Coding Mode setting will determine what Data Rate settings are available to you. For example, five channels require more bandwidth than two channels, and so Data Rate must be set higher in that case.

11 Set Dialog Normalization to -31.

This will ensure that the audio will not be modified during encoding or on playback. Other settings may cause the center channel volume to be attenuated during playback to account for louder sounds in the other channels.

All of the other settings may be left at default for this exercise.

12 Go back to the Batch window and click Submit to begin the batch processing.

Exporting QuickTime Files

When your show is finished, you will likely want to make many different kinds of output. We've already covered how to create a file for DVD or for the Web. There are reasons you may want to create a QuickTime movie at full resolution as well.

A QuickTime movie is a good archive of the finished project (along with your precious project file, of course). You can save a single file that contains your whole movie (in its native resolution) so you can archive or delete the bulky media files referenced by your project. You then can use that file in Compressor or any other QuickTime-compatible program to create more MPEG or H.264 files, or files in any other formats.

You can output that file to tape, just as you would output directly from your edited sequence. All the rendered bits will never become unrendered, and you enjoy the convenience of having all the data in one safe place rather than the reference movie that links to myriad files from all over your disk(s).

You might also want to deliver a full-resolution copy of your show to another editor, or use it yourself in a new project. For example, you might want to generate a trailer or promo spot based on the finished show, or to include a section in a show reel.

1   In the Browser, select **Showdown Sequence.**

2   Choose File > Export > QuickTime Movie.

The QuickTime movie export dialog appears.

3   Name the new file *Showdown.mov* and navigate to your desired destination.

By default, the Settings pop-up menu is set to Current Settings, which means the exported movie will have the same frame size, frame rate, audio, and compression settings as the sequence. The source footage that matches those sequence settings is displayed in gray in the Timeline render bar, and will not be re-compressed, thus preserving the highest quality possible.

In nearly all cases, you will leave the Setting pop-up menu unchanged. However, if you ever wanted to transcode your sequence into a different sequence preset you could do just that by changing this setting. In most cases, there is a better way of transcoding: by editing the clips into a sequence with the desired settings within Final Cut Pro, or by using Compressor.

4   From the Include pop-up menu, choose Audio and Video, and from the Markers pop-up menu, choose All Markers.

The Markers pop-up menu allows you to control which types of markers are included in the QuickTime movie. Many of the marker types are readable by other software such as Apple's DVD Studio Pro or Soundtrack Pro.

5   Select the Make Movie Self-Contained checkbox and click Save.

Creating Reference Movies

The Make Movie Self-Contained checkbox is a very powerful setting. It determines whether your exported movie is a huge file containing a copy of all of the video and audio clips used in your sequence, or whether you get a tiny *reference movie* that is merely a pointer to all of those files, wherever they may exist on your computer.

Reference movies are great. They're much quicker to make than regular movies, they're very small, and you can use them in Compressor just like a regular QuickTime movie, or any other QuickTime-compatible program. However, if you move, modify, or delete any of the video files that were used in the sequence from which you exported, the reference movie will no longer work. If that happens, opening it in any application may yield an error message and a search dialog (similar to Final Cut Pro's Offline Files dialog) asking you to locate the missing file.

Final Cut Pro's reference movies contain all of the audio data from the sequence, plus any frames that needed to be rendered at the time of the export. But raw video will be pulled from the files in your Capture Scratch folder and sections of the sequence that were previously rendered are pulled from the files in your Render Files folder. If any of those files are altered, the reference movie will become unplayable.

Reference movies are fine as long as you have no intention of taking them off the computer, and don't plan to make changes to the files they're based on (such as re-rendering a portion of your sequence).

1   Select **Showdown Sequence**.

2   Choose File > Export > QuickTime Movie.

    The QuickTime movie export dialog appears.

3   Name the new file *ShowdownRef.mov* and navigate to your desired destination.

4   Set the Settings pop-up menu to Current Settings, the Include pop-up menu to Audio and Video, and the Markers pop-up menu to All Markers.

5   Deselect the Make Movie Self-Contained checkbox and click Save.

The exported file will be a reference movie.

Transcoding Video Formats

It's not uncommon these days to need to provide versions of your finished show in a variety of formats. For example, although your show might have originated in NTSC format, you might need a PAL version for international exhibition. You might want to convert 29.97 fps interlaced video into 24p for output to HD, or just to create a more film-like look. You might even want to blow up an SD project to HD resolution, or vice versa.

Until recently, changing formats, or *transcoding*, could cause dramatic quality reduction, or required expensive dedicated hardware. With the latest version of Compressor, many of these types of transcoding are readily available. But be warned: they can take an extraordinarily long time to process depending on the specific settings you choose.

Transcoding from NTSC to PAL

One of the most common types of transcoding is converting between NTSC and PAL formats. This requires a frame rate conversion (NTSC is 29.97 fps and PAL is 25 fps) and a frame size conversion (NTSC is 720 x 486 and PAL is 720 x 576).

1   Select the **Turn To Stone** sequence in the Browser.

This sequence is an NTSC DV sequence.

2   Choose File > Export > Using Compressor.

Compressor launches and the sequence is added to the batch.

3   Open the Presets window in Compressor by choosing Windows > Presets or pressing Command-2.

4   Click the "Create a new setting" button and choose QuickTime Movie from the pop-up menu.

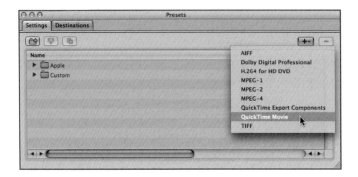

A new preset is added to the Custom bin.

5   Click the disclosure triangle to open the Custom bin (if it's not already open) and double-click the Untitled QuickTime Movie preset.

This opens the Inspector, in which you can modify the settings of the new preset.

6   Name the custom preset *DV NTSC to DV PAL* and add a short description.

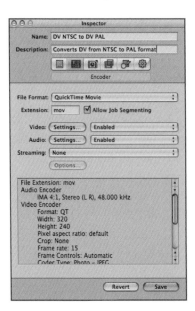

7   Click the Video: Settings button.

This opens the Standard Video Compression Settings window.

8   Set Compression Type to DV- PAL, and set Frame Rate to 25fps.

9   Click OK to close the window.

10   Click the Audio:Settings button.

This opens the Sound Settings window.

11   Set Format to Linear PCM, and set Channels to Stereo (L R).

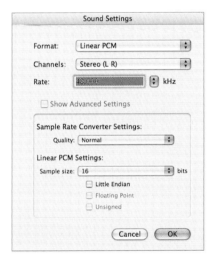

You can leave the rest of the settings in this window unchanged, since both DV NTSC and DV PAL use the same sample rate and bit depth.

12   Click OK to close the window.

13   Click the Frame Controls button in the Inspector.

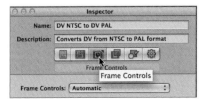

This is where you can customize the frame size conversion.

14 In the Frame Controls pop-up menu, choose Custom.

15 Set the Resize Filter to Better (Linear filter).

> **NOTE ▶** You can optionally set this to Best (statistical prediction) but it will dramatically increase the rendering time. In most cases Best will only provide a slight improvement in quality.

16 Leave Output Fields set to "Same as Source" and the Deinterlace setting to Fast.

In this case, because you are going from one interlaced format to another, no deinterlacing will take place.

17 From the Rate Conversion pop-up menu, choose Better (Motion compensated).

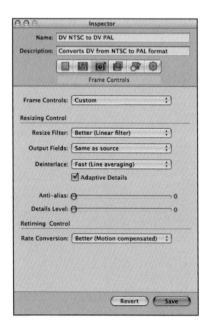

NOTE ▶ You can choose to set this to Best but the results tend to be only slightly better and it will take a considerably longer time to process. In general, only use the Best settings in Compressor after determining that the Better settings are inadequate.

18 At the top of the Inspector, click the Geometry button.

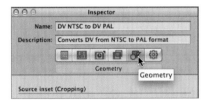

19 Set Frame Size to Custom and type *720* in Width and *576* in Height.

20 Set Pixel Aspect to PAL CCIR 601.

The Constrain to Display Aspect option would allow you to account for anamorphic 16:9 content, but in this case you can leave it set to None.

21 Click Save.

The preset is saved and is now ready to be assigned to the item in the batch list.

22 In the batch list, click the Settings pop-up menu and from the bottom of the list choose DV NTSC to DV PAL.

23 Click Submit and go to the movies.

If you wanted to convert a PAL movie to NTSC, you would use the opposite settings and set the frame size to 720 x 480 and Pixel Aspect Ratio to NTSC CCIR 601/DV.

Transcoding Interlaced to Progressive

Another common type of transcoding is turning interlaced video into progressive scan video. This frequently is done to create a more film-like look, but may also be essential if you are planning to output to a progressive format such as 24p HD or film.

Although you've long been able to deinterlace video using the Deinterlace or Flicker filters in Final Cut Pro, Compressor offers a much more robust deinterlacing tool that produces significantly higher-quality output. The filters in Final Cut Pro simply eliminated one of the fields or, at best, interpolated new lines based on the two fields. Compressor analyzes each pixel individually, and only affects areas of the frame where there is motion. This means that much less data is being eliminated. This is known as *adaptive deinterlacing*. Furthermore, Compressor offers detailed control over how motion is detected as well as how the newly generated pixels are created.

All this control is really incredible, and helps to create truly impressive results; but, like the other special settings described in this chapter, the render times can be prohibitive.

In this exercise, you will create a preset to turn 29.97 fps interlaced NTSC into 24p video, still in the NTSC DV codec. Although the 24p output file can't be recorded to a standard NTSC deck without conversion back to 29.97 fps, it will retain a more film-like appearance, even after the pulldown is reinserted. Furthermore, you could use the same technique for creating an optimized 24p MPEG-2 preset, or for converting a 29.97 HD movie to 24p.

1   In the Compressor Presets window, click the "Create a new setting" pop-up menu and choose QuickTime Movie.

   A new preset is added to the Custom Presets bin and the preset is loaded into the Inspector.

2   In the Inspector window, name the preset *29.97 DV to 24p DV*.

3   Click the Video: Settings button.

   The Standard Video Compression Settings window opens.

4   Set Compression Type to DV/DVCPRO NTSC.

5 Set Frame Rate to 24 and Scan mode to Progressive.

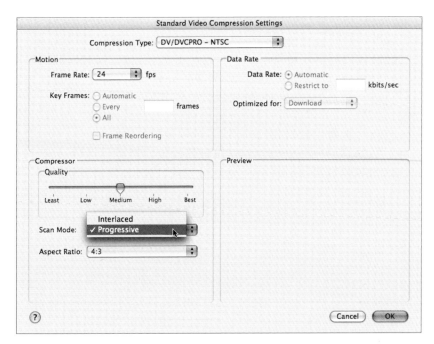

Although this seems like all you need to do, this is only the beginning.

6 Click OK to close the Compression Settings window.

7 From the Audio pop-up menu, choose Pass-through.

This will copy the audio from the source file into the destination file without modifying it.

8   Click the Frame Controls button in the Inspector and set the Frame Controls pop-up menu to Custom.

9   Set Resize Filter to Better (Linear filter), Output Fields to Progressive, and the Deinterlace setting to Better (Motion adaptive).

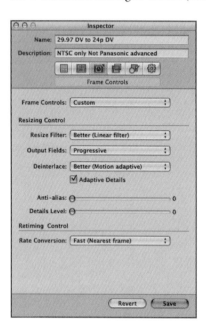

10   Make sure the Adaptive Details checkbox is selected.

11   Set the Rate Conversion pop-up menu to Fast (Nearest frame).

In this case, because you are reducing the frame rate, no advanced rate conversion is necessary. If you are performing a transcode in which you are increasing the frame rate (for example from 25 fps to 29.97 fps or from 29.97 fps to 59.94 fps) you will want to the Rate Conversion to a higher setting for maximum quality.

12 Click the Geometry button and set the Frame Size pop-up menu to "100% of source".

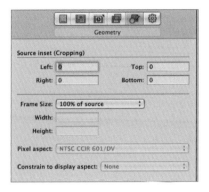

13 Click Save.

The preset is saved with all the settings you have selected.

Converting SD to HD

Another common conversion is to adjust frame size (with or without an accompanying frame rate change) to up-res from SD to HD or down-res from HD to SD.

Although Compressor has some powerful scaling technology, blowing up your picture from standard definition to high definition is going to come with quite a bit of quality reduction. Up-conversion is no substitute for shooting in HD from the outset, but if your client or film festival requires an HD master and all you have is an SD file, this will enable you to deliver what you're asked for.

In this exercise, you will create a custom preset designed to convert a standard-definition PAL clip into an uncompressed 1080i HD file at the same frame rate. This is only one example of how to do such a conversion. Depending on what your own source footage is and what format you want to transcode to, you may need to adjust the settings accordingly.

In this case, you will begin with the format preset and then modify it to maxi-mize quality.

1   In the Preset window, open the Apple bin and then open the Advanced Format Conversions bin.

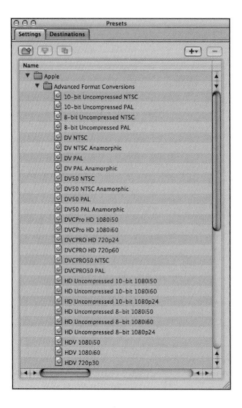

2   Select the HD Uncompressed 10-bit 1080i50 preset.

3   Click the Duplicate Selected Setting button.

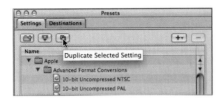

A duplicate of the preset is added to the Custom bin.

4   Double-click the new custom preset to open it into the Inspector.

Because you are beginning with the preset, the Encoder settings are already set for you.

5   Name the preset *SD PAL to 1080i50.*

6   Click the Frame Controls button and set the Frame Controls to Custom.

NOTE ▶ Leaving this setting on Automatic will instruct Compressor to attempt to set the Frame Controls by analyzing the source footage and comparing it to the destination format. This can be very helpful if you want to use one preset for a variety of source file types. However, you are more likely to get best results by customizing the Frame Control settings to optimize them for your particular source.

7   Set Resize Filter to Best (Statistical prediction).

Because this preset is intended to convert PAL SD to a 50i format, you can leave the Output Fields and Deinterlace settings at their default. Also, you can deselect Adaptive Details because this conversion will not be modifying the fields or interlacing. If you were converting from NTSC, or converting to or from a progressive frame rate, these settings would need to be adjusted accordingly.

8   Raise the Anti-alias slider to about 10 and the Details Level slider to about 15.

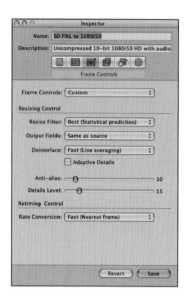

These controls affect the visual quality of the output image. The anti-alias setting softens the image slightly, and the Details Level setting enhances edges. The result of combining the sliders is similar to an adaptive noise reduction in which the edges remain sharp but solid fields appear less noisy. Be aware that these settings are very finicky and you may have to experiment to find the best setting for your shots. Also, the higher the anti-alias setting, the longer your render will take.

9   Click Save to store the settings in your custom preset.

Clips or sequences assigned to this setting will take a very long time to render. Very long. Earlier in this lesson, you were urged to go out and watch a movie while you compressed your clip. For this one, you should go out and *make* a movie.

This is why it's very important to select a small section of your movie and
test-export it with a variety of settings. Make sure the output looks acceptable before you begin compressing your entire show.

Making a Droplet

Rather than working through the whole Compressor interface every time
you need to compress a file, you can create *droplets* based on any of the presets. A droplet is a standalone application onto which you can drag and drop
QuickTime movies, automatically initiating the compression process.

1   If it's not already open, open the Compressor Presets window by choosing
     Window > Presets or pressing Command-2.

2   From the Custom bin, select the *DV NTSC to DV PAL* preset.

3   Click the Save Selection as Droplet button or choose File > Save as Droplet.

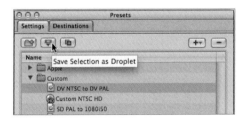

The Save Droplet dialog appears.

4   Choose a destination for the droplet (the Desktop is a good choice).

5   Choose where you want the droplet's output to be saved.

     By default, you have only four choices. You can add custom destinations,
     but you have to do it in the Presets window.

6   Click Cancel to close the Save Droplet dialog.

7   In the Presets window, click the Destinations tab.

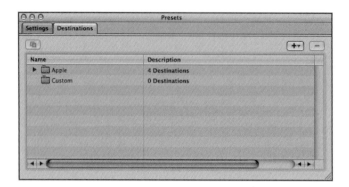

8   Click the "Create a new destination" button and choose Local.

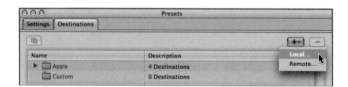

A File Open dialog appears.

9   Navigate to your Movies folder and click the New Folder button.

10   Name the new folder *NTSC to PAL Output* and click Create.

11   Click Open in the File Open dialog to set that folder as the new destination.

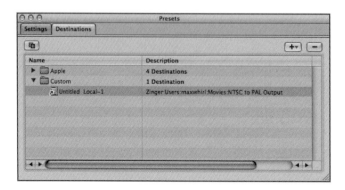

The new destination appears in the Custom bin.

12 Double-click the new destination.

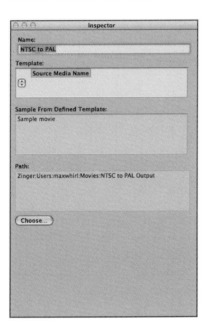

The Inspector shows the destination and associated information.

13 In the name field, type *NTSC to PAL* and press Return.

This names the destination within Compressor.

14 Click the Settings tab to return to the Preset list.

Now repeat Steps 2 through 5 to create the droplet and your new folder will appear in the Destinations pop-up menu.

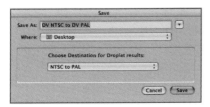

15 Click Save.

You can now drag and drop your QuickTime files directly onto the droplet to encode them. But let's automate the process one step further.

16 Navigate to the newly created droplet and double-click it.

17 Deselect the Show at Launch box and quit the droplet (Command-Q).

Now when you drag and drop QuickTime files onto the droplet for encoding, they will be sent directly to the Batch Monitor without any dialogs displaying.

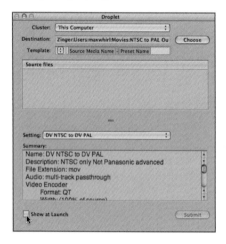

NOTE ▶   QuickTime files need to have a .mov extension on the end of the file name for droplets to recognize them.

Lesson Review

1. How do you export MPEG-2 files for use in DVD Studio Pro?

2. What is a GOP?

3. What codec is most commonly used for HD DVD encoding?

4. How do you create custom presets in Compressor?

5. Name ways to export audio data from a Final Cut Pro sequence.

6. What should always accompany an OMF export?

7. What is a "reference movie" and how do you make one?

8. How do you create a droplet in Compressor?

Answers

1. Choose Export > Using Compressor in Final Cut Pro and choose an MPEG-2 preset or create a custom preset.

2. GOP stands for *Group of Pictures* and describes the arrangement of keyframes and non-keyframes within an MPEG stream.

3. HD DVDs are usually encoded in H.264 format at high data rates.

4. Duplicate and modify an existing preset, or click the "Create a new setting" button in the Presets window.

5. As a mixed stereo AIFF; as a channel grouped AIFF; as a multitrack QuickTime movie; as an OMF; and as a compressed AC3 file.

6. OMF exports should always be delivered with a corresponding video file, preferably with BITC that matches the timecode in the OMF.

7. A reference movie is a tiny QuickTime file containing pointers to the media contained in the clips used in a sequence. You create one by deselecting the Make Movie Self Contained checkbox in the Export > QuickTime Movie dialog.

8. Select a preset and click the Save Selection as Droplet button.

15

Lesson 15
Working with Film Source

Cinema Tools is a collection of special Final Cut Pro settings, prepared film leaders, a utility for converting between a 24 fps and a 30 fps edit decision list (EDL), a reverse telecine and conforming program for QuickTime movies, and a list generator. At its core, it is also a database that keeps track of all the information for even the most complex feature film.

Popular software now exists that will give video a "film look," and as described in the previous lesson, Compressor can change NTSC or PAL video to a 24p scan. That is *not* the purpose of Cinema Tools.

There are many Final Cut Pro workflows that rely on, or that can benefit from, Cinema Tools. Originally, Cinema Tools was designed for projects shot on film, edited on Final Cut Pro, and finished on film. Now, it can be used for projects originating on 24p HD, edited at 29.97 fps or 25 fps SD, and then finished back on HD. You can even take advantage of Cinema Tools on projects that originate on SD video but finish on film or HD.

Rather than cover the myriad possibilities, this lesson will focus primarily on the most common situation: shooting on film, editing in Final Cut Pro, and then outputting the lists necessary to accurately cut—and possibly recut—the film negative.

Understanding the Film–Video–Film Workflow

First, it's important to understand the precise details of this workflow. When you shoot a project on film, the film must be telecined to video before it can be captured and edited in Final Cut Pro. In other words, the film has to be converted into a different format, and usually this means the film frame rate (24p) must be converted to either NTSC format at 29.97 interlaced fps or PAL at 25 interlaced fps.

That video is then brought into Final Cut Pro and edited, and, once the show is complete, those edit decisions need to be translated back to the film frames so that the film negative can be cut.

While you are already intimately familiar with video timecode, you may not be as versed in film's version of frame tracking: keycode. Keycode works just like timecode, except it's not malleable. With timecode you can switch from NDF to DF, or even apply one type of timecode to video of a different frame rate, and so on. With keycode, the numbers are physically attached to the frames on the film.

When the film is telecined, a list is generated that relates the keycode numbers on the film to the timecode numbers on the video. This list is called an *Evertz list* or a *FLEx file*, or more generically a telecine log. Without this list, it's impossible to get back to the film from Final Cut Pro's edited sequence (which is based on the timecode numbers on the video). Often these numbers will also be burned into the video image and, in that case, if you didn't have the telecine log, you could enter the numbers manually.

Just to make things extra complicated, film often has a separate set of frame-counting numbers called ink numbers. While keycode is physically embedded on the film (it's exposed when the film is developed), ink numbers are physically printed onto the film after developing. Ink numbers are generally used on workprints.

The EDL based on the keycode contains instructions to cut the negative. The EDL based on the ink numbers is used to cut the workprint.

Cinema Tools is the link between the Final Cut Pro project file and the instructions for how to cut the film based on those keycode or ink numbers. Those instructions are called a *cut list*.

Cinema Tools works by generating a database file that is basically a translation of the telecine log as it corresponds to the actual clips logged into Final Cut Pro.

If you feed Cinema Tools a Final Cut Pro sequence, it compares all the edits with the corresponding keycode or ink numbers and generates the cut list that can be sent to the film editor.

Over the years, more and more of Cinema Tools' features have found their way directly into Final Cut Pro's menus, and now, with Final Cut Pro 5, there's almost no need to launch Cinema Tools directly. But Cinema Tools is still working for you in the background, storing and managing those keycode or ink numbers.

Creating the Database

The Cinema Tools database is the only way to attach film-specific information to the clips you edit in Final Cut Pro. This includes those keycode and ink numbers, camera roll numbers, audio timecode and reel number, notes made during the telecine process, and other information specific to film.

Although you can type in all the information manually, it is far more practical to import a telecine log to avert the possibility of human error, as even a two-digit transposition can cause irrevocable damage to your negative. Cinema Tools can read most telecine formats, including FLEx, Evertz, Aaton, and ALE.

A telecine log is a simple text file, containing clip names and their corresponding reel and timecode numbers, and those all-important keycode or ink numbers. If you opened the telecine log included with this book in a text editor, it would look like this:

000 Manufacturer Aaton No. 021 Equip Keylink Version 6.91 Flex 1004 010 Title GOLD
FEVER TRAILER

012 Shoot Date 11-07-02 Transfer Date 11-07-02

100 Edit 0001 Field A1 NTSC

110 Scene 2K Take 1 Cam Roll A4 Sound 2A 09:48:49:01.0 120 Scrpt 200 35 23.98 000005
000038+01 Key EASTM KU262783 003957+12 p2 300 Assemble VT002 At 02:00:05:25.0
For 00:00:25:10.0

100 Edit 0002 Field A1 NTSC 110 Scene 2K Take 2 Cam Roll A4 Sound 2A 09:51:02:24.0
120 Scrpt 200 35 23.98 000005 000091+01 Key EASTM KU262783 003995+12 p2 300
Assemble VT002 At 02:00:31:05.0 For 00:01:00:20.0

...and so on.

It is basically just a batch list. With Final Cut Pro 5, you can import a telecine log directly into Final Cut Pro like any other batch list and generate a list of offline clips, ready for capture. Unlike an ordinary batch list, importing a telecine log automatically generates a Cinema Tools database as well, so if you ever need to conform the original film, you can.

Older versions of Final Cut Pro required you to create a new Cinema Tools database, import the telecine log there, export a Final Cut Pro batch list from Cinema Tools, and then import that batch list into Final Cut Pro. Same result, just a few added steps.

When importing any set of offline clips, Final Cut Pro uses the timebase of the default sequence settings. This can cause problems if you aren't careful. It's vitally important that you set your default sequence settings to the time-base of your telecined or downconverted videotape. This means 29.97 fps for NTSC and 25 fps for PAL. In this example, the telecined tape is at 29.97 fps.

1   Choose Final Cut Pro > Easy Setup and choose DV-NTSC. Click Setup.

    This sets your default sequence and capture settings to 29.97 fps.

2   Create a new Final Cut Pro project and save it on your Desktop as *Gold Fever Import*.

3   Choose File > Import > Cinema Tools Telecine Log.

The Import Telecine Log dialog opens.

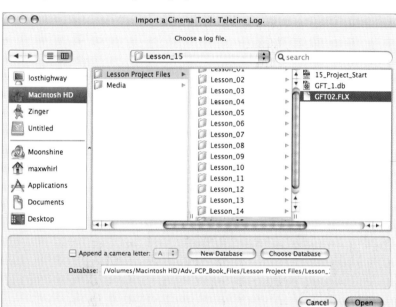

4   Navigate to the Lesson_15 project folder and select **GFT02.FLX**.

5   Deselect the "Append a camera letter" checkbox and click New Database.

A dialog opens.

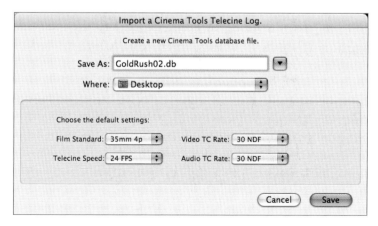

6 Name the new database *GoldRush02.db* and set the options to match the screen shot above.

7 Click Save, then click Open to select the FLEx file and import it.

A dialog appears to identify how many records were imported into the Cinema Tools database.

8 Click OK.

The list is automatically imported into the Final Cut Pro project and appears in the Browser as a set of offline clips.

9 Select one of the clips and choose Edit > Item Properties > Film.

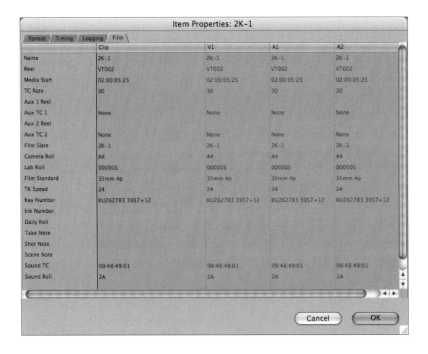

The Item Properties window opens to the Film tab, where you can see the camera roll, keycode, and other film-specific information.

10 Click OK to close the Item Properties window.

11 Press Command-Tab to switch to Cinema Tools.

Cinema Tools is automatically launched when performing the previous operation. Although you don't need to use the Cinema Tools database for anything at this point, it may be helpful to see how it works.

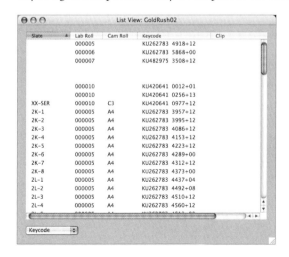

The List view shows all of the clips, and the Detail view shows all the data for the selected item.

12 Click the arrow at the top right of the Detail view to step through the events one at a time.

13 Press Command-Tab to switch back to Final Cut Pro.

You are now ready to capture the offline clips. Unfortunately, you don't have a copy of the source tape, and so you won't be able to complete that task.

Fortunately, the media DVDs included with this book provided you with a project file that contains a few of the clips from this show already captured. You will use this project for the next part of this lesson.

14 Close the **Gold Fever Import** project.

Editing a Project for Film

Thanks to the Cinema Tools database, you can safely edit your telecined clips at just about any frame rate and still generate an accurate cut list, but there are several advantages to cutting at the original 24 fps frame rate of the film. First of all, 24 fps files take less space and less bandwidth, which is always good. Second, Final Cut Pro can automatically generate 29.97 or 25 fps output for you to make preview copies or to view on a TV monitor. Third, you can forget all about the danger of editing on "imaginary frames," as discussed in Lesson 13.

However, the telecined clips were captured at 29.97 fps, so before you can begin editing, you need to convert them to 24 fps.

1 Open **15_Project_Start**.

This project has four clips from the Gold Fever trailer footage.

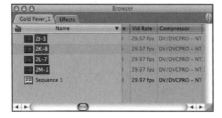

2 Select all four clips and choose Tools > Cinema Tools Reverse Telecine.

This automatically removes the 3:2 pulldown and converts the clips to 24p.

NOTE ▶ Be aware that this operation is not reversible, and permanently modifies your source footage. Alternatively, you could open Cinema Tools and use the Batch Reverse Telecine operation, which keeps your original files intact. This also gives you the ability to generate 23.98 fps files (used for material originated on HD instead of film).

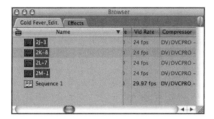

Now you are ready to edit your show in 24p. It's important that you edit in a 24 fps sequence that matches your clips' compression settings.

3 Press Option and choose File > New > Sequence to display the Select Sequence Preset dialog.

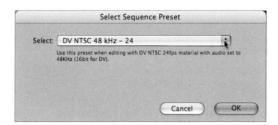

4 From the Select pop-up menu, choose the DV NTSC 48 kHz - 24 preset and click OK.

A new sequence is added to your project.

5 Name the new sequence *Gold Rush Trailer* and save your project.

6 Double-click the sequence to open it into the Canvas and Timeline.

7 Select all four clips and drag them into the Canvas window to add them to the sequence.

Dupe Detection

One important difference editing in film versus editing in video is that with film, you can't simply reuse a shot unless you instruct the lab to duplicate that section of the negative. Furthermore, because editing film requires actually splicing the negative, you must destroy one frame on either side of each clip you include. If you want to use frames 1–24 of a shot in one place, and frames 25–48 in another, you're in a bit of trouble. When the negative cutter prepares the first section, she will have to destroy frame 25, so it cannot be used in the second part. Again, the simple (though costly) solution is to have the lab generate a duplicate of that section of the negative so you can destroy frame 25 for the first section, and destroy frame 24 for the second. But wouldn't it be a lot easier if the editor simply used frames 26–49 instead?

Final Cut Pro offers a feature called dupe detection to alert you when you are using frames more than once in your show. Furthermore, it alerts you when you are using two shots based on adjacent frames as in the example above. It will even warn you if you have a dissolve or other transition that will require frames not visible in the sequence but that will be required for editing.

1 Choose Final Cut Pro > User Preferences and click the Editing tab.

2   In the Dupe Detection section, set the Handle Size option to 3 and click OK to close the window.

This is the minimum setting for working in 35mm film. Your negative cutter would probably appreciate it if you set this a bit higher, as it gives her a little more room for error. When cutting 16mm negatives, you should set this to at least 3 frames.

3   Select the **Gold Rush Trailer** sequence. Choose Sequence > Settings and click the Timeline Options tab.

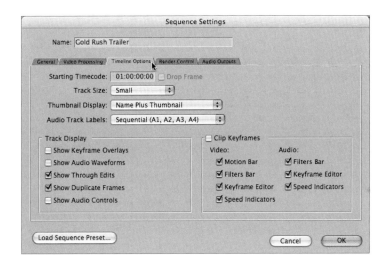

4   Select the Show Duplicate Frames checkbox.

Now, this sequence will indicate when duplicate frames are being used.

5   Select the Razor Blade tool (by pressing B) and add an edit to the middle of the **2K-8** clip in the Timeline.

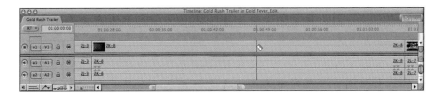

6   Zoom in on that new edit point.

NOTE ▶ You may need to force the Timeline to redraw to see the duplicate frames indicators. To refresh the window, click the tab containing the sequence name.

The red line on the bottom of the video track alerts you that you are now technically duplicating two frames (since that edit would require destroying the frame after the first part and the frame before the second part).

7   Press Shift-Z to zoom back out.

8   Select the **2K-8** clip from the Browser and edit it into your show at the end of the sequence.

TIP ▶ You may want to press Shift-Z again to view the entire Timeline at once.

This clip is now being used twice in this sequence. In fact, the middle section (where you made the edit) is now being used three times. The Duplicate Frames indicator appears on both instances of the clips and displays different colors to show the frames being duplicated.

You can identify exactly which frames are duplicated in the shortcut menu for the clip with the duplicated frame.

9   Control-click the second instance of the **2K-8** clip and choose Dupe Frames.

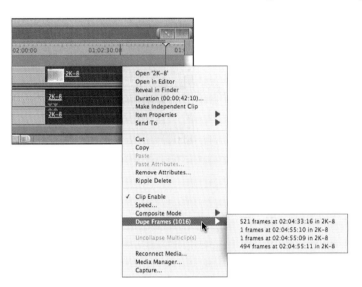

The submenu lists the areas of duplication and how many frames are in
each section.

As editor, it is now your choice to either live with the duplication (and force
the producer to cough up the extra dough to pay for a duplicate negative), or
reedit the show to eliminate the overlaps.

Generating Lists

For the most part, cutting a show for film isn't very different than cutting for
video. The difference mainly comes in what you deliver when you've finished.

Once you're done editing, there are several lists that you must output so the folks
handling the actual film can conform the film to match your finished sequence.
The most basic of these lists is the cut list mentioned earlier, but you may need
to generate other lists depending on the specifics of your project. If you used
duplicate frames, you can generate a *dupe list*. If you used visual effects, you can
output an *opticals list*. If someone is going to reedit the original audiotapes, you
can create an audio EDL based on the timecode from the audiotapes as indicated in the telecine log, and so on.

Creating a Cut List

The cut list is simply an EDL that indicates the keycode numbers for the original film. This is the most important file you'll provide to your negative cutter, and it's very easy to create.

1   Select the **Gold Rush Trailer** sequence and choose File > Export > Cinema Tools Film Lists.

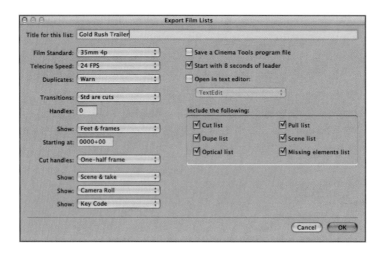

The Export Film Lists dialog appears.

The left side of the window lists all the settings that must correspond to the film you are cutting. In this example, all of the default settings are fine.

The right side of the window lets you choose which files to export.

2   Deselect the "Save a Cinema Tools program file" checkbox.

This option saves a special file that is a version of your Final Cut Pro sequence specifically for Cinema Tools. This will be covered a bit later.

3   Select the "Start with 8 seconds of leader" checkbox.

All films must begin with a standard academy leader. This is the familiar countdown that allows the projection and exhibition equipment to sync up and work properly. Selecting this option sets the program counter to account for the time that the leader will occupy. This is akin to putting bars and tone at the beginning of a video master.

4   Deselect the "Open in text editor" checkbox.

This setting will optionally open the finished lists in a text editor for you to examine and modify if necessary.

5   In the "Include the following" section, leave all the options selected.

These options will all be included in a single file.

6   Click OK.

The "Export a Cinema Tools film list" dialog appears.

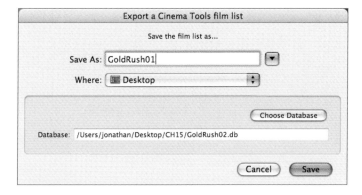

7   Name the list *GoldRush01* and navigate to the Desktop. Ensure that the database is pointing to the **GoldRush02.db** file and click Save.

Creating an Audio EDL

Audio EDLs are useful only for productions that use a separate audio recorder with timecode capabilities. Creating audio EDLs requires that sound rolls and timecode be entered into the Cinema Tools database. If the audio was logged and synchronized in telecine, this information will automatically be included in your telecine log.

Although audio files can be moved from the picture-editing system to the sound-editing system without losing a single bit of digital quality, there is still a big demand for audio EDLs. The reason is that not all sound editors prefer to use audio OMF exports from Final Cut Pro, and exporting tracks as AIFF files doesn't allow for the flexibility to make adjustments when exporting to a digital audio workstation.

In addition, going back to the original production tapes ensures that no extraneous noise gets into the mix due to sample-rate conversion, or a flaw in the analog-to-digital path.

Audio EDLs are very different from EDLs for online video edits. The first thing that a sound editor will do when importing an EDL into the audio workstation is remove all the dissolves, panning, volume mapping, filters, and any other effects put there by the picture editor. The reason is that the effects don't usually translate between systems, and the audio editing and mixing systems usually have better control over these effects.

The audio EDLs created by Cinema Tools automatically flatten all of these effects in order to give the sound editor a clean list. However, the downside is that much of the detail of the original edit is lost. Things like reverse audio or filtering effects to simulate, say, the sound from a telephone need to be explained to the sound editor because they don't show up on the list.

Try to use just the first four tracks for your production audio. Keep sound effects, music imported from CD or MP3, and other nonproduction sound out of these tracks. The audio EDL created by Cinema Tools can handle only four audio tracks per list. If you must use more than four tracks, export to a separate list.

1   Create a new 24 fps sequence. Remember to press the Option key with the File > New > Sequence pop-up menu or use the Command-Option-N shortcut, and choose the DV NTSC 48 kHz – 24 preset.

2   Make a few edits using the **Gold Fever** clips. Put sound on tracks 1 through 4 of the Timeline.

3   If you are planning to use audio filters, change the speed of audio clips, or perform other processing of your sound files, try these on your test edit to see what happens.

4   In Final Cut Pro, choose File > Export > Cinema Tools Audio EDL to create an audio EDL.

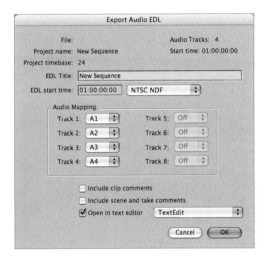

If you find yourself in a situation in which you need more than four tracks for an audio EDL, turn off the first four tracks and map tracks 5 through 8 to EDL tracks 1 through 4.

5   From the Modes Project pop-up menu, choose NTSC NDF.

6   Click OK.

7   Navigate to your **GFT_1.db** file in the Lesson_15 folder when prompted in the next dialog and click Choose.

8   Name the EDL *Audio.edl*, save it to the Desktop, and click OK.

If you selected Final Cut Pro as your text editor, then two text files windows should open automatically in Final Cut Pro. If not, choose File > Open in Final Cut Pro, navigate to the Desktop, and open both **Audio.edl** and

Audio.edl.txt. When Cinema Tools exports an audio EDL, it also creates a separate text file that shows how the tracks were mapped to the EDL.

If you put in filters and other audio effects, notice that they do not appear in the audio EDL.

Understanding Scene Lists

The scene list, another one of the lists that can be generated by Cinema Tools, is a somewhat special purpose item. Many independent filmmakers don't have the budget to print all of their dailies, so they wait until after editing to order a workprint. To facilitate this, Cinema Tools can create a list of every shot used in the sequence. The scene list includes the entire clip, not just the section of the shot that was used. This is a way to order just the takes that were used in the edit.

Note that in many cases, ordering prints this way costs more because they are considered reprints instead of the daily prints that are done right after the negative is developed. In addition, shots from various setups will be combined into a lab roll, and a one-light print from this lab roll will not be as consistent in color balance as a daily workprint.

Despite these disadvantages, it is a way to order the print for a film preview before committing to cutting the negative. This is highly desirable if the production can raise the money for the workprint.

Creating an Optical List

Fades, dissolves, flops, and other common effects are usually created on a specialized piece of equipment known as an *optical printer*. This device is basically a camera pointed at a film projector, but, of course, there is much more to it than that. Faithfully reproducing the effect from the Final Cut Pro project requires some instructions. These instructions are known as an *optical list*.

Cinema Tools can create accurate optical lists for many common effects like dissolves, wipes, and speed changes. However, it doesn't catch all the effects that should be included in an optical list. Effects like flops, resized images, and many others don't show up on the optical list. In addition, superimposed images are displayed in a second cut list instead of an optical. In other cases, such as combining a speed change with a dissolve, the optical will be listed in a way that may be hard for the optical printer operator to follow.

When making optical lists, it is important to examine every effect in the Timeline and determine if it is best to make an optical, make a digital effect, or process it when color correcting the final film print. Don't rely on Cinema Tools to make these decisions for you.

It is preferable to create all the opticals before attempting to cut the negative. The main reason is that you don't want the negative to be handled any more than necessary, and making the opticals first ensures that the shots needed to create the effects aren't cut into tiny pieces.

1   In Final Cut Pro, use any of the sequences from the previous exercises, or create a new sequence with several edits.

2   Add a Cross Dissolve transition effect on one of your edits.

3   Apply a filter on one of the shots. A common effect is a flop, and you can find it in the Effects tab in the Browser under Video Filters > Perspective > Flop.

4   Choose File > Export > Cinema Tools Film Lists.

5   Use the following settings to export an optical list. Be sure to set the Transitions option to "All are opticals", or the dissolve may not show up on the list.

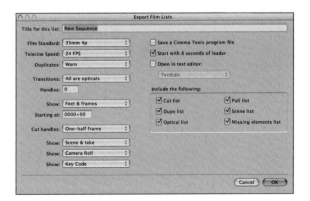

NOTE ▶ Setting Transitions to Standard is designed for creating fades and dissolves using the A- and B-roll negative-cutting method, and you must specify the amount of transition handles with this setting. The "All are opticals" setting is designed for conforming a workprint where effects will be marked on the print using a grease pencil.

6   Click OK. Name the list *Opticals.cut* and save it to your Desktop. Remember to specify the current **GFT_1.db** database.

7   Examine the list. Notice how the dissolve is listed graphically, detailing exactly where the effect starts, the length, and everything needed to re-create the effect on an optical printer—but what happened to the filter effect?

TIP ▶ If you have several effects shots in your project, you may want to put each effect into a separate sequence. This will make it easier to keep track of the effect, and if it doesn't show up properly in the optical list you can make a cut list and add notes for the company working on your effects.

Understanding Program Files

So far, all of the lists generated by Cinema Tools have been text files that you could view, modify, and print. A Cinema Tools program file is completely different. It is a special purpose file that you can't open up and view—it is designed for use only with Cinema Tools.

The main purpose of the program file is to archive a Final Cut Pro sequence. The program file is needed to create a change list (more on this in a moment), and it can also be used to generate an audio EDL. Ironically, it can't be used to create a film list, so you had better have the sequence saved in your Final Cut Pro project if you want to create a film list.

Creating a Change List

Feature films produced by the major studios go through a process in which they are previewed by an audience and their reactions are studied, then the film is reedited and once again previewed. This process is repeated until someone decides to release it. There is an old saying, "Films are never finished. They are merely surrendered to the projectionist."

Studio previews are usually shown in a regular movie theater using the cut workprint. To update a workprint to the new edit, you need a change list that shows where shots have been added, deleted, moved, trimmed, and extended.

Change lists only include edits that are needed to conform a film workprint. In addition, Cinema Tools assumes that all the opticals and visual effects have been finished on film and cut into the workprint; it cannot list changes in opticals. Changes in superimposed video tracks and audio tracks are not handled, and it doesn't help much if you are planning to preview on video. Still, change lists are extremely valuable when you're working on projects in which you want to see the film projected before making the commitment to cut the negative.

1   Using **15 Project_Start**, create a new 24p sequence.

2   Make a few edits; be sure to avoid any duplicate usage, and use cuts only— don't put in any effects.

3   In Final Cut Pro, choose File > Export > Cinema Tools Film Lists to open the Export Film List dialog. Choose "All are cuts" from the Transitions pop-up menu and select "Save a Cinema Tools Program File".

   You will be asked to save a regular list file, which is not important for this exercise. Next, you'll be asked to save the program file.

4   Name the file *Original Edit.pgm* and save it to your Desktop.

5   Next, make some changes to the sequence. Extend, trim, and move shots around. Try just about anything, but be sure not to put in any duplicate usage or effects.

6   Once you are satisfied with your new version, in Final Cut Pro choose File > Export > Cinema Tools Change List.

7   Cinema Tools will open a navigation window and ask you to point out the location of the program file for the previous version of the sequence. Select the **Original Edit.pgm** file on your Desktop.

8   Next Cinema Tools will open the Export Change List dialog. Notice that it is very similar to the Export Film List dialog, with the addition of some change list options. You can create a cut list of the new sequence along with the change list.

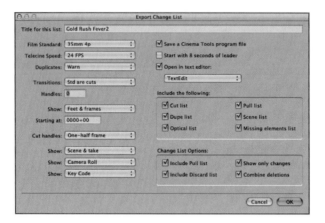

9   In most cases you will want to select all of the change list options. Click OK.

    The Save dialog appears.

10 Name the file *Change.cut* and save it to the Desktop.

11 Next, you'll be asked to save the changed program file. Name it *Change.pgm* and save it to the Desktop.

12 Open **Change.cut** and examine how it lists the changes to your sequence.

    The pull list will show which pieces of film you will need to complete the changes, and the discard list shows which pieces you no longer need. Of course, you shouldn't throw these pieces away—you might change your mind and need them again! Splice all of your discarded pieces of film back into their original rolls.

Another way to create a change list is from two Cinema Tools program files. This allows you to make a change list without having to access the sequences in Final Cut Pro. However, there is no option to create a cut list when using program files.

Lesson Review

1. What is Cinema Tools?

2. What information does a telecine log contain?

3. What is reverse telecine?

4. Why is dupe detection important?

5. What is a cut list?

6. What is an opticals list?

7. What are scene lists?

8. What is a change list?

Answers

1. A collection of film-related functions to aid in editing material originated on film or 24p HD at standard video rates.

2. A telecine log contains the keycode or ink numbers from the film original as well as the corresponding video timecode.

3. Reverse telecine is the process of reverting 24p footage that had previously been converted to 29.97(interlaced) back to 24p.

4. When a sequence contains duplicated frames, conforming the corresponding film negative will not be possible without creating a duplicate negative.

5. A cut list is an EDL for the original film based on the keycode or ink numbers stored in the Cinema Tools database.

6. An opticals list contains the information for each of the shots that will need special effects treatment such as fades or filters.

7. A scene list is a list of shots that are used in the program for the purpose of creating a film workprint.

8. A change list is a special EDL that describes only changes that have occurred since the last cut list was generated.

01:07:41:13
07:41:13
1:05:23
PROD. NO.
SCENE
TAKE
ROLL
DATE
PROD. CO.
DIRECTOR
CAMERAMAN
SOUND

Final Cut Studio Workflows

Apple's professional audio and video applications are designed to work together seamlessly, even in the most demanding postproduction workflows. The Final Cut Studio product line—a comprehensive and integrated postproduction package—comprises Final Cut Pro 5, Soundtrack Pro, Motion 2, DVD Studio Pro 4, Compressor 2, LiveType 2, and Cinema Tools 3. These tools, in conjunction with Shake 4 and Logic Pro 7, provide professional editors with the most comprehensive toolkit in the industry.

The appendix on the DVD accompanying this book details the roles of each application in the Final Cut Pro production process. You will also find a sample Final Cut Studio workflow and information on "round-tripping," the ability to embed and open project files while working in another application. See **Appendix-Final Cut Studio Workflows.pdf.**

01:07:41:13
07:41:13
1:05:23
PROD. NO.
SCENE
TAKE
ROLL
DATE
PROD. CO.
DIRECTOR
CAMERAMAN
SOUND

Glossary

16-bit A standard bit depth for digital audio recording and playback.

16x9 The standard display aspect ratio of a high-definition television set.

32-bit A four-channel image with each channel 8-bits deep. Typically, a CGI image with red, green, blue, and alpha channels.

4x3 The standard display aspect ratio of a standard video home television set.

8-bit For video, a bit depth at which color is sampled. 8-bit color is common with DV and other standard-definition digital formats. Some high-definition acquisition formats can also record in 8-bit, but usually record in 10-bit.

A

Action safe The area inside a border that is five percent smaller than the overall size of the video frame. Most of the time, anything in your video image that's outside of this border will not be displayed on a video screen.

Add Edit Working like the Razor Blade tool, adds an edit point to all clips in the Timeline at the current position of the playhead.

A/D converter box Equipment that changes an analog signal into a digital signal.

AIFF (Audio Interchange File Format) Apple's native uncompressed audio file format created for the Macintosh computer, commonly used for the storage and transmission of digitally sampled sound.

Alpha channel An image channel in addition to the R, G, and B color channels that is used to store transparency information for compositing. In Final Cut Pro, black represents 100 percent transparent, and white represents 100 percent opaque.

Ambience A type of sound that includes background room noise, traffic noise, and atmospheric sound effects.

Analog A signal that consists of a continuously varying voltage level, measured on a Waveform Monitor, which represents video and audio information. Analog signals must be converted to digital signals (digitized or captured) for use in Final Cut Pro. VHS and Beta SP are both analog tape formats.

Anamorphic An image shot in a widescreen format and then squeezed into 4x3 frame size. When played back in Final Cut Pro, the image is played wide screen.

Anchor point In the Motion tab, the point that is used to center changes to a clip when using motion effects. A clip's anchor point does not have to be at its center.

Animation The process of changing any number of variables such as color, audio levels, or other effects over time using keyframes.

Aspect ratio The ratio of the width of an image to its height on any viewing screen. Standard TV has an aspect ratio of 4:3; HDTV's is 16:9.

Attributes All of the unique settings that have been applied to either audio or video clips.

Audio meters A graphic display of the audio level (loudness) of a clip or sequence. Used to set incoming and outgoing audio levels and to check for audio distortion and signal strength.

Audio mixing The process of adjusting the volume levels of all audio clips in an edited sequence, including the production audio, music, sound effects, voice-overs, and additional background ambience, to turn all of these sounds into a harmonious whole.

Audio sample rate The rate or frequency at which a sound is sampled to digitize it. 48 kHz is the standard sampling rate for digital audio; CD audio is sampled at 44.1 kHz.

Audio waveform A graphical representation of the amplitude (loudness) of a sound over a period of time.

Autosave Vault A function to automatically save backup copies of all your FCP open projects at regular intervals. It must be turned on, and you can specify the intervals.

AVI A PC-compatible standard for digital video no longer officially supported by Microsoft but still frequently used. AVI supports fewer codecs than QuickTime.

Axis An imaginary straight line (horizontal, vertical, 3D diagonal) along which an object can move or rotate in space.

B

Backtiming Using In and Out points in the Viewer and only an Out point in the Timeline, the two Out points will align, and the rest of the clip will appear before or to the left of this point.

Batch capture Capturing multiple clips and or sequences with a single command.

Batch export The ability to export multiple clips and or sequences with a single command by being able to stack them up in a queue. It is particularly useful when exporting will take a lot of time.

Bars and tone A series of vertical bars of specific colors and an audio tone that are used to calibrate the audio and video signals coming from a videotape or camera to ensure consistent appearance and sound on different TV monitors.

Bezier handle The "control handles" attached to a Bezier curve on a motion path that allow you to change the shape of the curve.

Bin A file folder in the Browser window used to keep media clips grouped and organized. Derived from film editing where strips of film were hung over a cloth bin for sorting during the editing process.

Black level The measurement of the black portion of the video signal. In analog television, this should not go below 7.5 IRE units. In digital television, black may be 0 units.

B-roll A term used to describe alternate footage that intercuts with the primary soundtrack used in a program to help tell the story, or to cover flaws. B-roll is usually referred to as *cutaway shots*.

Blue screen A solid blue colored background placed behind a subject and photographed so that later the subject can be extracted and composited onto another image.

Broadcast safe The range of color that can be broadcast free of distortion, according to the NTSC standards, with maximum allowable video at 100 IRE units and digital black at 0 IRE, or analog black at 7.5 IRE units. FCP has a Broadcast Safe color-correction filter that provides a fast method of dealing with clips that have luminance and chrominance levels exceeding the broadcast limits for video.

Browser An interface window that is a central storage area where you organize and access all of the source material used in your project.

C

Cache A special high-speed memory area that the computer uses to store information that it can retrieve much faster than from main memory.

Canvas The window in which you can view your edited sequence.

Capture The process of digitizing media in the computer.

Center point Defines a clip's location in the X/Y coordinate space in the Motion tab of the Canvas.

Chroma The color information contained in a video signal consisting of hue (the color itself) and saturation (intensity).

Clip Media files that may consist of video, audio, graphics, or any similar content that can be imported into Final Cut Pro.

Clipping Distortion occurring during the playback or recording of digital audio due to an overly loud level.

Close-up Framing a subject so that it fills the frame. Usually used for dramatic storytelling.

Codec Short for compression/decompression. A program used to compress and decompress data such as audio and video files.

Color balance   Refers to the overall mix of red, green, and blue for the highlights (brightest), midtones, and shadow (darkest) areas in a clip. The color balance of these three areas can be adjusted using the Color Corrector 3-way filter.

Color correction   A process in which the color of clips used in an edited program is evened out so that all shots in a given scene match.

Color depth   The possible range of colors that can be used in a movie or image. In computer graphics, there are usually four choices: grayscale, 8-bit, 16-bit, and 24-bit. Higher color depths provide a wider range of colors but also require more disk space for a given image size. Broadcast video is generally 24-bit, with 8 bits of color information per channel.

Color matte   A clip containing solid color created as a generated item in the effects.

Composite Mode   One of the options in the Modify menu that offers many different methods of combing two or more images.

Compositing   The process of combining two or more video or electronic images into a single frame. This term can also describe the process of creating various video effects.

Compression   The process by which video, graphics, and audio files are reduced in size. The reduction in the size of a video file through the removal of redundant image data is referred to as a *lossy compression scheme.* A lossless compression scheme uses a mathematical process and reduces the file size by consolidating the redundant information without discarding it. See also *codec.*

Compression marker   A marker placed in a Final Cut movie that will flag DVD Studio Pro to stop so an I-frame can be changed.

Contrast   The difference between the lightest and darkest values in an image. High-contrast images have a large range of values from the darkest shadow to the lightest highlight. Low-contrast images have a more narrow range of values, resulting in a "flatter" look.

Crop tool   A tool used to slice a specified amount from the total frame size of a clip. You can crop the top, left, right, and bottom of a clip independently.

Cross fade A transition between two audio clips where one sound is faded out while the other is faded in. Used to make the transition between two audio cuts less noticeable.

Cut The simplest type of edit where one clip ends and the next begins without any transition.

Cutaway A shot that is related to the current subject and occurs in the same time frame; for instance, an interviewer's reaction to what is being said in an interview or a shot to cover a technically bad moment.

D

Data rate The speed at which data can be transferred, often described in megabytes per second (MB/sec). The higher a video file's data rate, the higher quality it will be, but it will require more system resources (processor speed, hard disk space, and performance). Some codecs allow you to specify a maximum data rate for a movie during capture.

Decibel (dB) A unit of measure for the loudness of audio.

Decompression The process of creating a viewable image for playback from a compressed video, graphics, or audio file. Compare with *compression*.

De-interlace filter Used to convert video frames composed of two interlaced fields into a single unified frame; for example, to create a still image of an object moving at high speed.

Desaturate To remove color from a clip. 100 percent desaturation results in a grayscale image.

Device control A cable that allows Final Cut Pro to control a video deck or camera. Three protocols are used most frequently to control video devices: serial device control via the RS-422 and RS-232 protocols, and FireWire for DV camcorders and decks.

Digital Data that is stored or transmitted as a sequence of ones and zeros.

Digital video Video that has been captured, manipulated, and stored using a digital format, which can be easily imported into your computer. Digital video can come in many different formats such as Digital-8, DVC Pro, DVCAM, or DV.

Digitize To convert an analog video signal into a digital video format. A method of capturing video. See also *capture*.

Dissolve A transition between two video clips where the first one fades down at the same time the second one fades up.

Distort An option in the Tool palette that allows you to change the shape of an image by moving any of its four corners independently of the others.

Dock A strip on the Desktop where you can store the program alias icons that you use most frequently.

Drop frame timecode A type of timecode that skips ahead in time by two frame numbers each minute, except for minutes ending in "0" (10, 20, 30 and so on). Although timecode numbers are skipped, actual video frames are not skipped. Drop frame timecode is a reference to real time.

Drop shadow An effect that creates an artificial shadow behind an image or text.

Dub Making a copy of an analog tape to the same type of format.

Duration The length of a clip or a sequence from its In to its Out point, or the length of time that it takes that piece of video to play.

DV A standard for a specific digital video format created by a consortium of camcorder vendors, which uses Motion JPEG video at a 720 x 480 resolution at 29.97 frames per second (NTSC) or 720 x 546 resolution at 25 fps (PAL), stored at a bit rate of 25 MB per second at a compression of 4:1:1.

DVD A disc that is the size of a CD, but uses higher density storage methods to significantly increase its capacity. Usually used for video distribution, DVD-ROM discs can also be used to store computer data.

DVD marker A location indicator that can be seen in DVD Studio Pro used to mark a chapter.

Dynamic range The difference, in decibels, between the loudest and softest parts of a recording.

E   **Easy Setup** Preset audio/video settings, including capture, sequence, device control, and output settings.

Edit point (1) Defines what part of a clip you want to use in an edited sequence. Edit points include In points, which specify the beginning of a section of a clip or sequence, and Out points, which specify the end of a section of a clip or sequence. (2) The point in the Timeline of an edited sequence where the Out point of one clip meets the In point of the next clip.

Edit to Tape The command that lets you perform frame-accurate Insert and Assemble edits to tape.

EDL A text file that uses the source timecode of clips to sequentially list all of the edits that make up a sequence. EDLs are used to move a project from one editing application to another, or to coordinate the assembly of a program in a tape-based online editing facility.

Effects A general term used to describe all of Final Cut Pro's capabilities that go beyond cuts-only editing. See *filters, generators,* and *transitions.*

Export A menu option that allows you to move files or media out of Final Cut Pro to a variety of destinations via a variety of codecs; lets you translate the current file format into a number of different formats.

Extend edit An edit in which the edit point is moved to the position of the playhead in the Timeline.

F   **Fade** An effect in which the picture gradually transitions to black.

Faders In the Audio Mixer, vertical sliders used to adjust the audio levels of clips at the position of the playhead.

Favorite A customized effect that is used frequently. You can create favorites from most of the effects in Final Cut Pro.

Field Half of an *interlaced video* frame consisting of the odd or the even scan lines.

Field Dominance The choice of whether field one or field two will be displayed on the monitor first. The default should be Lower (even) for DV and Targa captures.

Filters Effects you can apply to video and audio clips or group of clips that change some aspect of the clip content.

Finishing The process of fine tuning the sequence audio and video levels and preparing the sequence for output to tape or other destination, such as the Web or DVD. Finishing may also involve recapturing offline resolution clips at an uncompressed resolution.

FireWire Apple's trademark name for the IEEE 1394 standard used to connect external hard drives and cameras to computers. It provides a fast interface to move large video and audio files to the computer's hard drive.

Fit to Fill edit An edit in which a clip is inserted into a sequence such that its duration matches a predetermined amount of specified track space.

Frame A single still image from either video or film. For video, each frame is made up of two interlaced fields (see *interlaced video*).

Frame blending A process of inserting blended frames in place of frames that have been duplicated in clips with slow motion, to make them play back more smoothly.

Framing Composing a shot for the best presentation of the subject, taking into consideration the size of the subject in the frame and how it is centered.

Frequency The number of times a sound or signal vibrates each second, measured in cycles per second, or hertz.

Gain In video, the level of white in a video picture; in audio, the loudness of an audio signal.

G

Gamma A curve that describes how the middle tones of an image appear. Gamma is a nonlinear function often confused with "brightness" or "contrast." Changing the value of the gamma affects middle tones while leaving the whites and blacks of the image unaltered. Gamma adjustment is often used to compensate for differences between Macintosh and Windows video cards and displays.

Gap Locations in a sequence where there is no media on any track. When output to video, gaps in an edited sequence appear as black sections.

Generators Clips that are synthesized by Final Cut Pro. Generators can be used as different kinds of backgrounds, titles, and elements for visual design.

Gradient A generated image that changes smoothly from one color to another across the image. The change can occur in several ways horizontally, vertically, radially, and so on.

Green screen A solid green colored background placed behind a subject and photographed so that later the subject can be extracted and composited into another image.

H

Handles Extra frames of unused video or audio that are on either side of the In and Out points in an edit.

Head The beginning of a clip.

Histogram A window that displays the relative strength of all luminance values in a video frame, from black to super-white. It is useful for comparing two clips in order to match their brightness values more closely.

Hue A specific color or pigment, such as red.

I

Icon An onscreen symbol that represents a program or file.

Import File The menu option that allows you to bring one or more media files into an FCP project.

Import Folder The menu option that allows you to import a folder of media files into an FCP project.

Incoming clip The clip that is on the right-hand side, or B-side, of a transition or cut point.

In point The edit point entered either in the Viewer, Canvas, or Timeline that determines where an edit will begin.

Insert edit To insert a clip into an existing sequence into the Timeline, which automatically moves the other clips (or remaining frames of a clip) to the right to make room for it. An Insert edit does not replace existing material.

Interlaced video A video scanning method that first scans the odd picture lines (field 1) and then scans the even picture lines (field 2), which merges them together into one single frame of video. Used in standard-definition video.

IRE A unit of measurement for luminance in an analog signal established by the Institute of Radio Engineers (IRE).

J

Jog To move forward or backward through your video one frame at a time.

JPEG (Joint Photographic Experts Group) A popular image file format that lets you create highly compressed graphics files. The amount of compression used can vary. Less compression results in a higher quality image.

Jump cut A cut in which an abrupt change occurs between two shots.

K

Keyframe A point at which a filter, motion effect, or audio level changes value. There must be at least two keyframes representing two different values to see a change.

Keying The process of dropping out a specific area of an image, such as its background, in order to composite it with another image. You can key out information in a clip based on brightness and darkness, or color.

L

Labels Terms that appear in the Label column of the Browser such as "Best Take" and "Interview." Labels can also be assigned to clips and media to help distinguish and sort them. Each label has an associated color that is also applied to clips.

Letterbox When widescreen video is displayed to fit within a standard 4x3 monitor, putting black at the top and bottom of the picture.

Lift edit An edit function that leaves a gap when material is lifted from the Timeline.

Link (1) To connect an audio clip and video clip together in the Timeline so that when one item is selected, moved, or trimmed, all other items linked to it are affected. (2) The connection between a clip and its associated source media file on disk. If you move source media files, change their names, or put them in the Trash, the links break and associated clips in your Final Cut Pro project become *offline clips.*

Linked selection An option in the Timeline that, when enabled, maintains connections between linked clips. When linked selection is turned off, linked items behave as if they are not connected.

Lock Track control The lock icon in the Timeline tracks control area, which locks and unlocks tracks. See *locked track.*

Locked track A track whose contents cannot be moved or changed. Crosshatched lines distinguish a locked track on the Timeline. You can lock or unlock tracks at any time by clicking the Lock Track control on the Timeline.

Log and Capture The process of playing clips from a device and logging and capturing the clips you want to use in editing.

Log bin A specific bin where all the logged or captured clips go when using the Log and Capture window.

logging The process of entering detailed information including the In and Out points from your source material, log notes, and so on, in preparation to be captured.

Looping A playback mode of repeatedly playing the same portion of a clip or sequence from an In point to an Out point.

Lower third Lines of text used to identify a person, place, or thing in a clip.

Luma Short for luminance. A value describing the brightness part of the video signal without color (chroma).

Luma Key A filter used to key out a luminance value, creating a matte based on the brightest or darkest area of an image. See *keying and matte.*

M

Mark In The process of indicating with a mark in the Timeline the first frame of a clip to be used.

Mark Out The process of indicating with a mark in the Timeline the last frame of a clip to be used.

Markers Location indicators that can be placed on a clip or in a sequence to help you find a specific place while you edit. Can be used to sync action between two clips, identify beats of music, mark a reference word from a narrator, and so on.

Marquee When dragging the pointer over items in the Browser or Timeline, the dashed lines that create a rectangular area used to select items in that area.

Mark in Sync Placing a marker that labels the audio from another source as being in sync with a selected video clip. This disables the normal out-of-sync warnings.

Mask An image or clip used to define areas of transparency in another clip. Similar to an *alpha channel.*

Master clip The status given to a clip when it is the first time that clip is used in a project. It is the clip from which other affiliate clips, such as sequence clips and subclips, are created.

Master shot A single, long shot of some dramatic action from which shorter cuts such as close-ups and medium shots are taken in order to fill out the story.

Mastering mode A mode in the Edit to Tape window that lets you output additional elements such as color bars and tone, a slate, and a countdown when you output your program to tape.

Match Frame A command that looks at the clip in the Timeline at the playhead, and puts that clip's master into the Viewer. The position of the playhead in the Viewer matches that of the playhead in the Canvas, so both the Canvas and the Viewer will display the same frame, and the In and Out points of the clip in your sequence will be matched to those of the copy in the Viewer. In addition, all the original source material for this clip will also be displayed.

Matte An effect, such as a widescreen matte or a garbage matte, that hides or reveals a part of a clip.

Media file A generic term for captured or acquired elements such as QuickTime movies, sounds, and pictures.

Media Manager A tool that helps you manage your projects, media files, and available disk space quickly and easily in Final Cut Pro without using the Finder.

Midtones The middle brightness range of an image. Not the very brightest part, nor the very darkest part.

Mono audio A single track of audio.

Motion Blur An effect that blurs any clip with keyframed motion applied to it, similar to blurred motion recorded by a camera.

Motion path A path that appears in the Canvas when Image+Wireframe mode is selected and a clip has Center *keyframes applied to it.*

MPEG Acronym for *Moving Picture Experts Group.* A group of compression standards for video and audio, which includes MPEG-1, MPEG-2, MPEG-3 (referred to as MP3), and MPEG-4.

Multicam editing This feature lets you simultaneously play back and view shots from multiple sources and cut between them in real time.

Multiclip A clip that allows you to group together multiple sources as separate angles and cut between them, up to 128 angles, of which 16 can be played back at a time.

N

Natural sound The ambient sound that is used from the source videotape.

Nest To place a sequence that is edited within another sequence.

Non-drop frame timecode A type of timecode, in which frames are numbered. Non-drop frame timecode is off by 3 seconds and 18 frames per hour in comparison to actual elapsed time.

Noninterlaced video The standard representation of images on a computer, also referred to as progressive scan. The monitor displays the image by drawing each line, continuously one after the other, from top to bottom.

Nonlinear editing (NLE) An video editing process that uses computer hard disks to random access the media. It allows the editor to reorganize clips very quickly or make changes to sections without having to re-create the entire program.

Nonsquare pixel A pixel whose height is different than its width. An NTSC pixel is taller than it is wide, and a PAL pixel is wider than it is tall.

NTSC Abbreviation for National Television Systems Committee. Standard of color TV broadcasting used mainly in the North America, Mexico, and Japan, consisting of 525 lines per frame, 29.97 frames per second, and 720 x 486 pixels per frame (720 x 480 for DV).

Offline clip Clips that appear in the Browser with a red slash through them. Clips may be offline because they haven't been captured yet, or because the media file has been moved to another location. To view these clips properly in your project, you must recapture them or reconnect them to their corresponding source files at their new locations on disk.

Offline editing The process of editing a program at a lower resolution to save on equipment costs or to conserve hard disk space. When the edit is finished, the material can be recaptured at a higher quality, or an *EDL* can be generated for re-creating the edit on another system.

OMF (Open Media Framework) OMF is an edit data interchange format.

On the fly The process of setting an In or Out point as the clip is playing in the Viewer or on the Timeline.

Opacity The degree to which an image is transparent, allowing images behind to show through.

Outgoing clip The clip that is on the left-hand side of the cut point or the A side of the transition.

Out of sync When the audio of a track has been shifted horizontally in the Timeline from the video track causing it to no longer match the video track.

Out point The edit point entered in the Viewer, Canvas, or Timeline where an edit will end.

Overlays Icons or text that are displayed over the video in the Viewer and Canvas windows while the playhead is parked on a frame to provide information about that frame.

Overwrite edit An edit where the clip being edited into a sequence replaces an existing clip. The duration of the sequence remains unchanged.

P

PAL (Phase Alternating Line) The European color TV broadcasting standard consisting of 625 lines per frame, running at 25 frames per second, and 720x546 pixels per frame.

Pan To move a camera left or right without changing its position.

Parade Scope A modified Waveform Monitor that breaks out the red, green, and blue components of the image, showing them as three separate waveforms. Useful for comparing the relative levels of reds, greens, and blues between two clips, especially in a graphics situation.

Paste Attributes The ability to copy attributes from one clip and transfer (paste) them to another clip of the same type.

Patch panel The section of the Timeline containing the Audio, Source, and Destination, Track Enabling, Locking, and Edit Select controls.

Peak Short, loud bursts of sound that last a fraction of a second and can be viewed on a digital audiometer that displays the absolute volume of an audio signal as it plays.

Phase An attribute of color perception, also known as *hue*.

PICT The native still-image file format for Macintosh developed by Apple Computer. PICT files can contain both vector images and bitmap images, as well as text and an alpha channel.

Pixel Short for "picture element," one dot in a video or still image.

Pixel aspect ratio The width-to-height ratio for the pixels that compose an image. Pixels on computer screens and in high-definition video signals are square (1:1 ratio). Pixels in standard-definition video signals are nonsquare.

Playhead A navigational element on the scrubber bar that shows you on what frame you are in the Timeline, Canvas, or Viewer. You drag the playhead to navigate through a sequence.

Post-production The phase of film, video and audio editing that begins after all the footage is shot.

Post-roll The amount of time that a tape machines continues to roll after the Out point of an edit, typically between 2 to 5 seconds.

Poster frame The representative still frame of a clip that is the Thumbnail image.

Pre-roll A specified amount of time, usually 5 seconds, given to tape machines so they can synchronize themselves to the editing computer before previewing or performing an edit.

Preview To play an edit to see how it will look without actually performing the edit itself.

Print to Video A command in Final Cut Pro that lets you *render* your sequence and output it to videotape.

Proc amp (processing amplifier) A specific piece of equipment that allows you to adjust video levels on output.

Project In Final Cut Pro, the top-level file that holds all the media associated with a program, including sequences and clips of various kinds.

QuickTime Apple's cross-platform multimedia technology. Widely used for editing, compositing, CD-ROM, Web video, and more.

Q

QuickTime streaming Apple's streaming media addition to the QuickTime architecture. Used for viewing QuickTime content in real time on the Web.

QuickView tool Provides an alternate way of viewing your composition outside of the Canvas as you work. It takes advantage of Final Cut Pro's ability to cache frames of your sequence as you play it. This is useful for fast previews of complex composites and effects. It's also a good way to see how your final composite looks if you are zoomed into the Canvas while making adjustments.

RAID (Redundant Array of Independent Disks) drive A method of providing nonlinear editors with many gigabytes of high-performance data storage by formatting a group of hard disks to act as a single drive volume.

R

Range check Options that enable zebra striping to immediately warn you of areas of a clip's image that may stray outside of the broadcast legal range.

Razor Blade An option on the Tool Palette that allows you to slice the clip into two separate edits to be manipulated individually and is also used as a quick way to trim frames off of a clip.

Real-time effects Effects that can be applied to clips in an edited sequence and played back in real time, without requiring rendering first. Real-time effects can be played back using any qualified computer.

Record monitor A monitor that plays the previewed and finished versions of a project when it is printed to tape. A record monitor corresponds to the Canvas in Final Cut Pro.

Redo To reverse an undo, which restores the last change made to a project.

Render To process video and audio with any applied effects, such as transitions or filters. Effects that aren't real time must be rendered in order to play them back properly. Once rendered, your sequence can be played in real time.

Render file The file produced by rendering a clip to disk. FCP places it in a separate hidden folder so it does not show up in the Browser, but is retrieved with the Timeline.

Render status bars Two slim horizontal bars, in the Timeline ruler area, that indicate which parts of the sequence have been rendered at the current render quality. The top bar is for video, and the bottom for audio. Different colored bars indicate the real-time playback status of a given section of the Timeline.

Replace edit Allows you to replace an existing shot in a sequence with a different shot of the same length.

RGB An abbreviation for red, green, and blue, which are the three primary colors that make up a color image.

Ripple edit An edit in which the start and end times of a range of clips on a track is adjusted when the duration of one of the clips is altered.

Roll edit An edit that affects two clips that share an *edit point*. The Out point of the outgoing clip and the In point of the incoming clip both change, but the overall duration of the sequence stays the same.

Rotation To rotate a clip around its anchor point without changing its shape.

RT Extreme Real-time effects processing that scales with your system.

Ruler area The measurement bar along the top of the Timeline, which represents the total duration of an edited sequence. Also displays the timecode corresponding to the location of clips in the Timeline. You can move the playhead on the ruler in order to navigate through clips in a sequence.

S

Sampling The process during which analog audio is converted into digital information. The sampling rate of an audio stream specifies how many samples are captured. Higher sample rates yield higher-quality audio. Examples: 44.1 K, 48 K.

Saturation The purity of color. As saturation is decreased, the color moves towards pastel then towards a white.

Scale In the Motion tab of the Viewer, an adjustable value that changes the overall size of a clip. The proportion of the image may or may not be maintained.

Scratch disk The hard drive that is designated as the destination to hold your captured media, rendered clips, and cache files.

Scrub To move through a clip or sequence with the aid of the playhead. Scrubbing is used to find a particular point or frame or to hear the audio.

Scrubber bar A bar below the Viewer and the Canvas that allows you to manually drag the playhead in either direction to playback.

SECAM (Séquentiel Couleur à Mémoire) The French television standard for playback. Similar to PAL, the playback rate is 25 fps and the frame size is 720x546.

Selection tool The default arrow-shaped pointer, which allows you to select items in the interface. For example, you use it to select a clip or edit point. You can choose the Selection tool by pressing the A key.

Sequence An edited assembly of video, audio, or graphics clips. In Final Cut Pro, sequences can be up to four hours long and contain as many clips as you need to tell your story. A sequence can contain your entire edited program or be limited to a single scene.

Sequence clip A clip that has been edited into a sequence.

Shuttle control The slider control located at the bottom of the Viewer and the Canvas. This control is useful for continuous playback at different speeds, in fast and slow motion. It also shifts the pitch of audio as it plays at varying speeds.

Slate A small clapboard that is placed in front of all cameras at the beginning of a scene, which identifies the scene with basic production information such as the take, date, and scene. A slate or clapper provides an audio/visual cue for synchronization of dual system recordings.

Slide edit An edit in which an entire clip is moved, along with the edit points on its left and right. The duration of the clip being moved stays the same, but the clips to the left and to the right of it change in length to accommodate the new positioning of the clip. The overall duration of the sequence and of these three clips remains the same.

Slip edit An edit in which the location of both In and Out points of a clip are changed at the same time, without changing the location or duration of the marked media. This is referred to as *slipping* because you slip a pair of In and Out points inside the available footage.

Slug A solid black video frame that can be used to represent a video clip that has not yet been placed in the Timeline.

SMPTE (Society of Motion Picture and Television Engineers) The organization responsible for establishing various broadcast video standards like the SMPTE standard timecode for video playback.

Snapping A setting in the Timeline that affects the movement of the playhead. When snapping is enabled, the playhead "snaps," or moves directly, to markers or edit points when it is moved close to them.

Solo An audio monitoring feature in which one audio track from a group may be isolated for listening without having to remove it from the group.

SOT Acronym for *sound on tape.*

Sound byte (SOT, sound on tape) A short excerpt taken from an interview clip.

Split edit An edit in which the video track or the audio track of a synchronized clip ends up being longer than the other; for example, the sound is longer than the video at the head of the clip, so it is heard before the video appears. Also referred to as an *L-cut.*

Spread An audio control that allows you to adjust the amount of separation of stereo channels.

Square pixel A pixel that has the same height as width. Computer monitors have square pixels, but NTSC and PAL video do not.

Static region An area in a sequence in the Timeline that you lock so that it is visible even when you scroll to see other tracks. The static area can contain audio tracks, video tracks, or both.

Stereo audio Sound that is separated into two channels, one carrying the sounds for the right ear and one for the left ear. Stereo pairs are linked and are always edited together. Audio level changes are automatically made to both channels at the same time. A pair of audio items may have their stereo pairing enabled or disabled at any time.

Storyboard A series of pictures that summarizes the content, action, and flow of a proposed project. When using the Browser in icon view, clips can be arranged visually, like a storyboard. When dragged as a group into the Timeline, the clips will be edited together in the order in which they appear in the Timeline, from left to right, and from the top line down to the bottom.

Straight cut An edit in which both the video and audio tracks are cut together to the Timeline.

Streaming The delivery of media over an intranet or over the Internet.

Subclip A clip created to represent a section of a *master clip.* Subclips are saved as separate items within a bin in the Browser, but do not generate any additional media on the hard disk.

Superimpose edit An edit in which an incoming clip is placed on top of a clip that's already in the Timeline at the position of the playhead. If no In or Out points are set in the Timeline and Canvas, the previously edited clip's In and Out points are used to define the duration of the incoming clip. Superimposed edits are used to overlay titles and text onto video, as well as to create other compositing effects.

Super black Black that is darker than the levels allowed by the CCIR 601 engineering standard for video. The CCIR 601 standard for black is 7.5 IRE in the United States, and 0 IRE for PAL and for NTSC in Japan.

Superwhite A value or degree of white that is brighter than the accepted normal value of 100 IRE allowed by the CCIR 601.

Sweetening The process of creating a high-quality sound mix by polishing sound levels, rerecording bad sections of dialogue, and recording and adding narration, music, and sound effects.

Sync The relationship between the image of a sound being made in a video clip (for example, a person talking) and the corresponding sound in an audio clip. Maintaining audio sync is critical when editing dialogue.

T

Tab In Final Cut Pro, tabs delineate projects in the Browser, sequences in the Canvas and Timeline, and functions within the Viewer. You click a tab to open a project or go to a specified function window, such as Video, Audio, Filters, or Motion. Tabs can also be dragged out of the main window to create a separate window.

Tail The end frames of a clip.

Target track The yellow light that indicates which track is active.

Three-point editing The process of creating an edit by setting just 3 edit points that determine source content, duration, and placement in the sequence. With 3 edit points selected, Final Cut Pro calculates the fourth one.

Thumbnails The first frame of a clip, shown as a tiny picture for reference. In Final Cut Pro, the thumbnail is, by default, the first frame of a clip. You can change the frame used as that clip's thumbnail by using the Scrub Video tool.

TIFF (Tagged Image File Format) A widely used bitmapped graphics file format that handles monochrome, grayscale, and 8- and 24-bit color. There are two types of TIFF images: one with an alpha channel and one without.

Tilt To pivot the camera up and down, which causes the image to move up or down in the frame.

Timecode A unique numbering system of electronic signals laid onto each frame of videotape that is used to identify specific frames of video. Each frame of video is labeled with hours, minutes, frames, and seconds (01:00:00:00). Timecode can be drop frame, non-drop frame, or time of day (TOD) time-code, or EBU (European Broadcast Union) for PAL projects.

Timecode gap An area of tape with no timecode at all. Timecode gaps usually signify the end of all recorded material on a tape, but timecode gaps may occur due the starting and stopping of the camera and tape deck during recording.

Timeline A window in Final Cut Pro that displays a chronological view of an open *sequence*. Each sequence has its own tab in the Timeline. You can use the Timeline to edit and arrange a sequence. The order of the tracks in the Timeline determines the layering order when you combine multiple tracks of video. Changes you make to a sequence in the Timeline are seen when you play back that sequence in the Canvas.

Time remapping The process of moving a frame in a clip to another time relative to the Timeline. All frames in that clip from the beginning of the clip to that keyframe are either sped up or slowed down to accommodate the new duration that's been specified.

Title safe Part of the video image that is guaranteed to be visible on all tele-visions. The title safe area is the inner 80 percent of the screen. To prevent text in your video from being hidden by the edge of a TV set, you should restrict any titles or text to the title safe area.

Tool Bench A window that contains interface elements that supplement information displayed in the Viewer and Canvas. The Tool Bench can contain up to three tabs—QuickView, Video Scopes, and Voice Over.

Tool palette A window in Final Cut Pro that contains tools for editing, zooming, cropping, and distorting items in the Timeline. All tools in the Tool palette can also be selected using keyboard shortcuts.

Tracks Layers in the Timeline that contain the audio or video clips in a sequence. Also refers to the separate audio and video tracks on tape. Final Cut Pro allows up to 99 video and 99 audio tracks to be used in a single sequence.

Track Lock An icon that indicates a track has been locked to prevent accidental change.

Track Visibility A control in the track controls area of the Timeline that you click to turn track visibility on or off. Invisible tracks don't play in the Canvas or on an external monitor, nor will they be rendered or output to tape. When a track is invisible, it appears darkened in the Timeline, but its contents remain in your sequence and you can still edit them.

Transition A visual effect that is applied between two edits, such as a dissolve, wipe, or iris.

Transition Editor A specialized editor that appears in the Viewer when you double-click a transition in the Timeline used to make detailed changes to a transition's timing and effects parameters.

Trim Edit window A window in Final Cut Pro that displays both sides of an edit: the Out point of the outgoing clip on the left and the In point of the incoming clip on the right. You can use this window to adjust the edit point between two clips very precisely, frame by frame.

Trimming To precisely add or subtract frames from the In or Out point of a clip. Trimming is used to fine-tune an edited sequence by carefully adjusting many edits in small ways.

Two-up display A display in the Canvas that appears when using some type of trim or adjustment mode, such as Roll, Ripple, Slip, or Slide. Two individual frames appear to display either the frames being adjusted or the border frames.

Undo A feature that allows you to cancel out the last change made.

U

User Preferences The area where you to set up how you want to work with your media inside Final Cut Pro.

Variable speed Dynamic alteration of the speed of a clip, alternating among a range of speeds, in forward or reverse motion.

V

Vectorscope A window in Final Cut Pro that graphically displays the color components of a video signal, precisely showing the range of colors in a video signal and measuring their intensity and hue.

Video level The measurement of the level (amplitude) of a video signal. It is measured using the Waveform Monitor in FCP.

Video scopes Tools you can use to evaluate the color and brightness values of video clips in the Viewer, Canvas, or Timeline. Video scopes display an analysis of the video frame located at the current playhead position.

Video Scopes tab A tab in the Tool Bench that contains the four Final Cut Pro Video scopes: Waveform Monitor, Vectorscope, Parade Scope, and Histogram.

Viewer A window in Final Cut Pro that acts as a source monitor. You can use the Viewer to watch individual source clips and mark In and Out points in preparation for editing them into your sequence. You can also customize transitions, modify filters, and view and edit various effects. Clips from the current sequence in the Timeline can be opened in the Viewer to refine edits, effects, and audio volume.

Voice Over tool Allows you to record audio in Final Cut Pro while simultaneously playing back a specified section of a sequence from the Timeline. Audio can be recorded using any Sound Manager-compatible device, such as a USB audio capture device, PCI audio card, or the built-in microphone on a DV camcorder.

VTR / VCR Videotape recorder/Videocassette recorder. A tape machine used for recording pictures and sound on videotape.

VU meter (Volume Unit meter) An analog meter for monitoring audio levels.

W **Waveform Monitor** A window in Final Cut Pro that displays the relative levels of brightness and saturation in the clip currently being examined. Spikes or drops in the displayed waveforms make it easy to see where the brightest or darkest areas are in your picture.

White balance The reference to white that is made during recording. This reference can be changed within FCP to reset the white balance, correcting or improving it.

White level An analog video signal's amplitude for the lightest white in a picture, represented by *IRE units.*

Wide-screen An aspect ratio such as 16:9 or 2.35:1 that allows for a wider image, suitable for widescreen television or film projection.

Wide-screen matte filter Adds a mask, blacking out the top and bottom of a 4x3 image, which creates a wide-screen image, such as 16:9.

Wipe A type of transition that uses a moving edge to progressively erase the current clip to reveal the next clip.

Wireframe A visual substitute for a clip that simply represents the outline of the clip's video frame. Clips in the Viewer and Canvas can be viewed in Wireframe mode.

Window burn Visual timecode and keycode information superimposed onto video frames. It usually appears on a strip at the bottom or top of the frame, providing code information to the editor without obscuring any of the picture.

X **X axis** Refers to the x coordinate in Cartesian geometry. The x coordinate describes horizontal placement in motion effects.

Y **Y axis** Refers to the y coordinate in Cartesian geometry. The y coordinate describes vertical placement in motion effects.

YcrCb The color space in which digital video formats store data. Three components are stored for each pixel—one for luminance (Y) and two for color information, Cr for red portion of the color difference signal and Cb for blue color difference signal.

YUV The three-channel PAL video signal with one luminance (Y) and two chrominance color difference signals (UV). It is often misapplied to refer to NTSC video, which is YIQ.

Z axis Refers to the z coordinate in Cartesian geometry. The z coordinate describes perpendicular placement in motion effects.

Z

Zebra stripes Animated diagonal "marching lines" that are superimposed over illegal areas or areas that are very near the broadcast legal limits in an image. Zebra stripes are enabled when you use Final Cut Pro's range-checking options.

Zoom To change the view of your image or Timeline.

Zoom control Used to zoom in or out while keeping the material in the waveform display area centered. Clicking to the right of the control zooms out to show more of the duration of your clip; clicking to the left zooms in to show more detail.

Zoom slider The slider control that appears at the bottom of the Timeline. The Zoom slider allows you to navigate throughout the total duration of the currently displayed sequence; you can use the thumb tabs on the left and right of the slider to zoom in to and out of a sequence for a more detailed view.

Index

The Apple Pro Training Series

The official curriculum of the Apple Pro Training and Certification Program, the Apple Pro Training books are a comprehensive, self-paced courses written by acknowledged experts in the field.

- Focused lessons take you step-by-step through the process of creating real-world digital video or audio projects.
- All media and project files are included on the companion DVD.
- Ample illustrations help you master techniques fast.
- Lesson goals and time estimates help you plan your time.
- Chapter review questions summarize what you've learned.

**Apple Pro Training Series:
Final Cut Pro 5**
0-321-33481-7

In this best-selling guide, Diana Weynand starts with basic video editing techniques and takes you all the way through Final Cut Pro's powerful advanced features. Using world-class documentary footage, you'll learn to mark and edit clips, color correct sequences, create transitions, apply filters and effects, add titles, work with audio, and more.

**Apple Pro Training Series: Advanced
Editing Techniques in Final Cut Pro 5**
0-321-33549-X

Director and editor Michael Wohl shares must-know professional techniques for cutting dialogue scenes, action scenes, fight and chase scenes, documentaries, comedy, music videos, multi-camera projects, and more. Also covers Soundtrack Pro, audio finishing, managing clips and media, and working with film.

**Apple Pro Training
Series: Advanced
Color Correction
and Effects in
Final Cut Pro 5**
0-321-33548-1

This Apple-authorized guide delivers hard-to-find training in real-world color correction and effects techniques, including motion effects, keying and compositing, titling, scene-to-scene color matching, and correcting for broadcast specifications.

**Apple Pro Training
Series: Optimizing
Your Final Cut Pro
System**
0-321-26871-7

Written and field-tested by industry pros Sean Cullen, Matthew Geller, Charles Roberts, and Adam Wilt, this is the ultimate guide for installing, configuring, optimizing, and trouble-shooting Final Cut Pro in real-world post-production environments.

**Apple Pro Training
Series: Final Cut Pro
for Avid Editors**
0-321-24577-6

Master trainer Diana Weynand takes you through a comprehensive "translation course" designed for professional video and film editors who already know their way around Avid nonlinear systems.

The Apple Training Series:

Apple Training Series: iLife '05
0-321-33020-X
Apple Training Series: GarageBand 2
0-321-33019-6
**Apple Training Series: Mac OS X
Support Essentials**
0-321-33547-3

**Apple Training Series: Desktop and
Portable Systems, Second Edition**
0-321-33546-5
**Apple Training Series: Mac OS X
Server Essentials**
0-321-35758-2

**Apple Training Series: Security
Best Practices for Mac OS X v 10.4**
0-321-36988-2
**Apple Training Series: Mac OS X
System Administration Reference**
0-321-36984-X

To order books or find out about the Apple Pro Training Series, visit: **www.peachpit.com/appleprotraining**

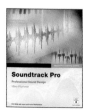

Apple Pro Training Series: Soundtrack Pro
0-321-35757-4

Apple Pro Training Series: Shake 4
0-321-25609-3

Apple Pro Training Series: Shake 4 Quick Reference Guide
0-321-38246-3

Apple Pro Training Series: Getting Started with Motion
0-321-30533-7

Apple Pro Training Series: Motion
0-321-27826-7

Encyclopedia of Visual Effects
0-321-30334-2

Apple Pro Training Series: Logic Pro 7 and Logic Express 7
0-321-25614-X

Apple Pro Training Series: Advanced Logic Pro 7
0-321-25607-7

Apple Pro Training Series: DVD Studio Pro 4
0-321-33482-5

Apple Pro Training Series: Getting Started with Aperture
0-321-42275-9

Apple Pro Training Series: Aperture
0-321-42276-7

Apple Pro Training Series: Color Management with Mac OS X
0-321-24576-8

Apple Pro Training Series: Final Cut Express 2
0-321-25615-8

Apple Pro Training Series: Xsan Quick Reference Guide
0-321-36900-9

To order books or find out about th
Apple Pro Training Series, visit:
www.peachpit.com/appleprotra